TAUNTON'S

Complete Illustrated Guide to

ROUTERS

Taunton's COMPLETE ILLUSTRATED *Guide to*

ROUTERS

LONNIE BIRD

The Taunton Press

The Taunton Press, Inc., 63 South Main Street, P.O. Box 5506, Newtown, CT 06470-5506
e-mail: tp@taunton.com

EDITOR: Paul Anthony
DESIGN: Lori Wendin
LAYOUT: Cathy Cassidy
ILLUSTRATOR: Mario Ferro
PHOTOGRAPHER: Lonnie Bird

LIBRARY OF CONGRESS CATALOGING-IN-PUBLICATION DATA

BIRD, LONNIE.
TAUNTON'S COMPLETE ILLUSTRATED GUIDE TO ROUTERS / LONNIE BIRD.
P. CM.
ISBN-13: 978-1-56158-766-7
ISBN-10: 1-56158-766-4
1. ROUTERS (COMPUTER NETWORKS) 2. INTERNETWORKING (TELECOMMUNICATION) I. TITLE: COMPLETE ILLUSTRATED GUIDE TO ROUTERS. II. TITLE.
TK5105.543.B57 2006
684'.083--DC22

2006001505

Printed in China
10 9 8 7 6 5 4 3 2 1

Working wood is inherently dangerous. Using hand or power tools improperly or ignoring safety practices can lead to permanent injury or even death. Don't try to perform operations you learn about here (or elsewhere) unless you're certain they are safe for you. If something about an operation doesn't feel right, don't do it. Look for another way. We want you to enjoy the craft, so please keep safety foremost in your mind whenever you're in the shop.

Acknowledgements

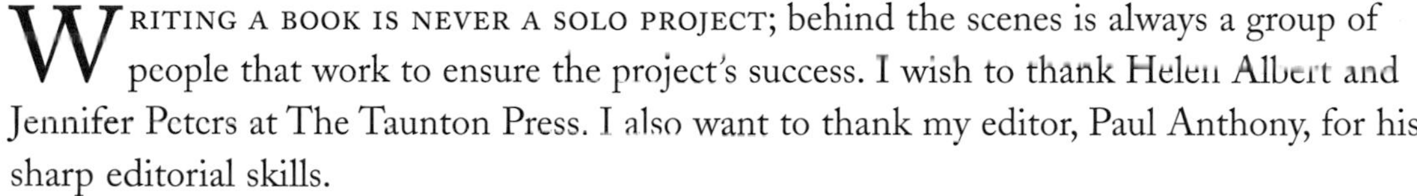

WRITING A BOOK IS NEVER A SOLO PROJECT; behind the scenes is always a group of people that work to ensure the project's success. I wish to thank Helen Albert and Jennifer Peters at The Taunton Press. I also want to thank my editor, Paul Anthony, for his sharp editorial skills.

Several corporations provided tools for photography, including Amana Tools, Jessem, Porter-Cable, Bosch, and BenchDog. My sincerest thanks to all. –L.B.

Contents

Introduction

The router is undoubtedly one of the simplest of woodworking machines—basically comprising just a motor, a base, and a collet. And yet it is one of the most versatile tools you can own. Back when the router was first invented, it was used primarily for shaping decorative profiles along the edges of tabletops and drawer fronts. It's still a great choice for those tasks, but the truth is, it can do a lot more, including grooving, flush-trimming, raising panels, and cutting almost any joint, including the all-important mortise-and-tenon and dovetail joints. In fact, the router can create all of the joinery necessary to make entire assemblies such as doors and drawers.

Unleashing all this versatility basically depends on two things: using the appropriate bit, and guiding the cut in the proper manner. That's a bit of an oversimplification, of course, but it really is at the heart of the matter, as I'll show you in this book.

For example, if you flip through the pages of any router bit catalog, you're sure to become overwhelmed by the assortment of bit styles and sizes, which range from simple straight bits to large, complex molding bits. However, you'll find that a judicious selection of a few essential bits will enable you to accomplish many of your routing tasks.

As for guiding the cut, I'll show you a range of options, including using the edge of the router base, fitting a bushing to the opening in the base, or using a guide bearing on the bit. You can also choose to attach a fence or edge guide to the base. For some tasks, such as excavating for hardware, you might choose to simply guide the router freehand to remove much of the waste stock, completing the job with hand tools.

Another option is to use a jig or router table. No other woodworking machine lends itself more to the use of jigs or table-mounting than the router. Many commercial jigs are available to help you perform simple or complex operations, but you can also construct jigs yourself. Router tables open up a whole other realm of possibilities, effectively turning the router into a stationary machine—a mini-shaper that's capable of routing large-scale jobs such as door panels. Although a table-mounted router lacks the power of a shaper, it's more versatile and economical, making it well suited to small-shop woodworkers on a limited budget.

So be prepared to expand your woodworking skills through the capabilities of this most remarkable tool. It's my hope that this book will provide you with a thorough understanding of the router and what you can achieve with it. –L.B.

Choosing Routers and Accessories, page 6

All About Bits, page 27

Router Tables, page 52

PART ONE

Tools

AS THE POPULARITY of woodworking has grown, so has the available variety of routers, bits, and accessories. Today, you'll find more types than ever before. Routers have become more sophisticated and often incorporate such features as soft-start and electronic variable speed control. Ergonomics have improved too, with handle placement, shape, and size all making it easier to get a good grip and improve control.

Like router choices, bit offerings are better than ever. Modern bits come in lots of shapes and sizes to suit just about any job. Larger bits can be paired up with powerful table-mounted routers for performing operations such as cutting profiles on raised panels or large moldings—jobs that formerly required a large industrial shaper.

In this part of the book, I'll help you sort out the routers, bits, and accessories that best suit your needs. I'll also show you how to maintain your tools, change bits and bearings, and how to build a router table and accessories.

Choosing Routers and Accessories

Custom Baseplates

Edge Guide

Maintenance

Open the pages of a woodworking tool catalog and you're sure to become overwhelmed with the selection of routers, tables, lifts, and other accessories. In the last 25 years, the router has changed the way we work wood, resulting in more choices in routers and accessories than ever before. Elaborate tables, router lifts with machine-shop accuracy, soft start, electronic variable speed (EVS) motors, and self-releasing collets have all made their débuts in the last 30 years. Having choices and options is great, but it can also be confusing—especially if you're new to woodworking.

In this section, I'll show you what's out there and help you to focus on matching your woodworking needs with the many available features and options.

Router Types

Take a close look and you'll see that routers are pretty simple machines; all comprise a motor, collet, and a base (see the photos on the facing page). Yet, if you've perused the pages of any tool catalog, no doubt you've been confused by the large assortment of routers. However, all routers can be divided into three main types: Fixed-base, plunge router, and laminate trimmers. Fixed-base

All routers have a motor, collet, and base.

Plunge routers are the best choice for mortising.

Fixed-base routers have been a popular style for many years.

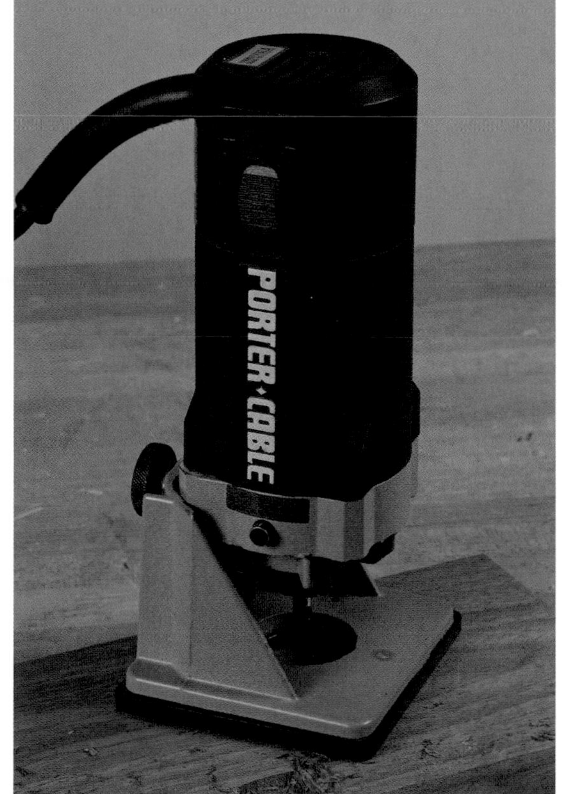

Laminate trimmers are scaled-down fixed-base routers.

The fixed-base router really has not changed much in the last 50 years.

The motor on this fixed-base router fits into a helical thread in the base.

routers have been around the longest and they're still the most popular, both for hand-held use and for equipping a router table.

Most fixed-base routers use a large helical thread to engage the motor to the base (see the drawing below). Adjustments to the cutting depth are made by spiraling the motor within the base and locking it in position with a thumbscrew or lever. A graduated ring helps in making accurate adjustments (see the photos on the facing page). Some newer models of fixed-base routers have a micrometer knob for making

FIXED-BASE ROUTER

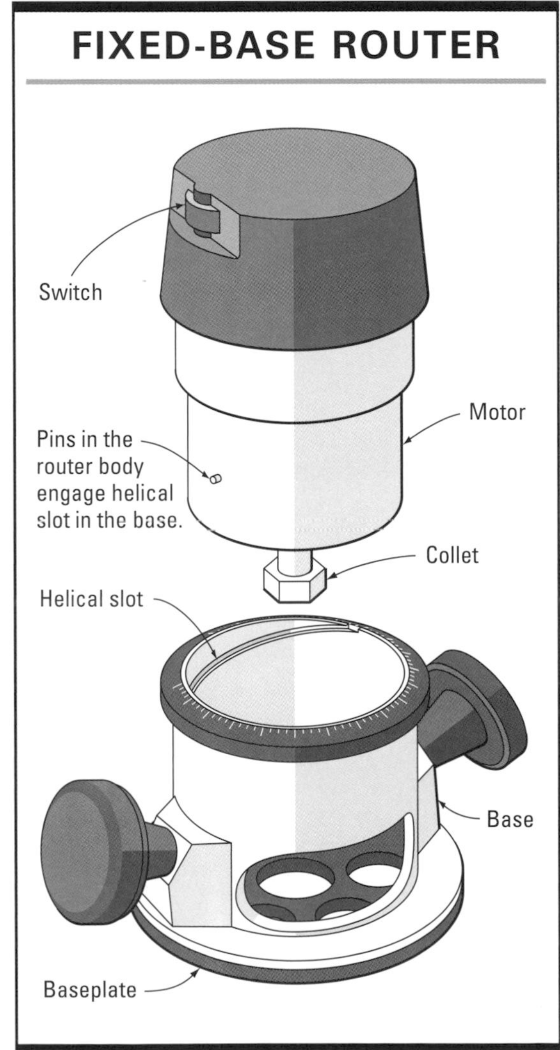

A lock lever has become standard on most new routers.

This graduated ring can be zeroed out for exact adjustments to the depth.

A BRIEF HISTORY

Although the popularity of routers has risen dramatically in recent years, they have been around awhile. In fact, one entrepreneur, R.L. Carter, had manufactured and sold nearly 100,000 of his machines when he was bought out by Stanley Tools sometime before World War II. Stanley worked to popularize the router with advertisements in early trade magazines such as Home Craftsman, and by the 1940s, sales were strong.

Surprisingly, the venerable fixed-base router has not really changed that much since those early days. Although modern motors are much larger and feature sophisticated electronics, such as soft start and electronic variable speed, routers are still guided as they were many decades ago, by the base, a bushing, pilot on the bit, or an edge guide. In the 21st century, the basic operations of the router remain unchanged.

A 1940s-era router is operated in much the same way as today's routers.

Stanley Tools popularized the router during the 1930s and 1940s.

A micrometer dial makes precise adjustments easy.

A series of notches provide a "ballpark setting," while a micrometer dial makes precise depth adjustments.

ultra-fine adjustments to the cutting depth and a lever to lock the setting. Although the degree of precision provided by a micrometer knob usually isn't needed for cutting decorative shapes, it's a real asset for setting up for routing dovetails or other fine joinery. Still other fixed-base routers use a rack and pinion for making height adjustments. Either way, after the setting is made, the motor is locked in position within the base and remains in a fixed position throughout the cut. Fixed-base routers are also the best design for use in a router table. Height adjustments are fast and convenient, especially compared to those of plunge-base routers. And if you choose to use one of the

This router uses a geared "rack" for depth adjustments.

This large, heavy-duty router is a favorite for use in a router table.

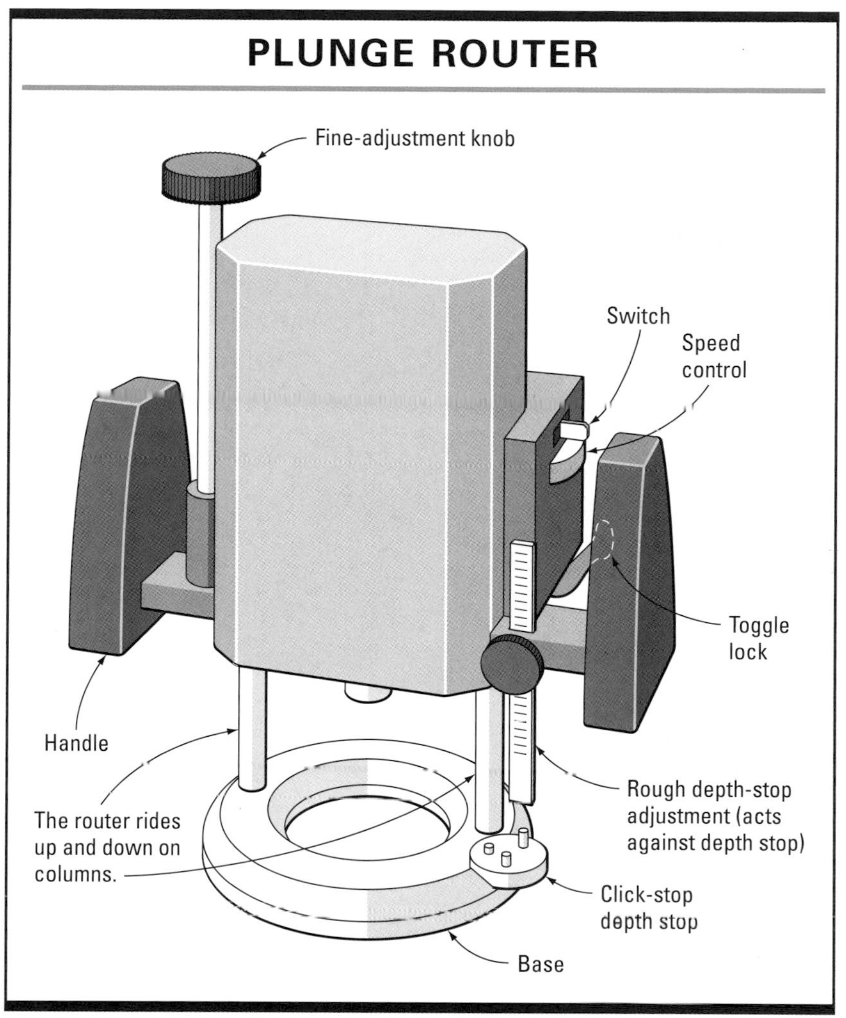

many router lifts in your table, you should realize that they are usually designed for use with a fixed-base router.

Plunge Router

Not long after the fixed-base router was first introduced, plunge routers made their way to the market. The motor of a plunge router slides up and down on a pair of posts attached to the base (see the drawing above). A spring suspends the motor on the posts, and a lever locks it in place (see the photo on p. 12). This design allows you to make depth adjustments as the router is running.

The motor of a plunge router is suspended on spring-loaded posts.

The lock lever on a plunge router should be within easy reach.

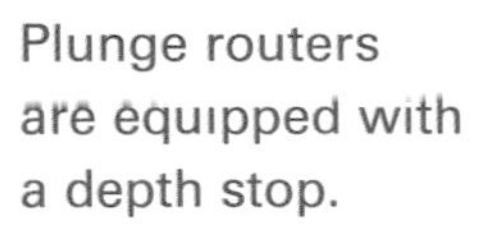

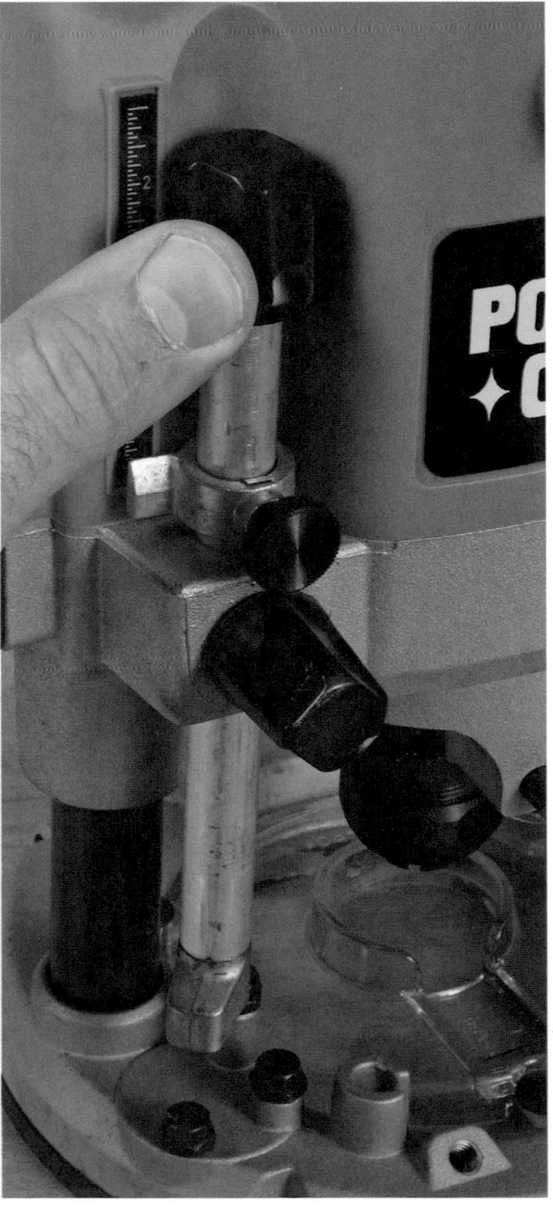

Plunge routers are equipped with a depth stop.

A three-position turret allows for multiple depth settings.

The plunge router is the best choice for routing mortises, grooves, and other joints that require starting and ending the cut at a specific point of layout. In order to lower the bit to a precise depth, plunge routers have a depth stop, which is simply a steel rod that positions against a screw on the router base. Plunge routers typically have three depth screws mounted on a turret. This allows you to make a deep cut, such as a mortise, in precise, incremental steps.

Laminate Trimmers

Laminate trimmers are best described as scaled-down fixed-base routers. As their name implies, these little routers are designed to trim plastic laminate when you install kitchen countertops. But don't let the name fool you; laminate trimmers are versatile routers that find a number of uses in my shop—from cutting shallow mortises for installing hardware to routing narrow grooves for scaled-down joinery (see the photo on the facing page).

FIXED-BASE OR PLUNGE BASE?

For many woodworkers, choosing between a fixed-base router and a plunge router is no easy task. Still the favorite choice of many woodworkers, fixed-base routers have a lower center of gravity, with handles positioned near the baseplate, making the router easier to control. In contrast, the handles of a plunge router are fastened to the sleeve that grips the motor. As the sleeve is vertically repositioned along the steel rods, the height of the motor and handles changes. Although this is precisely what allows you to safely plunge into a mortise (you don't want to try tipping a fixed-base router into a deep stop cut), it also changes the center of gravity. Because of this design, using a plunge router can take some getting used to. And when you don't need the plunge feature, which may be most of the time, you may find the fixed-base router easier to control. Fortunately, most manufacturers now offer a router kit that comes equipped with one motor and both plunge and fixed bases. Some are even designed with a built-in height adjuster for router table use.

This router comes with a wrench that allows for easy height adjustment when it's outfitted in a router table.

Router kits come supplied with with both fixed and plunge bases.

Laminate trimmers don't have a lot of power, and the chuck will only accept bits with a ¼-in.-dia. shank, so you don't want to overload these tools. But the light weight and small size make them ideal for light cuts, when a full-sized router would be awkward and difficult to control. And because laminate trimmers are compact, they'll route in confined spaces where a full-sized router can't. When shopping for a laminate trimmer, look for one with a square baseplate. The straight sides of a square baseplate will give the router a steady footprint and greater precision when used with a guide or template.

Laminate trimmers are versatile little multi-task routers.

Features

Although routers are pretty simple machines, their features can vary widely. Whether you're shopping for your first router or replacing an aging model, you'll want to be aware of the many available features so that you'll get the router that best suits your needs. Undoubtedly, the most important feature of any router is the motor, so let's take a look at what's available.

Motors

When comparing routers, one of the first criteria to consider is the motor horsepower. Bigger motors will handle bigger bits, allowing larger shaping, deeper grooves, etc. But horsepower ratings can be deceiving when you're selecting a router, because routers use universal motors rather than induction motors. Universal motors are the small, high-revving motors (about 20,000 rpm on routers) found on most small power tools such as drills and sanders, as well as on benchtop tools such as portable planers.

In contrast, induction motors are the relatively slow-turning motors (about 3,450 rpm) found on stationary tools such as tablesaws, planers, and jointer. Comparing horsepower ratings on universal motors to the horsepower ratings on induction motors is, as the saying goes, like comparing apples to oranges. A 2-hp induction motor will deliver 2 hp all day long, every day—such as in a manufacturing facility running three shifts. But a 2-hp universal motor is rated according to peak horsepower, not continuous horsepower. So you can expect your 2-hp router to provide 2 hp for only a brief period before it overheats and quits. Because of this, horsepower rating is simply not the best method for comparing universal motors. But manufacturers use it anyway, probably because most people are familiar with the term, although they may not truly know what it means.

When you're shopping for a router, a better representation of power is amperage rating. The higher the amperage rating, the more electrical current the router draws and the greater the power output. The efficiency of the router is a factor, too. Some of the electrical current is always turned into heat instead of power. Because of lower-quality bearings, less efficient windings, and even the design of the cooling fan, an inexpensive consumer-grade router will not have the power output of a professional router—even if the amperage rating is the same. In short, you get what you pay for. And when you purchase a router, most of what you're paying for is the motor. Remember, too, that although conventional wisdom often dictates

The sliding switch at the top of the router controls the speed of its universal motor.

Two-hp routers are a good choice for handheld routing.

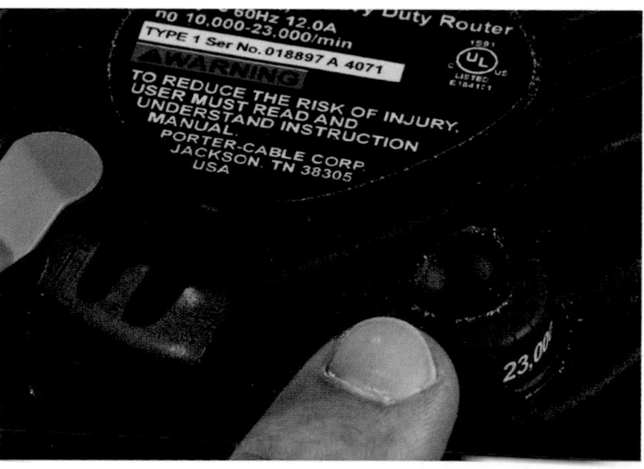

This infinitely variable speed dial allows you to adjust the speed for the job at hand.

that bigger is better, the extra power also adds extra weight and can make a large router awkward to use for handheld operations. Really big routers are best reserved for use in a router table.

Motor Options

Routers today have several options that were not available just a few years ago. Soft start, variable speed, and electronic speed control are all options worth considering. Soft start is an electronic feature that delays full rpm for a second to prevent the router from jerking as it instantaneously reaches full rpm at the flick of the switch. The one-second delay of a soft start router brings the motor rpm up gradually, reducing the jarring motion from the startup torque.

Electronic variable speed (EVS) is another option worth having. This feature allows you to adjust the motor speed to suit the bit diameter. Large-diameter bits have a much higher peripheral speed than do small bits when spinning at the same rpm. Spinning a 3-in.-diameter panel-raising bit at 22,000 rpm is dangerous and may scorch the wood and dull the cutting edges from excess heat. Electronic variable speed gives you a greater degree of flexibility with your router. Most EVS routers have a speed range of 10,000 rpm to 22,000 rpm or 15,000 rpm to 25,000 rpm, allowing you to slow the motor for large bits and speed it up again for smooth cutting with small-diameter bits.

Collets

The smallest part of the router has one of the toughest jobs. The collet of a router has to grip a bit securely while under the stress and strain of cutting through dense hardwood at speeds of about 20,000 rpm. Yet there is no mechanical interlock between

As the collet is tightened, the slots allow it to compress around the shank of the bit.

As the nut is tightened, the tapered end of the collet is drawn into the collet housing.

Because of its small size, the collet in a laminate trimmer is simple in design and must be kept clean to function.

This self-releasing collet uses a snap ring to join the collet and nut.

the bit and the collet as there is with most power tools; the collet simply squeezes the bit. It works like this: The collet has slits that allow it to compress. The outside of the collet is tapered to match the taper machined inside the end of the router motor spindle. As the collet nut is tightened, it forces the collet into the taper, putting the squeeze on the bit's shank. It works surprisingly well. In fact, it can squeeze so tightly that the bit can sometimes be difficult to remove later. That's why the best collets are self-releasing; some designs incorporate a snap ring that secures the collet to the lock nut (see the bottom left photo). As the nut is loosened, it pulls the collet and bit out, too. The better collet designs are also deep; this allows you to fully insert the bit without the shank bottoming out.

Years ago most routers had only 1/4-in.-dia. collets; now most have 1/2-in.-dia. collets (see the photo on the facing page.) When you shop for a router, look for one that accepts both; this will provide you with the greatest flexibility (see the photo on the facing page). Although I usually route with 1/2-in.-dia. shank router bits (more on that in the section on bits), many small profiles are

This deep collet provides a firm grip on large bits.

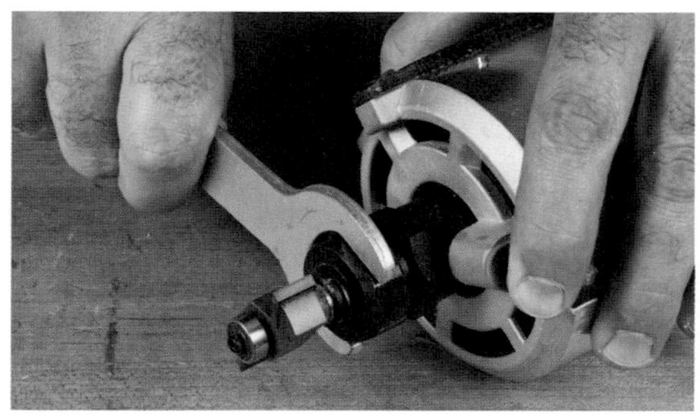

With a collet lock, only one wrench is needed.

Collets come in various sizes and configurations.

are only available in a 1/4-in.-dia. shank. I avoid using adapter sleeves, as they don't grip the bit as tightly as a collet that is made for the purpose.

Router Accessories

There are a number of worthy accessories for your router that will make it more functional and easier to use. The old favorites, such as edge guides and bushings, are still available.

ADAPTER SLEEVE

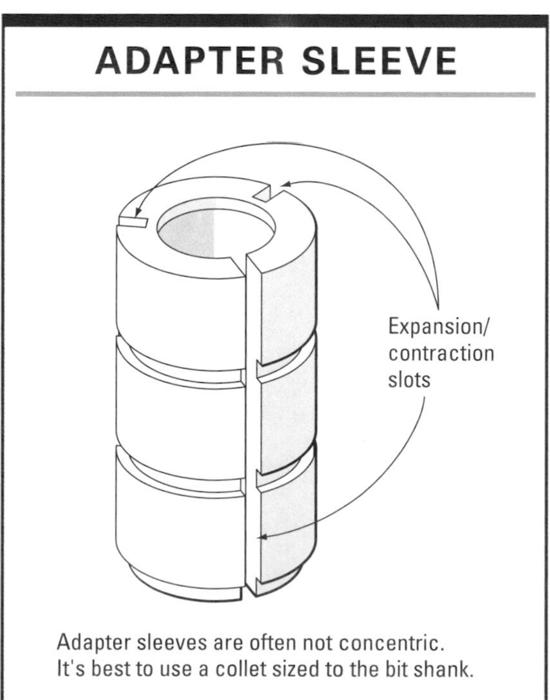

Adapter sleeves are often not concentric. It's best to use a collet sized to the bit shank.

COLLET MAINTENANCE

A little basic maintenance will keep your router's collet functioning well for a long time. The main culprits are dirt and pitch; they can form inside the threads of the collet nut or within the collet itself. When cleaning, it's important to avoid abrading the collet. Although you can use a mild plastic pad to polish the inside of a collet, anything coarser can put deep scratches in the surface and potentially hinder the holding power.

While you're at it, take a close look at the socket on the end of the motor shaft and clean it, too. If necessary, use a small amount of solvent such as mineral spirits to remove the grime.

Finally, it's important to realize that collets often wear out before the motor or other router components. If you're experiencing bit slippage, it can be a sign that the collet is dirty or worn. (It can also be a sign of an undersized bit, as discussed in Section Two.) If a light cleaning doesn't correct the problem, it's probably time to replace the collet.

Swapping baseplates on most routers is a snap.

Guide bushings allow you to use your router with templates and jigs.

But today's router tables, along with their sophisticated lifts, will transform your router into a stationary tool with an incredible degree of precision.

Custom Baseplates

In order to reduce friction and allow routers to glide smoothly across the surface of the workpiece, router bases are fitted with a slick plastic baseplate. The baseplate also works to support the router, and the opening in the baseplate provides a way to attach guide bushings for shaping or routing with a template. The bushing slips into the bit opening and is held in position with a threaded, knurled lock ring. Guide bushings are available in a variety of lengths and diameters (see the photo on the facing page).

Although the factory-supplied baseplate works well for most routing operations, the typical baseplate does have limitations. You may decide to swap it for an aftermarket baseplate or one that you make yourself. Hold onto the factory baseplate, however; it provides a template for making a custom baseplate.

This popular Porter/Cable bushing is held in place with a knurled nut.

Many woodworkers prefer a clear baseplate, which provides a better view when you're approaching a layout line. When you rout along an edge, much of the router overhangs the workpiece. If the router tips, the workpiece can be spoiled. A large, teardrop-shaped baseplate will enable you to easily keep the router balanced and upright.

There are also baseplates with larger openings to accommodate large-diameter bits. However, be aware that as the opening is enlarged, the router's footprint is reduced, which limits the stability of the router.

A set of guide bushings provides more versatility.

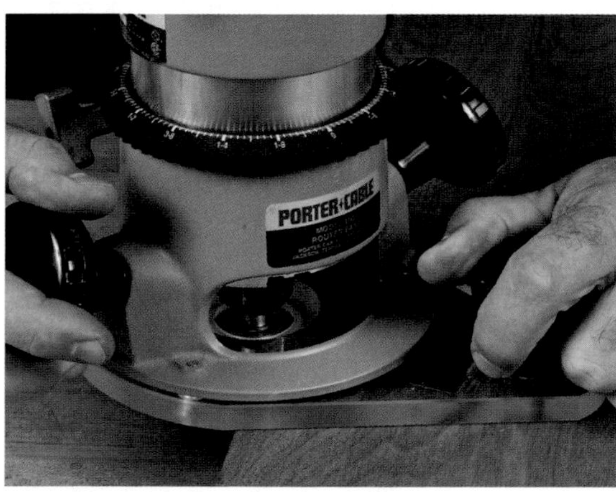

A teardrop-shaped baseplate helps maintain balance during edge routing.

MAKING CUSTOM BASEPLATES

Changing router baseplates is a fast and easy way to add greater versatility to an already versatile machine. You can swap out your router's standard baseplate for one of the many aftermarket varieties or you can make one of your own.

When making a custom baseplate, first choose your materials: plastic or plywood. Clear plastic will provide an unobstructed view, while plywood is easier to work and allows you to quickly attach a fence as a guide. Your local glass shop will have acrylic and polycarbonate plastics available, and you can save money by asking for available offcuts rather than purchasing a large sheet. These plastics are durable and inexpensive. Best of all, you can saw, file, and trim the plastic with the same tools you use for working wood.

When using plywood for a custom baseplate, select 3/8-in. or 1/2-in. thickness. Anything thinner flexes too easily; anything thicker costs you cutting depth. Remember to buy screws long enough to attach the new baseplate. If the stock baseplate screws have panheads, switch to flathead screws. Panhead screws require a counterbore, which weakens the plywood.

A clear baseplate offers a better view of the cut.

A router table baseplate will increase the footprint and provide a straight side for use with a guide.

A factory edge guide is precise and easy to set up and use.

Remember, too, that large bits belong in a table-mounted router and are not intended for handheld routing. A router-table insert plate works well for a straight-sided baseplate.

Edge Guides

Profile bits are usually guided by an integral bearing. But when cutting a groove with a straight bit or using a bit without a guide bearing, you'll need another method. One of the most common approaches is to attach an edge guide to the router base. Like custom baseplates, edge guides can be purchased from the company that made the router or you can make an edge guide of your own.

The edge guide offered as an accessory to your router has several worthwhile features. It's made to fit your router base, and so it takes just a minute or two to fasten it in position. The fence adjusts with no fuss and locks firmly in place. Best of all, some edge guides have a micrometer knob that makes fine settings a snap.

If you seldom have a need for an edge guide, you may just opt to construct one of your own (see the photo on the facing page). This allows you to customize it to suit the requirements of the job at hand. The easiest method is to replace your router's baseplate with one of plywood. You can attach a guide to the baseplate with screws for a quick and sturdy setup or make the guide adjustable with slotted holes and wing nuts.

Router Tables

Without a doubt, the router table adds more to the versatility of the router than any other accessory. By mounting your router table under a table, you create, in effect, a mini-shaper that's capable of shaping raised

A shopmade edge guide will allow you to produce a variety of cuts, such as this rabbet.

With a router lift, you no longer need to remove a heavy router from the table to change bits.

panels, crown molding, cope-and-stick framework for doors, and many other large, complicated cuts that would be difficult (if not impossible) to create with a handheld router.

Years ago, woodworkers made their own simple router tables with a sheet of plywood, as shown on p. 55. While that approach still works, especially if you're on a tight budget, there is now a full array of commercial models available, ranging from simple yet sturdy benchtop models to floor-standing versions complete with extruded aluminum components and height adjustments with machine-shop accuracy.

Lifts

Mounting your router in a table turns it into a stationary power tool with several advantages over hand routing. In many cases, it's easier to run the workpiece past the router than to run the router over the workpiece. If you're routing long pieces, a router table will provide plenty of support. Mounted in a table, the portable router becomes, in effect, a mini-shaper.

But once you mount your router in a table, you'll immediately encounter some problems. For example, the power switch and height adjustment mechanism are no longer easily accessible. And you'll have to remove the router to make bit changes.

A router lift solves these problems. Height adjustments are easily and precisely made from the top. And you no longer have to remove a heavy router from the table to change bits; just lift the router with a crank and make bit changes from above the table. For more on router tables and lifts, see Section Three.

A

Making a Custom Baseplate

Because the baseplate on many routers is designed for attaching a guide bushing, the center opening is too small to accommodate larger profile bits. The solution is to make a new custom baseplate using the factory baseplate as a pattern.

Begin by attaching the factory baseplate to the new baseplate material with double-stick tape **(A)**. Saw the excess material with a scrollsaw or bandsaw, cutting to within 1⁄16 in. of the factory baseplate **(B)**. Set up the router table with a flush trim bit and a stick for use as a starting pin or fulcrum **(C)**. Now, trim away the excess material **(D)**. Next, drill and countersink the holes for the baseplate screws **(E)** and fasten the new baseplate in place **(F)**.

B

C

D

E

F

Making a Straight-Sided Baseplate

Round baseplates are often not concentric with the collet **(A)**. This is usually unimportant, except when you're guiding the router from the base, where it can spoil the accuracy of the cut. The solution is to use a base with straight sides, which ensure that the distance from the edge of the baseplate to the collet is always constant **(B)**.

To make the baseplate, you'll need a template, such as a rectangle of ¼-in.-thick plywood. You can use the factory baseplate as a template for the bit opening **(C)**.

Attach the template to the baseplate stock with double-stick tape **(D)**. Carefully align the parts **(E)**.

(Text continues on p. 24)

A

B

C

D

E

Apply pressure to the tape for a secure grip **(F)**. Now trim the edges flush; a starting pin will enable you to ease into the cut **(G)**. Once the template has made contact with the guide bearing, you can maneuver away from the starting pin **(H)**.

Now, center the router base over the baseplate and mark the location of the mounting holes **(I)**. Attach the new baseplate to the factory baseplate **(J)** and trim the center bit opening **(K)**. Finally, mount the custom baseplate to the router base **(L)**.

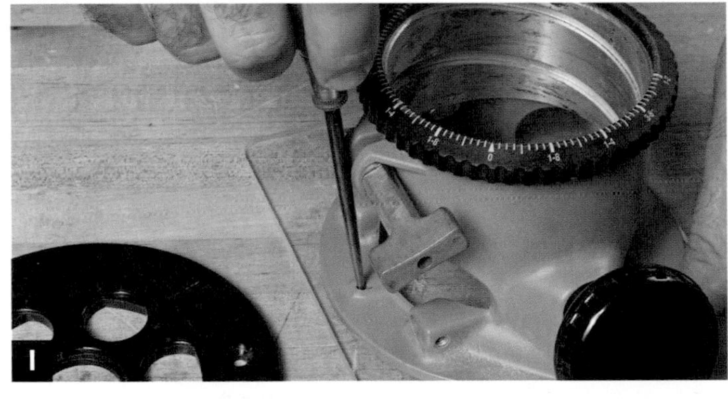

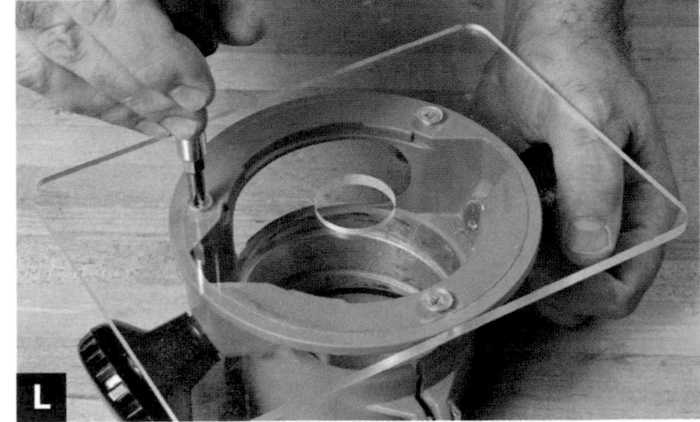

Constructing an Edge Guide

Manufactured edge guides are precise and easy to use. But if you seldom use an edge guide, you may prefer to devise one of your own using ⅜-in.-thick plywood, which has sufficient stiffness without adding excessive weight or thickness.

Begin by drilling holes for the bit and mounting screws **(A)**. Next, lay out the slots for the fence **(B)** and make the setup on a router table **(C)**. To make a plunge cut for the slots, first clamp a stop block to the fence **(D)**. Then, carefully lower the workpiece over the spinning bit **(E)**.

Now attach a fence to the base with machine screws and wing nuts **(F)**. Then, attach the plywood base to the router **(G)**.

A

B

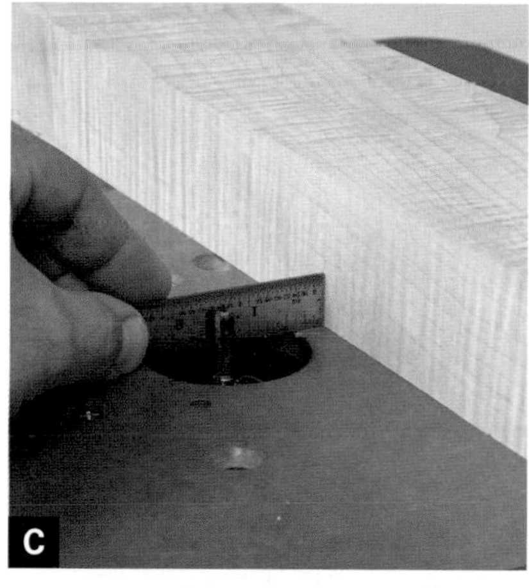

C

D

E

F

G

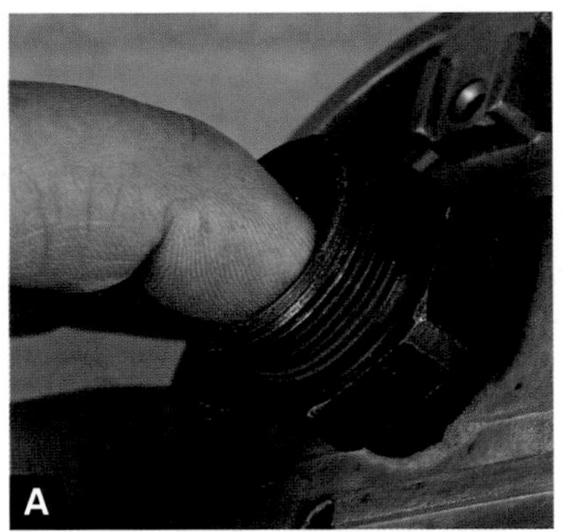
A

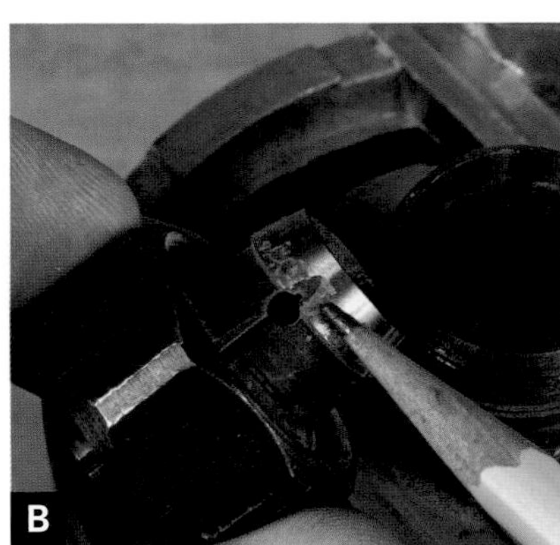
B

C

D

Router Maintenance

Routers quickly become dirty with dust and pitch. To ensure smooth cutting and the longevity of your router, it's a good idea to clean the collet and motor regularly.

Begin by removing the collet and inspecting the collet housing for pitch **(A)**. A rag dampened with mineral spirits will soften the grime so that you can more easily remove it. Also inspect the taper on the collet for pitch **(B)**. If necessary, you can use a mild abrasive plastic pad. However, avoid using steel wool, which can drop into the cooling vent and damage the motor windings.

The router motor will draw in dust and shavings, which can cause it to overheat **(C)**. To thoroughly clean this area, you'll first have to remove the cap over the end of the motor **(D)** and then use a vacuum to remove the dust **(E, F)**. I avoid using compressed air for this because it can force dust and dirt further inside the machine.

E

F

All About Bits

Setting Up Bits

ROUTER BITS have come a long way in the past 30 years; there are more choices in shape and design than ever before. And as router tables and routers have grown larger, so have the bits. The quality is better than ever, too. However, because of the surge of interest in woodworking, there are a few bits out there to avoid. As the saying goes, "You get what you pay for." The finest router will not cut cleanly and smoothly if you equip it with an inferior bit (see the top photo on p. 28).

If you're new to woodworking, you may be surprised at the cost of router bits. Depending on the size and shape, a half-dozen bits can easily add up to more than the cost of your router. Therefore, you'll want to make informed choices and purchase just what you need. In this section, I'll discuss the wide variety of choices and show you how to make smart buying decisions.

Design and Materials

So you purchased the 3-hp behemoth router and dropped it into the most expensive table on the market. You flip the switch and make the cut. Upon inspection, you notice that the cut is too deep on the trailing end and the work is ruined. What happened?

The bit slowly crept out of the collet;

The carbide tips, ball-bearing pilot, and ½-in.-dia. shank make the bit on the left far superior to the one on the right.

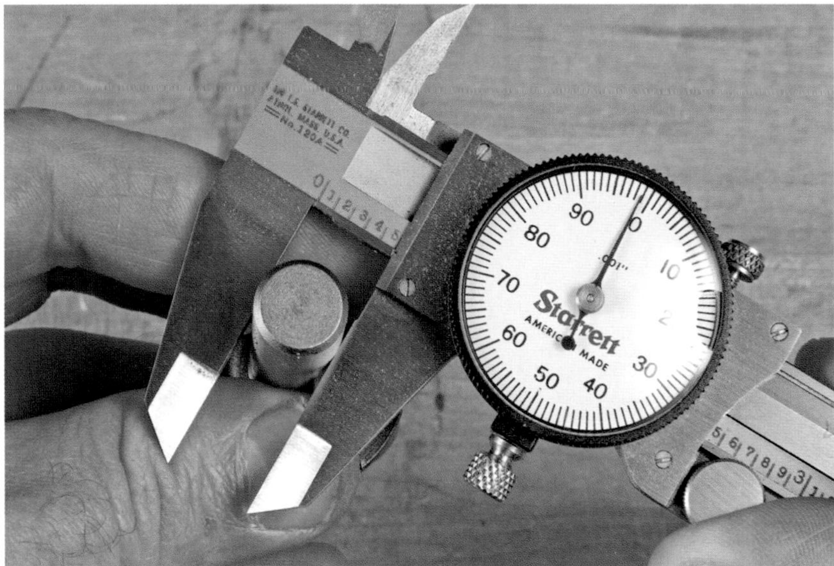

The shank of a bit should be no more than .002 in. smaller than the collet diameter. At .001 in. under, this shank is perfectly sized.

"Anti-kickback" bits help control overfeeding of the workpiece.

luckily, it didn't come completely out. A measurement of the bit shank with a dial caliper shows a reading of .494 in., which is about .005 in. less than it should be. As a result of the sloppy machining of the bit shank, the collet couldn't grip it tightly.

I'm not making up this story. It's true—and it happened to me. It comes down to this: The bit is the most important part of the setup. Skimp here and you might regret it. Although router bits appear pretty simple, there's more to manufacturing a high-quality router bit than you might think. And add to that the varieties of shapes, sizes, and materials, and the choices can be overwhelming. Let's take a closer look.

Flutes

Most router bits have two cutting edges, called flutes. However, some straight bits have one flute while others have three. Single-flute bits cut somewhat faster and are usually a little less expensive. Triple-flute bits are designed to provide a smoother surface, but the same effect can be achieved by slowing the feed rate while using a double-flute bit.

Some bits incorporate anti-kickback design. Kickback occurs when the workpiece is thrown back violently toward the operator. One potential cause of kickback is overfeeding the stock. Router bits that use an anti-kickback design work by limiting the projection of the cutting edge, which, in turn, limits the chip thickness (see the drawing on the facing page).

The smoothest-cutting router bits incorporate a shear angle. Viewed from the side, the cutting edge is tilted from the vertical plane of the bit shank (see the top photo on the facing page). This slight angle creates

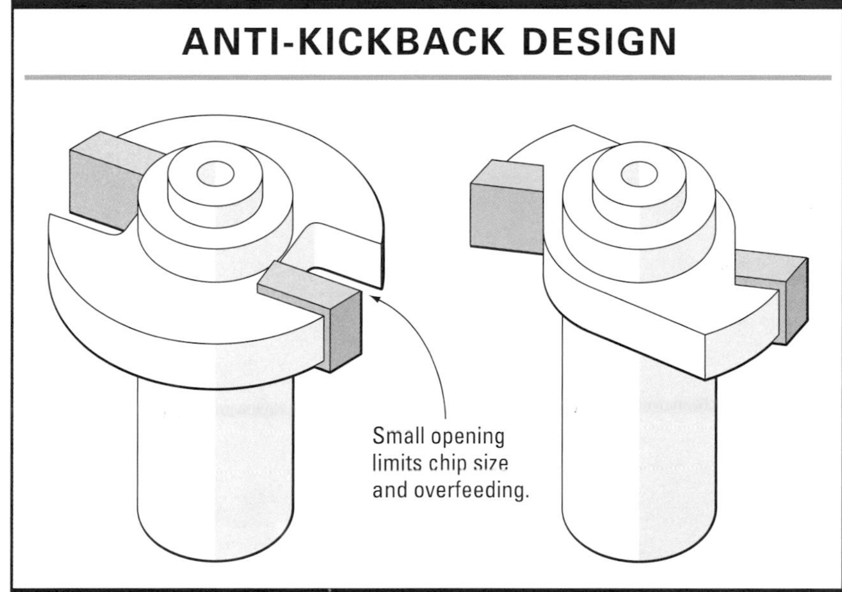

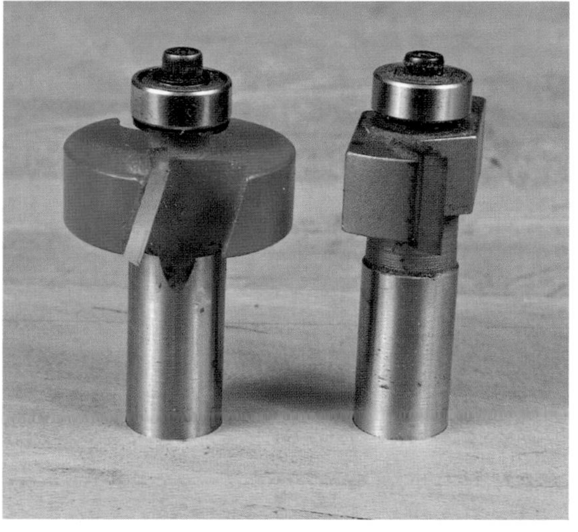

The bit on the left will cut more cleanly due to its skewed flute.

a shearing effect, as you do when you push a handplane across a board at an angle. Router bits that don't have a shear angle have a greater tendency to splinter and burn the wood.

For the smoothest possible finish, choose a spiral bit. The flutes of a spiral bit wind around the shank like the stripes on a barber's pole. This design's action is superior to the intermittent cutting action of the standard bit design. The cutting edges of a spiral bit are always in contact with the workpiece, leaving a phenomenally smooth surface.

Spiral bits without bearings are popular for mortising. They cut clean mortise walls, and the spiral flutes lift the shavings from the mortise. Spiral bits with guide bearings are used for either flush trimming or pattern trimming. On flush-trim bits, the bearing is mounted on the end of the bit opposite the collet. These bits are great for trimming a face frame flush to the cabinet with absolutely zero tearout. On spiral pattern bits, the guide bearing is mounted between the flutes

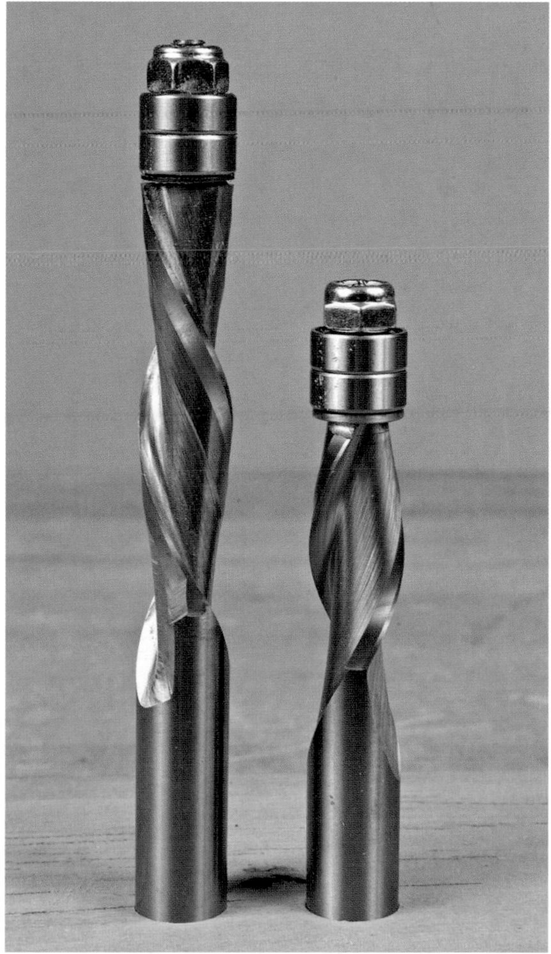

The flutes on spiral bits twist like the stripes on a barber's pole.

and the shank. A lock collar with a tiny setscrew keeps the bearing held firmly in position. Spiral pattern bits are ideal for trimming stock flush to a curved pattern where both short grain and end grain will likely be encountered.

When selecting spiral bits, you can choose from three styles: up-cut, down-cut, and compression. An up-cut pulls the chips upward toward the router. This provides fast cutting action and good chip removal for cutting mortises. Down-cut spirals cut more slowly but leave the top surface of the workpiece splinter-free. Compression spirals cut in both directions simultaneously to leave both top and bottom surfaces free of tearout.

[TIP] Spiral bits are expensive, so I use them only when I need the smoothest possible surface.

High-Speed Steel vs. Carbide

Years ago, most router bits were made of high-speed steel (HSS). Today, it has largely been replaced by carbide, although you can still find HSS bits at many hardware stores and home supply centers.

You may find HSS bits tempting because of their low price. But even though high-speed steel can be sharpened to a razor edge, it doesn't hold an edge for very long, especially on plywood. And don't even attempt to rout particleboard or MDF with it, because the hard, abrasive nature of these man-made boards will dull the HSS edge in short order.

On the other hand, carbide is very hard and resistant to both wear and heat. Although a carbide-tipped router bit may cost three or four times more than a comparable HSS bit, it will keep the sharp edge 20 to 25 times longer. And carbide-tipped

Carbide-tipped bits (at left in each pair here) will last 20 times longer than high-speed steel (HSS) bits.

The solid pilot on this HSS bit scorches the wood as it spins.

Don't insert a bit up to the fillet at the base of the profile.

router bits can also be resharpened many times, especially if the carbide tips are thick. So in the long run, carbide-tipped router bits are much more economical than HSS bits.

[TIP] When comparison shopping for carbide-tipped bits, consider that thicker tips allow many more sharpenings.

As an added benefit, carbide-tipped bits are fitted with ball-bearing guides. In contrast, the pilot of a high-speed steel bit is simply an extension of the bit itself. As the bit spins at 20,000 rpm, the pilot spins at the same speed. The result is that the steel pilot will burnish the edge of the workpiece and may even scorch it. The ball-bearing pilots on carbide-tipped bits don't create these problems.

Shanks

Most woodworking power tools use some sort of mechanical interlock to fasten the blade or cutter securely to the machine. For example, planer knives are held in the cutterhead with gibs and screws; sawblades are held securely on the arbor with a large washer and nut. However, routers are unique in that the collet simply squeezes the bit shank to hold it firmly in place. The system works well if the collet is clean and well designed and the bit shank is the correct diameter. When inserting a bit into the collet, don't allow the collet to contact the ramped area where the shank meets the cutting head.

For a secure grip in the collet, a bit shank should be within .002 in. of the collet diameter. For example, the shank of a 1/4-in.-dia. bit should measure no less than .248 in., and a 1/2-in.-dia. shank no less than .498 in. Better manufacturers grind and polish the shanks of their bits within .0005 in. (five ten-thousandths of an inch), but others are not so precise.

Once, when I was routing a groove, the bit slowly crept out of the collet. Needless to say, I was surprised, because the collet and

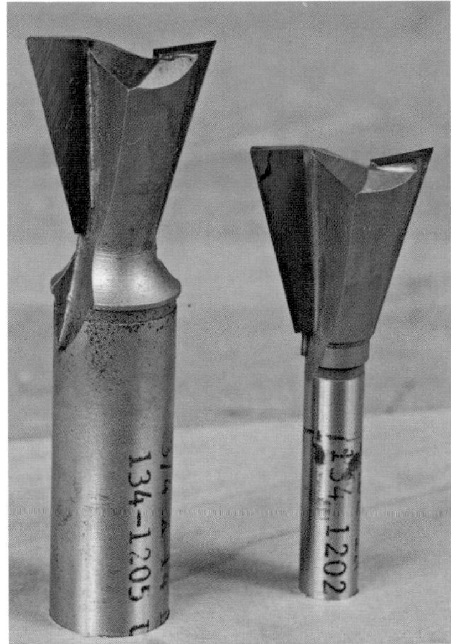

Unless you need a small bit for use in a laminate trimmer, it's best to purchase one with a ½-in.-dia. shank.

Small-profile bits with ¼-in.-dia. shanks are ideal for use in a laminate trimmer.

bit were both new and clean. So I measured the diameter of the bit shank; it was .006 in. less than the collet diameter. Because I had purchased a handful of these bits at a woodworking show, I decided to check each one. They were all undersized. Despite the low price, they weren't much of a bargain. With router bits, it's the things you can't see, such as carbide quality, brazing, and shank size, that determine how well they perform.

Years ago, most router bits had a ¼-in.-dia. shank, and the profiles were small, too. Today, routers have more power than ever before to drive the huge bits that are now available, and most router bits have a ½-in.-dia. shank. But when perusing a router bit catalog, you'll still often see router bits offered in both shank sizes. Unless my desired profile is very small, and I plan to use the bit in a laminate trimmer, I purchase a bit with a ½-in.-dia. shank. Remembering that the area of a circle is $\pi R2$; do the math and you'll see that it's an easy decision. I don't want to spin a hunk of steel and carbide at 20,000 rpm on a ¼-in.-dia. shank. If you're still using your 1970s router with a ¼-in.-dia. collet, then it's time to upgrade.

Although many router bit manufacturers offer bushings that allow you to mount a ¼-in.-dia. bit shank in a ½-in.-dia. collet, I've seen these bushings lose their grip. They don't seem to compress and squeeze the bit shank like a well-designed collet that's made for the purpose. So, on the occasion when you do use a ¼-in.-dia. shank bit, lock it into a ¼-in.-dia. collet. Most routers today come equipped with both ¼-in.- and ½-in.-dia. collets. If yours didn't come with a ¼-in.-dia. collet, check with the manufacturer. Perhaps you can order one.

Pilots and Bearings

There are several methods for guiding a router bit through the stock, but one of the most common is to use the pilot on the end of the bit. The process is stone simple: As the bit spins and cuts the stock, the pilot follows the edge of the workpiece, limiting the cutting depth. On HSS bits, the pilot is simply an extension of the bit, but on carbide router bits, the pilot is actually a miniature ball bearing that's held in place with a very small cap screw. You can change the cutting depth of the bit—and sometimes even the shape that the bit produces—just by swapping the bearing for a larger or smaller one. For example, most beading bits can be converted to a roundover profile by replacing the stock bearing with a slightly larger one. And rabbeting bits can be adjusted to cut a variety of different depths by using different-sized bearings. In fact, most router bit manufacturers offer rabbeting sets that consist of one rabbet bit with four or five bearings of different sizes.

This precision bearing ensures a consistent cutting depth without marring the work.

The one advantage of a steel bit is that the small-diameter pilot will reach deeper into corners.

Are there still uses for solid pilot bearings? Sure. When I want to shape further into a corner, I'll often use an inexpensive HSS bit with a solid steel pilot. The small diameter of the pilot goes further into the corner, and so the bit shapes more of the profile. The result is that you won't have to carve so much of the corner by hand. There are also a few specialty trimming bits on the market that still use a solid pilot. As for the tiny, ball-bearing pilots, I always keep a few replacements on hand for when a bearing begins to roll erratically.

Types of Bits

Routers have not really changed that much in 30 years, but there are more types and styles of router bits available than ever before. Besides many profile bits for producing moldings and table edges, there are spiral straight bits and adjustable grooving bits that work like a tablesaw stack dado head. And 20 years ago, those who didn't own a shaper would often shape raised panels on a tablesaw. But now there are router bits for

Large bits, when run at the same rpm as small bits, have a higher rim speed.

Edge-forming bits shape decorative profiles along the edge and face of the workpiece.

that, too. In fact, many of today's router bits are too large for hand held routing and must be run in a table-mounted router. Let's take a look at the wide variety of bits available to today's woodworker.

Edge-Forming Bits

Undoubtedly the most common form of router bit is the edge-forming bit. These are used to shape profiles such as ogees, chamfers, and roundovers. You can find them in every hardware store, home center, and catalog. Edge-forming bits add a decorative profile to a square edge, introducing style and detail. These are the bits that should be a part of every woodworker's kit. They include bits for making chamfers, roundovers, beading, and ogee bits.

The bead is a versatile profile, so it's good to have a bead bit assortment.

BUYING A SET

Most router bit manufacturers today offer router-bit sets comprising similar profiles, such as edge forming, grooving, etc. These sets can be a good deal because the cost of the individual bits would typically total more than the set. But before you lay down the cash, make certain that there is a reasonable likelihood that you'll use all the bits in the set. If the set contains just one or two bits of a size or profile that you'll never use, you're probably better off buying individual bits and getting just what you need.

Complex profile bits create two or more shapes in one pass.

When their height and cutting depth are adjusted, these bits can produce a number of different profiles.

Edge-forming bits are available in a variety of sizes in HSS and carbide. Some are quite large and require a powerful table-mounted router to safely operate them. Others consist of a combination of two profiles that create a complex molding. In fact, multi-profile bits have all the basic shapes (beads, roundovers, etc.) on one shank. Combination profile bits offer an economical alternative to buying several individual bits. Surprisingly, having all the profiles stacked on one shank can actually extend a bit's flexibility.

All of these bits shape a type of groove useful for joinery.

Grooving Bits

Grooves and dadoes are widely used in woodworking projects. Although both grooves and dadoes are identically shaped square-side channels, a groove technically runs parallel to the grain, and a dado perpendicular to the grain. For example, grooves are often used in drawer sides to accommodate the drawer bottom. Dadoes are often used to hold cabinet and bookshelf partitions in place.

There are variations on the standard grooving bit. For example, a corebox bit creates a type of groove. Large corebox bits are used to create coves for a molding, while smaller profiles can be used for shaping decorative flutes in a pilaster or column (see the top photo on p. 36). And when a divider and partition join at an intersection, a V-grooving bit is typically used to create a bird's-mouth joint. This elegant joint is simple to execute with router bits and looks

Corebox bits can be used to create decorative flutes.

Straight bits come in various sizes and configurations.

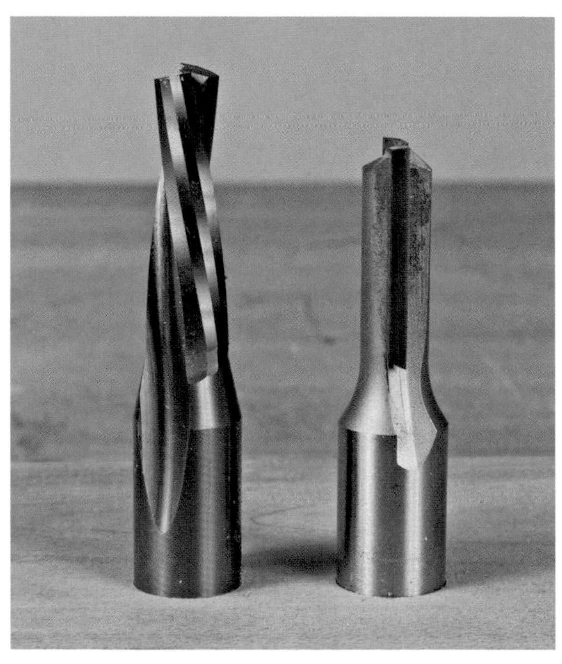

The spiral bit at left will create a smoother finish than the straight-flute bit at right.

refined, especially compared to a square groove from a standard grooving bit.

Straight Bits

Straight bits are among the most useful bits you can own. As the name implies, all straight bits are designed for cutting straight-sided grooves or dadoes. They will create a finished surface much smoother than that from a saw.

The best straight bits have skewed cutting edges that create a smooth surface free of burning and tearout. But for the smoothest surface, choose a spiral bit. A spiral bit, which resembles a twist drill, has a unique flute design that cleanly shears through even tough end grain. But that's not all: Spiral bits are superior for mortising because the spiral flutes actually lift the chips from the mortise for a faster cut with less load on the router.

There are three types of spiral bits: up-cut, down-cut, and compression. Of these, you'll probably find the up-cut style the most useful. The spiraling flutes of an up-cut bit will help clear away the cut chips during mortising. And when you're cutting or trimming in a table-mounted router, the bit will safely pull the stock toward the table surface rather than pushing it upward.

Straight, skewed-straight, and spiral-straight bits are all available with ball-bearing pilots for flush trimming (see the left photo on the facing page). Flush-trim bits are ideal for quickly and accurately trimming the excess edges of a face frame flush with a cabinet (see the drawing on the facing page). Some are designed specifically for trimming plastic laminate (see the right photo on the facing page).

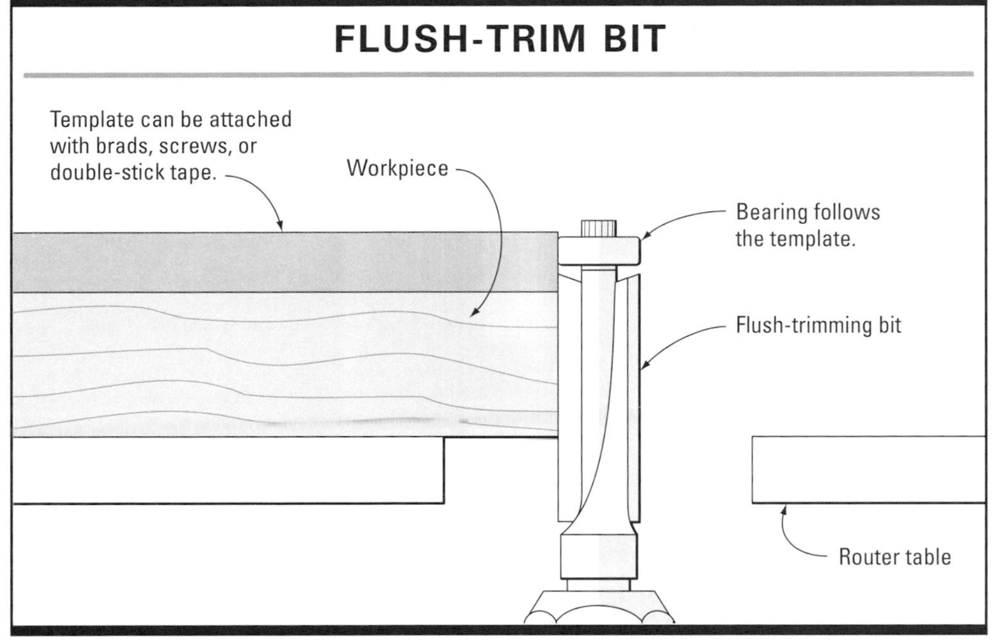

Flush-trim bits are available with (from left) straight flutes, skewed flutes, and spiral flutes.

These flush-trim bits are specifically designed for trimming plastic laminates.

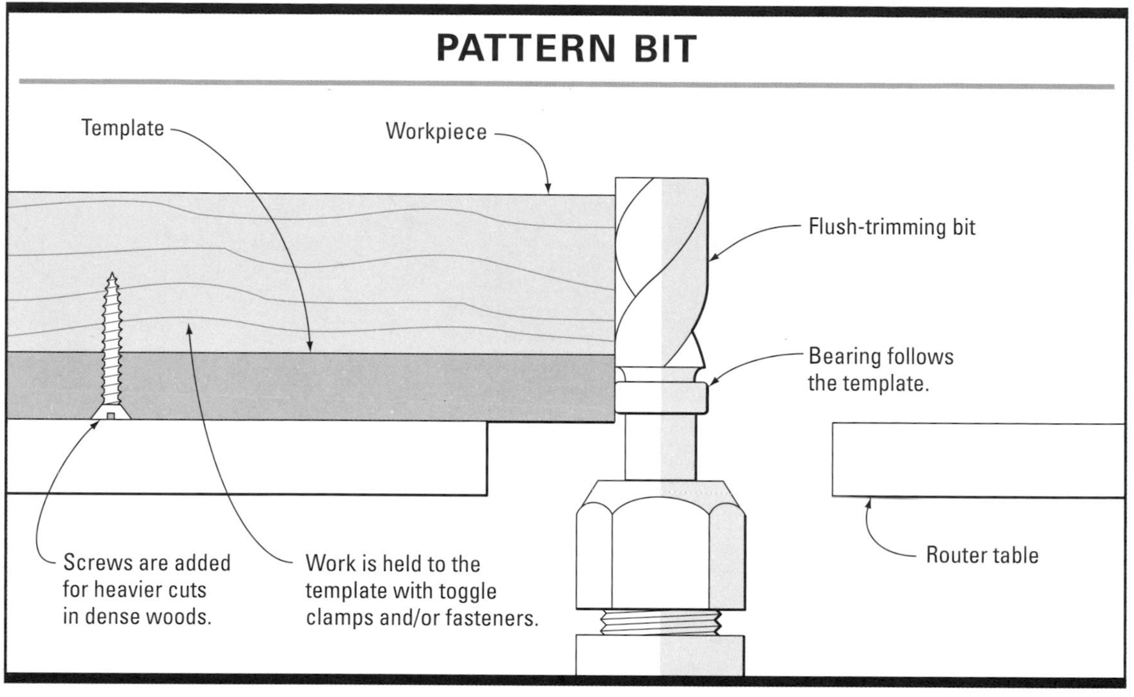

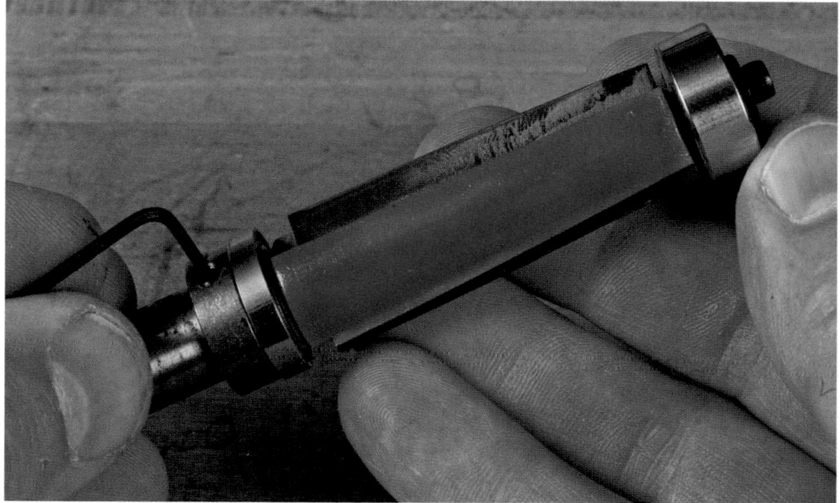

Adding a bearing on the shank allows you to position the template above or below the work.

Pattern bits are straight bits with a bearing at the shank end of the bit (see the drawing above). This style of bit is perfect for flush-trimming curved stock with a template. A lock collar and setscrew hold the guide bearing in position.

Slot-Cutting Bits

Like straight bits, slot-cutting bits cut a square-sided groove. The difference is that a slot-cutting bit cuts a groove parallel to the router baseplate. What's the significance? Slot-cutting bits can cut a groove along a curved edge, such as the top rail in an arched door. Straight bits can't (see the top left photo on the facing page.)

Slot-cutting bits are available in various sizes, for cutting grooves of different widths. To determine the depth of the groove, you simply choose a guide bearing of a suitable diameter. Slot cutters are also available in a stacking set, much like a dado head for a tablesaw. To adjust the cutting width, you just remove a nut and add or subtract cutters. Adjustable stacking cutters are available too. With this clever design, you simply turn a knurled screw to quickly and easily adjust the bit (see the bottom left photo on the facing page). There's no need to remove the

A slot-cutting bit will cut a groove into a curved edge.

This large rabbet bit can make smooth rabbets of any size.

The turn of a dial easily adjusts this slot cutter.

nut. This unique bit uses two mating cutters that interlock. A compression spring between the two pushes them apart while adjusting the bit for the desired setting.

Joinery Bits

There are a number of different styles of bits for producing accurate joinery with your router. Probably the most common is the rabbeting bit. Rabbet bits cut a square recess, or rabbet, along the edge of a board, often used to accommodate a door or backboard or to create a lip along the edge of a half-overlay drawer front. Because rabbets are used so often in woodworking, rabbeting bits can be found in every manufacturer's lineup. A rabbet bit set is extremely versatile, as it comes complete with an incrementally sized stack of guide bearings. Like straight bits, the best rabbet bits have skewed cutting edges.

By swapping the bearing, you can change the cutting depth of this rabbeting bit.

Dovetail bits cut the tapered pins and tails of this time-honored joint.

These bits are specially designed for use with dovetail jigs.

Dovetail bits cut a wedge-shaped slot for creating the interlocking tails and pins found on dovetail joints. Dovetail bits can be purchased in various diameters and pitch angles, most commonly 7 and 14 degrees.

Many woodworkers use dovetail bits with a jig. A bearing on the bit shank or a bushing attached to the base of the router guides the router bit along the "fingers" of a template that is part of the jig.

➤ See "*Commercial Dovetail Jigs*" on p. 137.

If you prefer to cut dovetails by hand, you might enjoy a method I use. I first lay out the dovetail in the usual manner. Then I use a dovetail bit and rout freehand to remove the waste between the pins. Afterwards, I saw the tails by hand to fit the pins. This method is efficient, yet unlike the jigs, it yields a dovetail joint with a hand-cut appearance (see the top left photo on p. 135).

Another popular bit is the drawer lock bit, used to create a simple interlock between mating drawer parts. A drawer lock joint appears deceptively strong. The short grain inherent to the joint breaks easily. If you choose to use this joinery bit, you may want to reserve its use for drawers that receive little abuse.

Finger joint bits cut rows of interlocking "fingers" for joining stock end-to-end. Because end grain doesn't create a strong glue bond, the idea behind a finger-joint bit is to join long-grain surfaces. This is a large bit that should be limited to use in a router table.

Panel-Raising Bits

Raised panels are a popular element in furniture and cabinets. However, until recently, if you didn't own a shaper, you would have to bevel the panel edges with your tablesaw. Now there are a number of panel-raising bits available in several sizes and shapes (see the top left photo on the facing page).

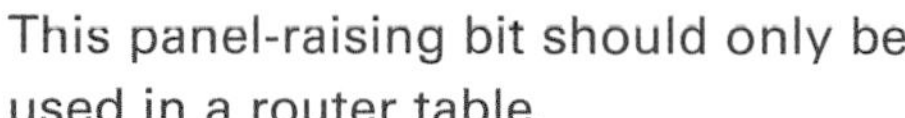
This panel-raising bit should only be used in a router table.

The vertical panel bit at left has a smaller diameter than the horizontal bit at right.

Matching stile-and-rail bits are used for making cabinet doors.

As you can imagine, router bits for shaping the edge of a panel are quite large. These bits deserve your respect and should only be used in a router table with a variable-speed router running at a lower rpm. Most panel bits come equipped with a guide bearing for shaping arched panels.

Vertical panel-raising bits are designed to cut a panel fed vertically rather than horizontally on the router table. Although they can be used with routers of smaller horsepower, they don't cut as smoothly as traditional panel-raising bits. It comes down to bit geometry: Small-diameter bits are too small to incorporate the effective cutting angle used by larger bits. So, unless you plan to bevel the edge of a coopered panel, I would stick to using the smoother-cutting horizontal bits.

➤ **See *"Raised Panel"* on p. 199.**

Sign-Making and Carving Bits

Router bits for sign making have a guide bearing mounted on the shaft with a lock collar to hold it in place. These bits are designed to follow the edge of templates to form letters. The most common sign making bits use a V profile; others use an inverted T that undercuts the letters to make them stand out from the background of the sign.

Matched Sets

Matched sets have become very popular. They typically consist of two complementary bits that make a complex joint. One example is the cope-and-stick, or stile-and-rail, set for making paneled doors. One of the two bits is used to make a decorative profile (sometimes referred to as "sticking") along the inside edges of a door frame. Shaping the sticking also cuts a panel groove.

A pair of bits can produce a complex molding or a drop-leaf edge.

This bit uses interchangeable cutters.

The complementary bit in the set cuts the cope on the ends of the rails. The cope is a reverse profile of the sticking. Along with the cope, a short tenon is also cut to fit in the panel groove. The two-piece set makes door making quick, simple, and precise. And if you glue a plywood panel into the frame, it will also be strong.

Similar sets are available for making divided light doors. Like the cope-and-stick set, a divided light door set shapes a decorative sticking along the edges of the door frame. This style of set cuts a rabbet instead of a panel groove to accept a glass pane, or "light." Divided light door sets are very popular for making doors for furniture or cabinets that display contents.

Still another style of matching bits is the drop-leaf set. This set shapes the matching cove and thumbnail profiles on drop-leaf table edges. The profiles allow the use of a special offset hinge to attach the leaf to the table.

Specialty Bits

There are a number of specialty bits from which to choose. If you're on a tight budget, you may want to consider bits that use interchangeable cutters. One design is best described as a diminutive shaper cutter bored to fit the bit shank. The idea is to put together an economical assortment of edge-forming profiles that use one shank.

These bits cut cost by sharing the same shank.

A newer style of interchangeable bit uses *replaceable carbide inserts*. The inserts are purchased in matching pairs that fasten securely into the body of the bit. Buying one body and several insert knives of various profiles allows you to build an assortment of shapes economically (see the top photo on the facing page).

An innovative bit features a mechanical interlock system to secure the replaceable carbide inserts.

Another style of insert bit is designed specifically for high-wear situations, such as routing abrasive sheet stock. The inserts have two or more cutting edges and are designed to be repositioned when the cutting edge becomes worn. Once all the sharp edges are used, the knives are replaced rather than resharpened. This ensures that the cutting diameter remains constant.

This bit features disposable carbide inserts.

Custom Profiles

Although there are certainly many more profiles to choose from, there are still times when you may not find the shape you need. However, many saw-sharpening shops can grind a custom router bit, complete with carbide tips. If that's the case, then consider high-speed steel. Although it wears faster than carbide, it holds an edge when used exclusively on natural wood and is easier to sharpen than carbide. For a short run of a special molding, a custom HSS bit is affordable.

For a custom profile, you may want to consider an inexpensive HSS bit.

Some specialty bits, such as the Crown Molding Set from CMT®, use standard profiles that are inverted on the bit shank. This allows you to shape segments of a large, complex molding that would be impossible with ordinary router bits.

This profile is inverted to shape areas that ordinary bits can't.

Swapping the bearing on a roundover bit converts the shape to a beading bit.

By rotating the profile 90 degrees, you can produce either shape here with the same bit.

Creative Uses for Bits

If you're creative, you'll often find several uses for the same one, which is obviously a great way to extend your woodworking budget. Often, just changing bearing sizes will alter the shape or depth of the profile. For example, switching to a larger bearing on a beading bit will convert it to a roundover bit. Other times, you can alter the shape of the finished profile by rotating the molding 90 degrees, a common technique with ogee bits. By changing the position in which the molding is applied, you can create a reverse ogee.

A chamfer bit is typically used to taper an octagonal post or leg or just to remove a hard, square edge. And when used in conjunction with a V-bit, a bird's-mouth joint can be created.

➤See *"Bird's Mouth"* on p. 172.

Beading bits can be used for an edge bead or a corner bead. And by removing the guide bearings and sometimes even

This bit can produce an edge bead or a corner bead.

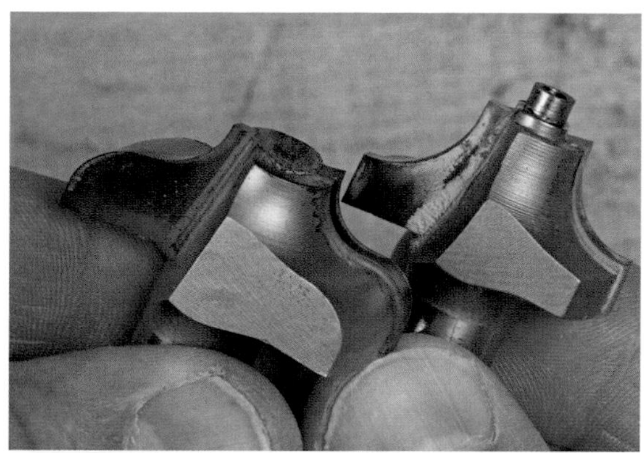

Sometimes the bearing and even the mounting stud can obstruct the desired cut.

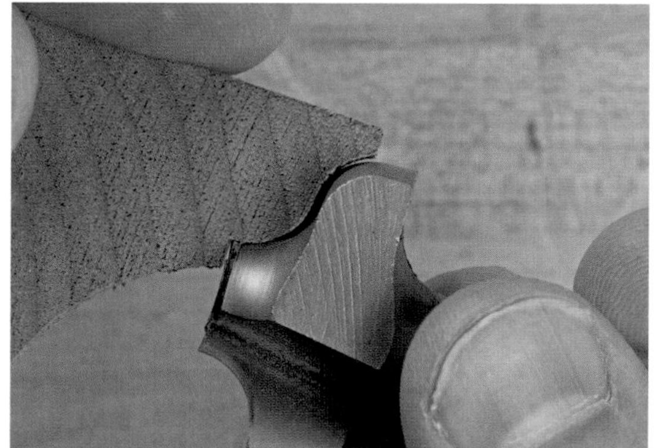

The bearing stud on this bit was purposely ground away to avoid marring the adjacent cove.

grinding away the mounting stud, you can increase the versatility of a bit.

Large Bit Safety

Shapers are expensive, and so are the cutters. But as the sizes of router bits have grown, you can now create many cuts with your router that were once done by a shaper. Raised panel bits and cope-and-stick sets are just a couple of examples of the large router bits that have become available to meet the demands of today's woodworkers. And when you compare the size of these huge bits to their much smaller predecessors of 20 years ago, they deserve your respect. Hold a panel-raising bit in your hand; that's a lot of steel and carbide to spin in a high-speed router. To use large bits safely, here are some guidelines:

Always follow the manufacturer's guidelines.

Mount the router in a table. Some bits are just too large for hand routing. A router table provides a massive, steady work surface to support the router and the large, spinning bit.

Large bits should only be run in a router table.

Lower the rpm. Large-diameter bits run at the same rpm as small bits have a much higher rim speed. So be safe and run these bits slowly (see the top photo on p. 46). Check with the bit manufacturer for a suggested speed. Of course, you'll need a router with electronic variable speed (EVS).

Use a soft-start router. Going from zero to 20,000 rpm in a fraction of a second causes a router to jerk suddenly, especially if equipped with a large bit. Soft-start routers have electronics that cause a router to develop full speed over the course of about one second, which all but eliminates the jerk.

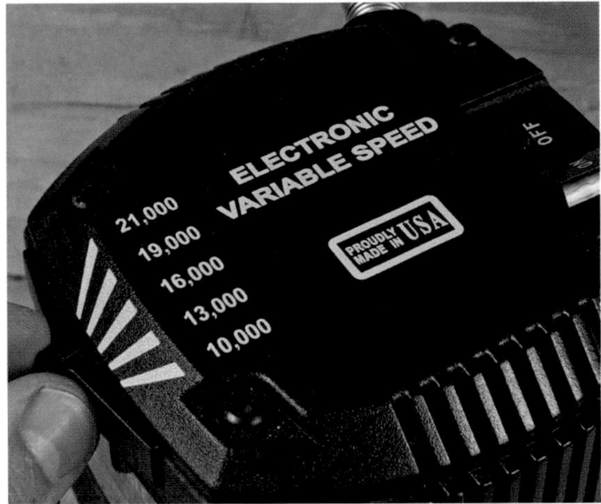

This multi-speed router can be slowed down for use with large bits.

This guard will shield your hands from large panel-raising bits.

This drawer protects the carbide and makes it easy to locate the bit you need.

Use light cuts. Even super-duty 15-amp routers don't have the power to make heavy cuts in a single pass. Heavy cuts can lead to kickback and overheating of the router motor. For best results, take several light cuts; listen to the router and don't bog it down by removing too much stock at once.

Use a guard. A well-designed guard, such as the Panel-Loc guard from Bench-Dog®, provides a protective barrier between your hands and the bit. It is also easy to set up and use. It simply fastens to the T slots in the fence. And if your fence isn't equipped with a T-slot, the Panel-Loc comes with one that easily attaches to your existing fence.

Bit Storage, Cleaning, and Sharpening

Router bits are not inexpensive; a dozen or so can add up to several hundred dollars. So it makes sense to take good care of them. In fact, a high-quality router bit will last for many years, with care. Depending on how often you use it, you may not ever need to purchase a replacement.

Proper storage is critical to the life of a router bit. Bits should be stored in a rack or compartmentalized box to keep them separate. If bits are tossed together in a drawer, the brittle edges of the carbide will be damaged. Clear plastic boxes compartmentalized for fishing tackle or small die-cast cars are ideal storage containers (see the top left photo on the facing page).

It's also important to keep bits clean. Dirt and resins will commonly build up along the cutting edges, causing a bit to overheat. There are a number of tool cleaners available that will easily dissolve the buildup without damaging the carbide or brazing (see the top right photo on the facing page).

A storage case keeps the bits separate to protect the carbide tips.

A commercial bit cleaner will dissolve built-up pitch on a bit.

For the best possible grip in the collet, the shank of a bit should be smooth and polished. You can polish the steel shanks with fine steel wool or a mild plastic abrasive pad.

Router bits will often last longer than their tiny guide bearings. When a bearing begins to show signs of rough, erratic movement, it's time to replace it. Attempting to prolong the life of a bearing by soaking it in a solvent will only shorten its life, because the solvent will penetrate the seal and dissolve the bearing grease.

Sharpening your router bits is best left to a professional sharpening shop. The cutting geometry of most router bits is complex. Attempting to hone the edges may change or even ruin the geometry. I send all my tooling—including planer knives, shaper cutters, sawblades, and router bits—to a local professional shop. Their prices are reasonable, and they have the knowledge, skill, and equipment to sharpen the tools correctly.

Surface rust should be removed with steel wool or a synthetic abrasive pad.

It's a good idea to keep an assortment of extra bit parts on hand.

A

B

C

Changing Bits

Before installing a bit in a router, make certain that the bit shank is smooth and free of rust, pitch, or burrs. New bits often have a thin coat of grease on the shank. This should be removed with mineral spirits.

As you tighten the collet, it simply compresses and squeezes the bit. Make certain it grips the shank and not the radius at the base of the shank **(A)**. Insert the bit fully and then withdraw it approximately ⅛ in. so that the collet makes contact only on the shank **(B)**.

Finally, snug the collet firmly against the bit shank by tightening the collet nut. Most routers have two wrenches. Position the wrench on the router against the benchtop for leverage as you apply pressure to the wrench on the collet nut **(C)**.

Changing Bearings

Why change bearings? A good-quality bit will often outlive the bearing. A bearing that feels rough as you spin it or one that whines during use should be replaced. Also, some bits, such as rabbeting bits, come supplied with several bearings so that you can alter the cutting depth.

To change a bearing, you'll want to first secure the bit in a collet **(A)**. Resist the temptation to grip the bit shank with pliers, as you'll scar the bit shank. Insert most of the bit shank **(B)** and tighten the collet firmly **(C)**.

Next, place a wrench on the router collet to prevent it from rotating, and remove the tiny cap screw with an Allen wrench **(D)**.

When replacing the bearing, make sure that the bearing shield is in place **(E)**. Replace the cap screw **(F)** and gently tighten it **(G)**.

A

B

C

D

E

F

G

A

Adjusting a Stacking Bit

A stacking bit has cutters of various widths that can be used alone or in combination to create a groove or a pair of parallel grooves **(A)**. Spacers are used to control the width of the cut and prevent the carbide tips from making contact. A guide bearing is included for template or curved work, and a nut holds all the parts onto the bit shaft.

Begin by mounting the cutter in a router **(B)** and locking it in place **(C)**. Resist any temptation to grasp the bit shank with pliers or place it in the jaws of a vise, which will damage the smooth surface of the shank.

B

C

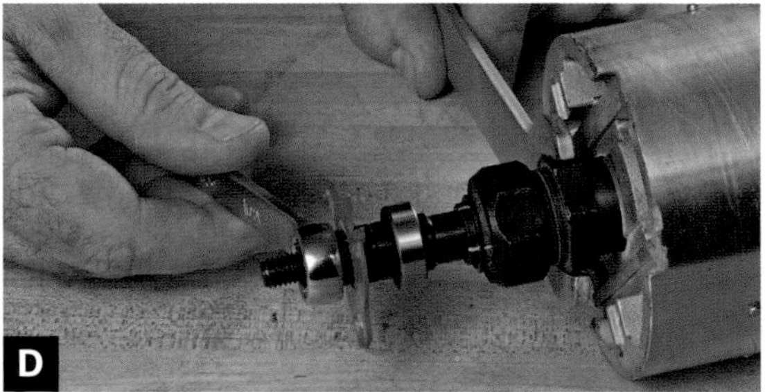

D

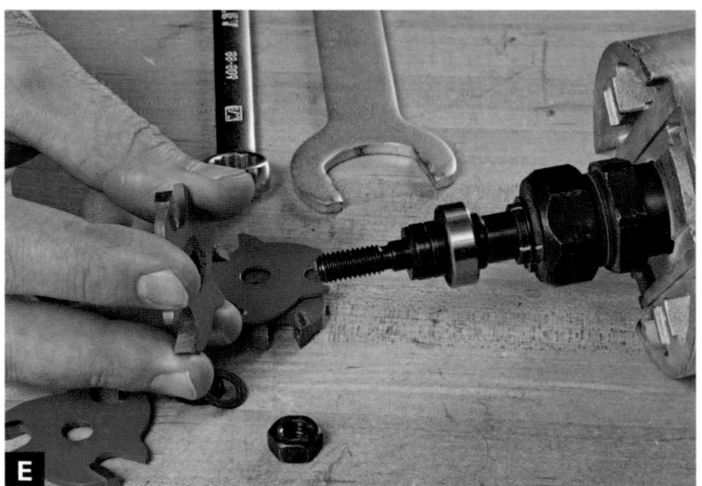

E

F

To remove the nut on the bit, place a wrench on the router and position it against the bench surface for leverage **(D)**. Now, carefully remove the cutter **(E)**. When stacking the cutters on the bit shank, make certain that the teeth are positioned to rotate counterclockwise as you're facing the end of the shank **(F)**. Place a spacer between cutters **(G)**, orienting the carbide tips so they don't touch **(H)**. Now place the washer on the shaft **(I)** and replace the nut **(J)**. Finally, lock the nut firmly in position **(K)**.

G

H

I

J

K

Router Tables

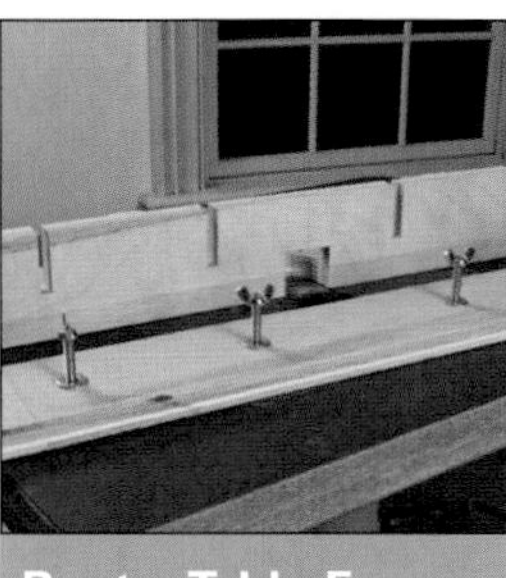

Router Table Fences

Benchtop Router Table

Router Table Sled

No other accessory will add more versatility to your router than a router table (as shown in the top photo on the facing page.) By inverting a router and mounting it in a table, you have, in essence, created a mini-shaper. With the small investment of a router table, you can shape large profiles, such as raised panels, straight and curved moldings, and a variety of complex joints.

There are other advantages gained by using a router table instead of a handheld router. For example, it's easier to shape small pieces on a table than to hold and balance the router over a small workpiece. Long workpieces, such as moldings, are also easier to shape because the table surface provides plenty of support. In addition, many large-profile bits, such as cope-and-stick sets and panel-raising bits, can be used only with a router table.

Router Table Designs

Like routers and bits, router tables have come a long way in recent years. The small, lightweight, vibration-prone, stamped-steel router tables of a few years ago have been replaced by large, sturdy cabinet models, complete with features such as accessible electrical switches, storage for accessories,

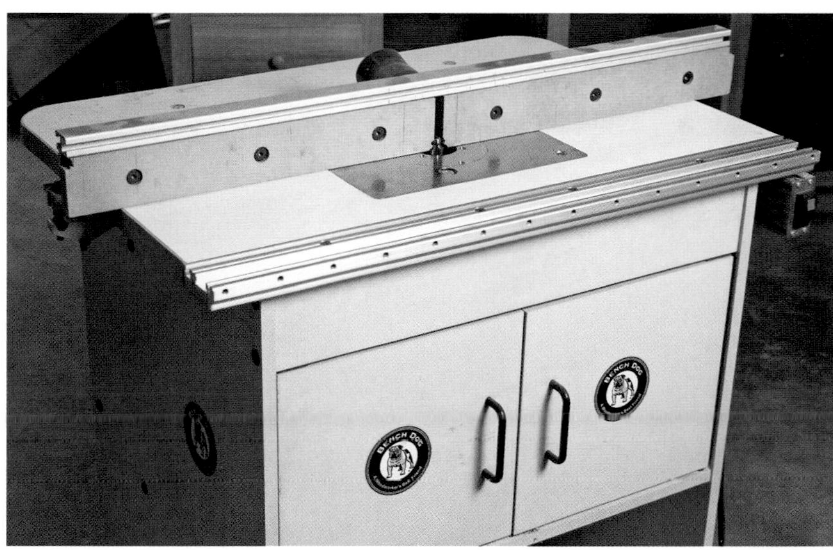

A router table adds tremendous versatility to your router.

and dust collection. Fences have seen vast improvements, too. The best fences are arrow-straight aluminum extrusions with T-slots for mounting accessory guards and featherboards.

You can even purchase cast-iron and phenolic tops that eliminate sag from heavy routers. And if you have limited space, you can purchase a router table wing that bolts onto the top of your tablesaw. Of course, if you're on a budget, you can build a table for a minimal investment of time and money. Let's take a closer look at your options.

Stationary Router Tables

If you have the floor space in your shop, then a stationary router table is definitely the way to go. Mount a large, 3-hp router under the top and you'll have a high-performance power tool. Stationary router tables have large tops for support of the work and extra weight to minimize vibration. You can also use the space underneath for storage. A stationary router table is definitely the best choice if you plan to do a lot of routing.

Like all benchtop tools, a benchtop router table can conserve valuable space and be easily transported to a job site.

Benchtop Router Tables

A benchtop router table will offer you the advantages of table routing without taking up more floor space in an already cramped shop. Benchtop router tables are typically more affordable than stationary models. And if you do job site work, the reduced weight and compact size make a benchtop router table truly portable. Even though they're small, the best models are loaded

BUILDING VS. BUYING

Open the pages of almost any woodworking catalog and you'll see an enormous selection of router tables. You may be wondering—why not just build a router table? My recommendation? Buy the top, and then build a cabinet to support it. Router tabletops, although not complicated, can be somewhat time-consuming to construct. And you'll need a fence as well. For most woodworkers, the nominal cost of buying a quality top and fence provides you with extra time for woodworking.

However, the best support stand is one that you build yourself. You can customize it to your height and equip it with doors and drawers for storage of all the stuff that you use with your router.

And don't feel that you have to blow your woodworking budget to have a sturdy, useful table. For a few dollars and a weekend of your time, you can construct a modest yet sturdy table that's capable of doing much of what the large, expensive tables will do.

This shopmade router table and sled are just as capable as many commercial models.

A sturdy yet inexpensive top was constructed from kitchen sink cutouts.

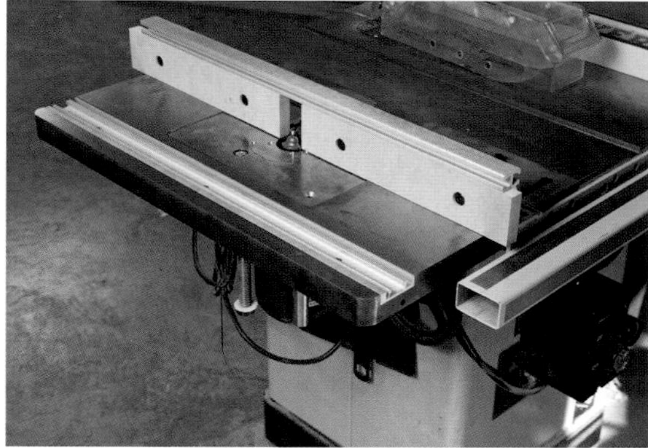

This space-saving cast-iron top bolts to the top of your tablesaw.

with features that enable them to go head-to-head with the floor models. The best benchtop router tables include a zero-clearance aluminum extrusion fence, a dust-collection port, and a miter gauge slot for end-grain routing.

Tablesaw Wing Tables

If you're looking to save space without losing convenience, you may want to consider a wing-type table. Wing tables replace the extension wing on your tablesaw without limiting the use of the saw. Wing tables are cast iron to reduce vibration and are outfitted with a high-quality fence with simple, yet solid fence locks. Think of it as the ultimate upgrade of your tablesaw.

The Top

The most important aspect of any router table is its surface flatness. Stripped to the essentials, a router table is just a flat top with an inverted router suspended underneath. It's the table that provides a reference surface, supports the workpiece, supports the router, and provides a surface on which to

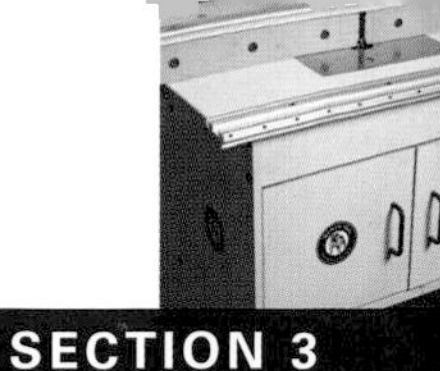

A micro-dial makes it easy to make height adjustments as fine as .001 in.

secure a fence. The top consists of the table, the insert plate, and possibly a router lift mechanism with a built-in height gauge.

The most important component in a router table, the top can also be the Achilles heel of the entire system. That's because many tops sag under the weight of today's high-powered, heavy routers. So let's take a look at material choices for tops.

Table Materials

The best router tabletop is one that stays strong and flat over time. Given that, the worst choice you can make is natural wood. It lacks sufficient stiffness across the grain, and it easily warps when the relative humidity changes. There are more suitable options, including plywood, particleboard, MDF, phenolic, and cast iron.

Plywood is a good choice because its laminated plies provide stiffness and stability. It's relatively inexpensive, and you can often buy a partial sheet of plywood at your local home supply center. For a stiff top that resists sagging, laminate two pieces of ¾-in.-thick plywood together, which will provide thickness and strength at the cutout.

As this simple plywood stand shows, there's no need to spend a lot of money to get started with table routing.

This sturdy top features accessory T-slots, a miter gauge slot, and insert-plate leveling screws.

Particleboard and MDF are flat and heavy—good qualities for a top. If you plan to build the top yourself, laminate two pieces together; the extra weight and thickness will absorb vibration and resist sagging. These materials can warp, so it's important to cover both faces with plastic laminate. If you plan to purchase a particleboard top, look for one that features a metal framework with built-in leveling screws to support the router insert plate. This design eliminates the wear

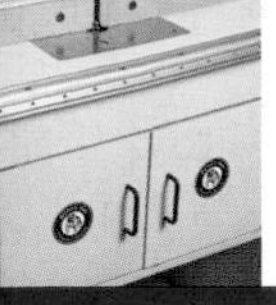

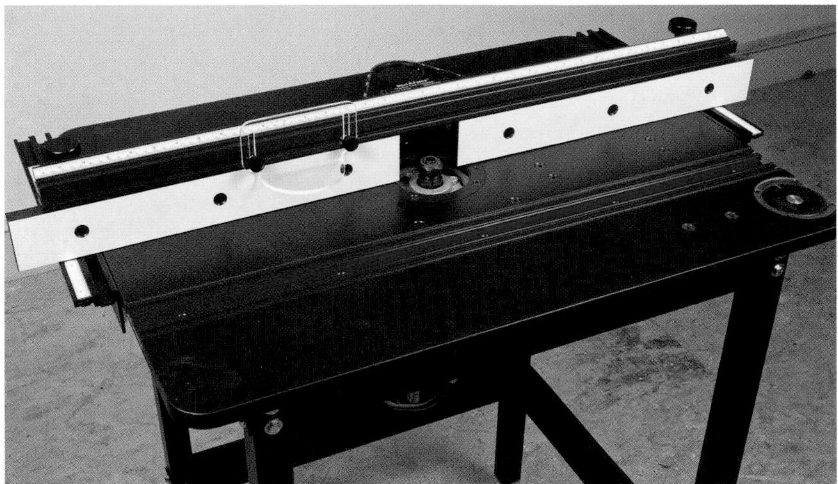

This phenolic table features a lift with a built-in crank for fast, precise adjustment.

Baseplates are available in plastic, phenolic, and aluminum.

that would otherwise occur on the particleboard from the leveling screws in the insert plate.

Phenolic is a relative newcomer among router-table tops. It is very hard, dense, and strong, making it well suited to the job. Phenolic is made by laminating layers of resin-impregnated paper or fabric. Heat and pressure is applied to cause polymerization, transforming the layers into a laminated plastic. Phenolic wears well, resists warping, and has sufficient strength and stiffness to resist sagging under the weight of a heavy router. It's a great choice for the job.

Cast-iron tops are available from several manufacturers. Cast iron wears extremely well and is stiff, strong, and heavy, which helps reduce vibration. Some commercial cast-iron tops are designed to be used on either a freestanding router table or as an extension wing of your tablesaw.

Baseplate Options

Most commercially available router-table tops feature a rectangular baseplate from which the router is suspended. The baseplate sits within a recess in the tabletop.

A baseplate gives you quick access to the router for adjustments and bit changes.

If you're making your own top, you'll probably want to use a baseplate as well, instead of simply drilling a bit access hole in the top. The baseplate allows you to quickly lift the router out of the table for making height adjustments and bit changes (see the bottom right photo above).

For best stock support when you're routing, the bit opening in the baseplate should suit the size of bit you're using without leaving a large space around its perimeter. Some baseplates are outfitted with insert rings that

This universal baseplate fits virtually every router without drilling.

This aluminum baseplate comes with an insert ring.

A phenolic baseplate includes insert rings for minimizing the bit opening.

allow you to quickly adjust the bit opening. Unfortunately, some baseplates don't have insert rings, forcing you to switch baseplates when changing from a very large-diameter bit to a small one. As you can imagine, this can quickly become a time-consuming chore.

Commercial baseplates are available in several different materials, including aluminum and various plastics. You can purchase a baseplate complete with mounting holes, or you can make your own.

Phenolic, an industrial laminated plastic mentioned earlier, is the best choice for a plastic baseplate because of its strength and stiffness.

Acrylic is also a good choice of plastics for baseplates. Although it doesn't have the stiffness of phenolic, acrylic works well with all but the heaviest routers and is usually available at your local glass shop.

Aluminum is another good choice for a baseplate material. Aluminum has greater stiffness than most plastics, to resist sagging from the weight of a heavy router. Also, aluminum baseplates are typically available with insert rings.

Lifts

A major drawback of router tables has always been the awkwardness of changing bits and making bit height adjustments. It usually requires that you either reach underneath the table or remove the heavy router. To solve

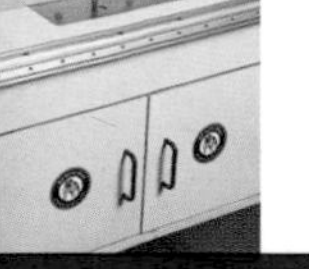

A lift is the ultimate upgrade for any router table.

this problem, some manufacturers now offer router lifts to make these adjustments fast, convenient, and accurate. The lifts also add extra weight, which helps limit vibration.

Router lifts eliminate the need for the router base. Instead, the router motor is fastened directly into the carriage of the lift, as shown in the drawing below. The lift, baseplate, and router motor become one unit, and, once installed in the tabletop, it does not need to be removed. Router lifts use a speed wrench or a crank (see the top right photo on the facing page) for making height adjustments from the top without having to reach underneath. To change bits, just crank

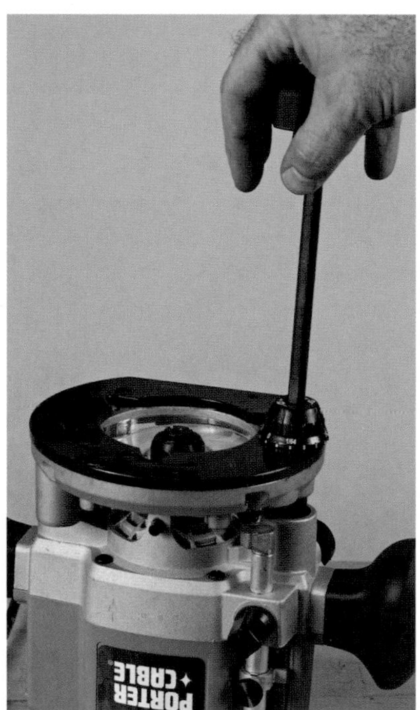

This unique plunge router, which incorporates a built-in lift mechanism, can be adjusted from above when used in a router table.

ROUTER LIFT

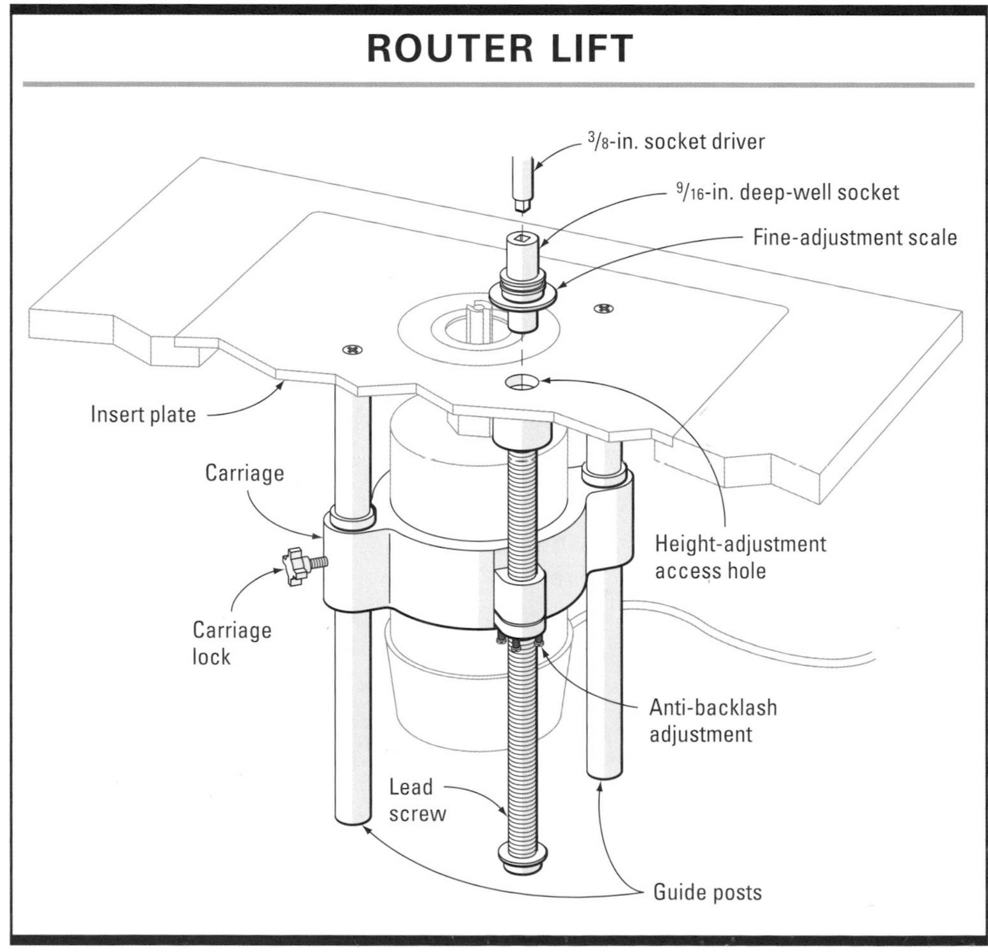

A lift allows for fast bit changes and adjustments from above the table.

This top includes a built-in lift and micrometer height adjustment.

A precision lift comes with a full set of insert rings.

the motor up, and you'll have easy access to the bit and collet. To adapt the system for a large bit, router lifts use insert rings to eliminate the need to swap out baseplates. Some router tables come equipped with a built-in lift and integral dust collection. A router lift provides the ultimate conversion of your router table into a true stationary power tool.

This lift features a dust collection fitting under the table.

Guiding Cuts

There are four tools for guiding the cut when you use a router table: the fence, a miter gauge, a guide bearing, or an overarm guide.

The Fence

The most common method for guiding cuts on the router table is to use a fence. If you're used to handheld routing, you'll find that using a router table and fence offers greater control and convenience. Besides guiding the cut, the fence provides a place to position a guard and featherboards. Cleanup is a snap too, because you can attach a dust-collection hook-up directly to the back of the fence.

A router table fence doesn't have to be elaborate or expensive to work; a plank and a pair of C-clamps will serve the purpose.

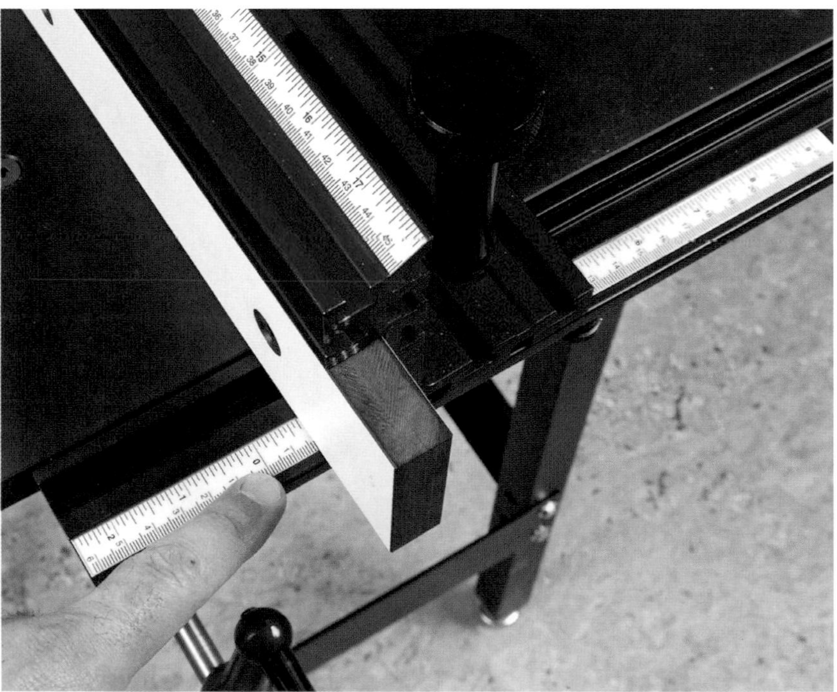

The graduations on this fence help with making fine adjustments to the setup.

Various dust-collection fittings are available for attachment to a router table fence.

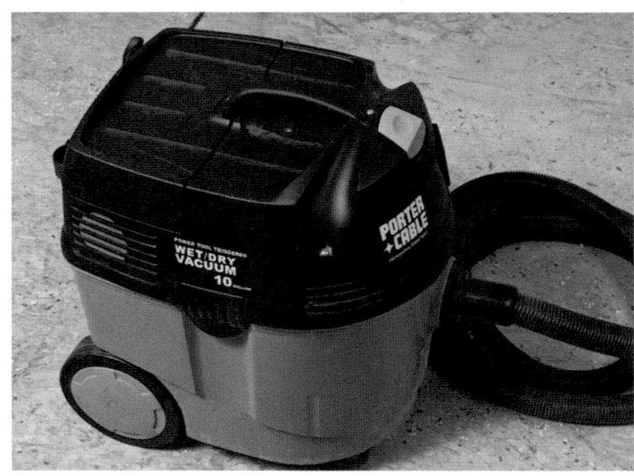

This shop vacuum can be switched to power up automatically when you start the router.

However, you can easily construct a fence with more support and features by attaching two strips of plywood at right angles to each other. Braces added behind the fence will stiffen it and keep it 90 degrees to the table surface.

Commercial fences are typically made from extruded aluminum. Aluminum fences are lightweight, strong, and include T-slots for quick and easy attachment of guards and accessories. MDF inserts in the face of the fences adjust laterally to accommodate different bit diameters and can be cut to cre-

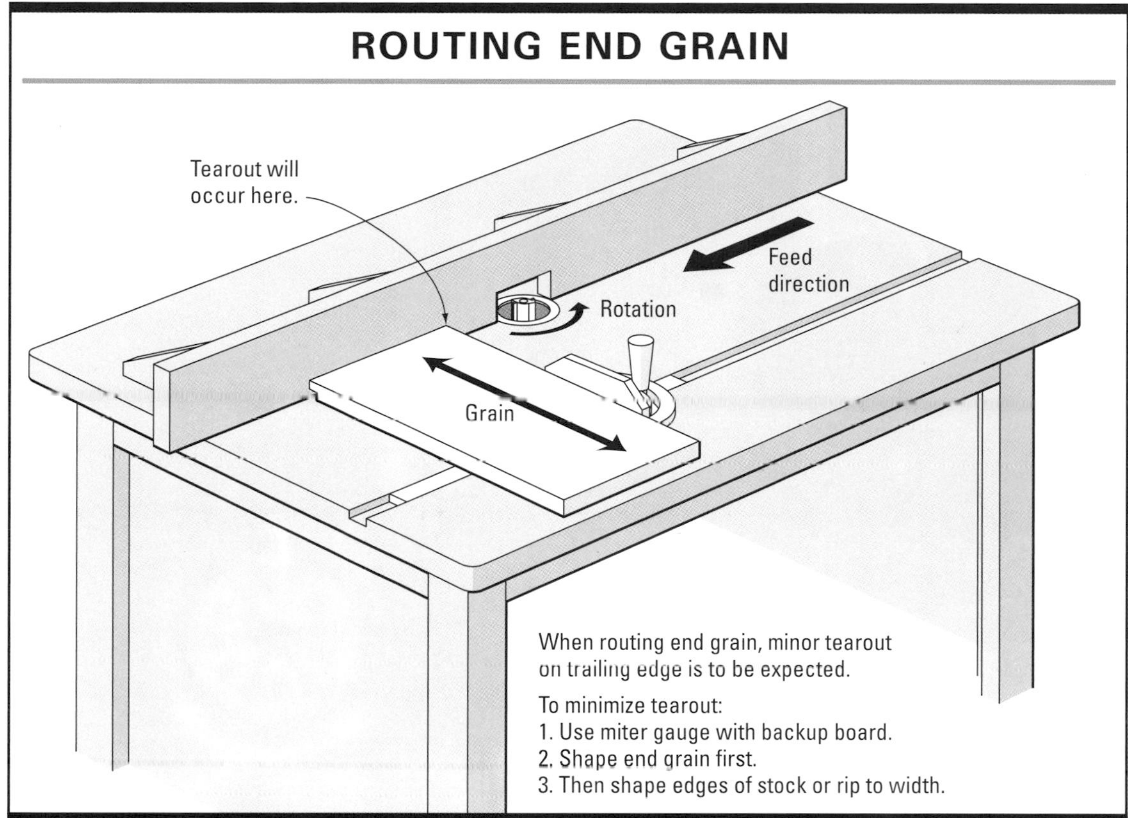

ate a zero-clearance opening. Commercial fences also have built-in clamps to securely lock them to the table.

The Miter Gauge

The miter gauge provides support when you're shaping the ends of narrow stock such as door rails. Of course, if you plan to use the miter gauge, you'll need a groove in the top of the router table to guide it in a straight path. If you make your own top, you'll probably want to purchase an aluminum insert for the miter-gauge groove for resistance to wear. When using a miter gauge, it's still important to use a fence. The fence serves as a guard to cover the unused area of the bit (see the drawing above).

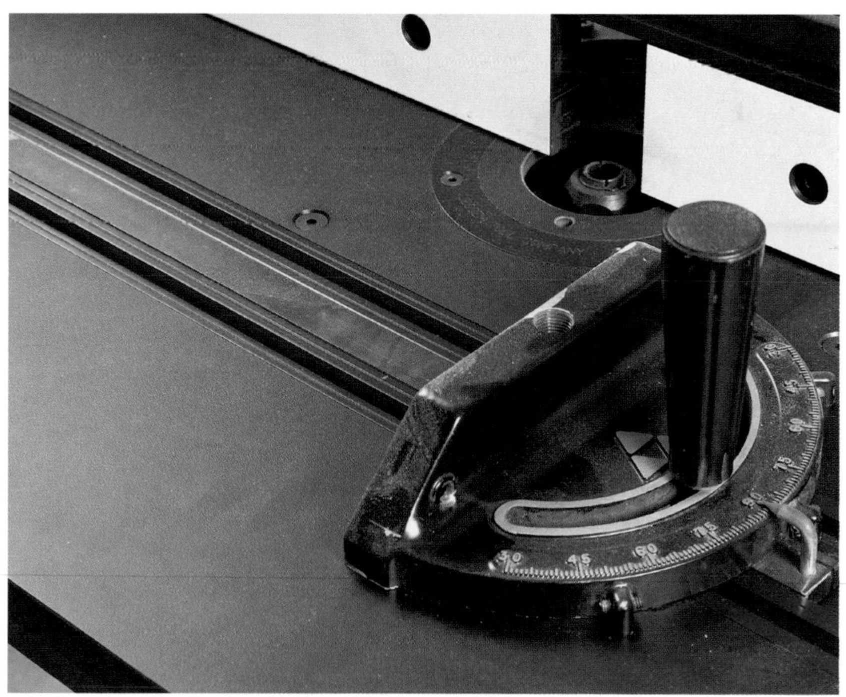

A miter gauge is useful when routing the ends of narrow stock.

A starting pin provides a fulcrum when you're routing curves.

TEMPLATE ROUTING

Stop blocks are glued and screwed to base of template.
Bit rotation
Feed direction
Block resists thrust of bit, preventing stock from moving laterally.
Stock
Template extends beyond workpiece, so starting pin is not necessary.
3/4-in. plywood
Toggle clamps hold stock to template.

Guide Bearing

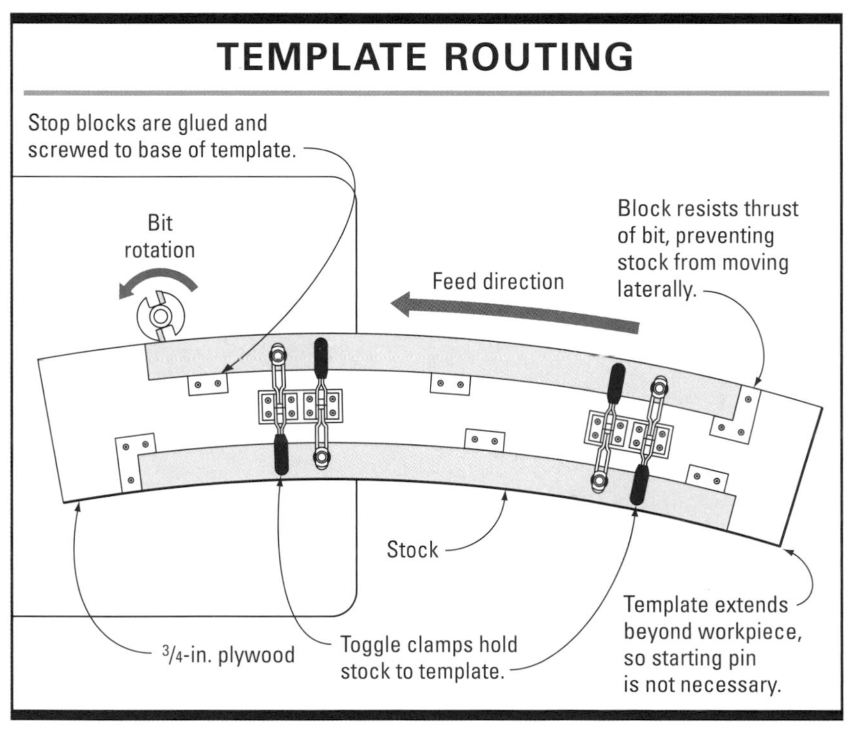

The guide bearing is one of the best guide tools for shaping freeform curves and arcs. As with handheld routing, the bearing can follow a pattern or the workpiece itself. The guide bearing even helps when used with the fence; just align the fence so that it is tangent to the bearing. This makes setting the fence fast and accurate.

When shaping curved stock with the bearing as a guide, it's important to use a starting pin. The starting pin threads into a hole in the tabletop and provides a fulcrum to safely lever the workpiece into the spinning bit. Without a starting pin, the bit can grab the stock and pull it from your grasp.

If you're shaping curved stock with a template, extend the template beyond the work, so that it contacts the bearing before the work contacts the cutting edge of the bit. This method provides a smooth entry into the cut without a starting pin (as shown in the drawing at left).

OVERARM GUIDE

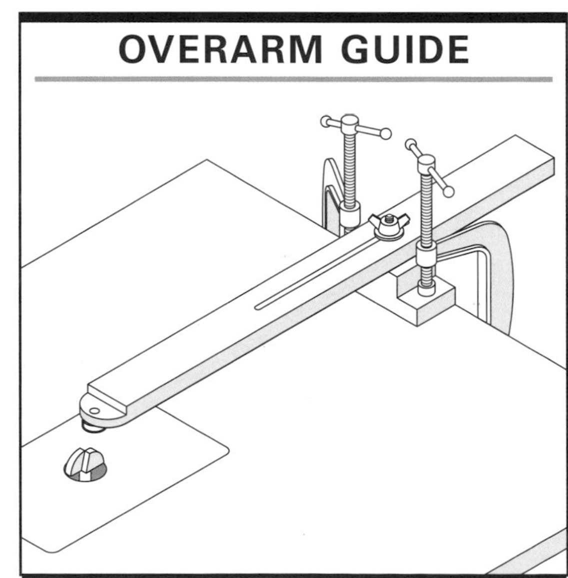

Overarm Guide

An overarm guide (as shown in the bottom right drawing on the facing page), works much like a bearing. The difference is that unlike a guide bearing, the overarm guide can be positioned off-center to the bit. This allows you to make internal cuts on curved stock, as when coving a gooseneck molding.

➤ See *"Curve with Template"* on p. 215.

Base Designs

Even if you choose to purchase a top and fence for your router table, the best base is one that you build yourself. By building the base, you can customize its height and enclose it to create a useful storage area. Unless your shop has lots of room to spare, you'll probably want to avoid mounting the top on an open base or leg set. The space below the table is an ideal storage area for bits, wrenches, and accessories. Plus, the added weight of a cabinet-style base (and its contents) adds to the stability of the router table.

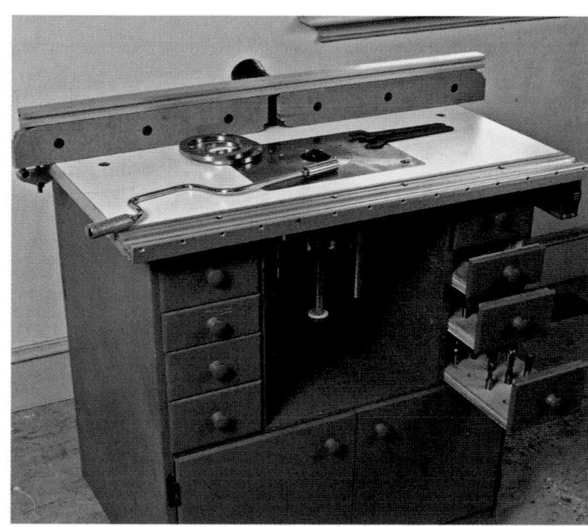

A custom cabinet provides plenty of storage for bits and accessories.

Router Table Accessories

Of all the accessories you can add to your router table, the most important are safety devices such as guards and featherboards. Many of these are designed to fasten to a T-slot in the fence. (If your fence doesn't have a T-slot, you can add a T-track.)

Guards provide a barrier between your hands and the spinning bit, while featherboards hold the stock firmly against the fence and table. This helps prevent kickback and offers greater control and a smoother cut. The Panel-Loc barrier guard by Bench Dog is a large aluminum extrusion designed

A T-slot in a router table fence allows attachment of guards, featherboards, and other accessories.

This unique guard is effective when you're routing curved stock.

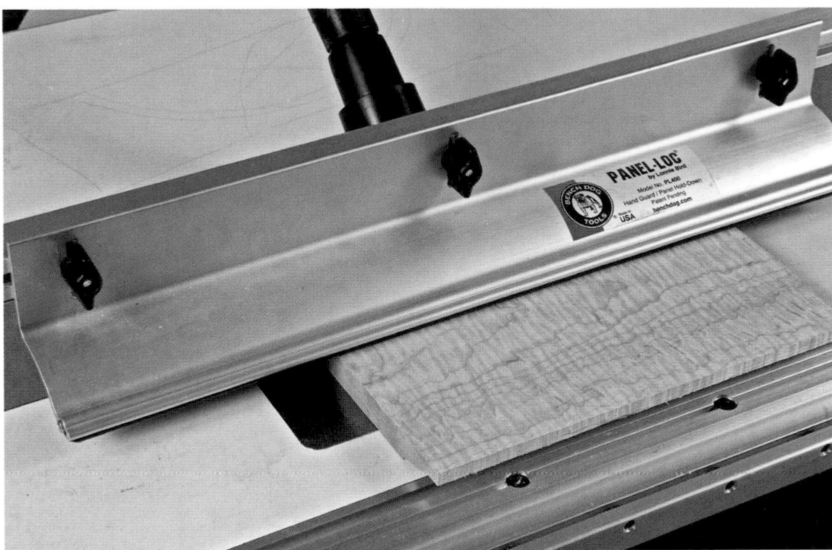

This guard provides an effective barrier when you're using large bits.

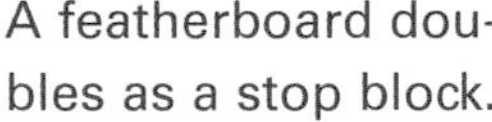

A featherboard doubles as a stop block.

An external switch eliminates groping under the table for the power switch on the router.

for shaping panels. The heavy extrusion shields large panel-raising bits from your hands while working as a hold-down to keep the panel firmly positioned on the table.

Other worthy accessories include stop blocks used to limit kickback when you're making stopped cuts, and an exterior power switch, which eliminates groping under the table for the switch on the router.

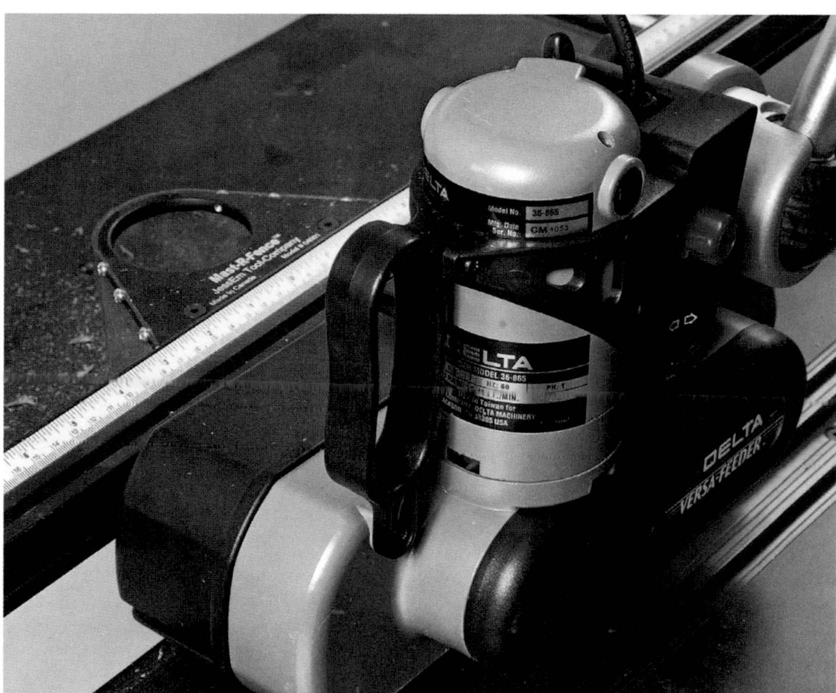

While providing a uniform feed rate, this scaled-down power feeder keeps your hands clear of the bit.

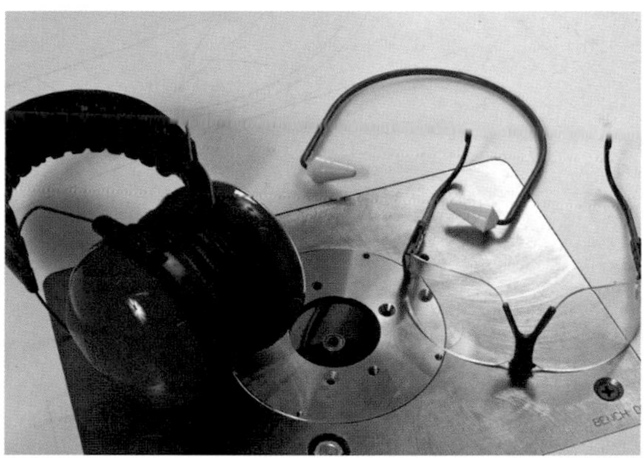

Eye and hearing protection are critical when you're using routers.

Power Feeder

One of the best accessories you can add to your router table is a power feeder. This tool keeps your hands safely distanced from the bit, while the constant feed rate provides a smoother, more uniform surface than you can achieve by hand feeding. Today there are small, lightweight feeders that are perfectly suited for router table use.

Router Table Safety

Although most router bits are small, routers and bits deserve your attention and respect. As with all power tools, you can enjoy them safely by following a few safety guidelines:

- Large-diameter bits are for use only in a router table. Using bits over one in. in diameter in a handheld router can easily cause you to lose control.
- Always wear eye and hearing protection.

FEATHERBOARD

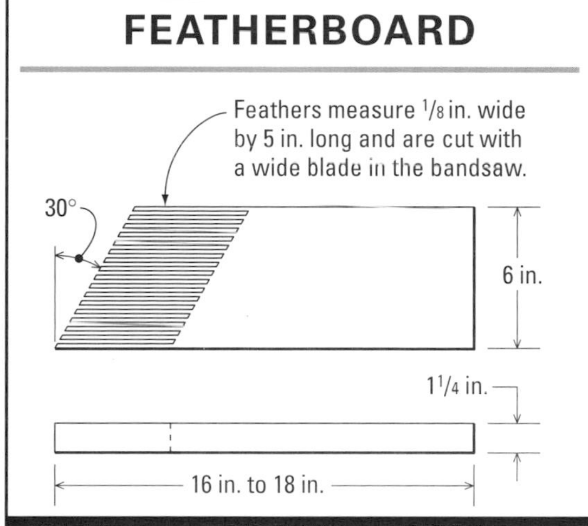
Feathers measure 1/8 in. wide by 5 in. long and are cut with a wide blade in the bandsaw.
30°
6 in.
1 1/4 in.
16 in. to 18 in.

- Take light cuts. Heavy cuts invite kickback. If necessary, move the fence closer to the bit or switch to a larger guide bearing.
- Use a featherboard to support the workpiece (as shown in the drawing above).

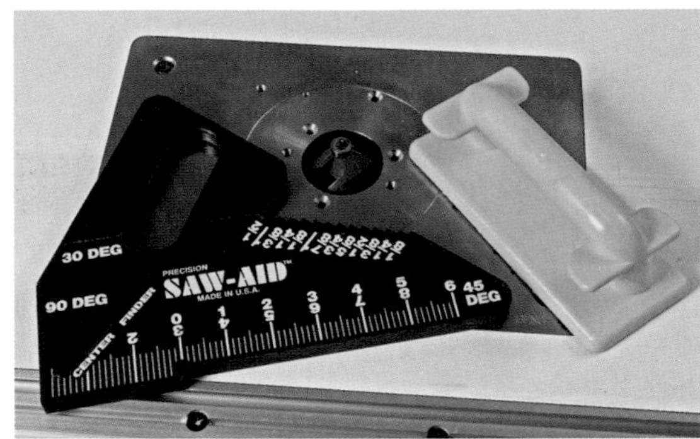

Push blocks and sticks distance your hands from the spinning bits.

ROUTER TABLE FEED

Router bit rotates into stock (against feed direction) and pushes stock away from fence and back toward operator. Stop blocks must be positioned to resist these forces.

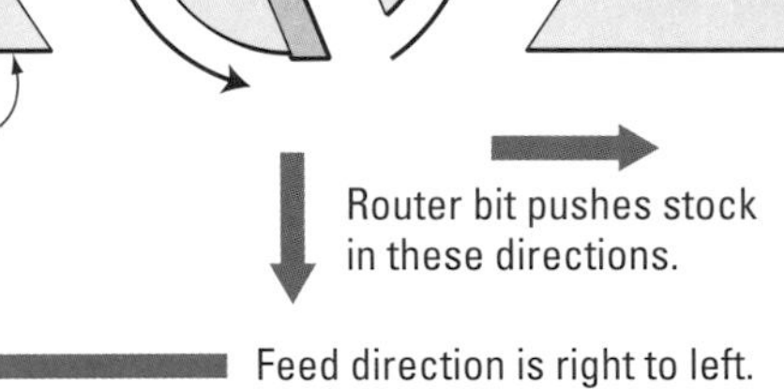

Router bit rotation

Fence

Router bit pushes stock in these directions.

Feed direction is right to left.

If your router table doesn't have a guard, you can make one of your own.

- Never climb-cut. Always feed the stock from right to left, as shown in the drawing above.
- Use push blocks and featherboards to position your hands a safe distance from the bit.
- Avoid shaping small stock. Instead, shape a larger piece and reduce it in size afterwards. If you must shape a small piece, build an appropriate jig or secure the work within the jaws of a wooden handscrew clamp.
- Always use a guard. If the fence didn't come with a guard, purchase an aftermarket guard or devise one of your own.
- Never start the router with the bit in contact with the stock.
- Don't force the bit or overload the router.
- Secure the motor in the base before starting the router.
- Don't bottom out the bit in the collet or partially insert the bit. Instead, completely insert the bit, and then back off approximately 1/16 in.

Simple Fence

If you've built your own router table, here is a simple fence that works well for routing edges and grooves **(A)**. Select a plank of hardwood and mill it slightly thicker than the average piece of stock you plan to rout. Use a scrollsaw or saber saw to cut a notch in which to fit the router bit **(B)**. Fasten a rectangle of Plexiglas® to the top of the fence to serve as a guard **(C)**. Two small clamps are used to secure the fence to the table **(D)**. The opposite side of the fence is used for routing grooves and dadoes **(E)**.

A

B

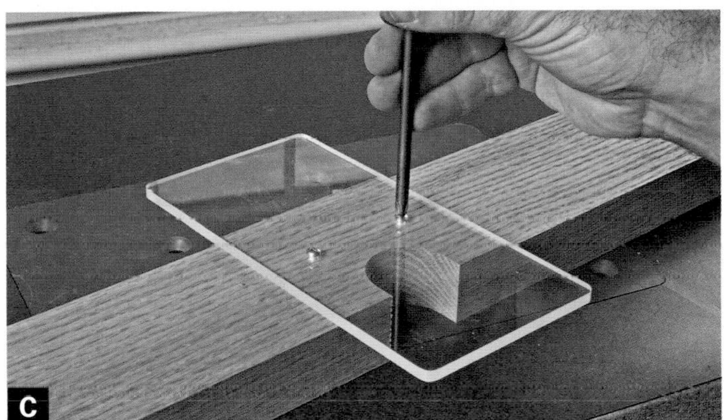

C

D

E

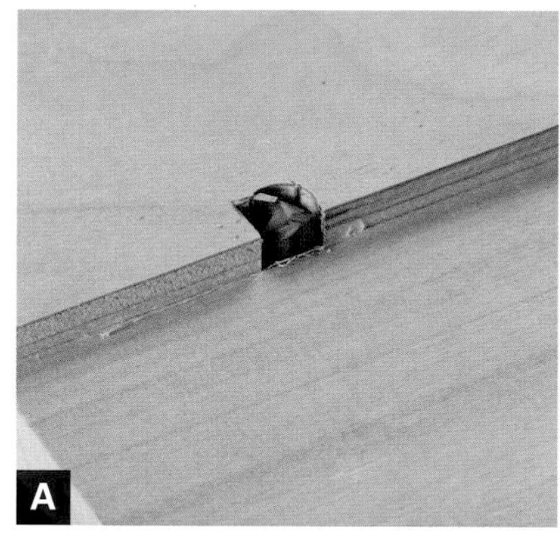
A

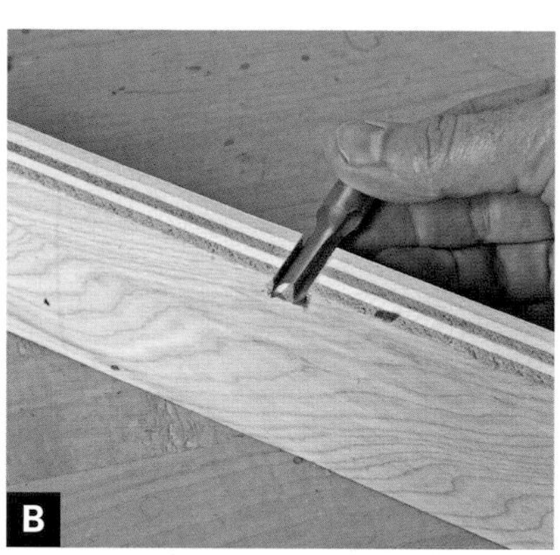
B

C

D

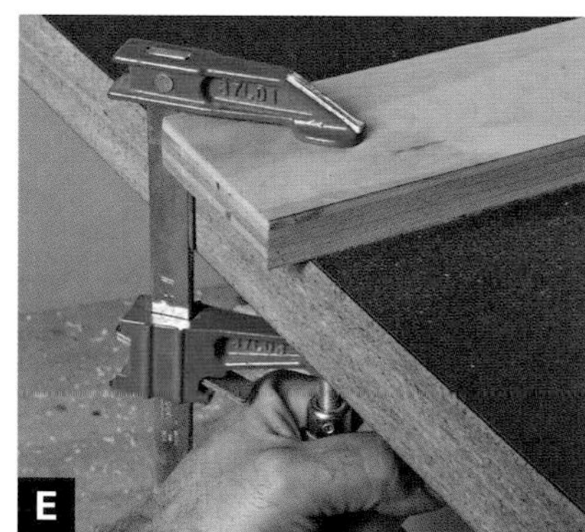
E

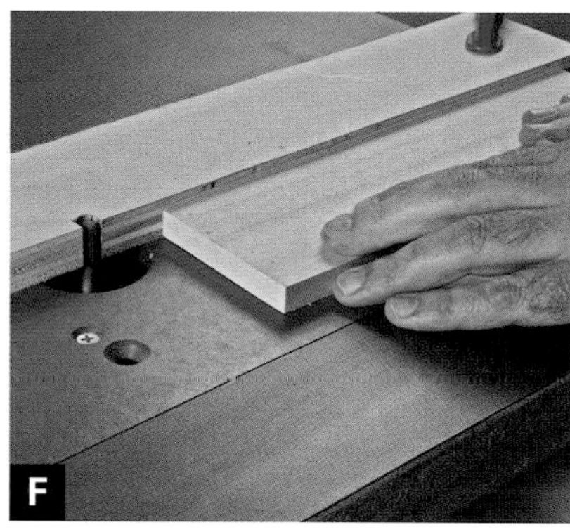
F

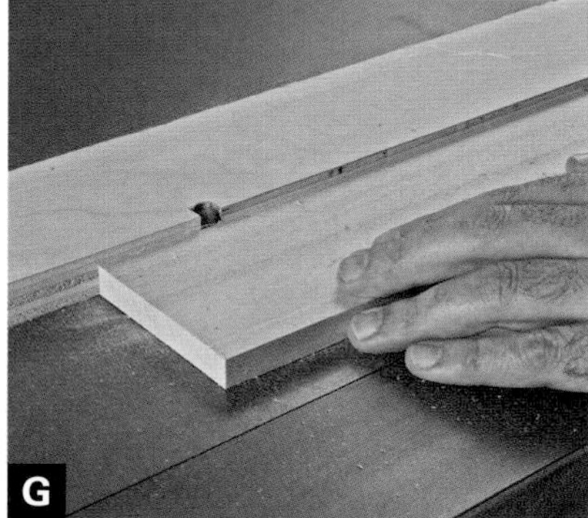
G

Jointing Fence

You can joint the edges of stock too short to safely run through a jointer by using your router table and a jointing fence **(A)**. A jointing fence is one in which the two halves are parallel but not in the same geometric plane. Instead, the outfeed fence is forward by a small amount, say $1/32$ in., to support the stock after it passes the router bit. The setup works like a mini-jointer with a vertical bed.

The first step is to cut a strip of plywood and cut a small notch in the center to contain the bit **(B)**. Next, use the router table and a straight bit to remove $1/32$ in. from half of the fence **(C)**. As you make this cut, maintain pressure against the infeed side of the router table fence and stop cutting when you reach the bit opening **(D)**.

To use the fence, first clamp it to the router table **(E)**. With a straight bit installed in your router **(F)**, joint the edge of the work, maintaining pressure against the outfeed half of the fence **(G)**. This method ensures that the jointed edge will be straight.

'L' Fence

Although a plank or strip of plywood can serve as a fence, in many situations you'll most likely want a taller fence. A tall fence gives greater support for feeding stock on edge and also provides a place to position guards and featherboards (as shown in the photo at left below). Construction is simple—two plywood strips are joined at 90 degrees **(A)**. Biscuits increase the glue surface area **(B)** and glue blocks at the back stiffen the fence **(C)**.

Begin by laying out and cutting the slots on the face of the fence **(D)**. Machine screws and wing nuts fit in the slots **(E)** for mounting a guard or sacrificial fence **(F)**. Next, cut a bit opening, and glue the two main parts of the fence **(G)**. Finally, attach the glue blocks **(H)**.

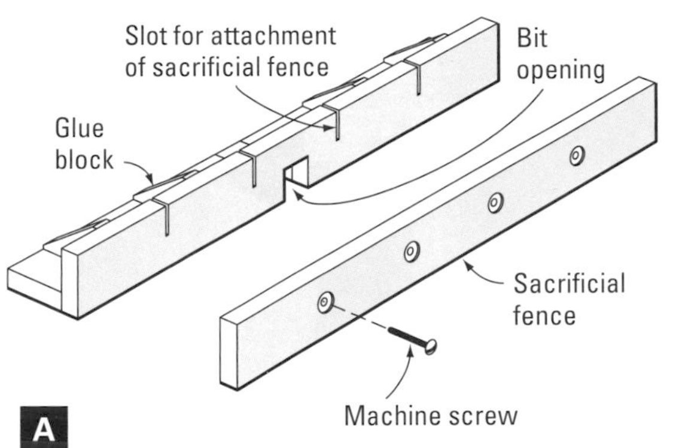

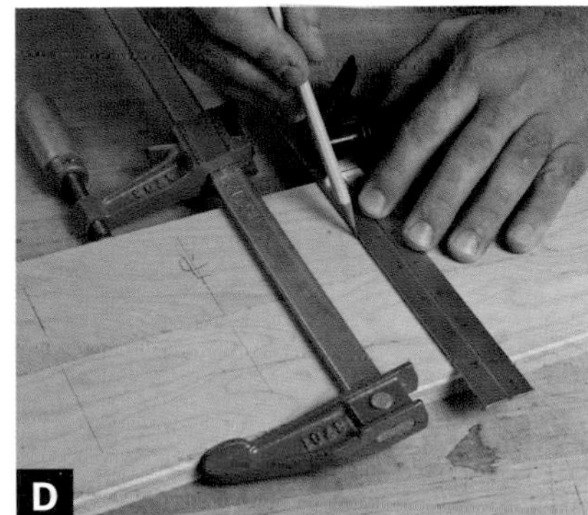

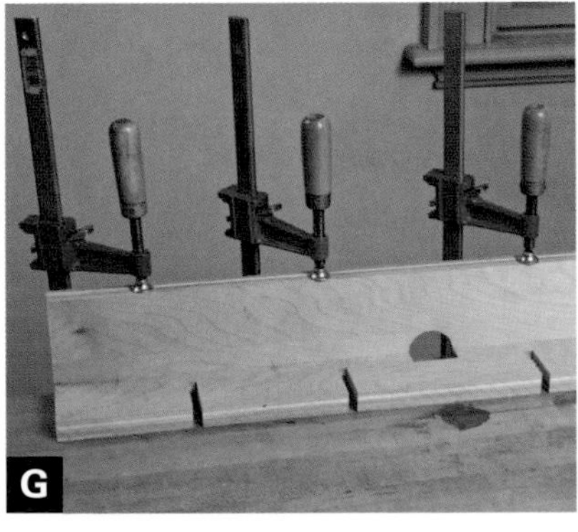

A

B

C

Zero-Clearance Fence

To get maximum support from a fence, you'll want its bit opening to be as small as possible. A zero-clearance fence has no opening for the work to drop into because the bit is used to cut an opening.

The first step is to adjust the height of the bit **(A)**. To avoid spoiling the standard fence, attach a sacrificial fence **(B)** that fits into the slots on the L-shaped fence (see previous photo-essay) **(C)**. Now clamp the outfeed end of the fence to the table **(D)** and pivot the infeed half of the fence into the spinning bit **(E)**. Remember to clamp the infeed end of the fence in place before use. If the bit has a guide bearing, the procedure is to first secure the fence to the table. Then loosen the locknuts that hold the fence insert. Next, slowly feed the fence half into the spinning bit. Now repeat the process for the second half of the fence.

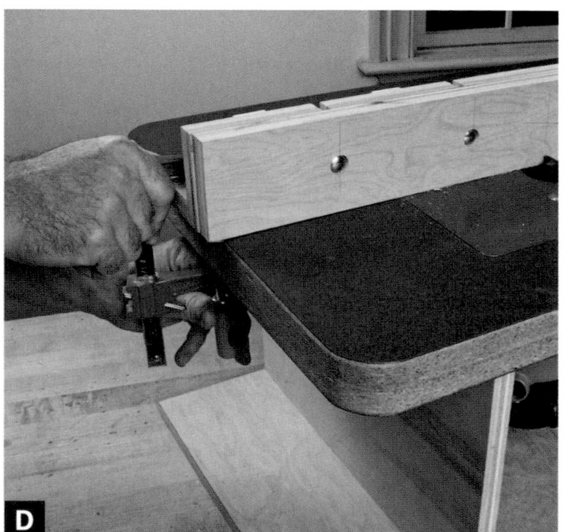
D

E

Support Stand

If you would like a router table but your woodworking budget is tight, you may want to consider building this support stand **(A)**. The stand can be used for hand routing, but it also serves as a benchtop router table when outfitted with a top. The unit is inexpensive, lightweight, and compact for easy storage. You can equip it with a plywood top or construct a thick, sturdy top from sink cutouts.

➤ See *"Two Dollar Top"* on p. 72.

After cutting the parts and sawing or routing the dado joints, assemble the table with glue and screws **(B)**. Drill a hole in the side of the cabinet for the cord **(C)**. This will keep it out of the way during routing operations. Fasten a top from underneath **(D)** and drop the router in from the top **(E)**.

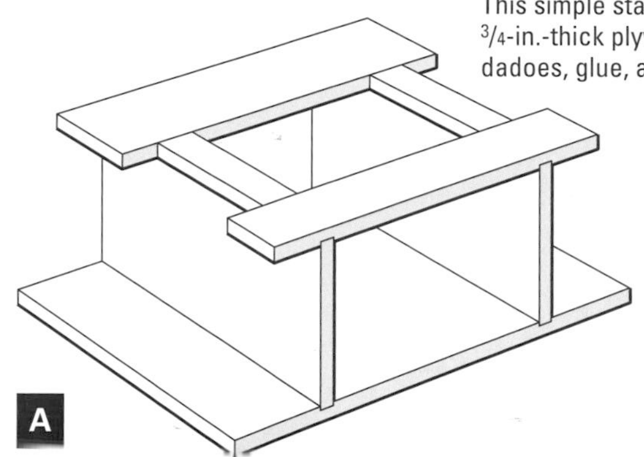

This simple stand is made of ¾-in.-thick plywood joined with dadoes, glue, and screws.

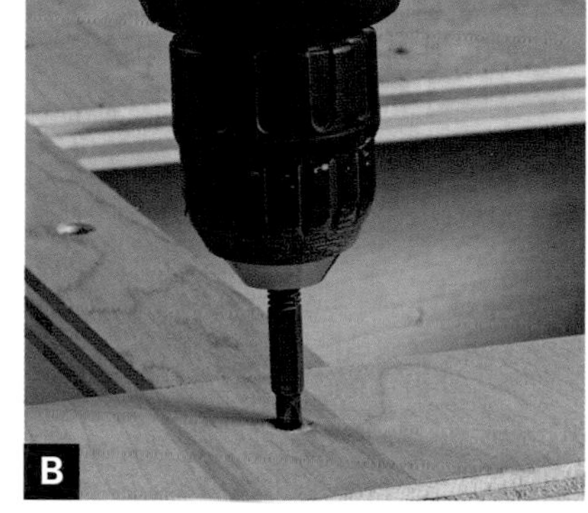

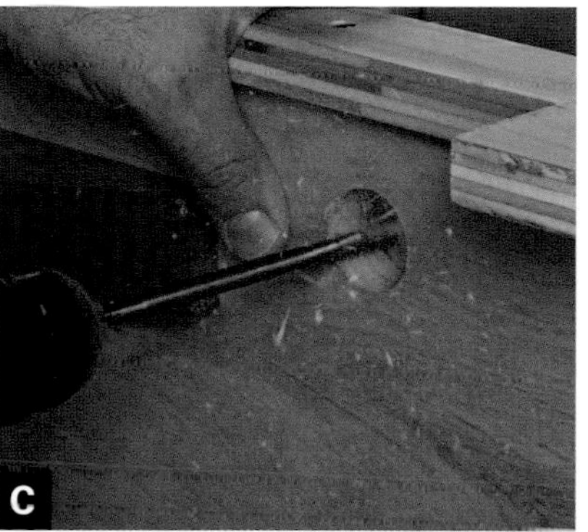

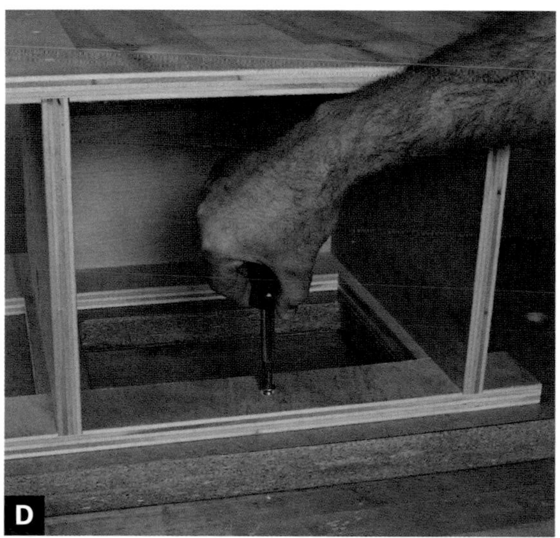

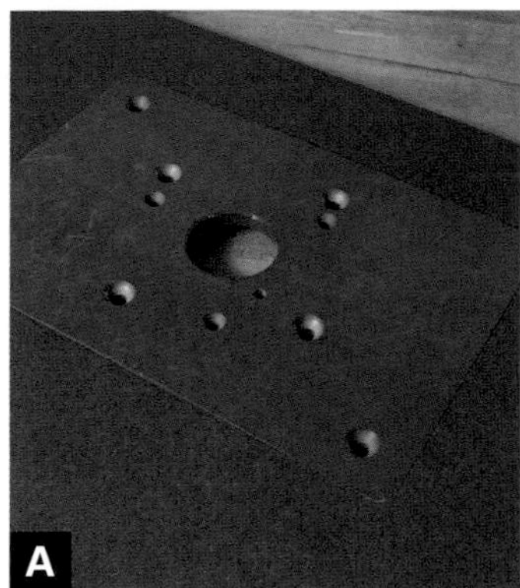

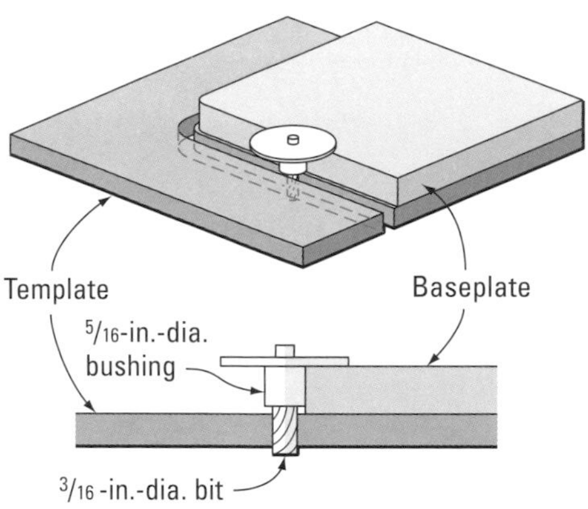

Step 1: Rout template from baseplate.

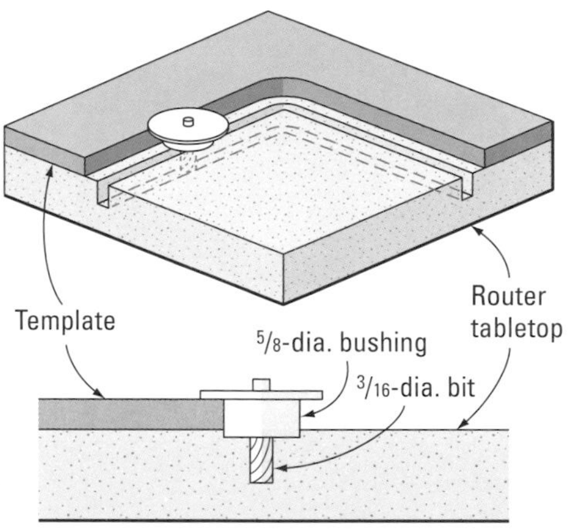

Step 2: Rout opening perimeter in top.

Two-Dollar Top

If your woodworking budget is limited, you'll like this top; it's constructed from two sink cutouts obtained from a local cabinet shop for a dollar apiece **(A)**. Your local shop may even give them away.

For this router-table top, I laminated two ¾-in.-thick cutouts back-to-back, making an extra-thick top that won't sag. It's less likely to warp too, because it has plastic laminate on both faces.

You can rout a shallow recess for the router on the underside of the top, but you'll probably want the advantages of a baseplate, which will allow you to lift the router out of the table to make bit changes or adjustments to the bit height. Routing for a baseplate isn't difficult, but get or make the baseplate first, because you'll need it to make a template from ¼-in.-thick plywood for routing the opening in the top **(B)**.

The first step is to set up the router. Remove its baseplate **(C)** and install a 5⁄16-in.-dia. guide bushing in place with the lock ring **(D)**. Next, install a 3⁄16-in.-dia. straight bit in the collet **(E)**.

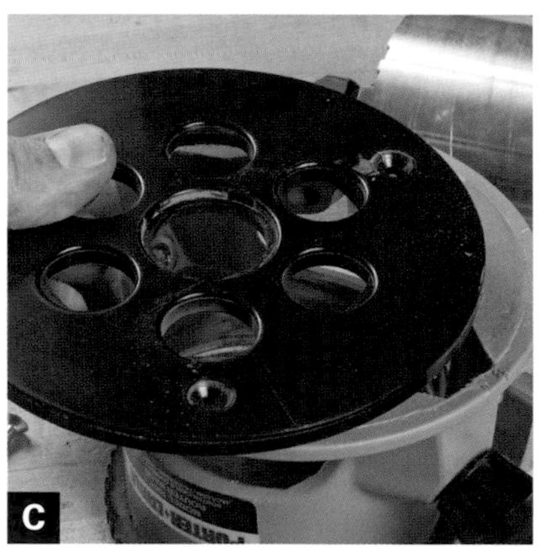

Double-sided tape works well to secure the baseplate to the template and the template to the underlayment **(F)**. Once it is in position, drill a starter hole in the template material to accept the router bit **(G)**. Now rout around the perimeter of the baseplate in a clockwise direction **(H)** and remove the baseplate and attached offcut **(I)**.

The next step is to use the template to rout the baseplate recess in the top. Begin by equipping the router with a ⅝-in.-dia. bushing, while leaving the ³⁄₁₆-in.-dia. straight bit in the router. Then set the cutting depth to equal the baseplate thickness **(J)**. Now lay out the baseplate location on the top, and secure the template to the top with double-sided tape **(K)**. Apply pressure to the tape with clamps or a mallet to increase its holding power **(L)**. Now rout around the inside perimeter in a clockwise direction **(M)**. After routing the perimeter of the cutout **(N)**, use a

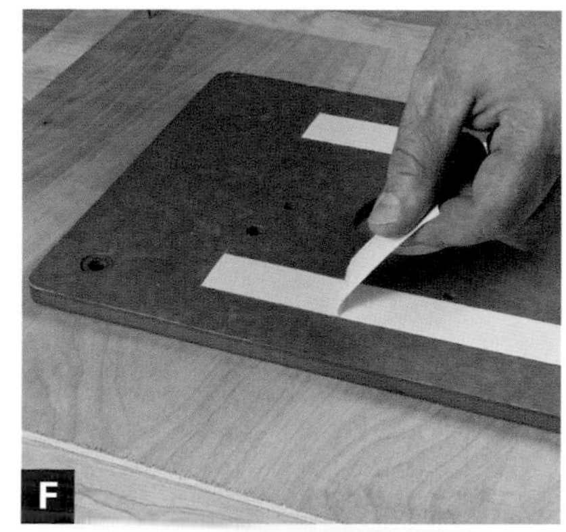
F

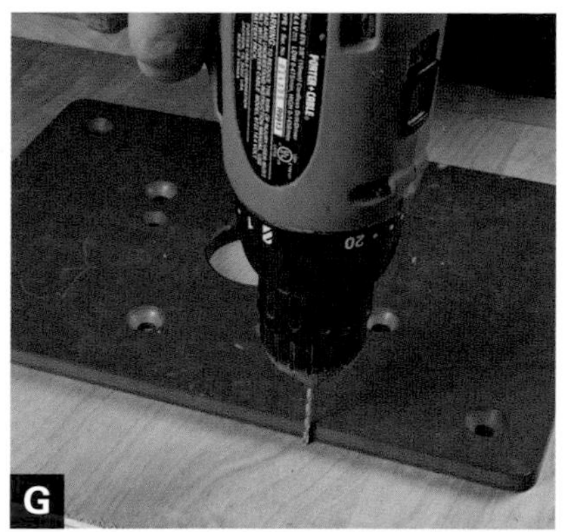
G

H

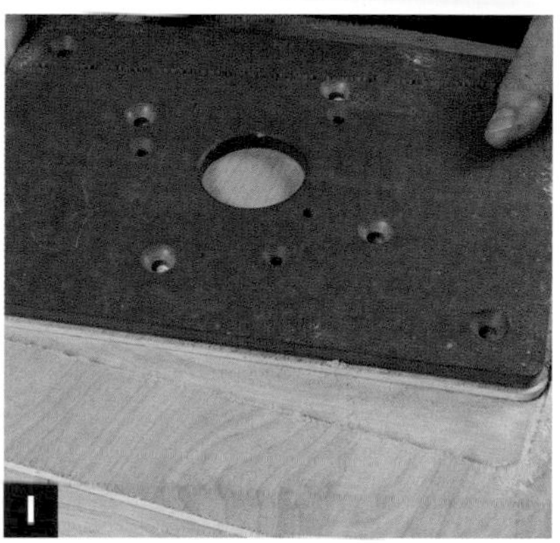
I

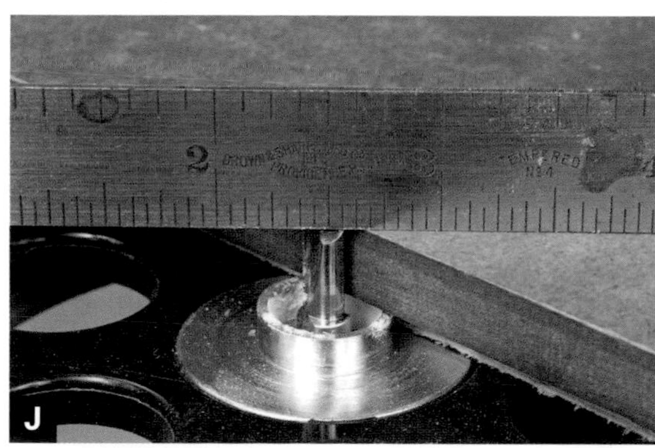
J

K

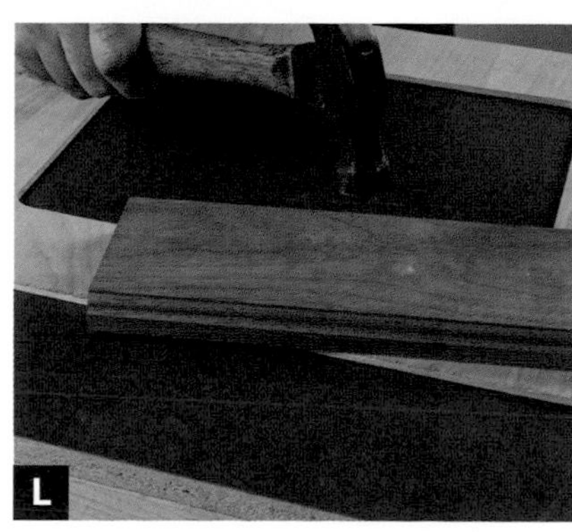
L

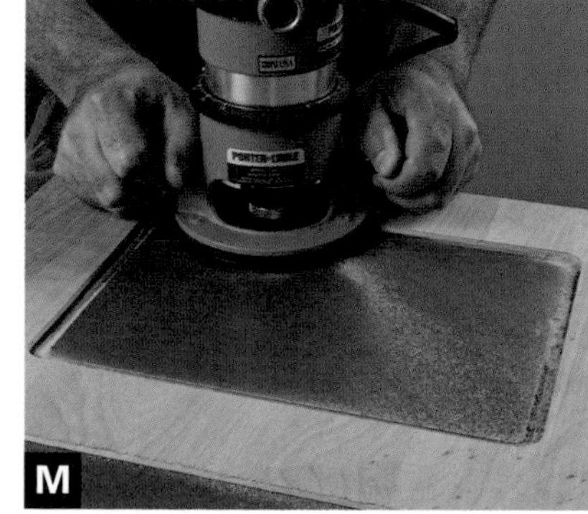
M

N

O

P

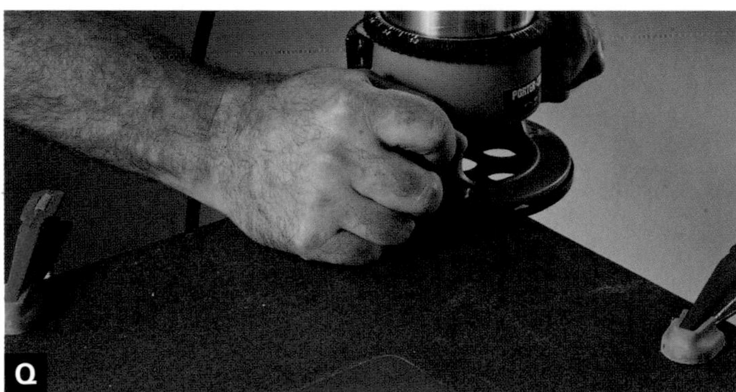

Q

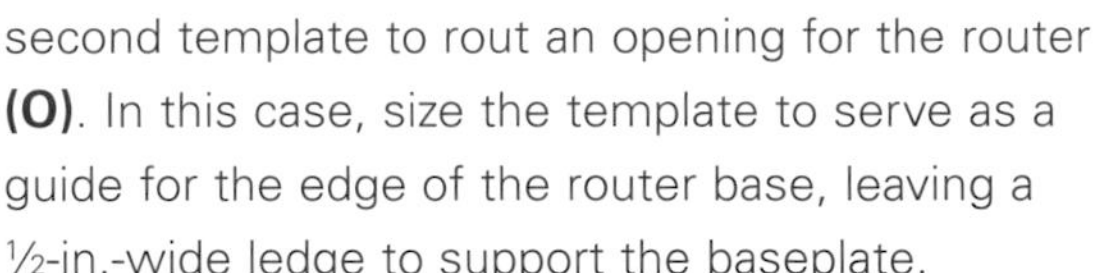

second template to rout an opening for the router **(O)**. In this case, size the template to serve as a guide for the edge of the router base, leaving a ½-in.-wide ledge to support the baseplate.

Next, make a template for rounding the corners of the table, and install a flush-trim bit in the router **(P)**. (In the photo, the top and template are staggered for clarity. When you're routing, the template is aligned with the edge of the top.) Clamp the template to the top and then rout a radius on the corners **(Q)**. Now laminate the second sink cutout to the underside of the top **(R)**, using plenty of glue and clamp pressure. Once the glue dries, rout the opening for the router with a flush-trim bit **(S)**, and trim the outside edges of the top flush **(T)**.

To complete the top, chamfer the edge to make it user-friendly **(U)** and seal the edges of the particleboard with a couple of coats of shellac **(V)**.

R

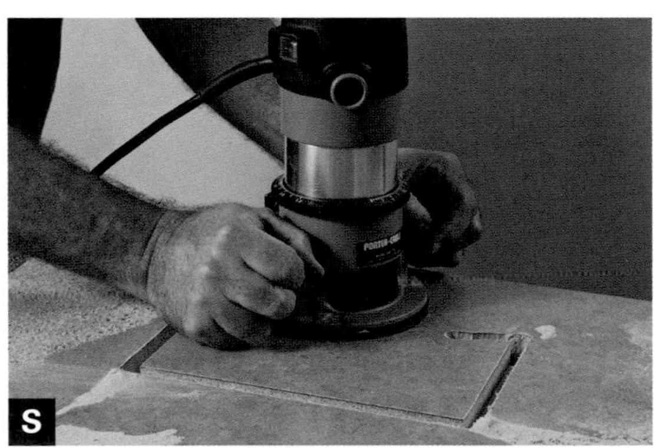

S

T

U

V

Making a Sled

When you're routing the ends of narrow stock such as door rails, the fence doesn't provide adequate support. The common solution is to feed the workpiece using a miter gauge. However, you may not want to cut a miter-gauge groove in your top, because even with an aftermarket metal insert, a groove exposes the raw edges of the substrate, inviting warping.

An alternative solution is to build a sled that rides the edge of the tabletop **(A)**. This is a simple jig that takes just a few minutes to construct.

Begin by cutting a rectangular piece of plywood for the base of the sled. Size the plywood to equal the distance from the router table fence to the front edge of the table. Remember to add a couple of inches of overhang for the runner. Next, fasten the runner in place with glue and screws **(B)**. Now attach the backing board to the top of the base the same way **(C)**. The last step is to fasten a toggle clamp to the backing board. Adjust the clamp so that its pad is compressed when the handle is in the closed position **(D)**.

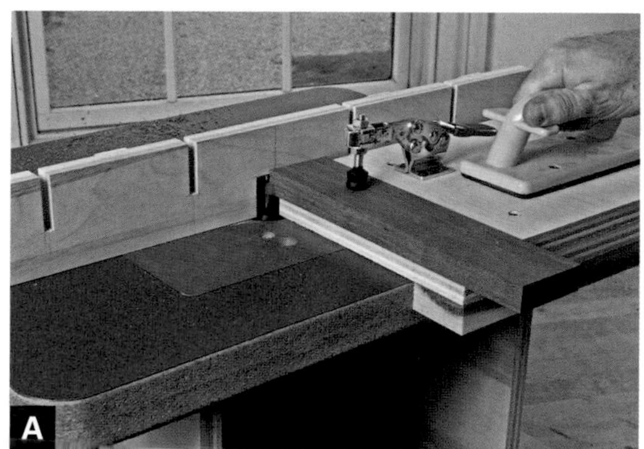
A

B

C

D

Common Cuts, page 78

Edges and Moldings, page 101

Flush-Trimming, page 123

PART TWO

Basic Operations

IF YOU HAVE NEVER USED A ROUTER, the information in this part of the book will show you how to begin. And even if you've owned a router for several years, you may find valuable insights here as well as a few new ways of routing.

In Section Four, I'll show you how to perform some of the router's most fundamental and useful operations. Along the way, I'll offer lots of information on making these common cuts, which range from routing stop cuts and narrow edges to making coves and small parts. In Section Five, you'll learn how to use the router for making moldings, which are used to add decoration, provide transitional elements, and even define particular furniture styles. Lastly, in Section Six, I'll cover flush-cutting—an invaluable technique for which you'll continue to find uses over time.

Common Cuts

Plunge Cuts

Guided Cuts

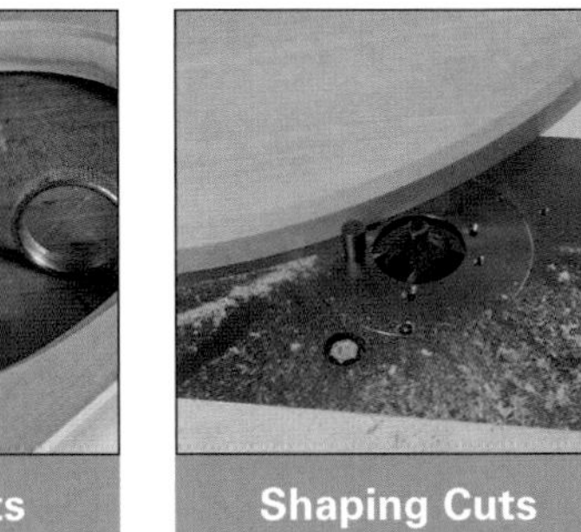

Shaping Cuts

Routing Small Parts

Routers are incredibly versatile tools, capable of cutting everything from decorative shapes to fine joints. They're efficient too. The speed at which they can shape a delicate curved molding is unmatched. But let's face it, routers can also destroy a beautiful piece of wood in a heartbeat. That's why it's so important to spend time on setup before turning on the power.

And there's more to setup than locking the bit in the collet. The work must be secured to a bench at a comfortable height, with clamps or hold-downs positioned out of the path of the router. It's important to have good lighting too. In this section, we will take a look at routing essentials as well as some tips for making your work with the router safe and accurate.

The Work Area

A large, sturdy workbench is an essential part of any shop, and it's especially important for routing. The workbench provides solid support for the workpiece as well as a way to secure the work with clamps or hold-downs. As you push and pull the router along the stock, the workbench should be steady and immovable.

Of course, a power supply should be nearby, yet out of the way. As you rout a groove or shape the perimeter of a tabletop, you don't want to risk routing into the cord. You may opt to attach a power strip to a leg of the bench or bring the power in from overhead.

Good lighting is critical for safe, accurate work. Natural light works well if you're fortunate enough to have lots of windows. However, if your shop is in a basement or garage, you may not have enough natural light. Regardless, it's important to add task lighting. A reflector-type lamp with a spring clamp is my favorite. It's inexpensive and I can easily position it where I need it by attaching it to a pipe clamp. I secure the pipe clamp to the edge of the bench and reposition it as the position of the work changes.

This inexpensive shopmade stand serves as a router table and a support base for hand routing.

Securing the Work

It's not enough to have the support of a solid workbench; the workpiece must be immobilized. Routers generate a considerable amount of force, which can easily launch a small piece of stock. Clamps are an easy solution, although it's usually necessary to stop halfway and reposition the clamps and the workpiece.

If you're routing completely through the stock, you'll need to position the work so that it overhangs the bench. Alternatively, you can lay it on riser blocks to lift it off the bench.

Sometimes the work is so small that there just isn't room for clamps. One option is to purchase a rubber routing pad to grip the stock. Although routing pads work well when new, they gradually lose their tackiness as the surface becomes infiltrated with fine dust. I don't care for the spongy feel created by the pad as I'm guiding the router. Instead, I prefer to pinch small work between bench dogs. The height of the dogs can be adjusted below the stock surface. This method solidly secures a small workpiece, yet keeps the area free of obstructions.

Hand routing does not require a router table or expensive jigs.

Bearings and bushings are common tools that help guide the cut.

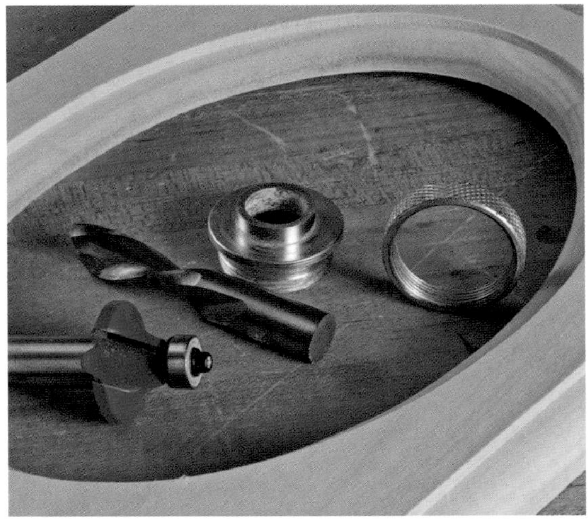

Many bits include a bearing for guiding the cut.

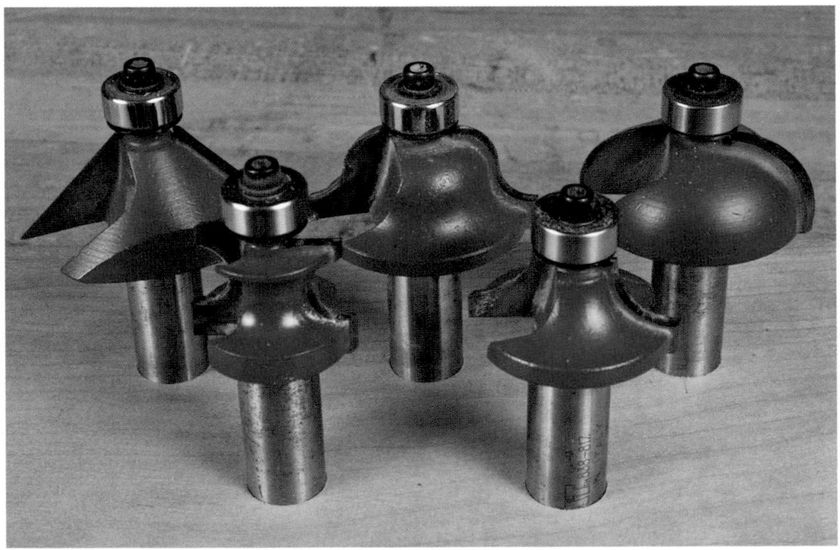

Handheld Routing

The most common and inexpensive method for using the router is hand routing. And even if you have a router table, at times handheld routing is still the best option. For example, sometimes the workpiece is too large or awkward to push across a router table. And if you need to cut a groove for a partition or divider inside a cabinet, handheld routing may be your only option.

The most basic of cuts is to shape a decorative profile (such as an ogee or thumbnail) along the edge of a straight-sided surface. This is also a common technique that's used for shaping the edge of a tabletop or drawer front or for making a strip of molding. The most common guide method is to simply allow the guide bearing on the router bit to follow the edge of the stock.

Internal cuts, such as grooves and mortises, are somewhat more complicated, because you'll need a guide system separate from the bit. Also, internal cuts often start and/or end at a specific point. There are four common approaches for guiding the cut: guide bearings, the baseplate, bushings, and an edge guide or fence. As you might expect, each approach has its advantages and disadvantages.

Bearing-Guided Cuts

The easiest solution for guiding the cut is to use the bearing that is fastened to the end of the bit. The bearing simply rolls along the edge of the workpiece to guide the bit along the edge while limiting the cutting depth. In addition to straight edges, guide bearings will also follow curves (as shown in the drawing on the facing page).

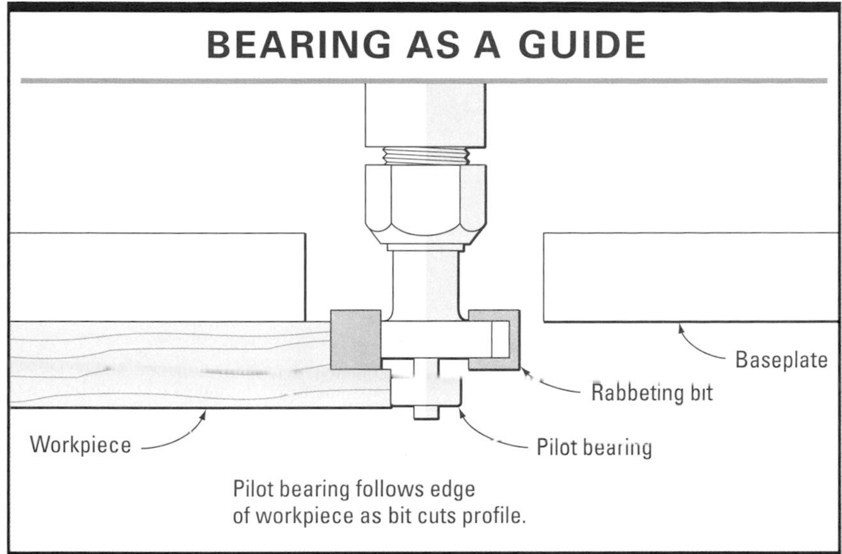

Guiding from the baseplate is fast and easy.

This makes it easy to shape a decorative profile along a circle or arc. If the entire edge is to be cut in the process, you'll need a template for the bearing to ride on.

Although edge shaping is the most frequent use for a guide bearing, it can also be used to guide a straight bit for flush-trimming one surface adjacent to another. A guide bearing can also be used at the base of a straight bit to make an internal cut.

➤ See "*Internal Cut*" on p. 214.

Baseplate-Guided Cuts

Another way to guide internal cuts is to use the edge of the baseplate. This is a quick and practical method for cutting grooves. A guide strip is first secured to the workpiece with clamps or brads to serve as a fence. The position of the fence from the center of the groove must equal one-half the width of the baseplate. Using the baseplate as a guide isn't as foolproof as the bearing method, however. For example, as long as you keep the router baseplate in contact with the fence, the bit will cut a straight path. If the baseplate wanders, the cut is spoiled. You can solve the problem by using two parallel fences and trapping the router base between them. Also, when guiding the router from the baseplate, it's important to realize that the baseplate of most routers isn't concentric with the collet. So if you rotate the base along the guide as you push the router, the location of the cut may be inconsistent. You can easily overcome this potential problem by keeping the same point of the base in contact with the fence throughout the cut. Or you can replace the round baseplate with a square one.

Edge Guide

Another method for guiding the cut is to use an edge guide (as shown in the top photo on p. 82). The edge guide has been around nearly as long as the router. It has a rod or a pair of rods that attach to the router base. A fence or guide attaches to the other end of the rod and rides the edge of the workpiece.

Edge guides allow for internal cuts.

Bushings require a jig or template to bear against.

Although it is still useful at times, an edge guide can be somewhat awkward to use, especially when positioned several inches from the router base. As when you guide the bit from the baseplate, you can quickly spoil the cut if the fence wanders even slightly from the edge of the stock.

Bushings

Still another method for guiding the cut employs a bushing, also called a template guide (as shown in the drawing below). A bushing is a metal collar or sleeve that fits within the baseplate opening, with the bit passing through it. Like a guide bearing, a bushing can guide the cut along the edge of both curved and straight stock. But guide

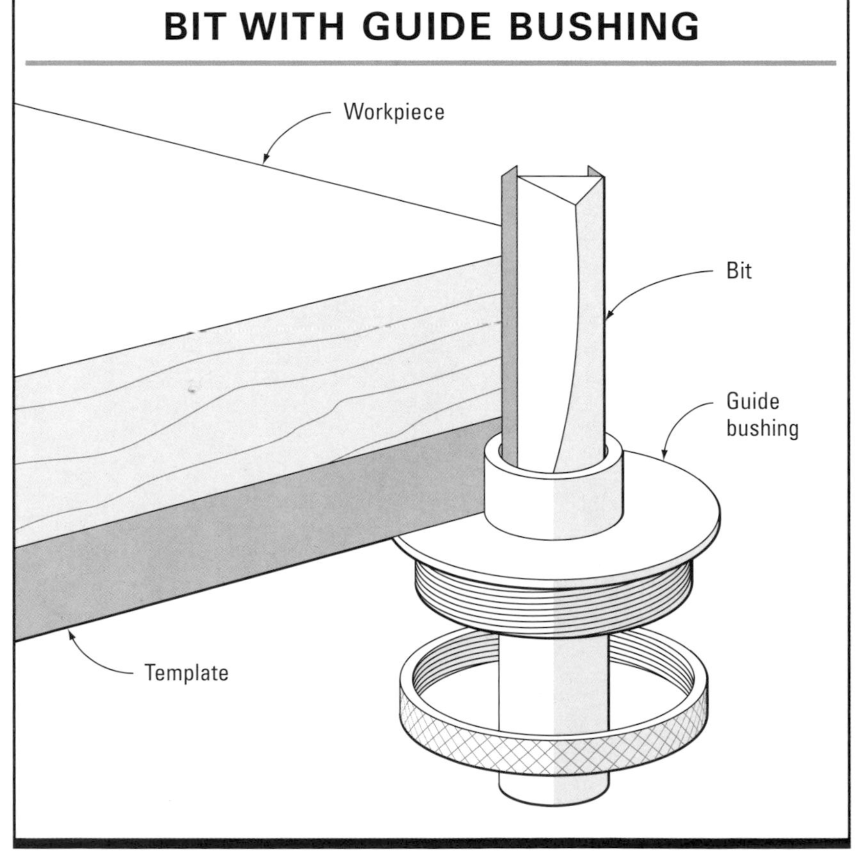

bushings excel at guiding internal cuts such as grooves. They're also used extensively with jigs for making accurate joinery such as dovetails. To use a guide bushing, you'll need to first make a template. The template can be curved or straight, but it's important that it be sized to accommodate the offset between the bushing and the bit (see the drawing below). Realize too that bushings are typically not concentric with the router collet (or the bit). So for the greatest accuracy, you'll need to guide from the same portion of the bushing throughout the cut.

Freehand routing is a great yet often overlooked option with several applications.

Freehand Routing

There are times when I rout freehand, without a guide. For example, when routing a shallow mortise for a lock or hinge, I just rout within the layout lines. Afterwards, I pare to the lines with a chisel. Also, when I cut half-blind dovetails, I usually rout the dovetail sockets freehand and then saw the

CALCULATING OFFSET

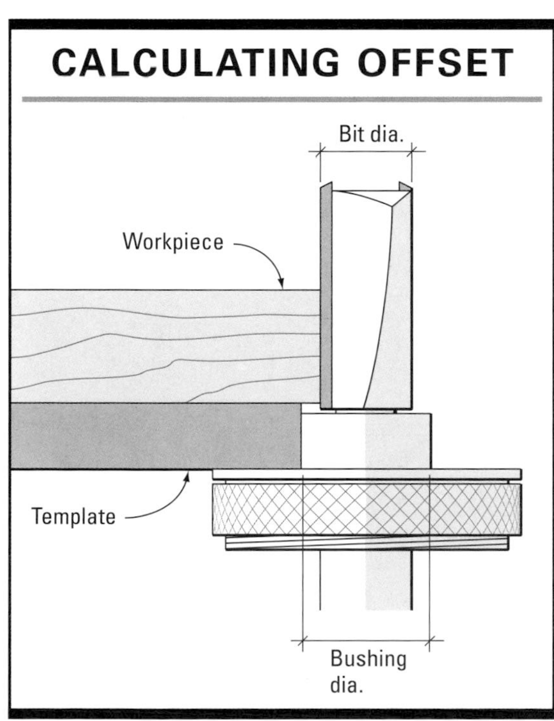

HANDHELD ROUTER SAFETY

The router is a relatively small, portable machine. But in spite of its size, it is capable of inflicting serious injury. As with all power tools, it's important to carefully follow safety guidelines.

- Always read and follow the manufacturer's safety guidelines.
- Large bits are not intended for handheld routers. If in doubt, check with the bit manufacturer.
- Don't attempt to climb-cut. The bit can grab the stock violently and pull the router from your grasp.
- Wear hearing protection. The high-decibel scream of the router will damage your hearing.
- Wear eye protection. Routers propel dust, chips, and wood fragments that can cause serious eye injury.
- Never start the router with the bit contacting the stock. Allow the router to develop full speed before making contact with the workpiece.
- Use the appropriate speed. Check with the bit manufacturer for the recommended rpm, and don't exceed it.
- Don't cut the power cord. Plan the route you'll use and position the cord out of the cutting path.

tails by hand to fit the sockets. Before routing, I lay out the joint with a sharp knife, and then I follow the knife lines with a router and dovetail bit. Routing freehand may sound difficult, but the key is to use only sharp, small-diameter bits.

Clean, Safe Cutting

To make clean cuts safely, it's necessary to approach the workpiece in a certain fashion and to feed the tool at the appropriate speed and in the correct direction. Following are a few general guidelines.

Entering the Work

As with all power tools, never turn on a router with the cutter contacting the workpiece. The workpiece or the router could jerk violently, and the bit could snap. Instead, allow the tool to develop full speed before making contact. Also, the router base should make contact before the bit. This approach ensures a smooth, stable entry into the cut. If you plan to cut mortises with a router, then you'll need a plunge router. You can't safely make a deep, plunging cut with a fixed-base router. However, an optional method is to first bore a hole that is larger than the bit and start the cut with the bit in the hole.

You can, however, cut shallow stopped grooves and flutes with your fixed-base router. But first replace the round baseplate with a square one. The long, straight edge of a square base will stabilize the router as you tip it into the cut.

CLIMB-CUTTING

Woodworking has many rules of thumb that keep us on track and help us avoid potential problems or safety issues. But sometimes the guidelines contradict each other. For example, it's always important to work wood with the grain to achieve the smoothest possible surface and avoid tearout. And a rule of thumb when routing is to work the perimeter of a board in a counterclockwise direction. In other words, don't climb-cut. But what do you do if the latter advice has you routing against the grain and tearing and splintering the stock? There are solutions, but I don't consider climb-cutting one of them. Sure, you can usually climb-cut relatively safely with smaller bits, but where do you draw the line? At some point, when you least expect it, the bit can grab and pull the router from your grasp. The solution? Take lighter cuts. Take three or four light passes if necessary. If the cut is guided with a bearing, take the first pass with a large-diameter bearing, then switch to smaller bearings until the final depth is reached.

Still another method for avoiding splintering is to first make several short, intermittent cuts along the edge. This severs the grain at each cut to limit splintering.

Feed Rate and Direction

The speed at which you push or pull the router through the stock has a direct effect on the surface quality of the cut. If you feed too quickly, each wing of the bit will take larger bites and create a rippled, washboard surface that is difficult to sand out. An excessively slow feed rate will overheat the bit as well as the stock and scorch the surface. Scorching or burning is especially a problem for certain wood species, such as cherry and maple, because of their chemical composition. The key is to listen to the router, observe the finished surface, and practice. In just a short period of time, you'll gain a feel for the proper feed rate.

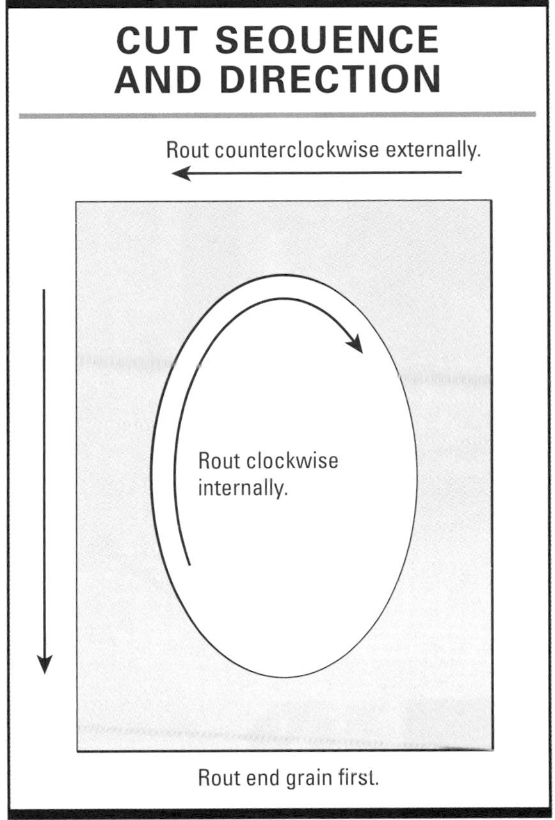

Feed Direction

Workpieces are always fed across tablesaws, jointers, shapers, and other woodworking power tools in the direction opposing the cutter rotation. Otherwise the workpiece would be grabbed and launched across the room. The same principle holds true for a router.

So with a handheld router, always push it counterclockwise around the perimeter of a board or frame and clockwise around the interior (as shown in the drawing above). Just remember, the feed direction is always the opposite of the direction the router wants to feed itself. This way, you'll be in control.

Avoiding Splintering

Anytime you plane, saw, chisel, or rout an end-grain surface, there's a possibility that the unsupported wood at the trailing end of the cut will splinter. When routing, you can minimize or eliminate any splintering by using a sharp bit and reducing the feed rate, especially as you approach the end of the cut. Even so, despite your best efforts wood will still sometimes splinter. There are several solutions. One is to shape or rout the ends of a board first. In that case, the subsequent cuts along the perpendicular edges will remove the splintered corners.

Another method for avoiding splintering is to rip the board to its final width after routing. If this method isn't feasible, you can clamp a backing board to the stock to support the trailing edge as you rout.

A

Plunge Cut with Edge Guide

With its motor mounted on spring-loaded posts, the plunge router has the unique ability to start and stop a mortise or groove at any point on the workpiece **(A)**. But before turning on the power, it's important to first set the cutting depth.

Loosen the locking screw that holds the depth stop rod, and position the rod against the depth stop **(B)**. At this point, the stop rod should be positioned against the base casting, which allows for the deepest cut.

Next, plunge the router until the bit touches the surface of the work **(C)** and lock the depth stop rod in position **(D)**. Then lock the depth indicator

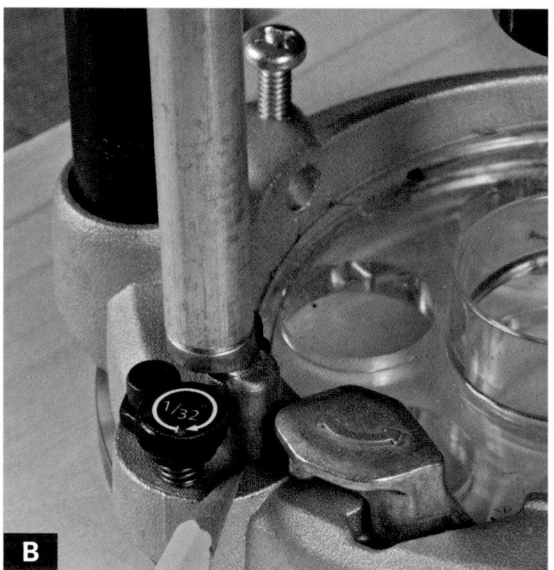

B

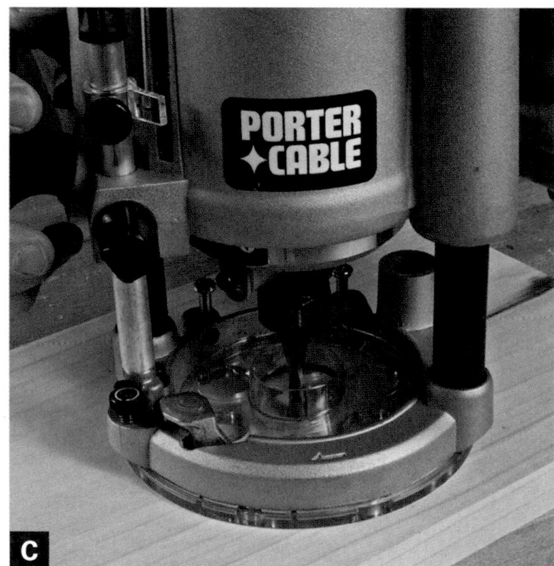

C

at "O" **(E)**. Now loosen the depth rod locking screw and raise the depth rod until the depth indicator is positioned for the cutting depth **(F)**. Finally, tighten the depth rod locking screw.

With the depth stop setup complete, you're ready to make the cut. Power up the router, position the edge guide against the workpiece, and lower the spinning bit **(G)**. While maintaining contact between the edge guide and workpiece, push the router to the ending point of the cut **(H)**.

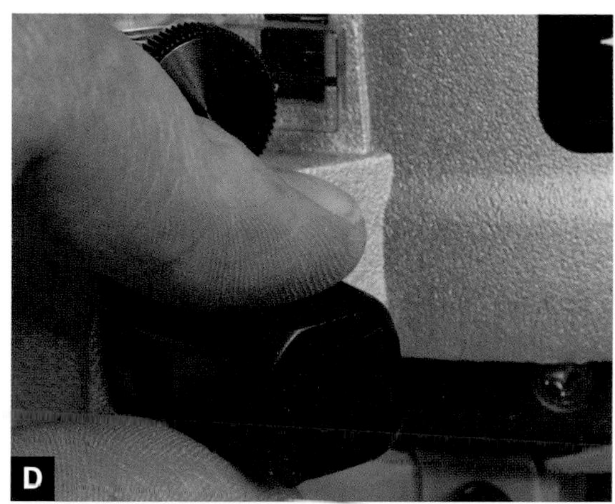

D

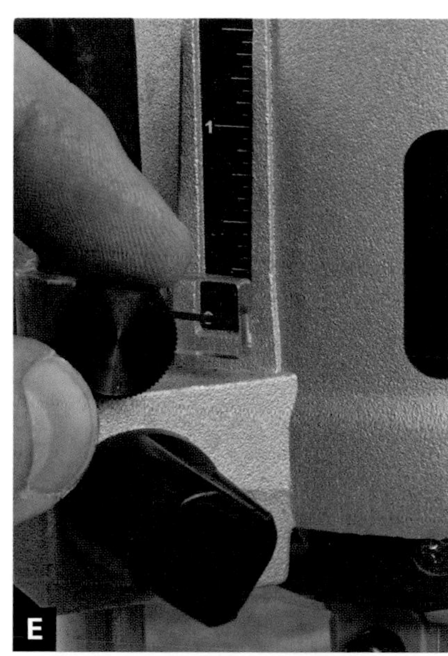

E

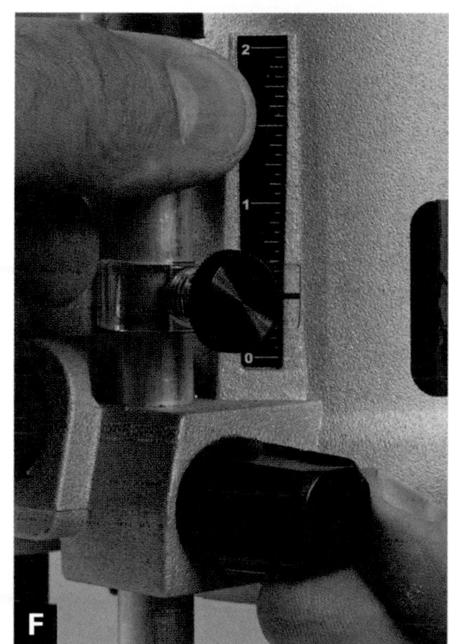

F

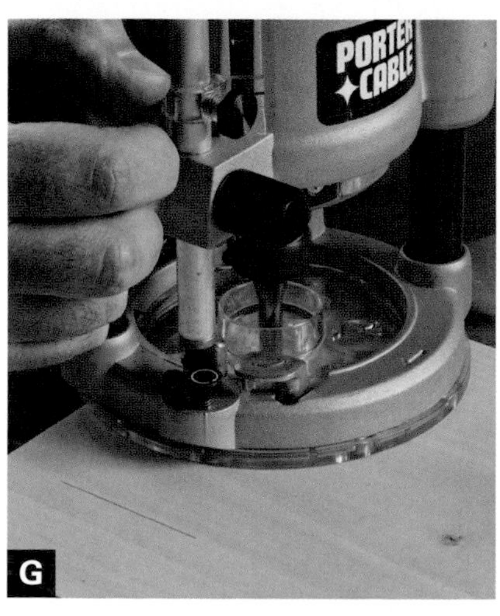

G

H

Internal Cut with Guide Bushing

Before using a guide bushing, you'll first have to calculate the offset (bushing diameter minus bit diameter divided by two) and make a template. In this case, I'm cutting a rectangular-shaped recess into the back of a frame that has an oval opening **(A)**.

Fasten the template with small nails or double-stick tape **(B)**. Secure a straight bit in the router collet **(C)** and install the guide bushing in the router baseplate **(D)**. Set the cutting depth **(E)** and make the cut in a clockwise direction **(F)**.

A

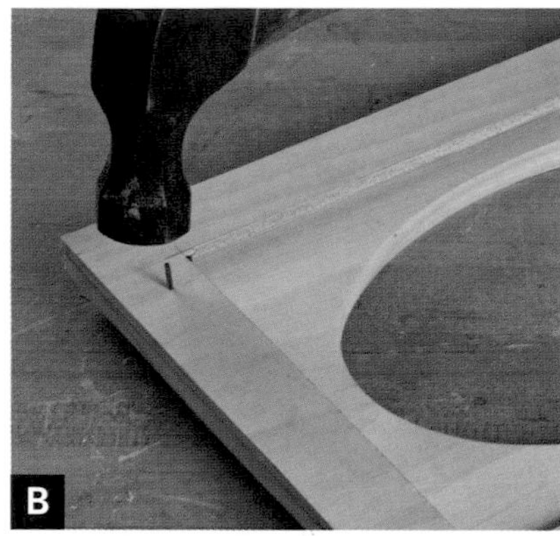

B

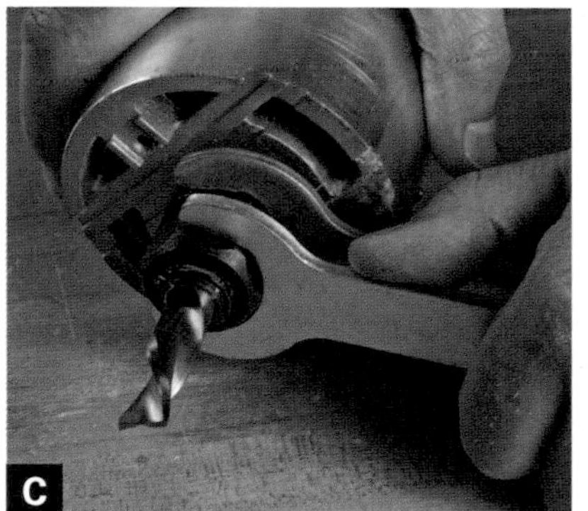

C

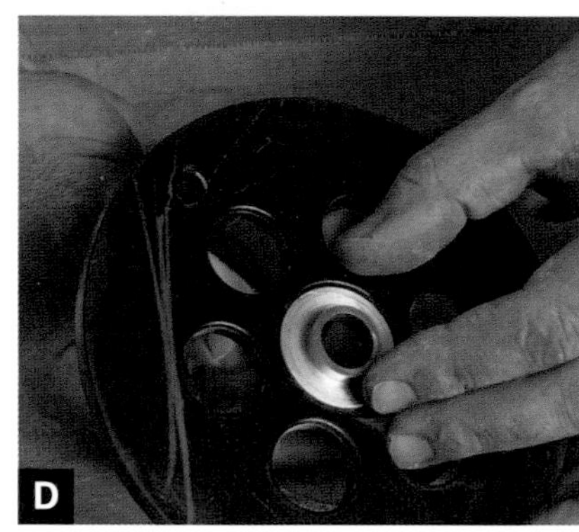

D

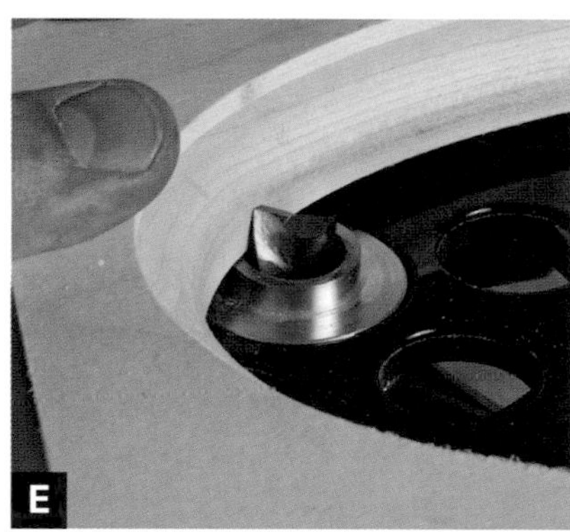

E

F

Baseplate as a Guide

Using the baseplate as a guide is pretty straightforward. For increased accuracy, I've replaced the factory baseplate with a custom baseplate with straight sides.

➤ See *"Making a Straight-Sided Baseplate"* on p. 23.

A T-square fence ensures that the cut is perpendicular to the edge of the workpiece, and it makes setup a snap **(A)**.

Begin by laying out the cut on the face of the workpiece **(B)**. Next, align the fence and clamp it in position. A cut in the T-square fence makes setup fast and accurate **(C)**. Finally, make the cut **(D)**.

A

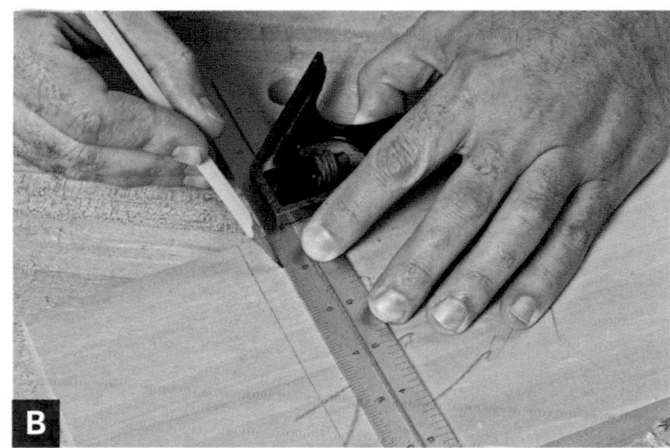

B

C

D

Bearing as a Guide

Probably the simplest and most common routing method is to use the bearing on the bit to guide the cut. It's often used to shape decorative edges, such as in this example **(A)**.

Begin by using the workpiece to gauge the cutting depth **(B)**. Shape the outside edge, starting with an end and moving in a counterclockwise direction **(C)**. As you approach the corner, it's common to experience minor tearout **(D)**. But as you shape the edge, the tearout will be cut away **(E)**. To avoid climb-cutting, remember to rout in a counterclockwise direction **(F)** on the outside and in a clockwise direction on the inside **(G)**.

A

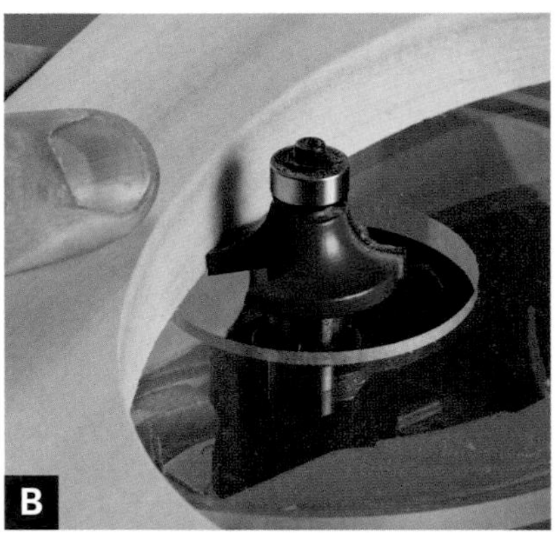

B

C

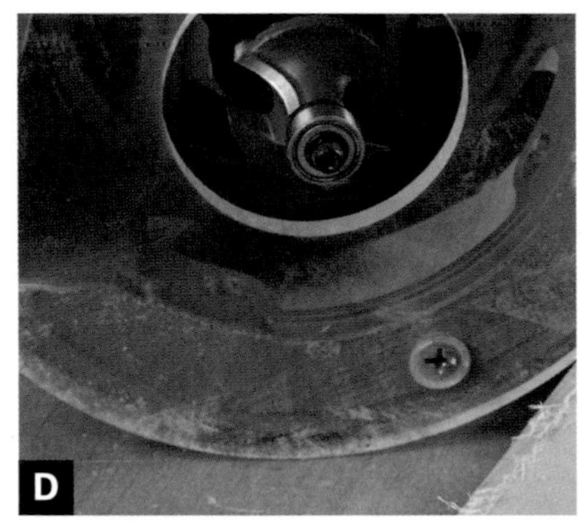

D

E

F

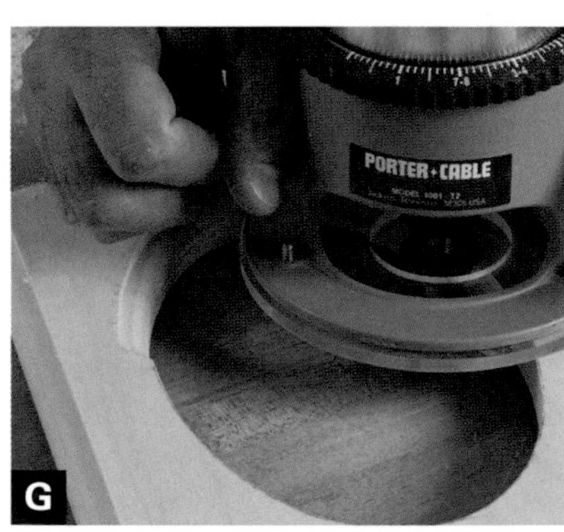

G

Making Stop-Cuts

A stop-cut begins and/or ends before it reaches the end of the workpiece **(A)**. To make a stop-cut along the edge, the workpiece is pushed sideways into the spinning router bit. It's very important for your personal safety that you use a stop block clamped to the fence to prevent kickback as well as to accurately position the board.

To begin, disconnect the router from the power source. Next, locate the point at which the router bit begins to project through the fence opening on the outfeed side of the bit. Position the workpiece against the fence and slide it until it makes contact with the bit **(B)**. Now mark a line at that spot **(C)** and repeat the process on the infeed side of the bit.

The next step is to position the stop block. Align the layout mark on the workpiece with the outfeed mark on the fence **(D)**.

(Text continues on p. 92.)

E

Now clamp the stop block to the infeed side of the fence directly behind the workpiece **(E)**.

To make the cut, first position the workpiece against the stop block and away from the bit **(F)**. Now pivot the work into the spinning bit until it makes full contact with the fence **(G)**. Feed the stock right to left until the stop line on the work aligns with the mark on the outfeed fence **(H)**.

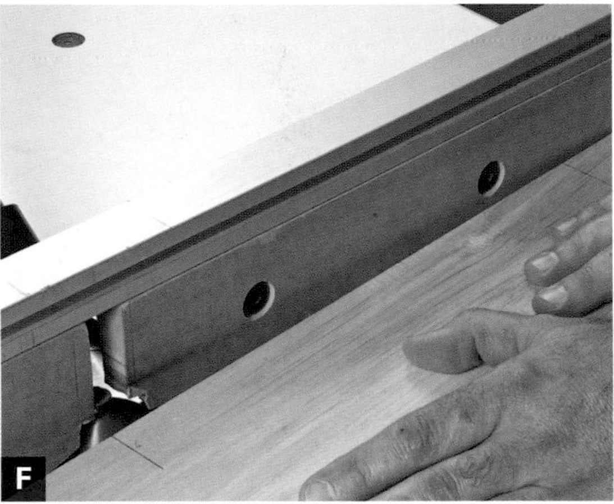
F

G

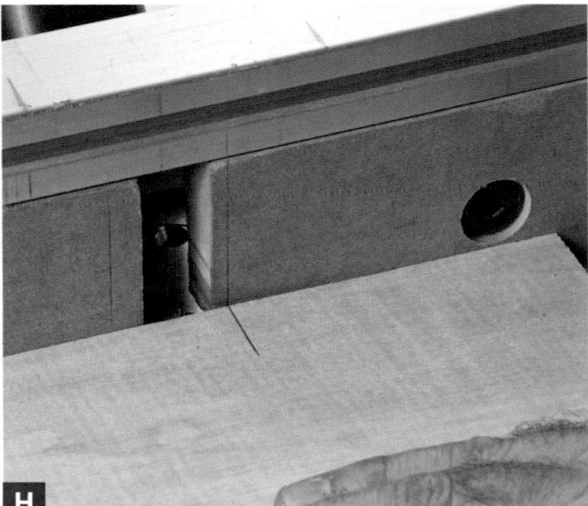
H

Shaping Edges

Shaping edges on a router table is much easier than shaping them with a handheld router **(A)**. There is no need to reposition the clamps halfway through the process or precariously balance the router as you push it along the workpiece. Instead, the workpiece is pushed along the fence with the full support of the table.

Begin by positioning the fence tangent to the bearing on the bit **(B)**. Then lock the fence securely in place **(C)**. Next, position a barrier guard **(D)**. If your router table isn't equipped with a guard, you can construct the one shown in the photo or just clamp a thick plank to the fence.

Position the board behind the bit on the infeed side of the fence **(E)** and begin routing one end of the workpiece **(F)**. The corners will often tear out **(G)**, but the splintering will shape away when you're routing the long-grain edge **(H)**.

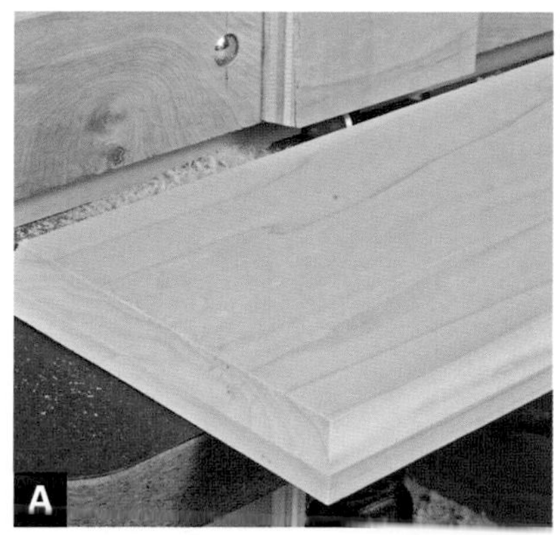

A

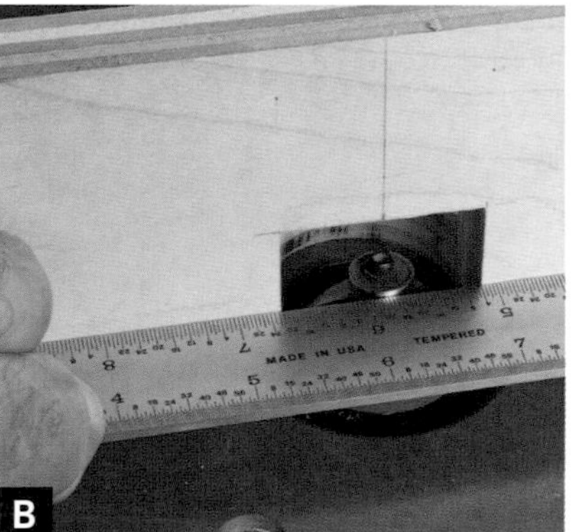

B

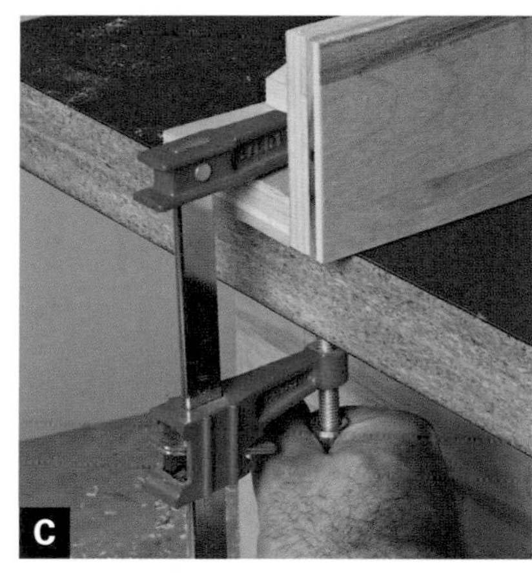

C

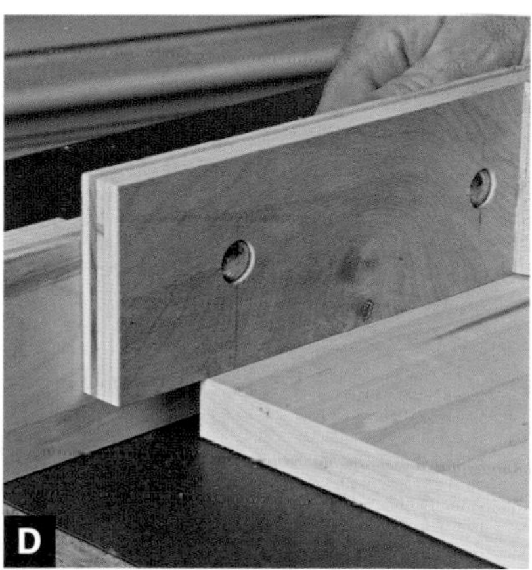

D

E

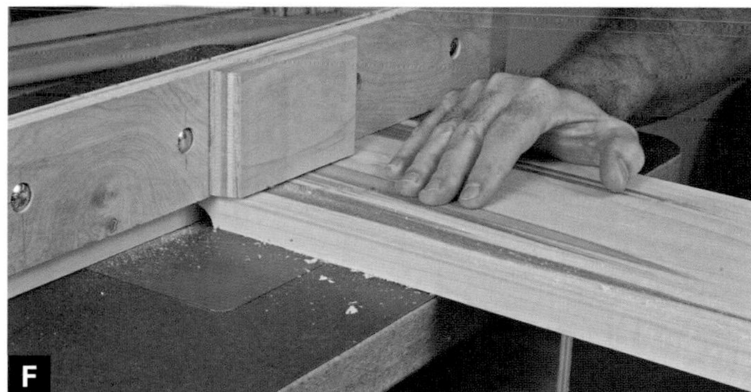

F

G

H

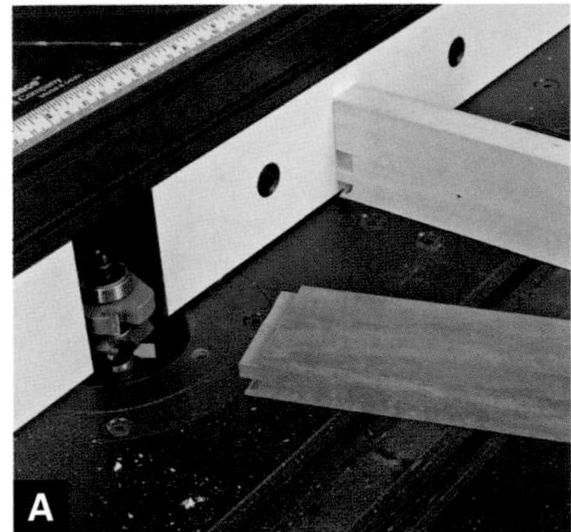

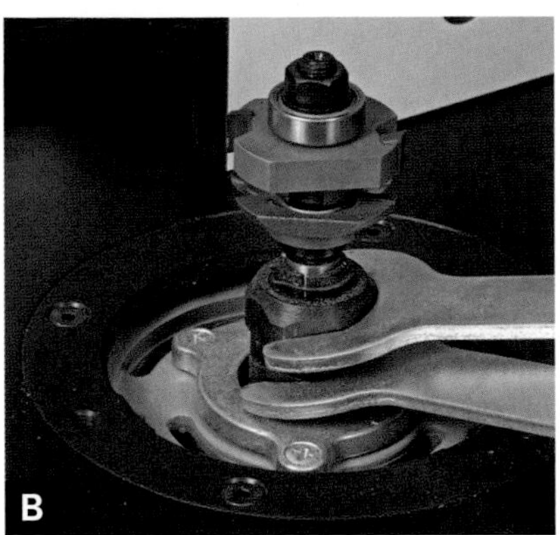

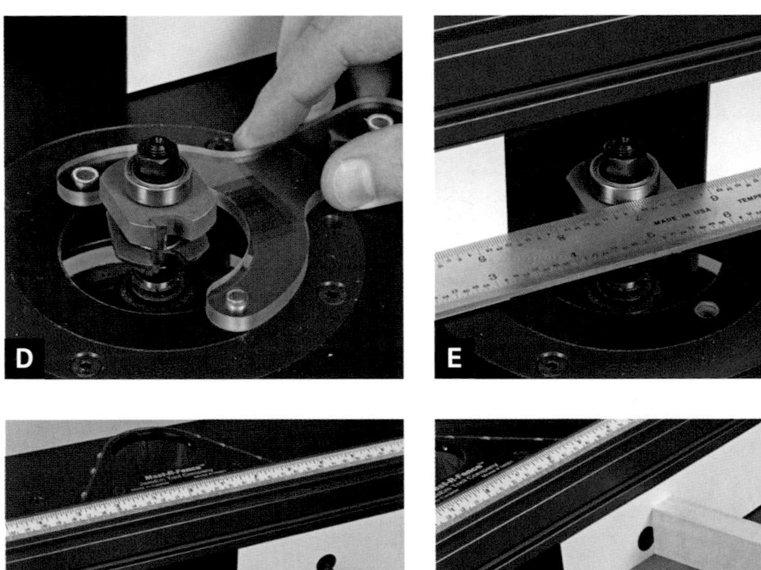

Shaping Narrow Ends

Many cuts on the router table are guided by the fence. However, narrow stock such as door rails doesn't receive adequate support from the fence. The solution is to use a miter gauge **(A)**. Remember: It's still important that the fence be locked in place. It serves as a stop to position the workpiece, it adds a measure of safety by placing a barrier around much of the bit, and it directs shavings toward the dust collector.

Begin by locking the bit securely in the collet **(B)**. Then adjust the bit to the necessary height **(C)**. Next, place an insert ring around the base of the bit to provide extra support for the workpiece **(D)**. Position the fence tangent to the guide bearing and lock it in place **(E)**. Loosen the screws that hold the fence inserts, and reduce the opening around the bit **(F)**.

Press the end of the work against the fence to correctly position it **(G)**. Hold the workpiece firmly against the miter gauge and make the cut **(H)**.

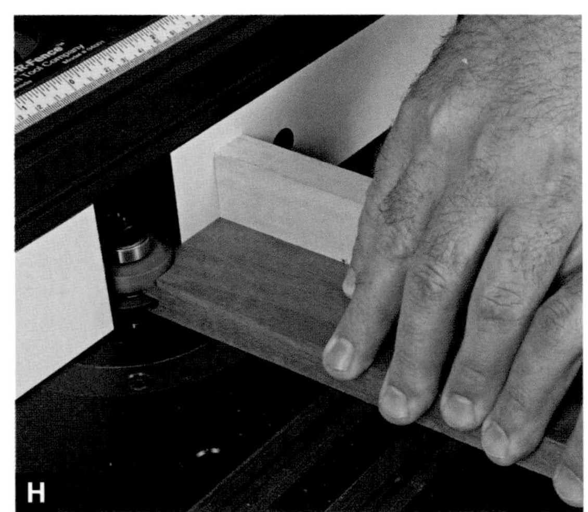

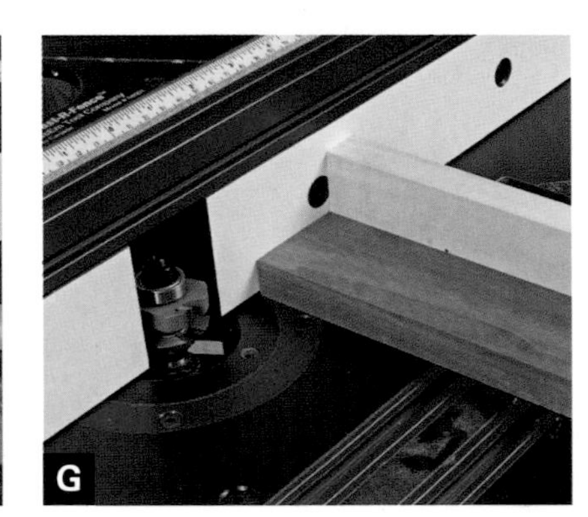

Using a Starting Pin

When you're routing the edge of a curve, the common guide method is to use the bearing on the bit. Because the bearing rolls along the stock, it's important that the workpiece be smooth and free of bumps or ridges from bandsawing.

The starting pin is an important part of this type of setup **(A)**. As you enter the cut, the cutting portion of the bit makes contact with the workpiece before the workpiece makes contact with the guide bearing. The potential is for a kickback to occur, especially with the large router bits available today.

The safe solution is to position the workpiece against the starting pin to enter the cut. The pin acts as a fulcrum on which to pivot the workpiece into the spinning bit **(B)**. Once the workpiece makes contact with the guide bearing, pivot the work away from the starting pin **(C)** and proceed with the remainder of the cut **(D)**.

A

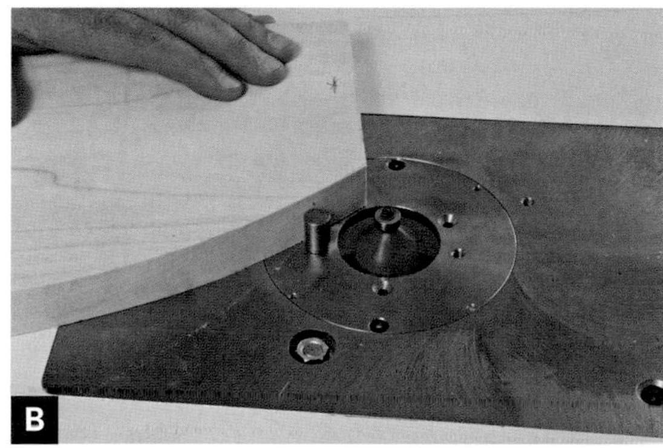

B

C

D

Cove Cut on the Router Table

Even the largest router bits will not cut a very deep cove. But there's a practical way to increase the size of the cove. Use two bits of different radii and create an elliptical cove **(A)**. This will greatly increase the depth and width of the cove and enable you to create a large molding profile. As an added benefit, an elliptical cove is more appealing than one with a constant radius.

Begin by making multiple light passes with the first bit **(B)**. It's important to keep each cut light; heavy cuts are prone to kickback and tend to cause overheating of the router. Use featherboards to keep the workpiece in position.

After making the first portion of the cove, switch bits and complete the cut **(C)**. Adjust the fence position and the bit height to blend the curves from each of the two router bits. The final cove should be a smooth, continuous curve **(D)**.

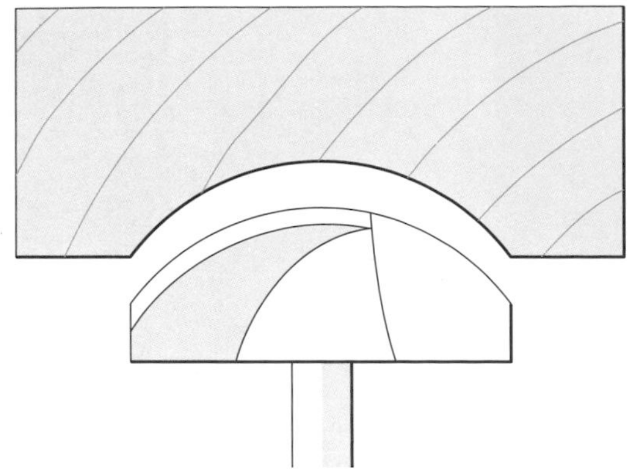

Even a large router bit can't shape a very large cove.

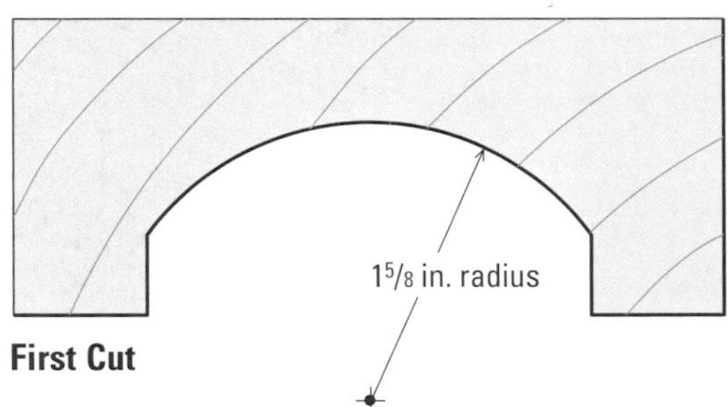

Instead use two large router bits with different radii to create a large elliptical cove.

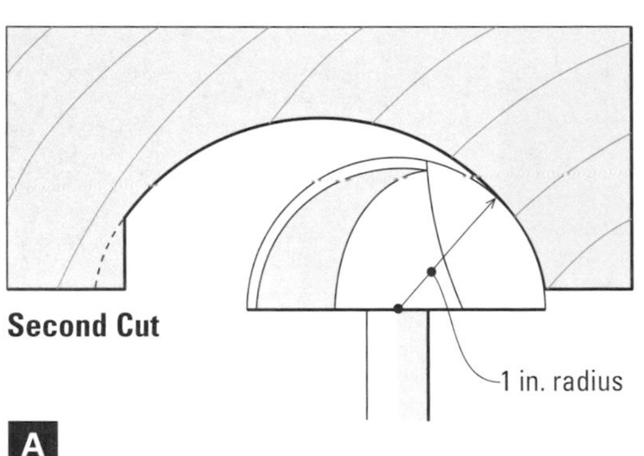

A

B

C

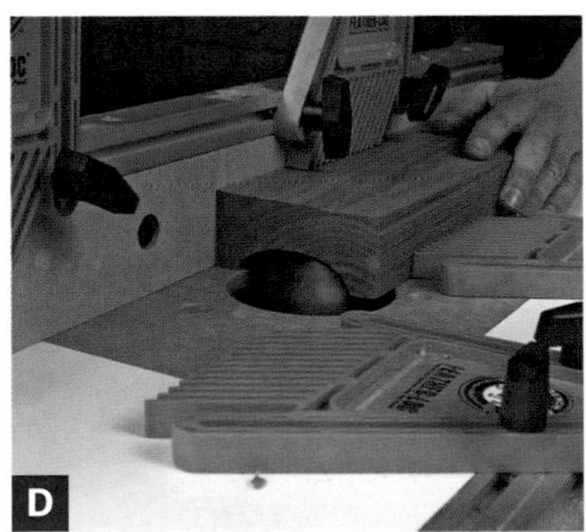

D

Template Shaping Small Parts

These tiny blocks **(A)** measure approximately ½ in. by ⅞ in. by 3 in. and require a thumbnail profile along one edge and both ends. Because the entire edge is shaped, the setup requires either a fence or a template to limit the cutting depth. After shaping, the blocks will be mitered on the ends and carefully fitted into a notch in the seat board.

Begin by milling the stock to the final thickness, but leave it oversize in width and length. Next, glue the stock to a piece of ¼-in.-thick plywood with heavy paper in the joint **(B)**. The plywood will provide a template for the router bearing during the shaping process. After shaping, the paper will allow you to separate the plywood easily from the workpiece.

After the glue has dried, joint the edge of the assembly with a bench plane or jointer **(C)**. Then rip the stock to final width and crosscut it to final length **(D)**. The next step is to shape the profile.

(Text continues on p. 98.)

A

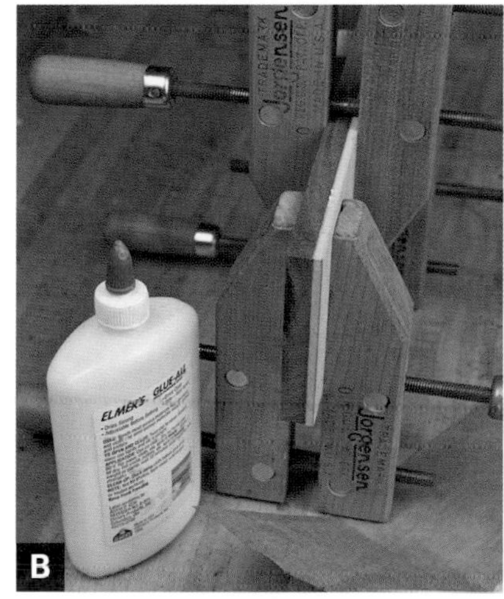

B

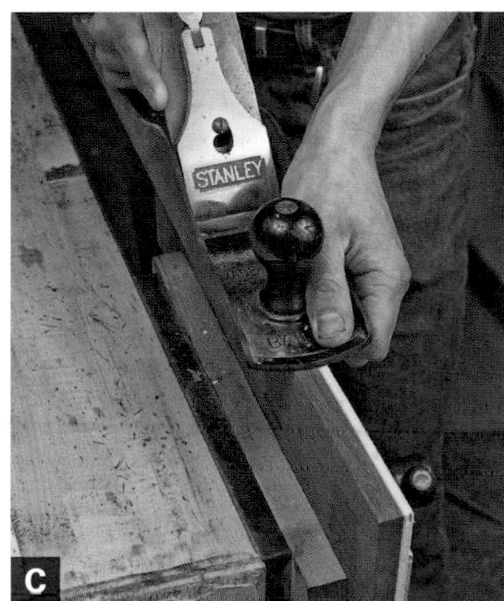

C

D

E

F

G

There are a couple of keys to shaping such a small piece: add mass to reduce chatter and provide a method to grasp the part safely for shaping. One solution is to grip the part within the jaws of a wooden handscrew. The heavy wooden clamp effectively adds mass and positions hands a safe distance from the spinning router bit. Also, if the bit inadvertently contacts the jaws of the clamp, there's no dangerous metal-to-metal contact.

Begin by shaping the ends. Tighten the jaws of the clamp firmly around the stock. Next, feed the work into the spinning bit until the plywood template makes contact with the bearing **(E)**. After shaping the ends, shape the edge using the same procedure **(F)**.

After the shaping is complete, gently pry the plywood from the workpiece by placing a chisel into the seam along the back edge **(G)**.

Shaping Small Parts with a Jig

Here's a second method for shaping the entire edge of a small part. It involves a simple jig that is designed for shaping multiple parts, such as the candle-slide front for a desk. The jig is a piece of ¾-in.-thick plywood with pockets for holding the work **(A)**. A rabbet holds the first workpiece as it is shaped along the edge; the second workpiece is held within a groove as the end is shaped. The fit of the workpiece within the groove must be snug; a finger hole in the top of the jig provides a way to push the work free from the jig after shaping.

Furthermore, the rabbet that secures the work for shaping the edge must be slightly less in dimension than the stock being shaped. This way pressure is applied to the stock as it is shaped, preventing chatter.

After making the jig, mill the stock for a snug fit within the groove of the jig **(B)**. Next, shape the ends of the stock. Then place it into the rabbet for shaping an edge. If you are shaping multiple pieces, you can also position a second piece into the jig for end shaping **(C)**. As you use the jig, maintain firm pressure against the router table and fence **(D)**.

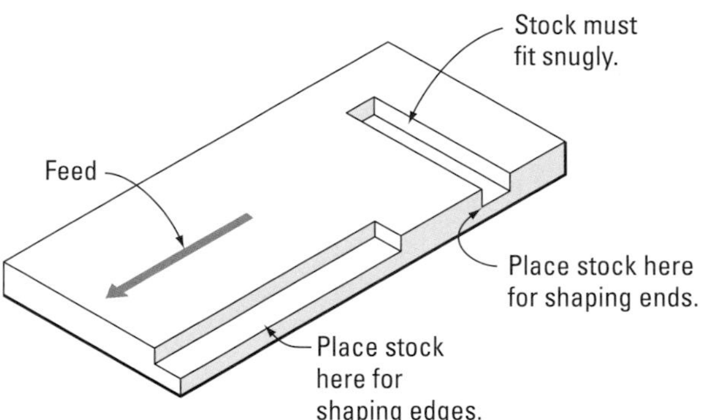

A

B

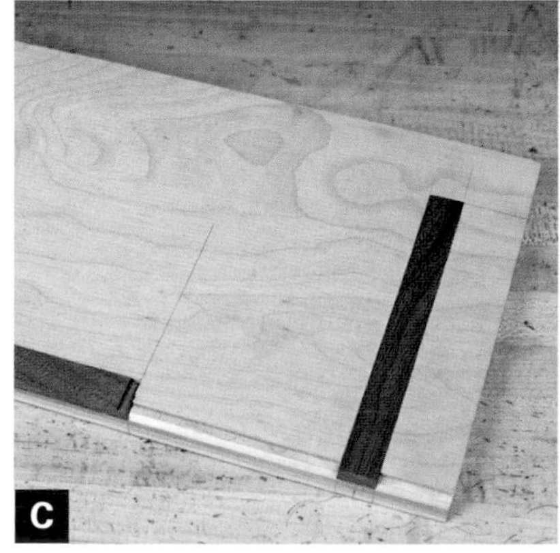
C

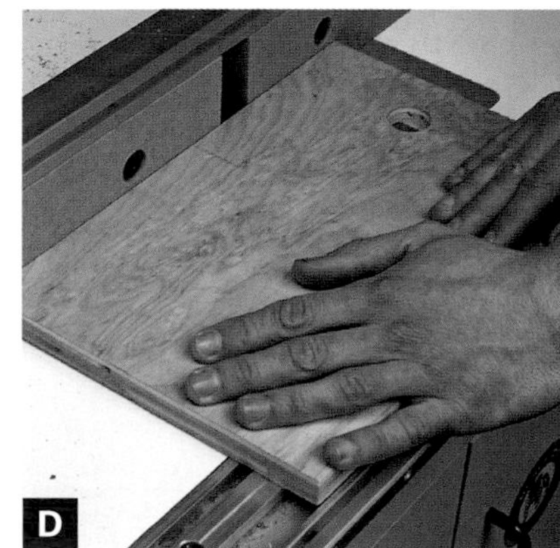
D

B

Shaping Small Parts with a Miter Gauge

This small-part setup uses a miter gauge in conjunction with a backup board, which is fastened to the head of the gauge with a pair of screws. The router table fence is first secured parallel to the miter gauge slot; the small workpiece is then clamped to the backup board for safe shaping. The parts being shaped in this example are the base and capital for a pilaster, or flat column. After shaping, the complete pilaster is added to the interior of a desk.

See *"Small Stock Fluted on the Router Table"* on p. 224

The first stage in this process involves shaping a strip of molding.

After shaping, short blocks of the molding are cut from the strip for use as the base and capital **(A)**. But first, the ends of the blocks must be shaped, or "returned," with the same profiles used on the face of the block. This setup allows safe and accurate shaping of very small workpieces such as these.

For each profile, orient the stock on the edge **(B)** or end **(C)** and firmly clamp it to the backup board on the miter gauge.

Edges and Moldings

Routing Edges

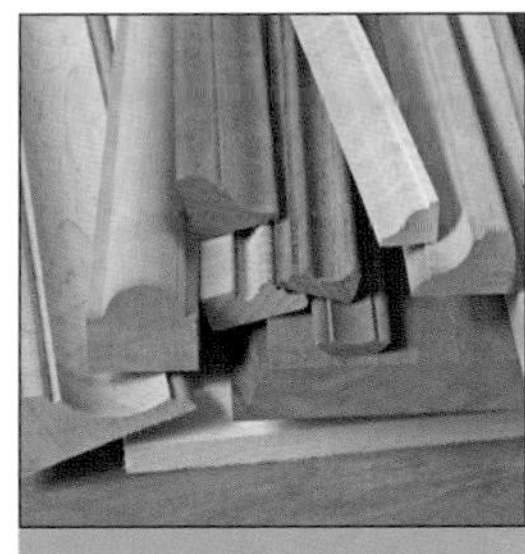

Making Moldings

Moldings and edge treatments have been used throughout the ages to create visual interest and to add detail to furniture and architecture. In fact, furniture styles are often dictated by their moldings, among other things. While most period pieces are embellished with elaborate moldings and cornices, even simple furniture styles use basic molding profiles or chamfers to soften an edge and add a small degree of detail, as shown in the top drawing at left on p. 102.

There are two basic methods for adding a molding profile to a piece of furniture or cabinetry, as shown in the drawing at right on p. 102. The first is to shape a strip of molding and attach it to the work with glue and/or fasteners. The second is to shape the edge of the work. Each method yields a different effect. For example, applied moldings stand proud of the surrounding surfaces and create a strong visual effect. A good example is a crown molding on a chest of drawers, which provides a visually powerful,

ARCHITECTURAL CORNICE

This cornice can be made with a router from six separate molding strips using simple profiles. Dentil can be made on tablesaw with dado head.

Crown
Fascia
Reverse ogee
Fascia
Soffit
Cove
Tongue-and-groove knives cut this profile.
Ovolo
Dentil
Reverse ogee
Front view

MOLDINGS IN FURNITURE

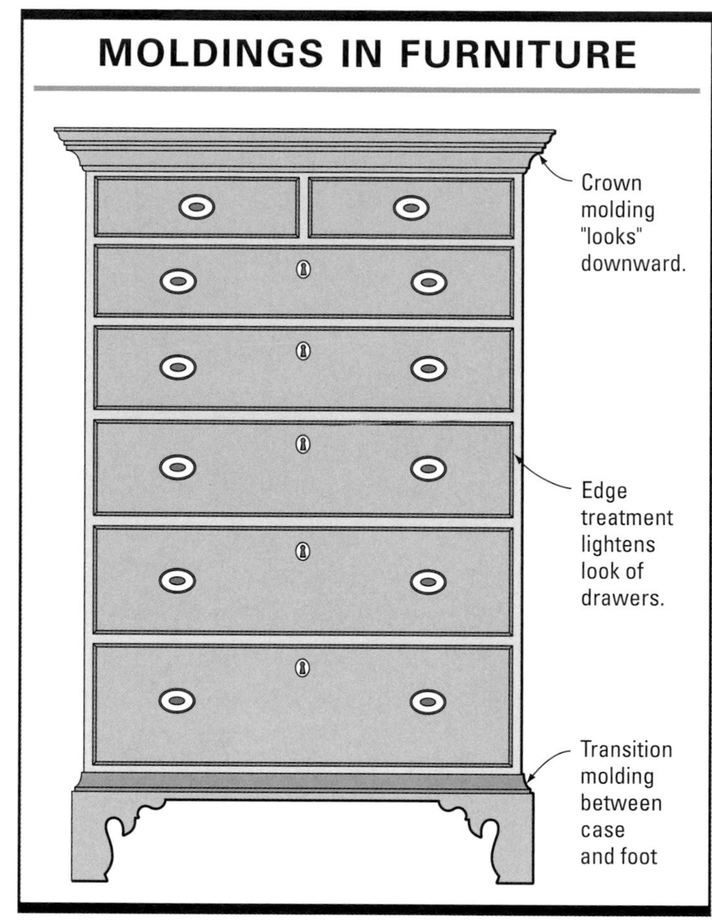

LIPPED DOORS AND DRAWERS WITH THUMBNAIL PROFILE

Hinge
¼ in.
⅞ in.
Door
Face frame
Thumbnail
Double doors
Expansion gap

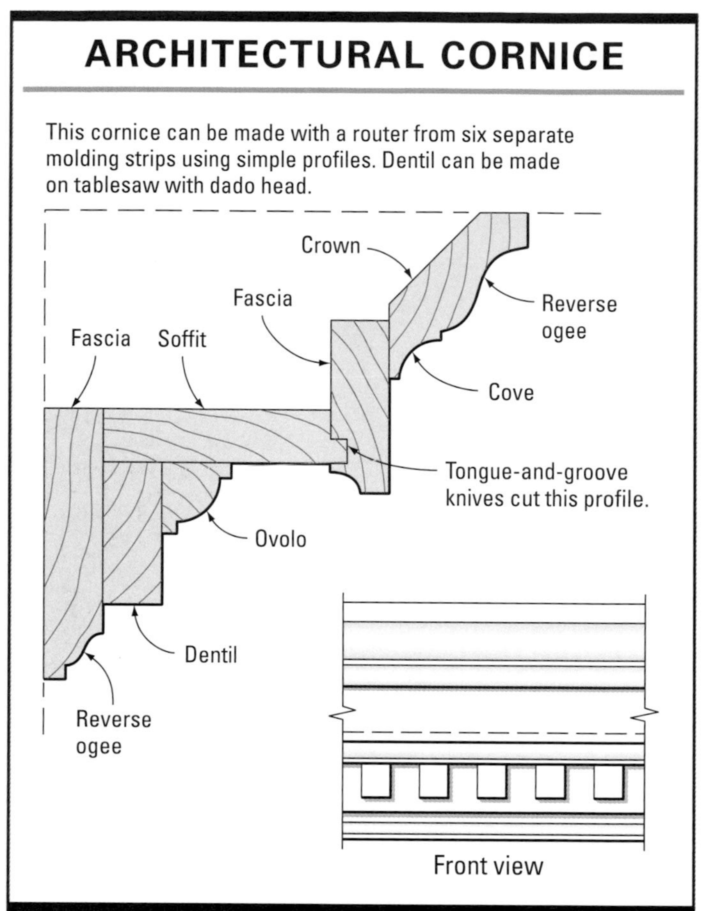

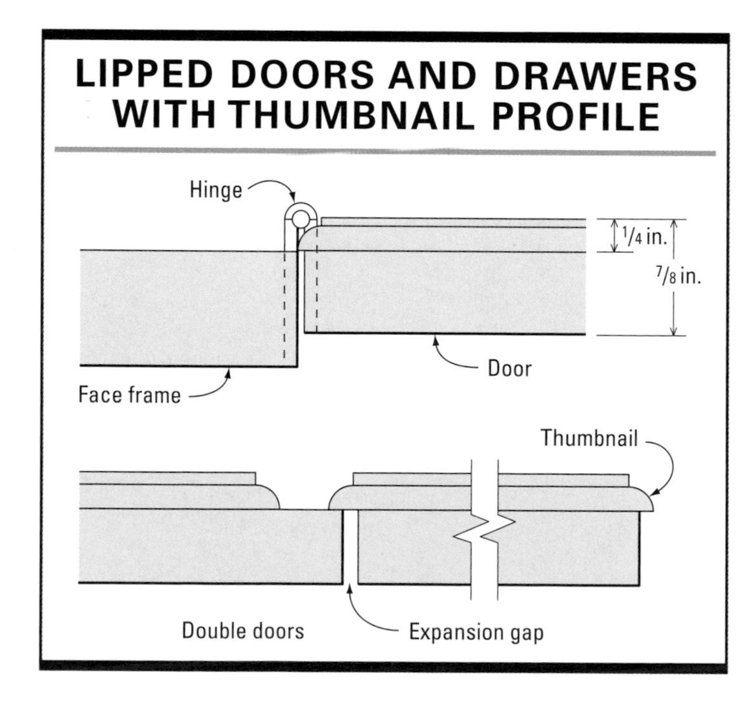

distinctive terminus to the top of a case piece. In contrast, edge treatments can reduce visual weight or thickness and create a lighter appearance. For example, lipped doors or drawer fronts can benefit from a simple roundover along the edges, which creates a thin, almost delicate appearance and reduces visual weight (see the drawing at left).

One of the most efficient and productive tools for creating both edge treatments and moldings is the router (see the photo on the facing page). The edge of a large tabletop is more easily shaped by pushing a router along the edge. On the other hand, the router table is a better choice for shaping long strips of

When you're shaping edges, the router table provides support for the workpiece.

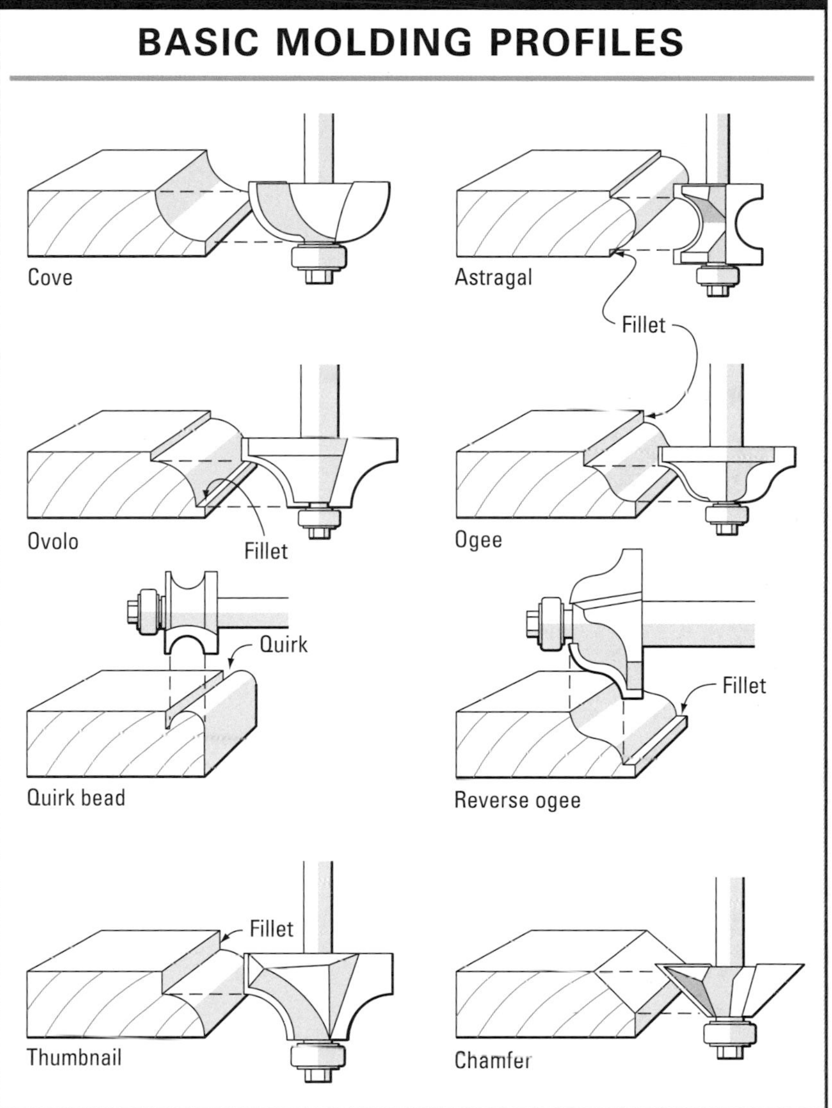

moldings. The fence and the tabletop provide support, and featherboards can be used to hold the stock and guide it past the bit in a straight path. In fact, a small power feeder is ideal for routing strips of moldings on a router table. It will keep your hands a safe distance from the bit and allow you to safely rout even narrow pieces of stock.

Using Edge Treatments

All the moldings that we use, from simple beads to complex crowns, comprise basic profiles that have origins in ancient Greek and Roman architecture (see the drawing at right). The ogee, bead, cove, and ovolo are a few examples. Of course, there are router bits available to create each of these basic profiles in a number of different sizes. The profiles can be used individually or combined to create a complex molding. Complex moldings are a combination of two or more simple profiles. Good examples are found in many of the crown moldings for furniture and architecture. Many crown moldings comprise a large central cove or ogee flanked by smaller profiles. As the molding steps upward, it also "looks down" toward the viewer, as shown in the left photo on p. 104.

Simple profiles are often used along the edges of tabletops and drawers (see the

This clock construction combines shaped edges and applied moldings.

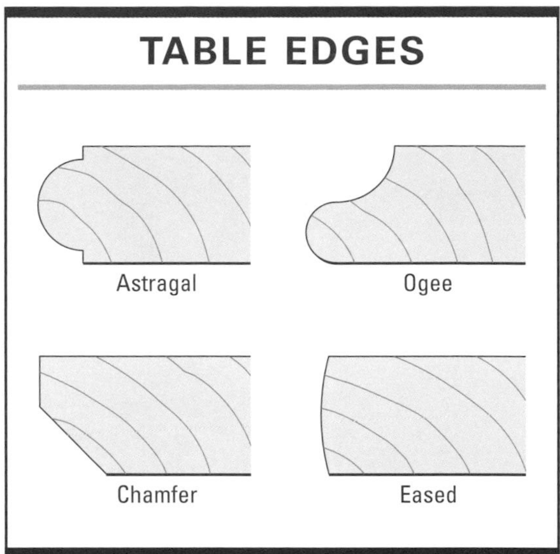

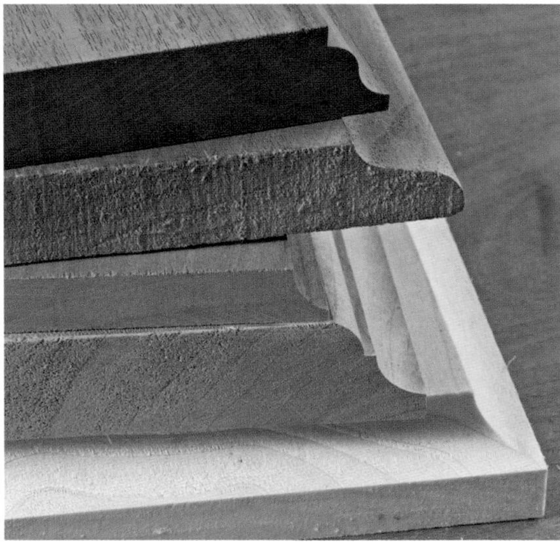

Tabletops and drawer edges are profiled to reduce their visual weight.

drawing above right). They are an effective way to eliminate a hard, square edge while adding a degree of style. Often a strip molding of a simple profile is used in casework to provide a transition between the upper and lower cases.

Combining Profiles

There are three methods for combining profiles to create a large, complex molding, as shown in the drawing on the facing page. The first method is to shape individual strips of wood of various widths and thicknesses and stack them. This is a great way to create a large architectural molding with a router.

The second method is to shape one large piece of stock. Unlike architectural moldings, which are often painted, furniture moldings are usually finished in a natural stain, and stacked strips can result in visually

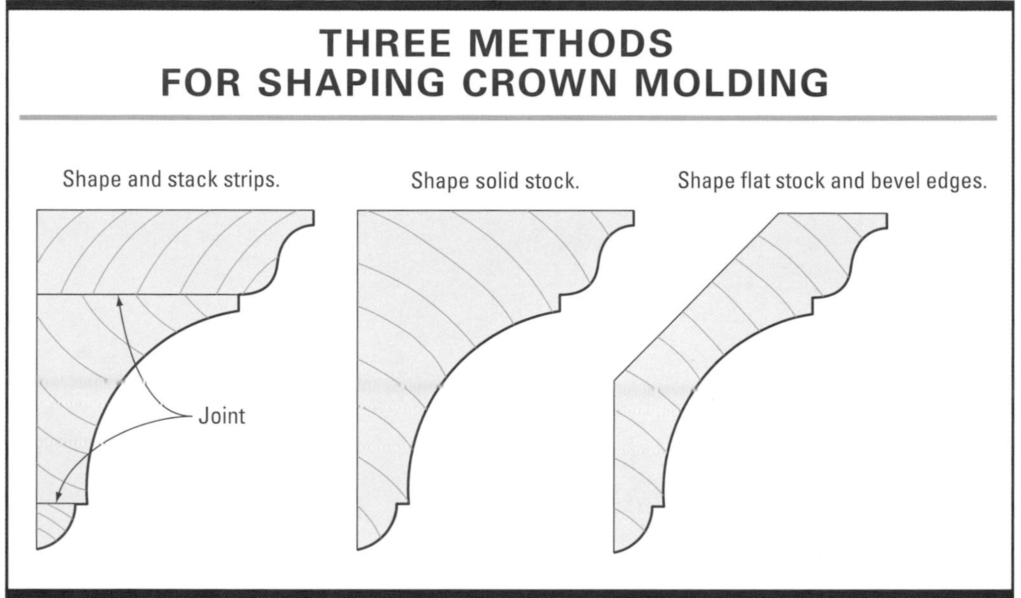

distracting, mismatched grain. In contrast, shaping a solid piece of stock eliminates this problem. Also, when used as a furniture crown, solid stock fills the void that would otherwise result from using a thin strip of architectural crown molding. This is also the best way to shape curved moldings, as shown in the top photo on p. 106.

The third method is to shape a strip of flat stock, bevel the edges, and attach it at an angle. This method gives the appearance of a large molding without the need for heavy stock. Although a flat molding is not useful at the top of a case where it would create a visual void, it works well as a transition molding between two stacked cases, as in a tall clock.

The drawback to the last two methods is the limited size of router bits. A good solution is to cut a large cove on the tablesaw and flank it with smaller routed profiles.

This crown molding bit set has special inverted router bits and a tablesaw cove cutter.

You can combine several bits to make a complex molding.

Most furniture styles use moldings, even if they're just simple edge beads.

Shaping Complex Profiles

Remember, complex molding profiles are just combinations of two or more basic profiles. You can shape a complex profile with a dedicated multi-profile bit, or you can use individual bits and make several cuts to achieve the same results.

Although a dedicated multi-profile bit may take the guesswork out of routing a complex molding, these bits are large and expensive. They also provide you with less flexibility. In other words, because a multi-profile bit is dedicated to making a specific profile, it can be somewhat limiting.

In contrast, a collection of individual single-profile bits gives you more design creativity. With an assortment of basic profile bits, you'll have greater flexibility to design a complex molding to match the project at hand.

Handheld vs. Router Table

The choice of whether to use the router freehand or in a router table depends on the size and shape of the workpiece. Whenever possible, I prefer to shape moldings and edges on the router table (see the photo on the facing page). It's an easy decision. In most cases, it's simply easier to manipulate the workpiece across the router table than to support the router above the work. The broad surface of the router table provides support for the work, and the fence allows use of guards and featherboards.

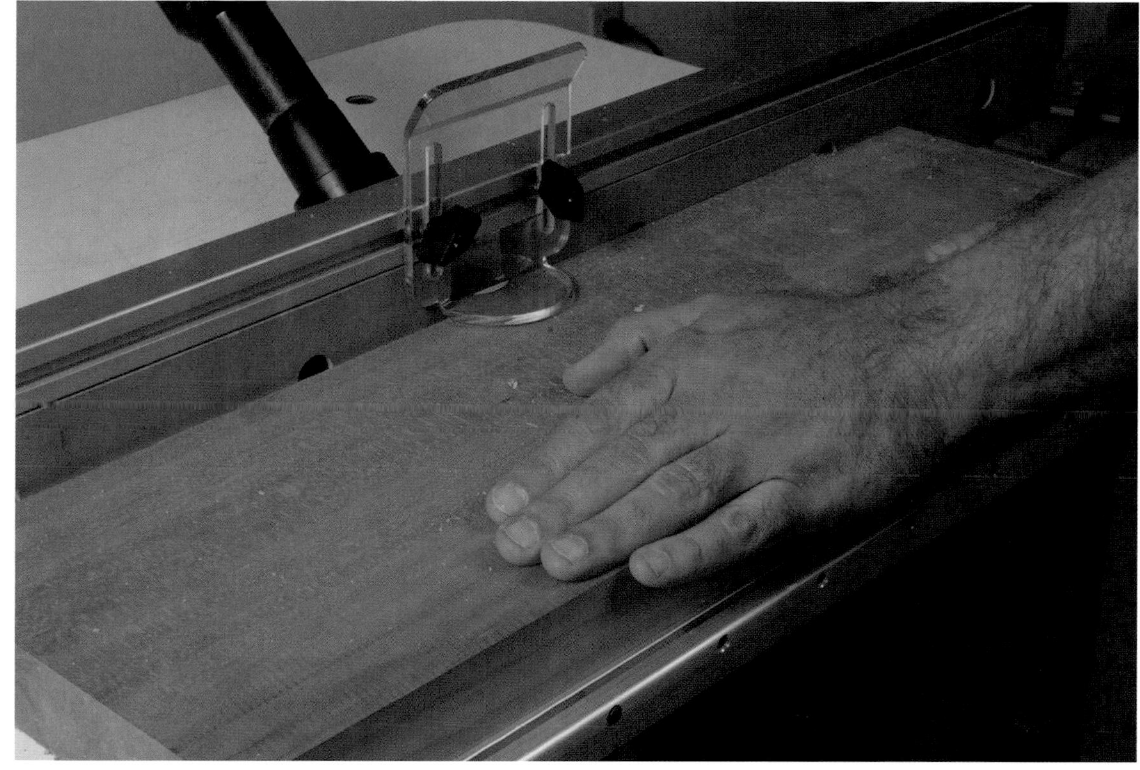

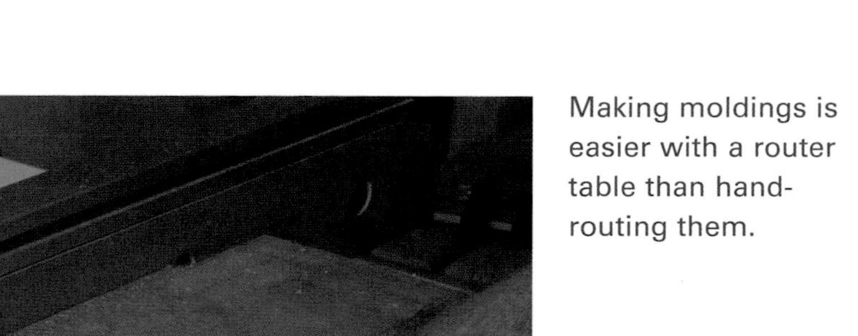

Making moldings is easier with a router table than hand-routing them.

This is a great advantage when you're shaping lengths of moldings. In fact, a power feeder used in conjunction with the router table allows you to safely and accurately shape even narrow molding strips—something you don't want to attempt with a handheld router. Of course, the router table is always cleaner because of the ease of attaching dust collection.

So why use a handheld router for edges or moldings? A large workpiece such as a tabletop may be too heavy or awkward to maneuver across the router table. With a large, heavy workpiece, you'll instead find it's easier to push a handheld router along the edge of the stock.

Stock Selection

Stock selection plays an important role in the visual success of moldings and edge treatments. It's also important to the success of the shaping process. A rule of thumb is to use straight-grained stock for moldings and figured stock for show surfaces, such as tabletops, drawer fronts, and door panels.

When you're making moldings, straight-grained stock produces less tearout. For safe routing, thin strip moldings are shaped on wide stock and ripped free afterwards. Straight-grained stock will be less likely to twist and distort as it is ripped. It's always a good idea to shape an extra piece or two of strip molding to avoid coming up short in case you miscut a piece while fitting. It can be difficult to mill an identical strip of a complex molding.

Large Coves

As mentioned earlier, many moldings are based upon a large central cove flanked

This spice cabinet features a large bead as part of the crown molding.

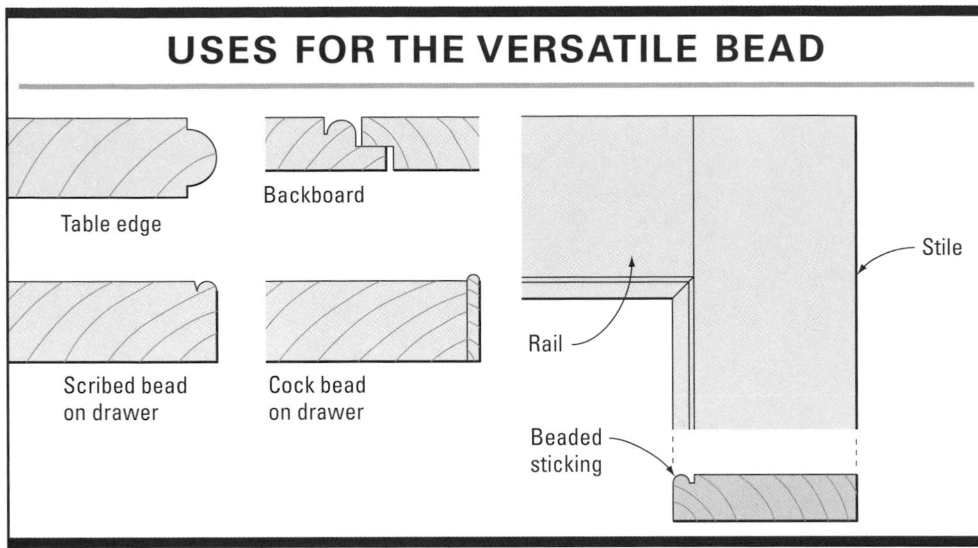

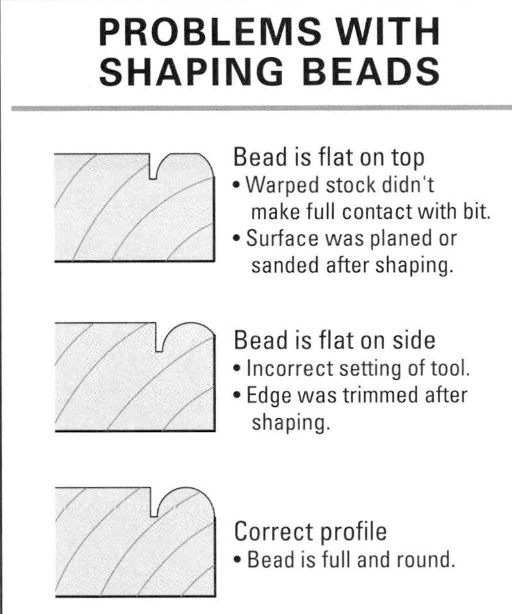

by smaller moldings like beads, coves, and ogees. By combining cove bits, you can shape a large, elliptical cove that is larger than the individual bits used to create it.

Another method for shaping large coves uses the tablesaw. This time-honored technique is as old as the tablesaw itself and, when combined with router profiles, is an effective method for creating large-scale moldings with small-shop tools. To shape a cove on the tablesaw, attach a fence to the saw table at an angle. A greater angle produces a wider cove. The depth of the cove is determined by the height of the blade on the final pass. Coves cut with this method require scraping and sanding to remove the saw marks. However, you can reduce the sanding time by using a specially designed cove cutter available from CMT.

The Bead

Undoubtedly, the bead is one of the most useful edge and molding profiles available (see the top drawing above). It's used to form the edge of drawers, dividers, and backboards, and to soften the corners of square stock, such as table legs and stretchers. Fortunately, there are router bits available to cut beads in a number of different sizes. When shopping for beading bits, I look for those that shape a narrow quirk, which is the shallow groove that flanks a bead. Unfortunately, many beading bits cut a large quirk that appears disproportionate to the bead.

Bullnose in Two Cuts

Although you can purchase bullnose router bits, you can shape the same profile with two passes of a roundover bit. This process is best done on a router table, because on the second pass, the bearing will not receive support from the workpiece **(A)**. Instead, the fence is used to guide the cut.

Begin by setting the height of the bit **(B)**. Set the fence tangent to the guide bearing and make the first pass **(C)**. Then shape the opposite face to complete the bullnose profile **(D)**.

A

B

C

D

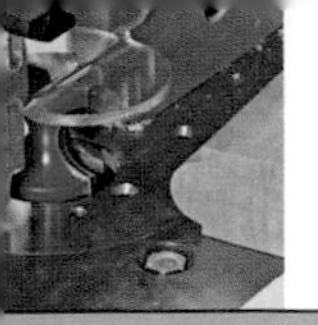

Edge Bead

Although quite simple, the edge bead is a good choice for adding a small embellishment to a table apron or the backboards in a cabinet **(A)**. Begin by setting the height **(B)** and then the depth of the profile **(C)**. When properly set up, the bead will be 180 degrees of a circle with no flat spots on the side or top **(D)**.

Edge with Fence

Conventional wisdom dictates using a split fence when you're shaping the entire edge of a workpiece **(A)**. The idea is to shape away a little more than really needed to ensure that the full profile is shaped. To avoid sniping of the trailing edge due to the loss of stock width, the outfeed half of the fence is positioned forward to support the workpiece.

The problem with this method is that it requires an offset fence and a fussy setup, and afterwards the fence must be reset to its original position. It's much easier to adjust the fence so that the full profile is tangent to the stock. You won't need a split fence, and, of course, there is no need to reset the fence at the end of the process.

When using a large bullnose bit like this, be sure it is secure in the collet **(B)**. Next, adjust the bit height **(C)** and minimize the fence opening **(D)**.

(Text continues on p. 112.)

A

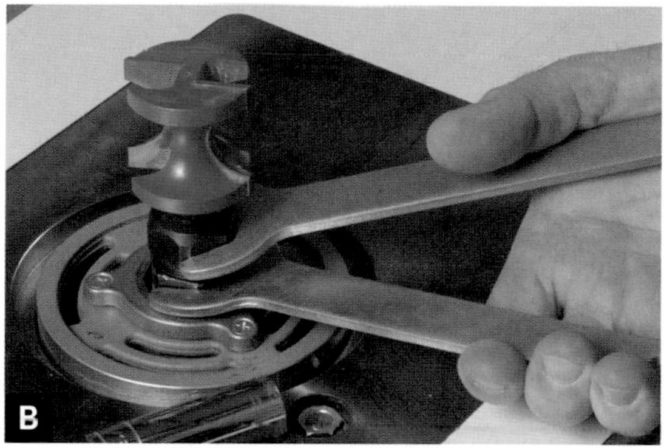

B

C

D

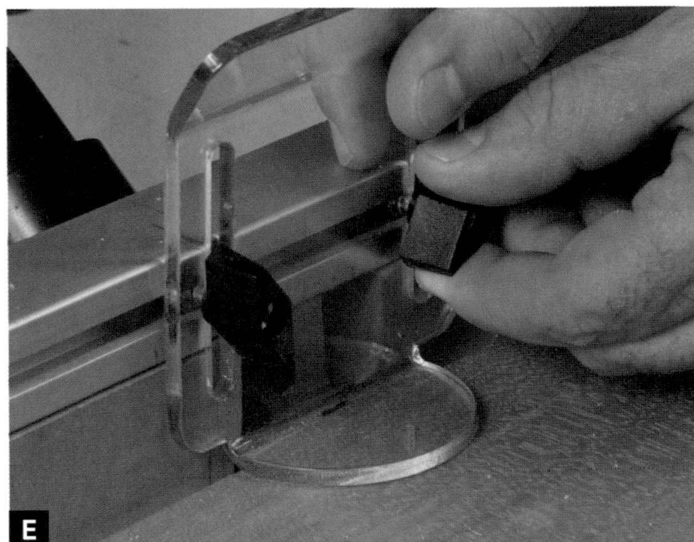
E

A guard is always important, especially on a large bit like the one pictured here **(E)**. After a first pass **(F)**, the fence is adjusted tangent to the smallest cutting circle of the bit **(G)**. When properly set, the bit cuts the full profile without reducing the size of the stock **(H)**.

F

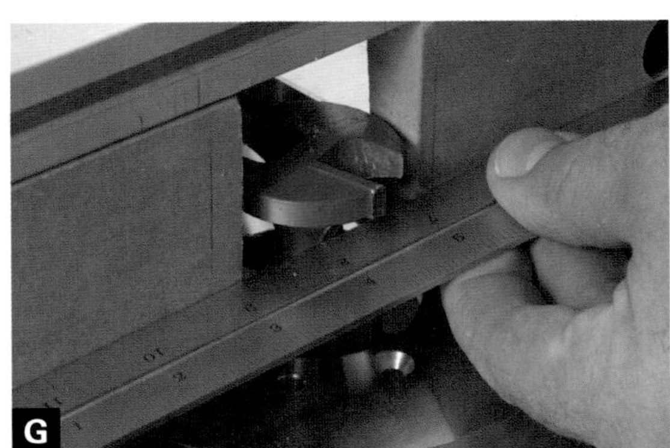
G

H

Beveling Curved Edges

Beveling the edges of curves is a centuries-old technique for making the stock appear thinner than it actually is. This detail creates an illusion of lightness without sacrificing strength. The splat (the back center area) of a chair is a good example. The difficulty is that the work of beveling all those tight, interconnected curves is extremely tedious.

To help speed the process, first bevel the edges with a modified router bit. Beginning with an inexpensive high-speed steel router bit **(A)**, grind away most of the steel to create a chamfer bit with a 15-degree angle **(B)**.

Next, mount the bit in a laminate trimmer, which is really a small router **(C)**. The small base will easily follow the curved surface of the splat, and the small-diameter pilot on the bit reaches into the corners **(D)**. Before beginning the cut, adjust the depth so that the pilot of the bit just grazes the edges of the surface.

After routing, you will still need to carve the corners **(E)** and complete the bevel. But much of the tedious handwork has been eliminated.

A

B

C

D

E

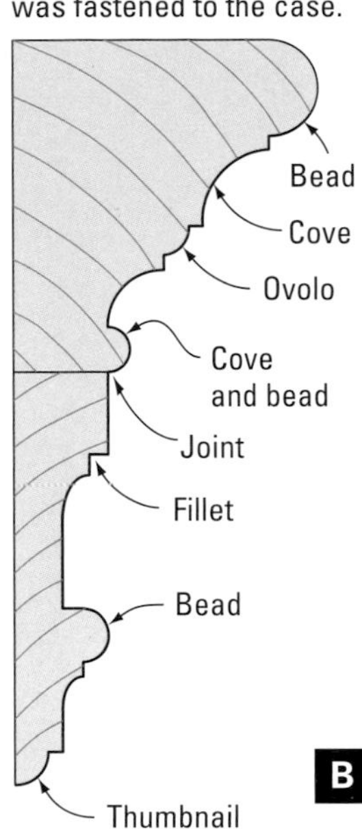

This corner cupboard cornice was shaped as two separate strips to avoid waste; then it was fastened to the case.

Molding on Face

By shaping the face of a board, you can create a wide molding, such as this cornice base **(A, B)**. Before beginning, it's important to make a sketch of the molding and plan the cutting sequence so that the workpiece has sufficient support from the table and fence during each step of the routing process **(C)**. It's also important to use featherboards to hold the stock firmly in place as you feed it past the bit.

The first step is to shape the small thumbnail profile at the base of the molding with a roundover bit **(D)**. For a smooth surface, it's best to make this cut in two passes **(E)**. Next, turn the

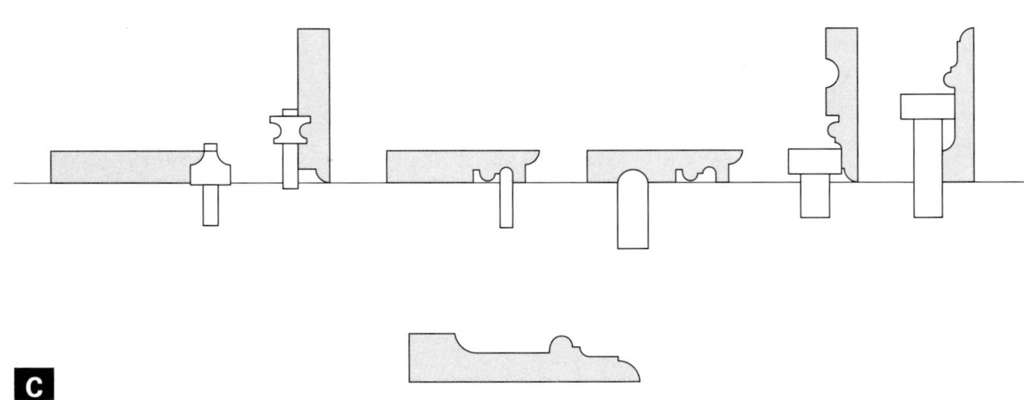

workpiece on edge and shape the bead **(F)**. Clamp a featherboard in place to hold the work to the fence and prevent it from tipping **(G)**.

The next step is to shape the small coves on the molding face **(H)**. Two sizes of corebox bits are used, along with featherboards, to control the cut and the feed rate **(I)**. Finally, shape the flat areas between the profiles **(J)**. To safely shape the "step" at the top, invert the molding **(K)**.

F

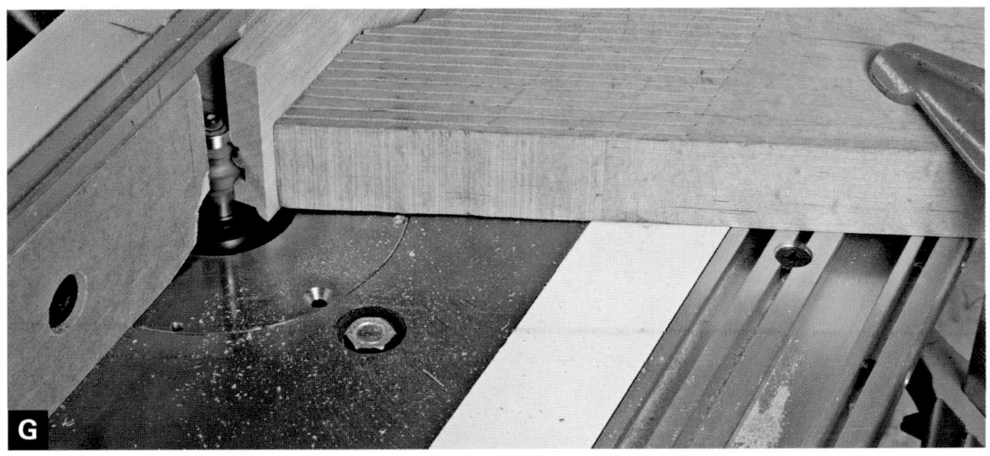

G

H

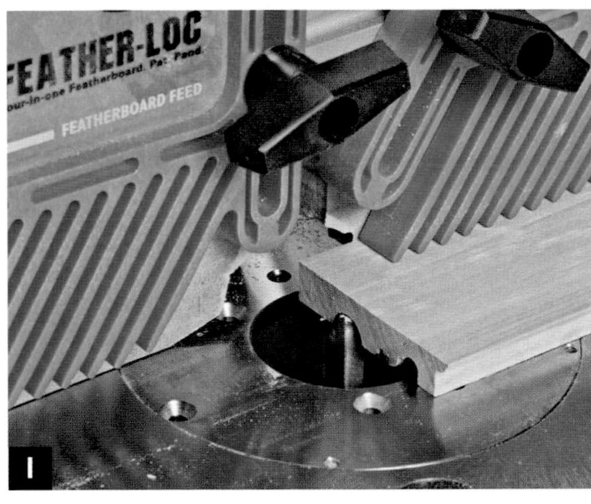

I

J

K

Complex Molding

This small crown molding **(A)** is from a spice box. It looks best when shaped from one piece of stock as opposed to combining several strips. It provides a good example of how to use your router table and a number of different bits to make a complex molding.

Before routing a complex molding, it's best to make a sketch, plan the cutting sequence, and gather the bits you'll need. Sometimes you'll find that it's necessary to remove the bearing to create an undercut **(B)**. As always, it's important for your safety that you shape a plank and rip the molding free afterwards. This technique positions your hands a safe distance from the bit during routing, and adds workpiece mass for a smoother, safer cut.

Begin by shaping the bead at the top of the profile. Inverting the stock enables you to reach the area with the short bit **(C)**. Two light passes ensure a clean cut without burning **(D)**. The next step is to shape the cove. Start with a light cut **(E)**. Then, raise the bit and take a second pass **(F)**. A third light pass **(G)** ensures that this cherry routs cleanly with no tearout or burning.

A slot cutter will create the fillet between the cove and bead. First set the height **(H)** and the fence so that the fillet will properly flank the bead **(I)**. The last step is to turn the stock on edge and shape the thumbnail profile with a roundover bit **(J)**.Featherboards support the stock as it passes through the router table on edge **(K)**.

F

G

H

I

J

K

A

Complex Molding II

This reverse ogee and ovolo **(A)** is cut using just two bits. However, to create the deep ogee along with the fillet, you'll first need to remove the guide bearing and grind away the mounting stud **(B)**.

Set the fence in position and make the ogee in two passes **(C)**. Then invert the stock and rout the ovolo **(D)**.

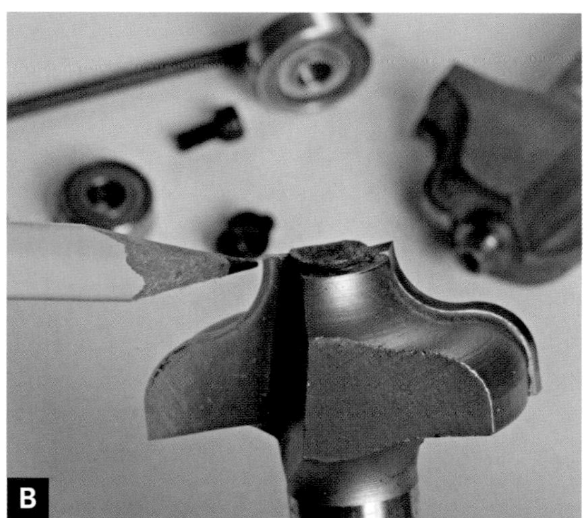
B

C

D

Built-Up Molding

To avoid the need for thick stock, you can stack separate strips to make a large molding. For the best results, take care to match the grain and color before you begin **(A)**.

In this case, I'm using a large multiple-profile bit. By adjusting the fence, bit height, or both, you can create a a number of shapes with one bit.

First, lock the bit securely in the collet **(B)**. Then set the height **(C)** and minimize the fence opening **(D)**. After an initial light pass **(E)**, position the

(Text continues on p. 120.)

A

B

C

D

E

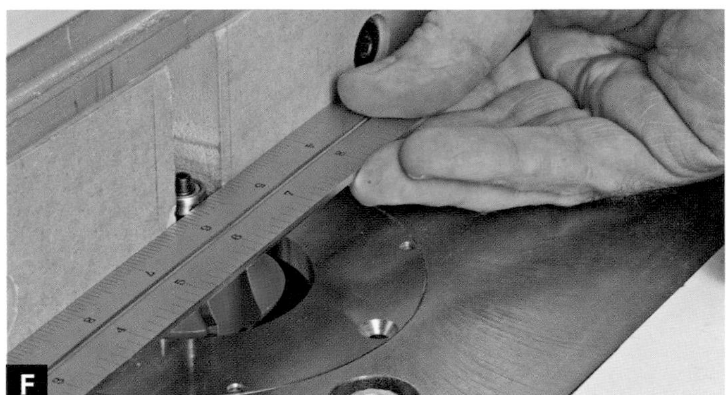
F

fence tangent to the guide bearing **(F)** and make a second pass to the full depth of the profile **(G)**.

To make the cove on the top of the molding, begin by raising the height of the bit **(H)**. To position the fence, set it tangent to the fillet underneath the cove profile **(I)** and then make the cut **(J)**.

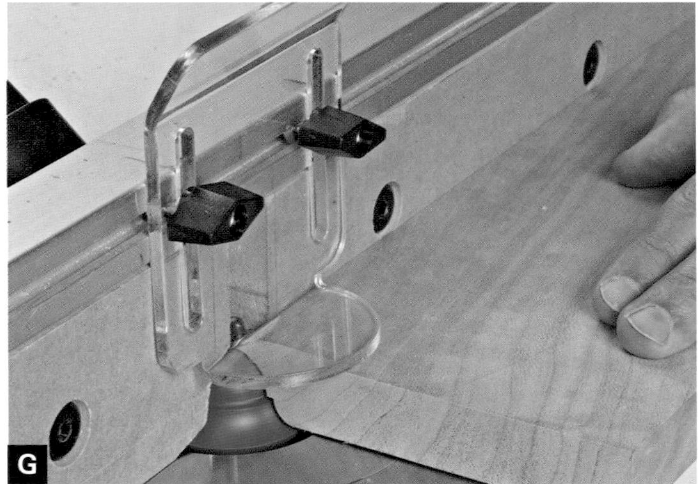
G

H

I

J

Arched Molding Face

This technique is useful anytime the profile has a quirk that can't be shaped from the edge. It involves making a curved jig, or cradle, in which the stock travels in an arc during shaping **(A)**.

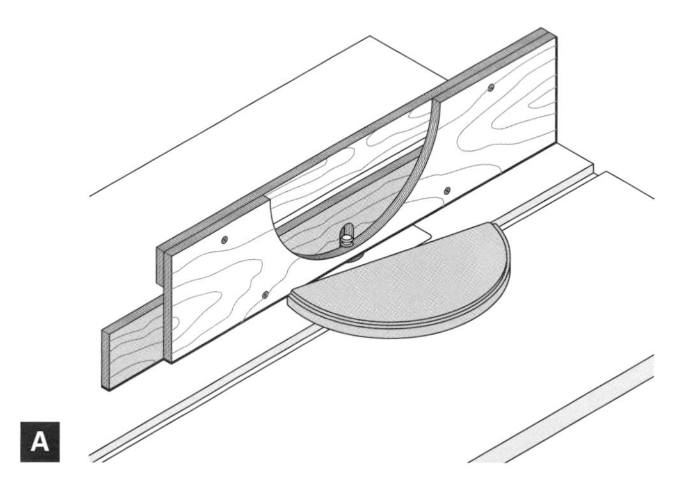

After milling the stock, strike the radius of the outside edge of the molding onto the face. Using the same compass setting, strike the radius onto a rectangle of plywood to serve as a cradle.

Now bandsaw the outside (convex) curve of the molding stock **(B)** and the inside (concave) curve of the cradle. Smooth the edge of the stock with a spokeshave **(C)** and fasten the cradle to the router table fence with screws **(D)**. Now mount the bit and adjust the height to align with the edge of the stock—and you're ready to begin **(E)**.

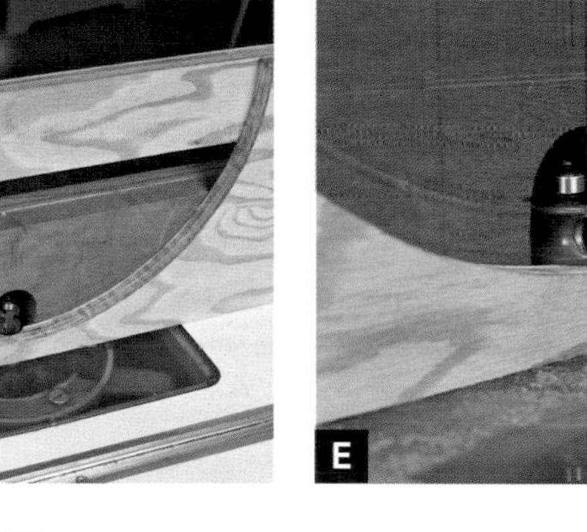

To shape the curve without spoiling the profile, it's necessary to keep the face of the stock against the fence and the edge of the stock against the cradle **(F)**.

[TIP] To get a feel for the technique, make a practice run without power.

You may find it helpful to use a featherboard to maintain pressure against the fence. After cutting the bead, shape the cove using the same process **(G)**. When you're finished, bandsaw the inside radius to complete the molding.

A

B

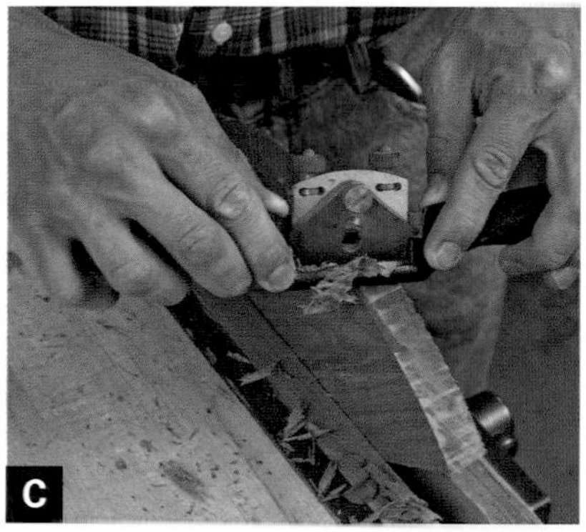

C

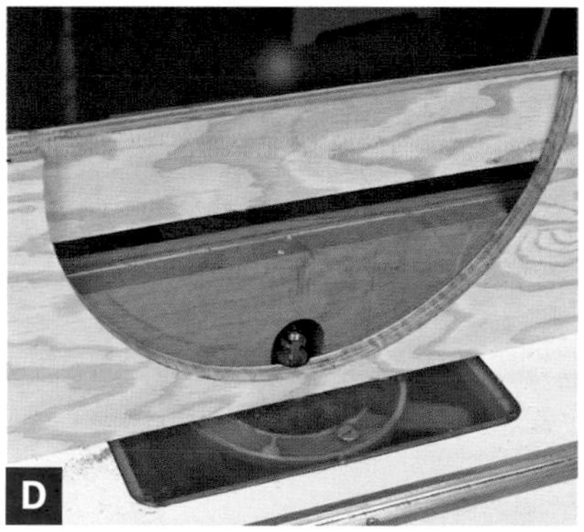

D

E

F

G

A

B

C

Arched Molding Edge

The process of shaping a curved strip of molding is much like shaping a straight strip of molding. The difference is that you'll first have to bandsaw the curve into the stock **(A)**. Then, when shaping, you'll guide the workpiece against a bearing instead of a fence **(B)**.

After shaping, bandsaw the outside radius of the curved molding and smooth the edges **(C)**.

WARNING **Remember to use a starting pin as a fulcrum to enter the cut safely.**

Flush-Trimming

One of the most useful techniques you can perform with the router is flush-trimming, which is the process of routing a surface level or flush to an adjoining surface. For example, it can be used to trim the face frame of a cabinet flush to the box to which it is attached. Of course, flush-trimming isn't needed if you align the surfaces when you join them. But attempts to construct a face frame to exactly the same dimension as a box or cabinet to which it is attached are tedious and time-consuming at best. It requires much less effort to make the frame about 1/16 in. oversized and then to trim 1/32 in. from each edge after assembly.

Flush-trim router bits are just straight bits with a guide bearing, as shown in the left photo on p. 124. The diameter of the guide bearing equals the cutting diameter of the bit. As the bearing rolls along the original surface, the spinning bit trims any excess from the adjoining surface. Once you use the technique a few times, you'll begin to discover other uses for it that will give you greater efficiency and accuracy in your woodworking. For example, you can flush-trim curves after bandsawing, which is much faster than filing or spindle sanding and yields better results. You can also flush-trim work that has an unusual shape, such as

A flush-trim bit in any form is basically a straight bit with a guide bearing.

For the smoothest cut, choose the shortest bit that will do the job.

shelves for a corner cupboard. By trimming each shelf flush to a template, you'll be guaranteed that all the shelves are identical.

If you plan to use plastic laminate in a kitchen or for a router-table top or shop cabinet, you can flush-trim the laminate to the substrate after assembly.

Bits for Flush-Trimming

You can choose from quite a variety of flush-trim bits. Open a router-bit catalog, and you'll see straight, shear, and spiral flush-trim bits in a wide selection of diameters and lengths. Choosing the best bit for the job ensures that you'll achieve the results you are after.

Length

When selecting a straight bit of any sort, the rule of thumb is to choose the shortest bit that will perform the job. Flush-trim bits are no exception. Because router bits are only supported at one end, you'll get less deflection with a short bit than with a long one. Also, for the greatest accuracy, it is important that the guide bearing contact the original surface as close as possible to the surface to be trimmed.

Straight, Shear, or Spiral?

The least expensive straight bits have cutting surfaces that run parallel to the bit shank. These are the least effective at cutting cleanly, especially when trimming difficult woods. That's because the small diameter of router bits doesn't allow for the effective cutting angle found on larger shaper cutters. Ordinary straight flush-trim bits work well on soft, straight-grained wood but have a tendency to splinter and tear dense, figured stock.

For improved cutting geometry and surface quality, some manufacturers offer a shear flush-trim bit. Instead of being parallel to the shank, the cutting surfaces are skewed. This minor change in the design dramatically improves the quality of the cut.

However, for the smoothest possible cut that is absolutely free of tearout even on difficult grain, I use a spiral flush-trim bit. You can't mistake the distinctive look of a spiral flush-trim bit—it looks like a twist drill with a bearing on the end. The unique design slices and shears and leaves behind an incredibly smooth surface that is free of chatter, burning, and tearout. The only drawback to spiral flush-trim bits is their cost. Because of the steep price, I reserve their use for when the lesser-priced shear bit isn't effective.

Flush-Trim Bits for Laminate

Flush-trim bits for trimming plastic laminate are small, with a ¼-in.-dia. shank to fit in laminate trim routers. They are available in straight as well as beveled profiles. Plastic laminate is hard and brittle and tends to wear down even carbide rather quickly. Some bit manufacturers make laminate bits with replaceable carbide inserts. The inserts are locked in place in the body of the bit with tiny screws. As the cutting edge becomes dull, the insert can be repositioned to expose a fresh edge. Eventually the inserts are replaced. Replaceable insert cutters ensure that the cutting diameter always matches the bearing diameter.

Templates for Flush-Trimming

One of the most efficient routing techniques is flush-trimming with a template. The method is fast, and every piece from the first to the last is identical. But before you begin, you'll need to make a template and decide how to attach it to the workpiece. Here are some ideas.

TOP OR BOTTOM BEARING?

Flush-trim bits are available with either a top or bottom bearing to suit the job at hand. For example, if you're flush-trimming with a handheld router, you'll want a bit with the bearing at the end—a bottom bearing. However, if you're using a router-table setup with the workpiece locked into a template jig that rides on the router-table top, you'll need a bearing on the bit shank—a top bearing. Want the greatest flexibility? Choose a ¾-in.-dia. bottom bearing bit and purchase an extra top bearing along with the lock collar. Now you can swap out bearings and use the bit either way.

Materials

Materials for templates must be stiff, free of voids, stable, and easy to shape with shop tools. Of the materials from which to choose, my favorite is cabinet-grade plywood. Although an entire 4-ft. x 8-ft. sheet can be somewhat expensive, 32 sq. ft. makes a lot of templates. Of course, most home centers also sell partial sheets.

A lower-priced alternative to plywood is tempered hardboard. However, I don't care for the nasty dust that it produces, and sharp corners tend to wear quickly after a

Curves can be flush-trimmed with a template jig.

few passes with a router, which results in soft, rounded corners on the work instead of crisp, distinctive corners.

Positioning the Template and Workpiece

Whether I'm flush-trimming with a handheld router or on a router table, I prefer the template positioned below the workpiece, where it doesn't obstruct the view. Of course, this also means that I need flush-trim bits with top and bottom bearings.

Positioning a workpiece on a template is often simple—just allow an edge to overhang the template slightly and fasten in place. Other times, the exact location is critical. For example, when trimming parallel edges, it is usually important that the overall dimension is exact after trimming. To obtain consistent dimensions, I use stop blocks to position the workpiece in the jig. The blocks also counteract the pushing force of the bit, especially when the work is dense and the cut is large.

Fastening the Template

Whenever you flush-trim with a template, you'll need a method for securing the template to the workpiece. Depending on the work at hand and the size of the cut, I use a variety of fasteners, including small brads, screws, double-sided tape, and/or toggle clamps.

Small brads work well when the subsequent nail holes can be hidden from view after the workpiece is assembled. For larger work, screws serve the same purpose. Nails and screws can be quickly attached and removed after trimming. Obviously, it is important to locate a metal fastener well out of the cutting path.

Although it's expensive, double-sided woodturner's tape is a good choice when the hole from a fastener would be seen in the finished work. The grip of woodturner's tape is surprisingly strong. For the greatest strength, initially squeeze the taped pieces together using a clamp.

When the cut is somewhat large and the workpiece is small, the best option is to construct a jig and secure the work with toggle clamps. The base of a jig can also serve as the template. Stop blocks are used to accurately position the workpiece, and toggle clamps apply pressure to hold the work in place throughout the cut. It is critical for safety that the steel clamps be positioned clear of the path of the spinning bit.

When making a cut, keep it light. You'll get the best possible surface if the bit is skimming off no more than 1⁄32 in. In contrast, aggressive cuts tend to leave the surface rough and torn.

Flush-Trimming Face Frames

When you're making cabinets, a common technique is to make the face frame slightly proud of the casework and trim it flush after assembly **(A)**. Begin by selecting the shortest bit for the job and setting the height **(B)**. When trimming with a handheld router, push the router in a counterclockwise direction around the perimeter of the cabinet. Smaller cabinets can be trimmed on a router table, pushing the work against the rotation of the bit **(C)**.

A

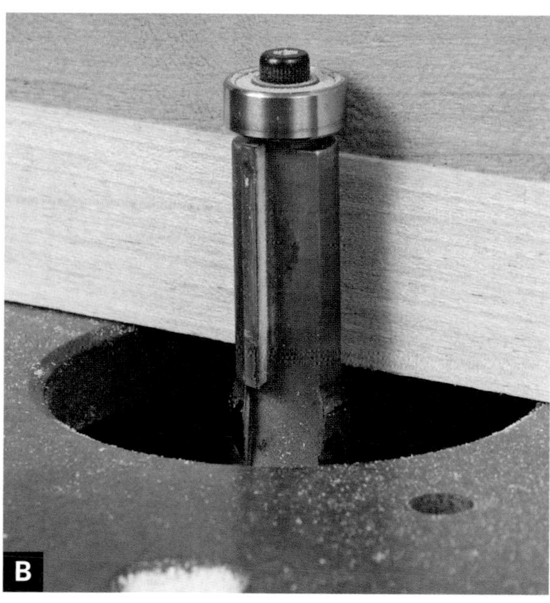

B

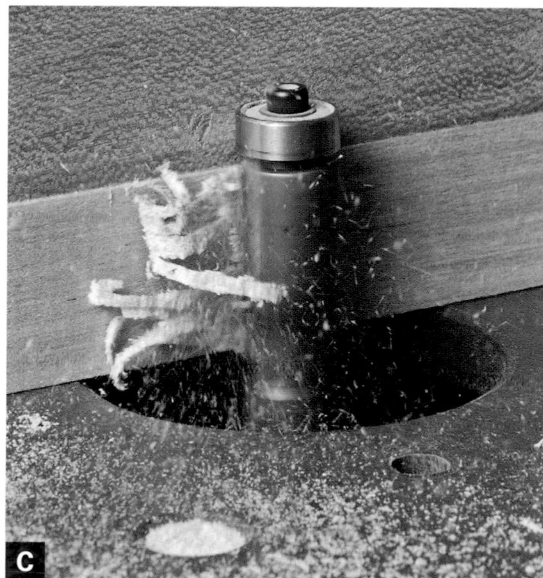

C

Flush-Trimming a Curve

After bandsawing a curve, it's standard practice to smooth away the saw marks with a file or spokeshave. Another option is to flush-trim the surface smooth **(A)**. Because this method requires making a curved template, it's best for efficiently smoothing multiple identical pieces.

Begin by securing the workpiece to the template/jig and setting the height of the bit **(B)**. The guide bearing should follow the template, and the cutting surfaces of the bit should extend slightly above the workpiece. Remember, the template should extend beyond the work on the starting end of the cut **(C)**. And a stop block should be fastened to the jig on the trailing end to provide support for the stock **(D)**.

A

B

C

D

Flush-Trimming Interior

There are times when you need to flush-trim an opening to a template **(A)**. Begin by laying out the interior cut on the workpiece by tracing the template **(B)**. Next, use a scrollsaw or jigsaw to cut the opening in the interior, sawing about ⅛ in. shy of the final cutline **(C)**. Before flush-trimming, it's necessary to secure the template to the workpiece. Small brads work well if the holes will not show in the completed work **(D)**. Otherwise, you can use double-sided wood-turner's tape.

Next, position the workpiece and the template adjacent to the bit and adjust the bit height **(E)**. As with any routing operation, it's important to feed the workpiece against the rotation of the bit. When you're routing the interior, this means working in a counterclockwise feed direction **(F)**.

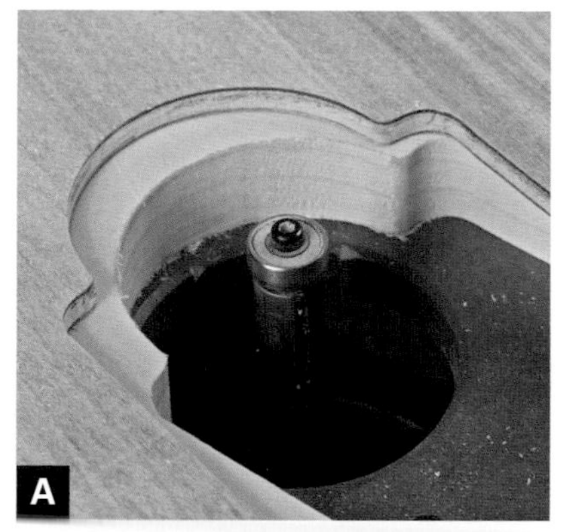

A

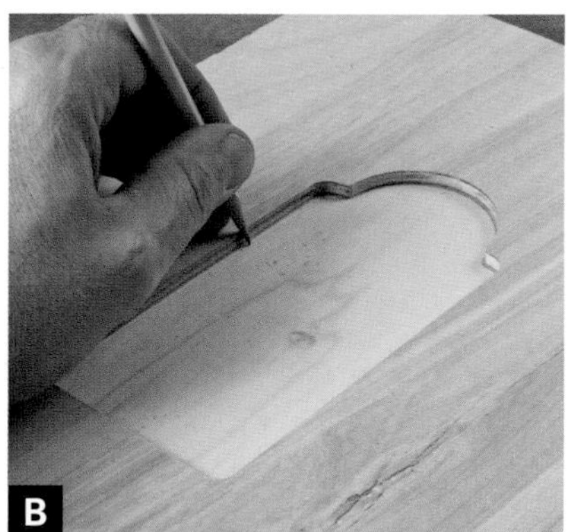

B

C

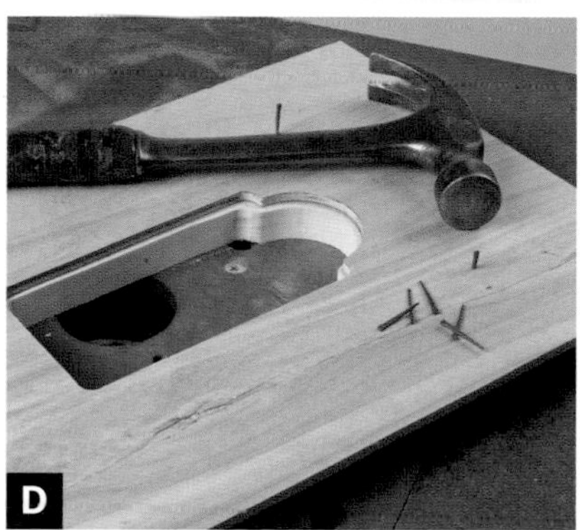

D

E

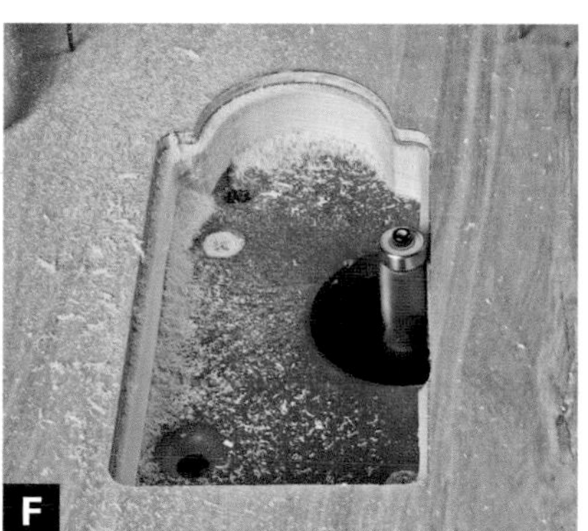

F

Router Joinery, page 132

Doors and Drawers, page 180

PART THREE

Joinery

THE ROUTER is among the most efficient joint-making tools available. Although cutting some joints may require an expensive bit and perhaps a jig, many others can be made with just a simple straight bit and a fence.

In this part of the book, I'll show you how to make a variety of essential joints, ranging from basic dadoes, grooves, and rabbets to mortise-and-tenon joints and dovetails. I've devoted considerable attention to the latter two because of their importance in the realm of furniture making and cabinetry. Due to their interlocking nature and extensive long-grain glue surfaces, mortise-and-tenon joints and dovetails have tremendous strength as well as broad applications. Because so much router work these days is devoted to building cabinet doors and drawers, I have also addressed those techniques at some length, describing how to make a variety of cabinet doors, as well as a very efficient approach to making drawers.

Router Joinery

Grooving

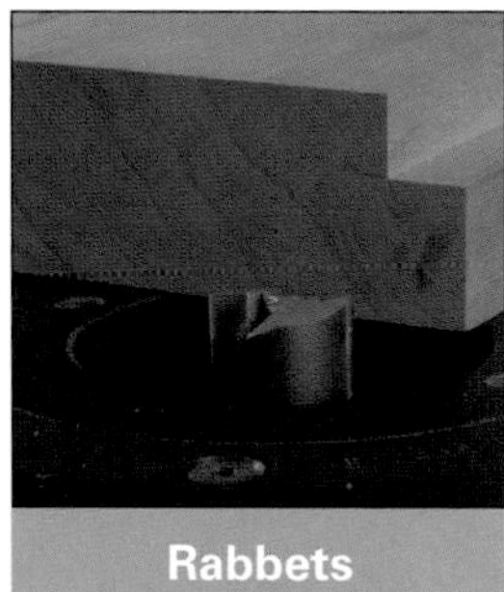

Rabbets

Dovetails

Other Joints

With a few exceptions—such as carvings or baseball bats—most woodworking projects involve joinery. As woodworkers, we use edge joints to make wide panels, mortise-and-tenon joints for door frames, and dovetails for casework and drawers. And no other power tool can match the versatility of the router for making joints. With your router and a selection of bits, you can cut grooves, dadoes, mortise-and-tenon joints, box joints, and even dovetails (see the top right photo on the facing page). Of course, making many of these joints requires a jig. Some jigs you'll want to purchase, but many you can make yourself. Let's begin by looking at the bits available for router joinery, and then I'll discuss various jigs.

A stopped groove is easy to cut on the router table.

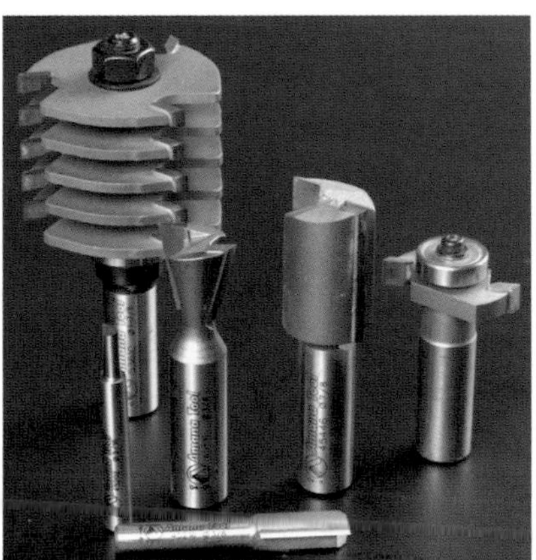

There are router bits available to cut almost any joint.

Bits for Joint Making

Regardless of the joint you want to make, there's probably a router bit for it. The number of router bits for joint-making has increased dramatically in the past few years. The most common joinery bits are straight bits, dovetail bits, and rabbeting bits. But nowadays there are also a number of sophisticated bits that will enable you to quickly and easily create complex cuts such as those for box joints and lock miters. However, it makes sense to choose carefully, as some specialty bits are high-priced, and you may not want or need them. Instead, choose the bits based upon the quality and integrity of the joint and how it fits with your style of woodworking.

Straight Bits

Every bit drawer should contain several straight bits in various diameters and lengths. Hands down, straight bits are among the most versatile that you can own. I use straight bits for cutting grooves, dadoes, and even rabbets. You can also use them for cutting mortises and the fingers of a box joint. And when I'm installing hinges

Straight bits can cut a wide variety of joints, including this rabbet.

and locks, I'll use a 1/4-in.-dia. straight bit in a laminate trimmer to quickly cut the recesses. If you want to cut mortises, it's best to use a spiral up-cut bit along with the jig.

➤ See *"Mortise"* on p. 164.

Rabbet Bits

Sure, you can cut rabbets on your tablesaw, but they won't be nearly as smooth as those cut with a rabbet bit. Rabbet bits are versatile, too. You can cut curved rabbets with a guide bearing. (Don't try that with your tablesaw!) To adjust the dimensions of

This rabbet bit comes with a set of bearings to cut rabbets of any size.

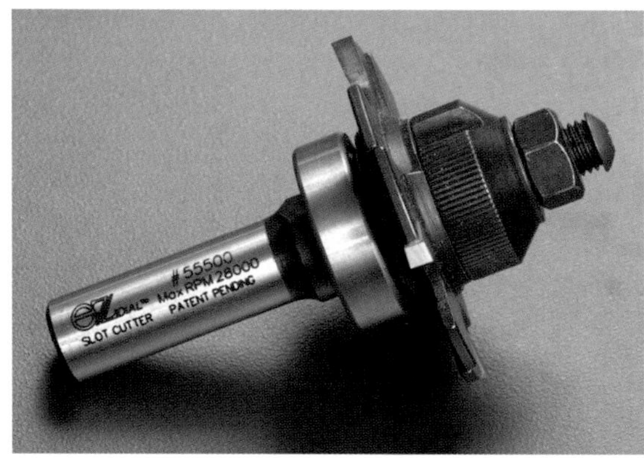

This grooving bit adjusts quickly to within .004 in.

the rabbet, just swap out the guide bearing for one of a different size. In fact, you can purchase rabbeting sets that come complete with an incrementally sized selection of bearings.

Wing Cutters

Similar to rabbeting bits are wing-type bits for cutting grooves. The cutters are not as wide as those on a rabbet bit. Instead, these are designed for cutting the narrow grooves into a door frame to accommodate a panel edge. Like dado heads for the tablesaw, some grooving bits come as stacking sets of cutters that can be arranged for a specific size groove. Still others adjust simply with a turn of a knob with .004-in. accuracy. These new grooving cutters are just what's needed for working with today's undersized plywood. If you have an occasional need for plate joinery (otherwise known as biscuit joinery) but don't want to invest in a biscuit joiner, you can instead purchase a router bit that cuts a narrow slot to accept a biscuit.

Dovetail Bits

Nothing speaks of fine craftsmanship like the time-honored dovetail joint. It has both strength and good looks. The long grain of the tails and pins provides plenty of surface area for glue, and the precise interlocking fit gives the joint unmatched strength even before the glue is applied.

My preferred method for cutting dovetails is by hand. Of course, this method requires both time and skill. However, to make the process of cutting half-blind dovetails more efficient, I use a dovetail bit to first remove most of the waste between the pins. Afterwards, I scribe the tails from the pins and complete the joint with handwork. This method of combining router cuts with handwork is more efficient than cutting the joint entirely by hand, yet it results in a "handcrafted" joint, as shown in the top left photo on the facing page.

If you prefer, there are a number of commercial router dovetail jigs on the market. They typically each require that you purchase a special bit that fits with that brand of jig. Be aware too that some require a 1/4-in.-dia. shank bit in order to slip inside the bushing that guides the router through the jig, as shown in the bottom left photo on the facing page.

Dovetail router bits are available in several angles, too—most commonly either 7 or 14 degrees. I prefer the look and strength of the more pronounced 14-degree pitch.

Routing freehand allows greater spacing flexibility than using a dovetail jig.

Many jigs require a small shank bit like the one at right, which should be fed slowly through the wood to prevent chatter.

Specialty Joints

There are a number of specialty joints that you can make with your router. Some require a special bit, while others can be easily made with bits you may already own.

Drop-leaf tables have extensions that hinge upward for use. The mating edges of the table and leaf use what has come to be known as a rule joint. To make a rule joint, the main tabletop is shaped with a roundover, and the underside of the leaf is shaped with a cove of the same radius as the roundover. After shaping, the top and leaf are joined with a special offset hinge.

The rule joint is easily made with a router.

Rule joints are both practical and attractive. When the leaf is up, it's partially supported by the roundover profile. When the leaf is down, the edges of the table form an attractive ovolo profile. You can purchase matching router bits to produce a rule joint, or you can simply use 1/2-in.-radius roundover and cove bits.

The bird's-mouth joint is a V-shaped groove that accepts a 90-degree point, hence the name "bird's mouth" (see the top photo on p. 136). It is used to join thin dividers and partitions. Like a square-edged shelf fit into a groove, the bird's mouth joins shelves and partitions, yet it looks much more refined. The bird's mouth is also the only method for effectively joining shelves or partitions that are profiled. The joint is easily created with a 90-degree V bit and a 45-degree chamfer bit.

Another useful joinery bit is the lock miter. This bit shapes a tongue-and-groove

The bird's-mouth joint is an attractive method for joining small partitions.

The lock miter bit ensures perfect alignment of a 90-degree corner.

joint on 45-degree surfaces to prevent the mating parts from slipping out of alignment as the joint is assembled. It's a perfect choice for casework and mitered bracket feet.

Jigs for Joinery

Jigs allow you to cut fine, precisely fitted joints without the time and skill it often requires to cut them by hand. Jigs can be simple shopmade guides or elaborate multi-functional tools that are capable of creating a variety of complicated joints. All jigs perform the same basic function in that they guide the router and bit or the workpiece in a linear path.

All jigs require careful setup. First, the jig is either secured to the workpiece or the stock is clamped within the jig. The cutting depth of the bit is important too. And there must always be a system in place to guide the bit. If the router is handheld, the bit can be guided by the router base, a guide bushing, or a bearing on the end or shank of the bit.

If a router table is used, the jig may be guided by the fence and/or miter-gauge slot. Sometimes the jig may be as simple as a backing board attached to the miter gauge.

One type of routed joint that is often made using a jig is the dovetail joint. Dovetails are considered by many to be the hallmark of finely crafted furniture. They're both strong and beautiful—which is why everyone wants to make them (see the drawing below). They also require lots of skill to master. That's where dovetail jigs come in.

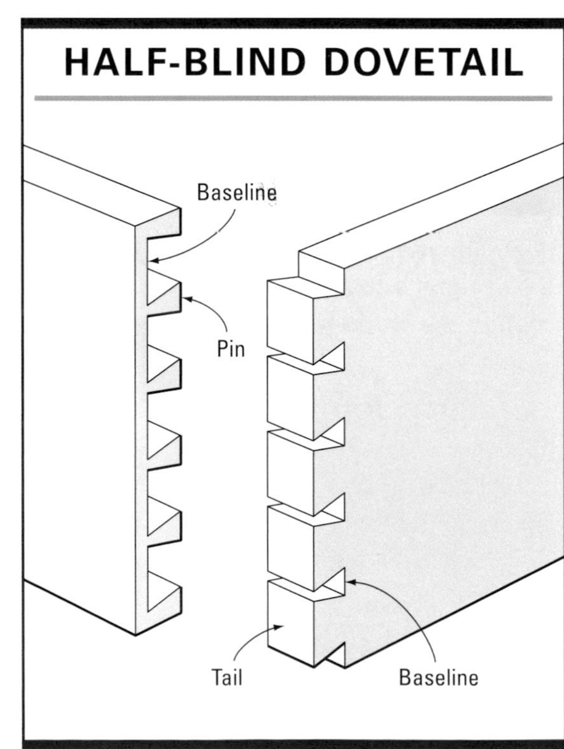

They have a strong selling point—allowing you to quickly master a difficult joint with a jig.

Although I prefer to cut dovetails by hand, for some woodworkers dovetail jigs may be the best approach. Cutting dovetails by hand requires skill, and it takes time and patience to master. But if you've never used a dovetail jig, realize that they have a learning curve too. And although commercially available dovetail jigs will cut an accurate joint, they take time to set up.

Realize too that no dovetail jig will cut joints with an authentic hand-cut appearance. The narrow pins, subtle variations in angles and spacing, and the sharp, distinctive baselines of a hand-cut dovetail are all important details that are not duplicated with a jig.

Another option is to use a router along with hand tools to create an authentic joint more efficiently than with hand tools alone.

➤ See *"Freehand-Routing Dovetails"* on p. 150.

Commercial Dovetail Jigs

Dovetail jigs use machined "fingers" to guide the spinning bit through the stock. The best jigs use adjustable guide fingers that allow for greater variation in spacing. The stock is secured in the jig with an integral clamping system, and the router is fed in a precise path between the fingers. Some jigs use a guide bushing mounted to the router baseplate. Unfortunately, because of the imprecise fit between the bushing, router base, and baseplate, the bushing is typically slightly eccentric to the bit. This can create errors in the final fit if the router is inadvertently rotated during the routing process. One solution is to mark a point of reference on the router baseplate with a dab of brightly colored paint. As you feed the router through the jig always keep the mark oriented in the same direction.

In contrast, other dovetail jigs use a bearing-guided bit instead of a base-mounted bushing. Because the bearing is concentric with the bit shank, it's usually

The interlocking fingers of the Akeda® jig make it one of the easiest to set up.

The Akeda jig has fingers that snap into position.

easier to achieve a precise joint with jigs that use this system.

There are three types of commercially available dovetail jigs—half-blind, through, and combination, which will cut both. Half-blind dovetail jigs have been around almost as long as the router. These jigs cut the mechanical-looking joints that are associated with mass-produced furniture. Both the pin board and the tail board are clamped into the jig and routed simultaneously. A guide bushing on the router base directs the path of the bit between the "fingers" or guides on the jig. There is absolutely no flexibility with the spacing on these jigs, so you'll often end up with an unattractive termination at one end of the joint. To solve the problem, you would have to change the depth of the box.

The fit of the joint is determined by the cutting depth of the bit. Mill several test pieces and be prepared for several trial runs in order to get the friction fit you're after.

Through dovetail jigs require using two bits: a straight bit to cut the pins and a dovetail bit to cut the tails. The tail board and pin board are each routed separately, using a different set of guides. The fit of the joint is determined by the thickness of the backer board. Although this type of jig is fairly simple to use once set up, the setup itself can be time-consuming. Unfortunately this type of jig doesn't cut half-blind joints. So if you want half-blind dovetails, such as those used in drawer construction, you'll have to cover the joint with a separate piece of stock once the dovetails are assembled.

This Porter Cable Omnijig is one of the most versatile dovetail jigs available.

This Katie® jig is well constructed and versatile.

Combination jigs, as the name implies, will cut both half-blind and through dovetails, while allowing you to vary the spacing of the tails and pins. The designs of these jigs are ingenious, but their setup and use are complex. By the time you've read the manual and made a series of trial-and-error cuts, you could probably have learned the basics of cutting dovetails by hand. And you'll likely have a much higher level of personal satisfaction from the hand process.

Shopmade Jigs

There are a number of router jigs for cutting precise joinery that you can make in

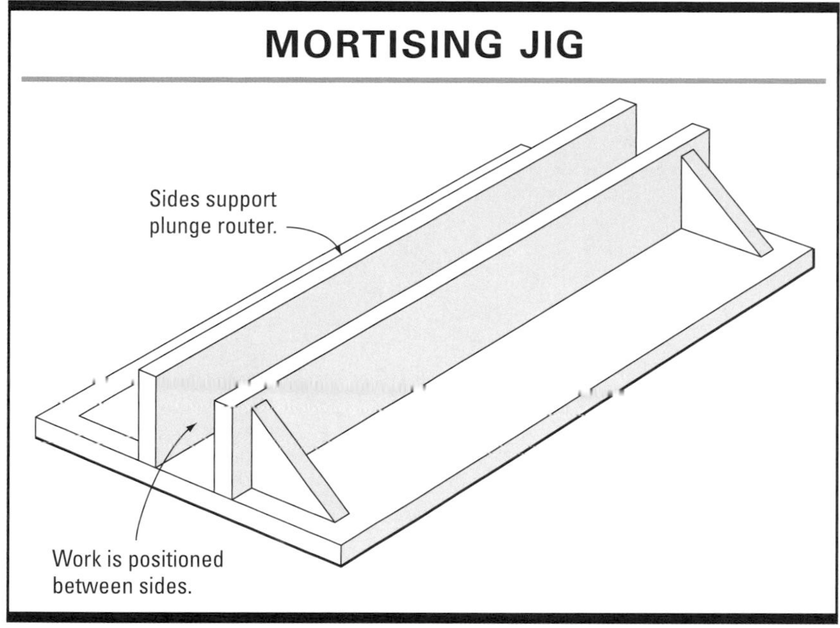

your own shop. For example, if you'd like to frequently use the router for mortise-and-tenon joinery, you'll probably want to make a dedicated mortise jig. The jig holds the workpiece securely while guiding the router in a linear path. It's simple to construct and it accommodates stock of a variety of sizes, as shown in the drawing above.

Although some woodworkers use a T-square-type jig to guide the router when cutting dadoes, this type of jig has a major drawback. It requires that you first carefully lay out each dado and then position the jig according to the layout prior to each cut. The entire process is error-prone. A much simpler method is to rout the dadoes in the box after assembly with a strip of thin plywood to guide the router. By positioning the guide against the inside of the box, perfect location is assured and mating joints match perfectly. This method is a real time-saver too, because there's no need to measure and mark the location of each joint.

Routing sliding dovetails with a template ensures perfect spacing.

The space between the pins on half-blind dovetails can be routed quickly with a dovetail template. A guide bushing follows the template to keep the spacing accurate and the cuts uniform. The tails are marked out from the pins and cut with a dovetail saw.

Box joints can be easily cut with a straight bit on the router table. A miter gauge and backing board makes a simple yet effective jig. A block glued into the backing board ensures perfect spacing.

A

B

Stopped Groove

Tongue-and-groove joints are strong and useful, but not necessarily attractive, especially when viewed from the end of the workpiece **(A)**. But they're easy to hide just by making a stop cut. Depending on the project, you can stop the groove at one end or both ends. A straight bit works best for a stop cut because it creates an abrupt, distinctive stopping point for the groove, thereby eliminating most of the handwork required when you're completing the wide arc left by a grooving bit.

Begin by adjusting the bit height **(B)**. Typically the depth of the groove is one-third to one-half of the bit diameter. In order to provide the greatest support for the stock and provide for your safety, close the fence halves **(C)**. Next, position the fence the correct distance from the bit and lock it in place **(D)**. To make a stop cut safely and accurately, it's important to secure a stop to the fence. Otherwise, you risk kickback while plunging the workpiece onto the spinning bit.

C

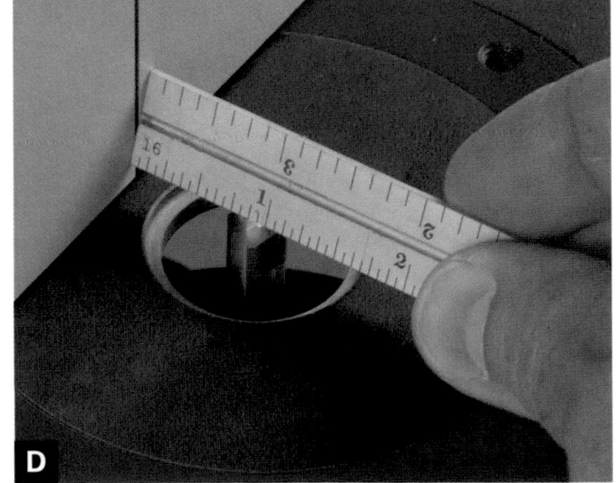

D

To locate the position of the stop block, first lay out the groove and make marks at the starting and stopping points **(E)**. Next, make a pair of marks on the fence to indicate the parameters of the bit **(F)**. Finally, align the leading layout line on the workpiece adjacent to the forward mark on the fence and clamp the stop block in place **(G)**.

To cut the groove, position the stock against the stop block and slowly lower it onto the spinning bit **(H)**. Now push the stock forward **(I)**. Stop when the trailing layout mark on the stock aligns with the mark on the fence **(J)**.

E

F

G

H

I

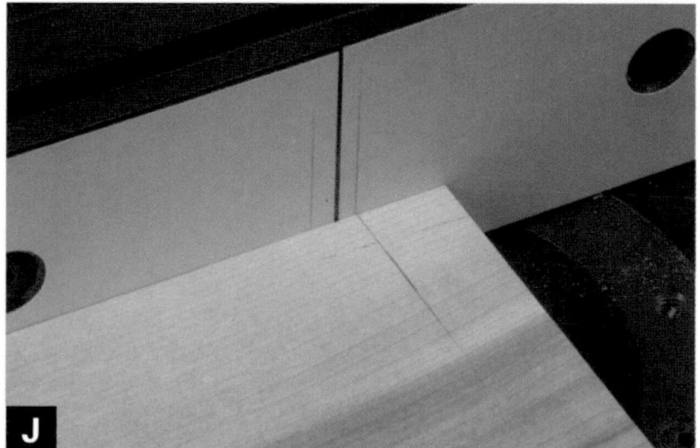
J

A

Panel Groove

When constructing cabinets for the shop or kitchen, it's typical to join solid wood with plywood. For example, plywood is often used for door panels and drawer bottoms. Because much of today's plywood is dimensioned undersized, it's necessary to adjust the panel groove for a precise fit **(A)**. Otherwise the panel will rattle in the framework each time the door is opened. This bit from Amana® uses two interlocking cutters, much like a stacking dado head. The cutters are separated by a compression spring and are easily adjusted by turning a knurled adjusting screw. This is a unique bit that makes cutting odd-sized grooves quick and precise **(B)**.

Begin by securing the bit in the router collet and loosening the lock nut **(C)**. Turn the nut counterclockwise until it stops against the limiter **(D)**. Next, turn the adjuster to dial in the size of the

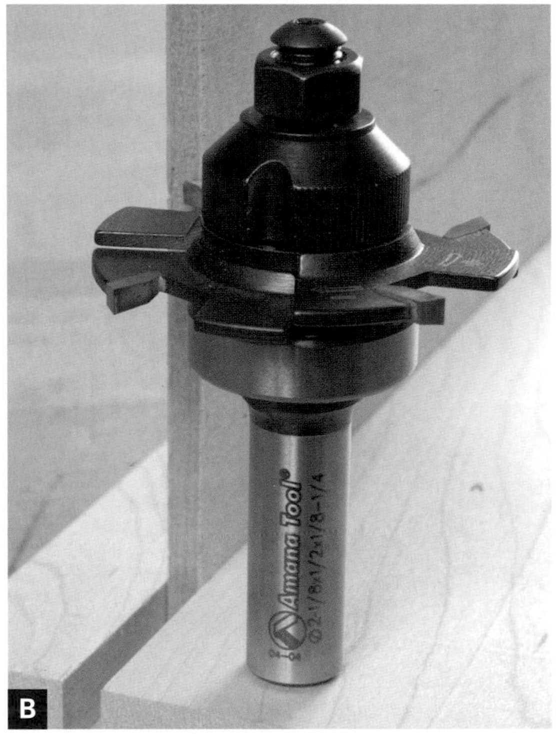

B

C

groove **(E)**. Marks are etched on the bit to make it easier to make precise settings. Each mark represents .004 in. Remember to tighten the lock nut once you've adjusted the bit.

Now adjust the cutting height by placing a graduated square next to the bit **(F)**. To adjust the bit for grooving in one pass, position the guide-bearing tangent to the fence **(G)**. Remember to reduce the fence opening as much as possible for maximum safety and stock support **(H)**. Finally, position featherboards to hold the stock against the fence, and then make the cut **(I)**.

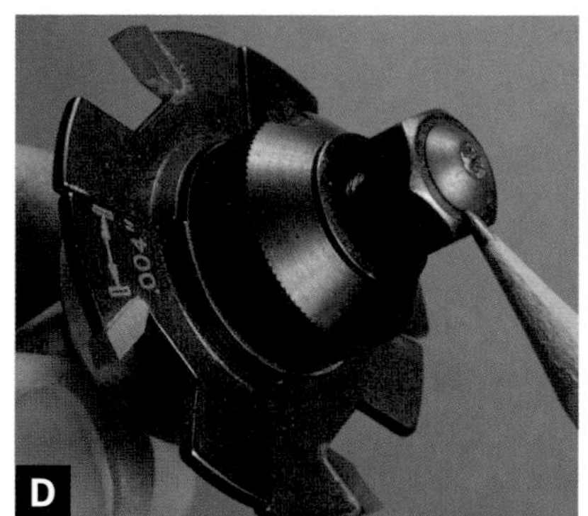
D

E

F

G

H

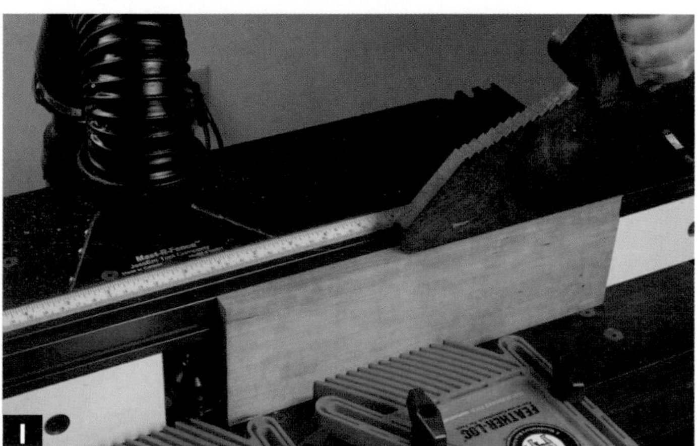
I

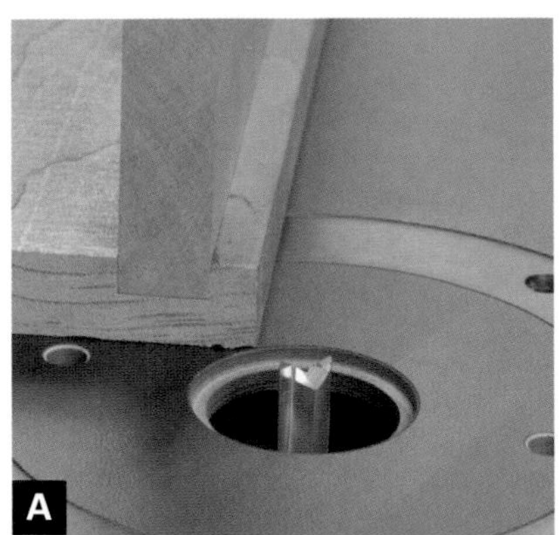
A

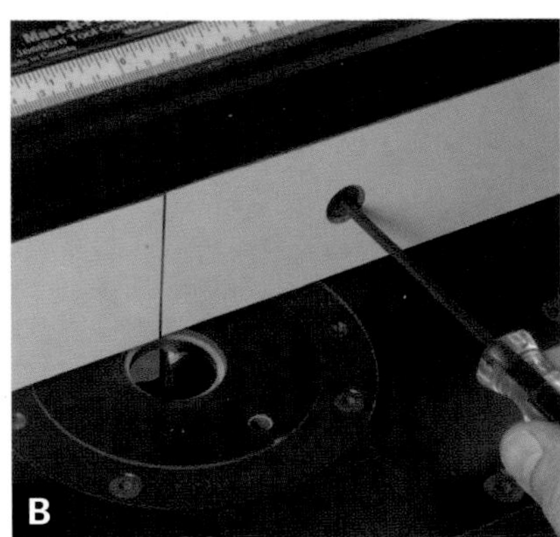
B

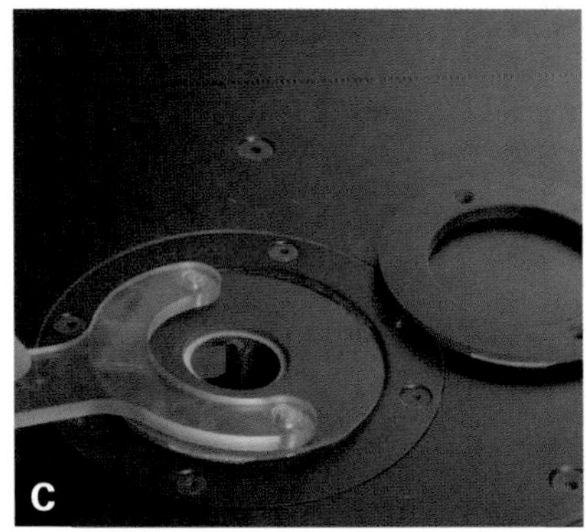
C

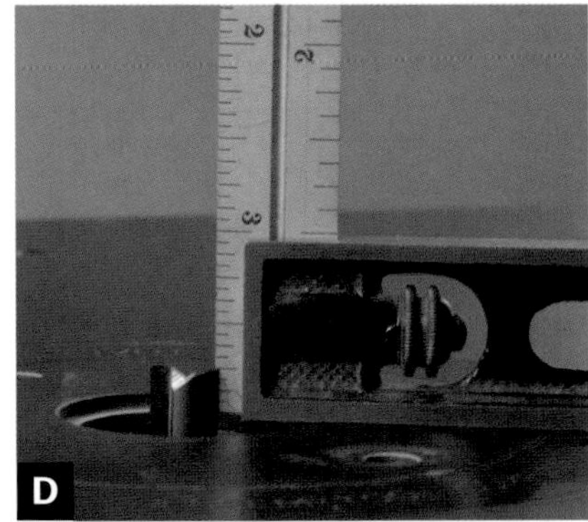
D

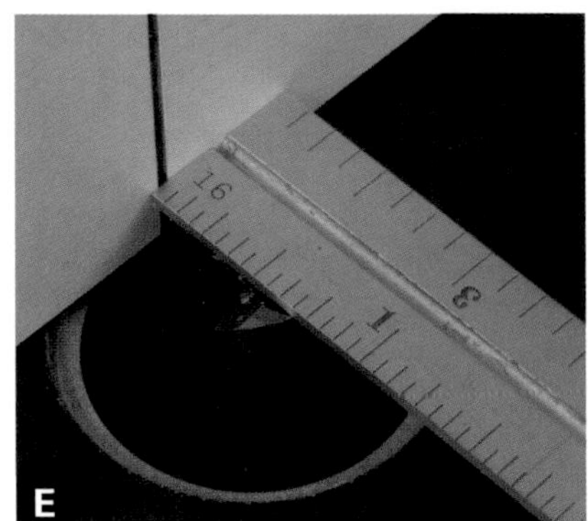
E

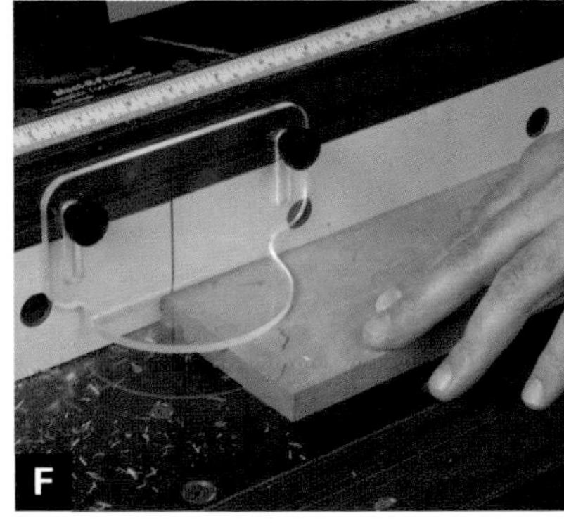
F

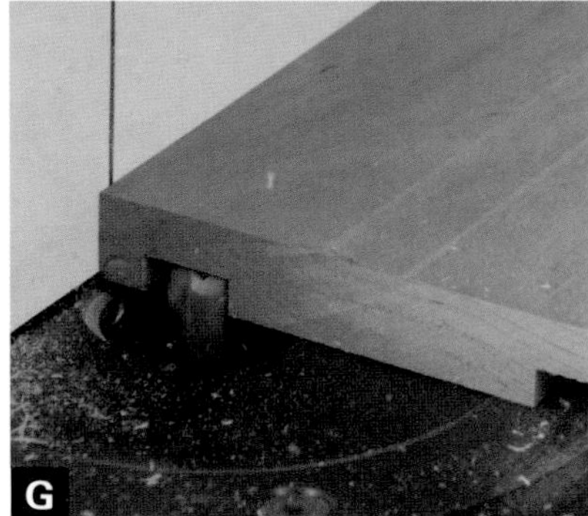
G

Two-Pass Groove

Sometimes it's necessary to cut a groove in two passes because either the bit you're using is too small or the groove may be an odd size for which there is no bit with the proper size cutter **(A)**. To make the second pass safely, it's important to position the bit to cut on the outside of the groove. If the bit is positioned to cut on the inside of the groove, the router will grab the work and possibly draw your hands into the spinning bit. So let's take a look at the safe approach for widening a groove.

Begin by closing the fence opening **(B)** and reducing the table opening **(C)**; these two steps are always important for providing safety and maximum support to the workpiece. Next, set the bit height **(D)**, position the fence, and lock it in place **(E)**. Now cut the initial groove **(F)**. To widen the groove, move the fence back, away from the bit **(G)**. Using this method, you'll cut against the bit rotation, the standard method for avoiding potentially hazardous kickback.

Tongue-and-Groove

The tongue-and-groove joint is commonly used for joining panels edge to edge. Tongue-and-groove joints are often assembled without glue; the dry joint keeps parts aligned while allowing for seasonal wood movement, such as in wood floors **(A)**. With glue added, the tongue-and-groove is useful for aligning the corners of a box **(B)** or joining a face frame to a carcase. Although the joint can be cut with multiple passes of a straight bit, a dedicated bit like the one used in this photo-essay makes the process more accurate and efficient.

With the bit set up to cut a tongue, adjust the bit height so that it is centered on the stock thickness **(C)**. Now use a straightedge to position the fence tangent to the guide bearing, and lock the fence in place **(D)**. (If the stock is very dense, you may want to initially position the fence forward, for taking two passes. This way you'll avoid the tearout associated with a too-heavy cut.) Now you're ready to cut the tongue **(E)**.

(Text continues on p. 146.)

A

B

C

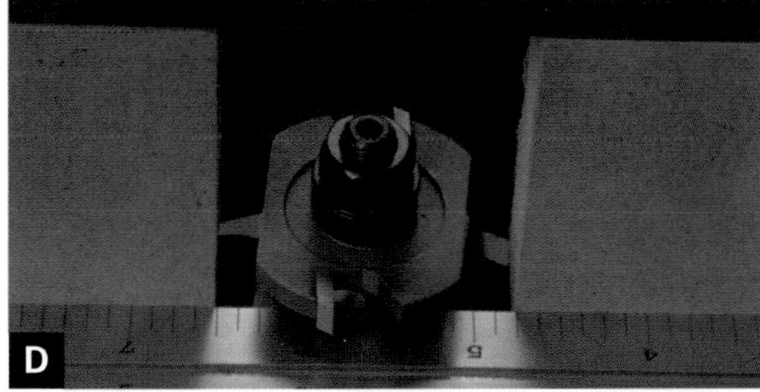

D

E

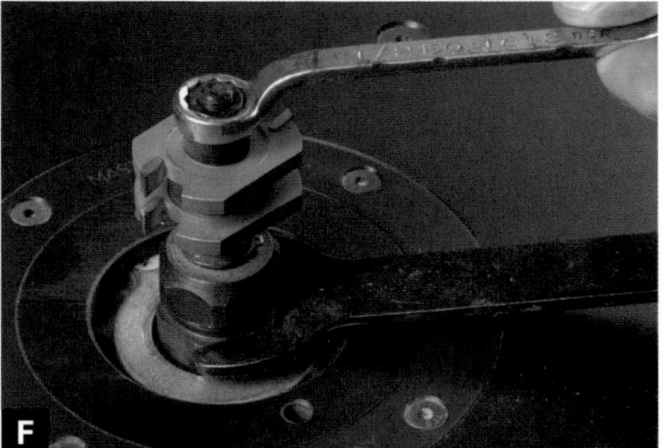
F

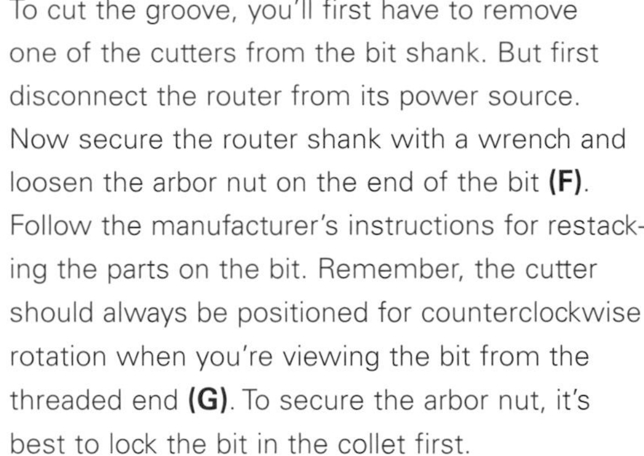
To cut the groove, you'll first have to remove one of the cutters from the bit shank. But first disconnect the router from its power source. Now secure the router shank with a wrench and loosen the arbor nut on the end of the bit **(F)**. Follow the manufacturer's instructions for restacking the parts on the bit. Remember, the cutter should always be positioned for counterclockwise rotation when you're viewing the bit from the threaded end **(G)**. To secure the arbor nut, it's best to lock the bit in the collet first.

The next step is to adjust the height of the bit to correspond to the first half of the joint. For the greatest accuracy, position the stock with the tongue next to the bit, and adjust the bit height **(H)**. Now make the cut **(I)**. To cut a groove on the corner, position the stock on edge and support it with featherboards to keep it firmly against the fence throughout the cut **(J)**.

G

H

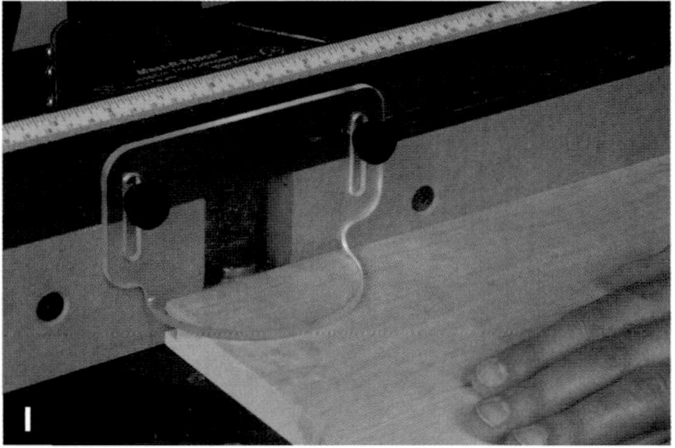
I

J

Rabbet with Straight Bit

A rabbet is a recess along the edge of the stock that's used for a variety of purposes—from creating door and drawer lips to cutting a recess in case sides to hide the back of a cabinet. Although a dedicated rabbet bit works best for the job, a straight bit works well too, and you may already have one in your kit **(A)**.

Begin by laying out the height and depth of the rabbet on the corner of the workpiece. Next, position the layout adjacent to the bit and adjust the bit height to correspond with the layout **(B)**. Minimize the fence opening to maximize the support for the stock **(C)**. As with any setup, it's important to use a guard **(D)**. Begin by making a light scoring pass **(E)**, which will make a light incision on the stock and limit the possibility of tearout on the final pass.

To accurately set the fence for the final pass, I position a board on the layout line as it contacts the cutting edge of the bit **(F)**. Two or more light passes eliminate the tearout that can easily occur when you're routing hard, brittle stock in one large pass **(G)**.

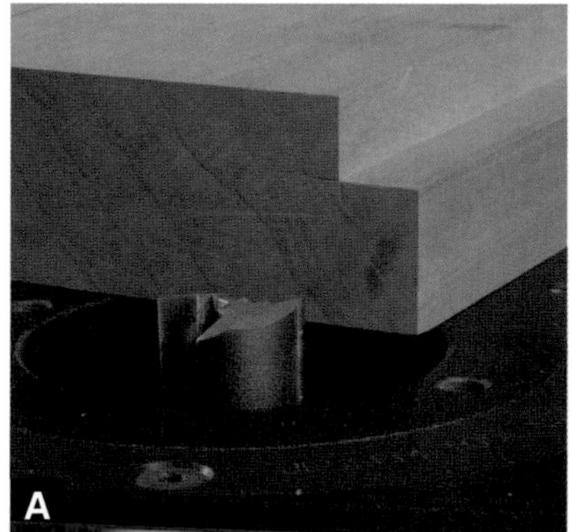
A

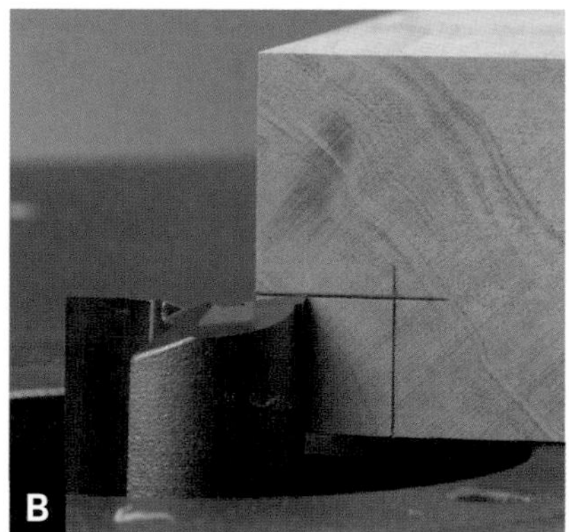
B

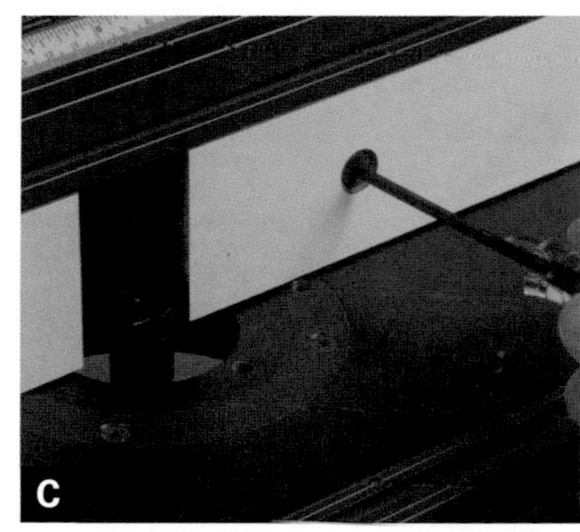
C

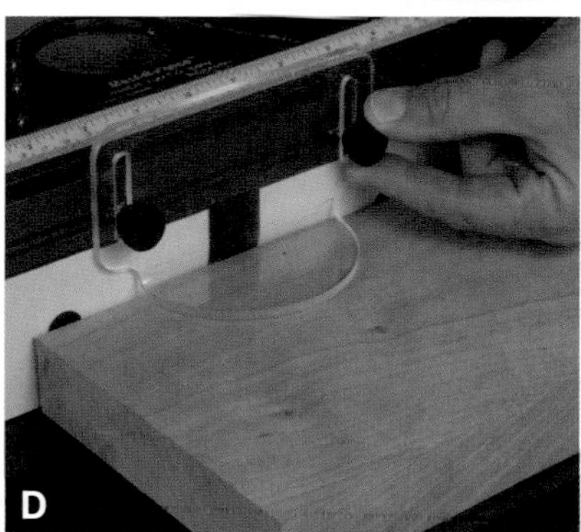
D

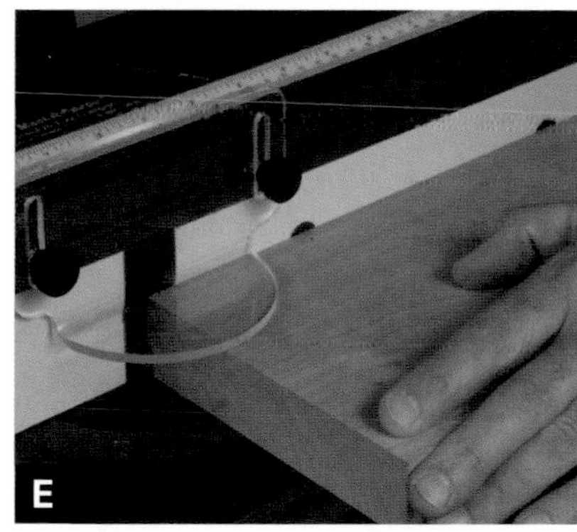
E

F

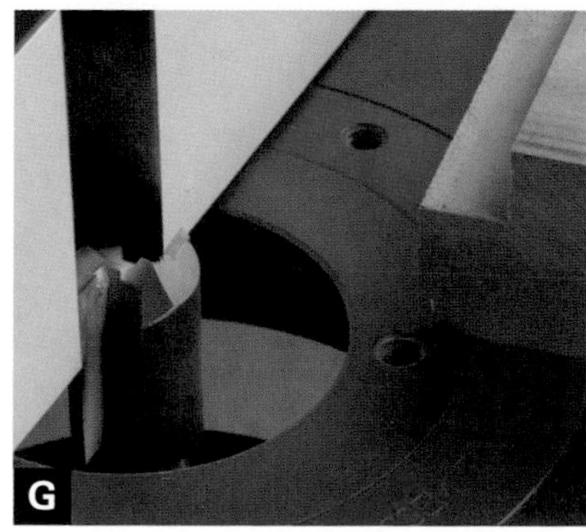
G

Dedicated Rabbet Bit

For cutting lots of large rabbets in hardwood, a rabbet bit is the best choice. Rabbet bits have cutting angles superior to those of straight bits, and so they'll create a smooth, clean joint free of tearout **(A)**.

Begin by mounting the bit securely in the collet **(B)**. Next, use a ruled square to accurately adjust the cutting height **(C)**. In order to provide the maximum support for the workpiece, reduce the size of the fence opening as much as possible **(D)**. Now position the workpiece adjacent to the bit and adjust the fence for the cutting depth **(E)**. To shield your hands and help hold the stock, position a guard over the bit **(F)** Remember, always feed the workpiece from right to left, against the rotation of the bit **(G)**.

B

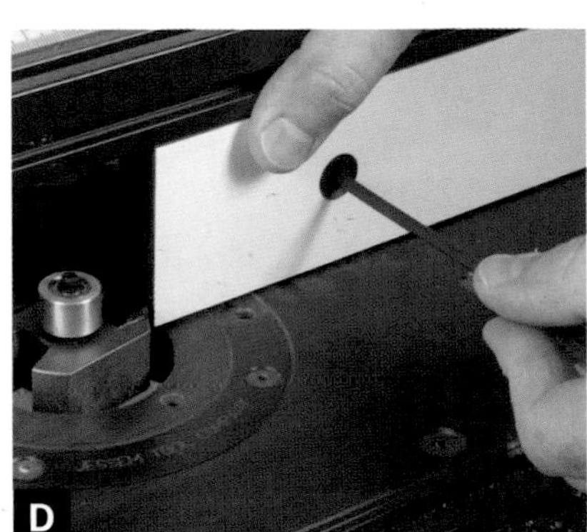

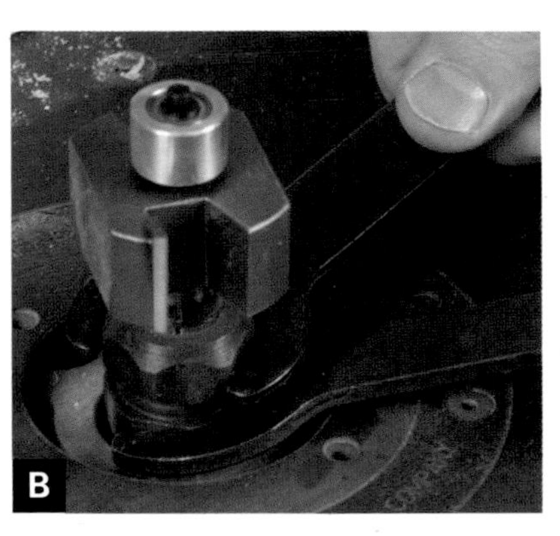

Lap Joint

A lap joint can be substituted for a mortise-and-tenon joint or, as shown here, used to join backboards in casework **(A)**. Like the tongue-and-groove joint, the completed lap joint is commonly assembled without glue to allow for seasonal wood movement without a gap between mating boards.

A lap joint is essentially two rabbets of equal dimension. The key to making the joint is to cut away one-half of the stock thickness from each of the mating boards. After layout, position the stock next to the bit as an aid for adjusting the bit height **(B)**.

If you're using a straight bit, as pictured here, it's best to first take a light scoring cut to avoid splintering along the edge **(C)**. Next, position a guard over the bit **(D)** and make the cut **(E)**. I use a second piece of stock aligned with both the layout marks and the bit to set the fence for the final pass **(F)**.

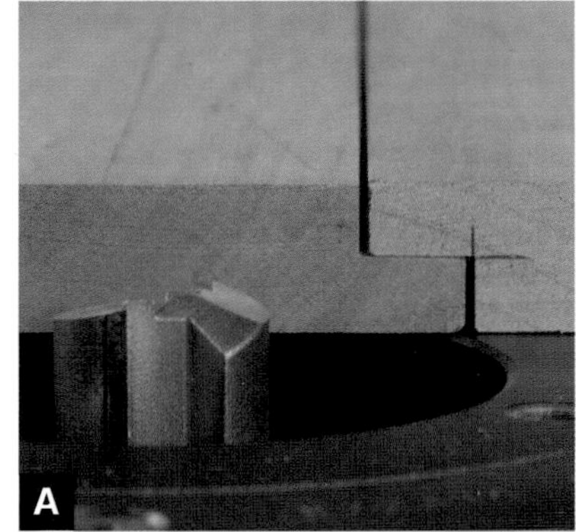

A

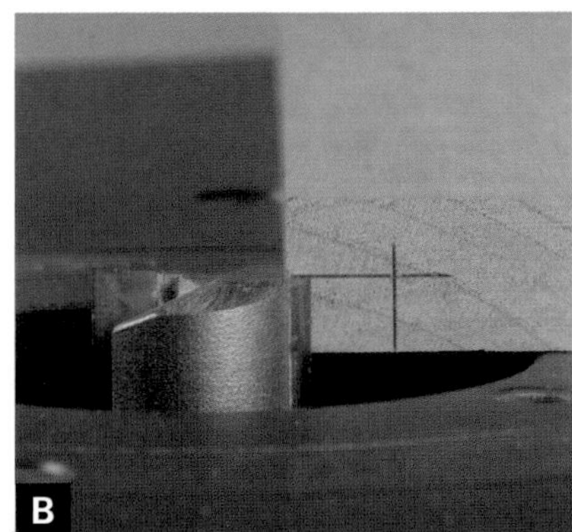

B

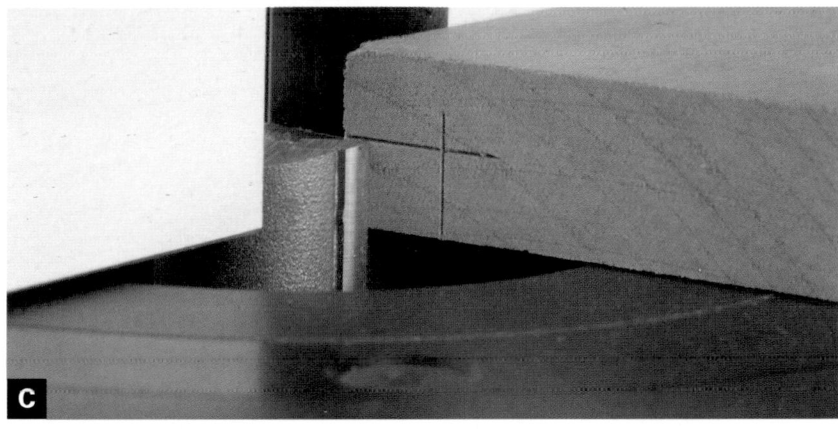

C

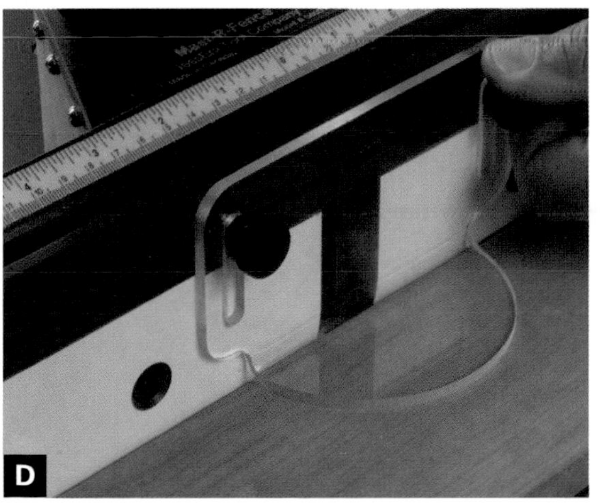

D

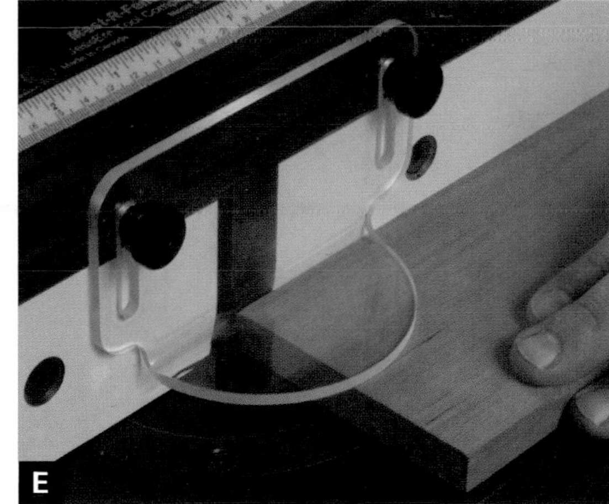

E

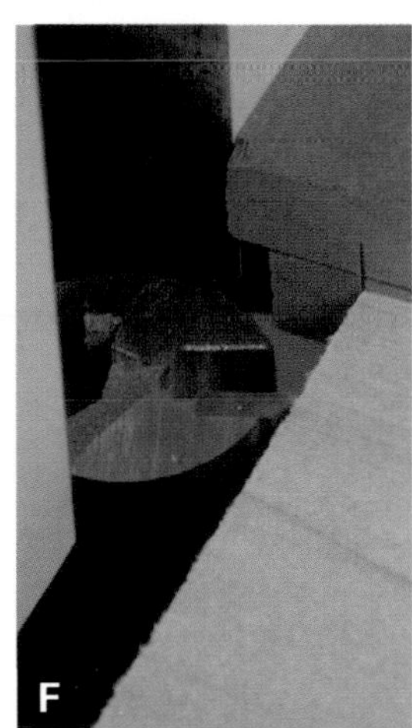

F

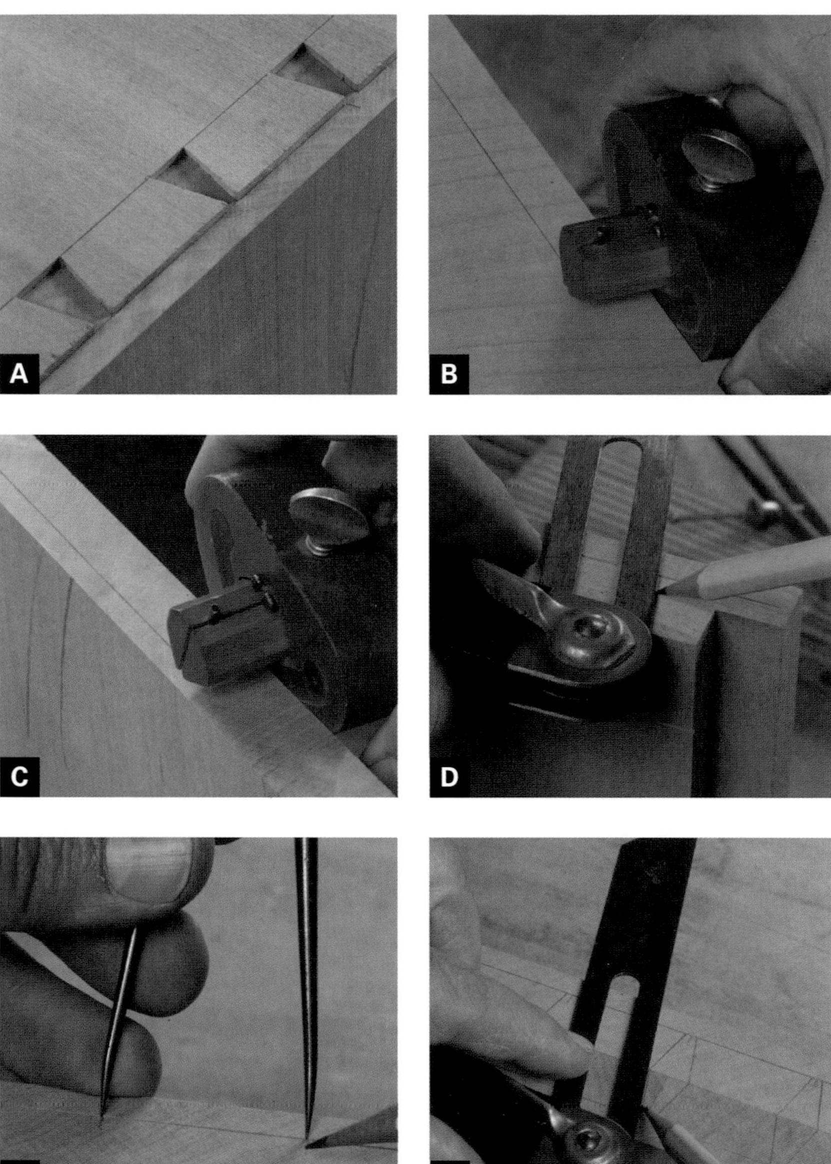

Freehand Routing Dovetails

Dovetails undoubtedly have a mystique associated with them. In reality, they're quite easy to cut—it's essentially just sawing and chiseling to a line **(A)**. Although jigs may be an efficient method of creating dovetails, especially in a production setting, there's a special satisfaction that comes from cutting them by hand. However, to ease the tedium that can come from chopping all the waste from between the pins of a half-blind dovetail, I use a router to quickly remove the excess wood. Although there is still handwork involved with this method, using the router to remove the excess stock makes this a very efficient process for creating authentic dovetail joinery with a hand-cut appearance. Here are the steps I use:

The first step is to mark the baselines with a sharp gauge **(B)**. After marking the tail board, use the same measurement to mark the pin board **(C)**. Using the same measurement on each of the adjoining pieces ensures a precise fit. As you pull the gauge across the stock, use light pressure to avoid tearing the grain. A sharp, crisp baseline is critical to setting the router bit depth.

The next step is to lay out the pins. One of the advantages of this method over using a jig is that you can make the pins any size you wish. I begin by marking the pins at the edges of the stock **(D)**. For strength, I make the end pins wider than the rest. Afterwards, I locate the center of the remaining pins with dividers **(E)**. Each step of the divider represents the center of a pin. You can easily increase or decrease the pin size during this step by adjusting the setting on the dividers.

Now mark the slope of each pin with an adjustable bevel **(F)**. I use a 14-degree angle, which matches the slope of the dovetail bit. Use a square to mark the face of each pin to the baseline **(G)**. Photo **(H)** shows the complete layout.

The next step is to rout the space between the pins. First set the depth of the dovetail bit so that it just touches the incised baseline **(I)**. A router with a micrometer depth adjuster makes this step much easier. Clamp the stock securely to the benchtop and rout between the layout lines **(J)**. As you rout, work from left to right against the rotation of the bit. Also, to avoid undercutting the joint, don't attempt to rout up to the baseline. Instead, leave a small amount of stock to trim away with the chisel afterwards. A small degree of undercut is OK because it is an end-grain surface, but a severe undercut may weaken the base of the joint. Don't worry about minor variations in pin width or spacing; it only adds to the "hand-cut" look. Besides, you'll be cutting the tails to fit.

Now use a chisel and mallet to complete the socket between each pin **(K)**. Once you've completed chopping to the baseline, a quick check with a small square will show you if you have any errant surfaces that need to be trimmed further.

Although routing freehand may seem difficult, it is actually quite easy to create smooth, 90-degree pins if the layout is accurate and the bit is sharp. In fact, with just a small amount of practice, you'll be surprised at how accurately you can perform this step of the process. Notice how the router

(Text continues on p. 152.)

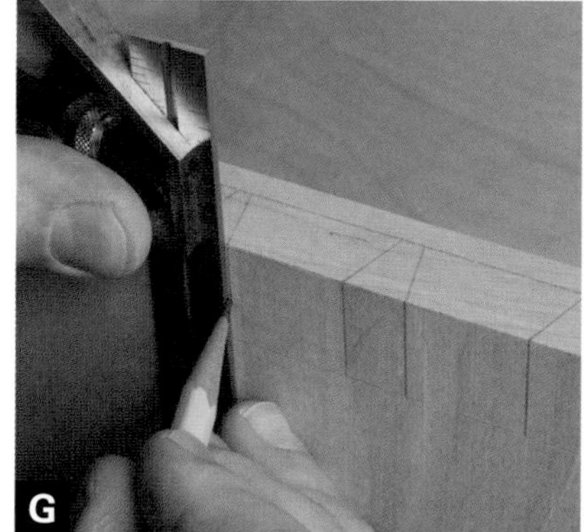

G

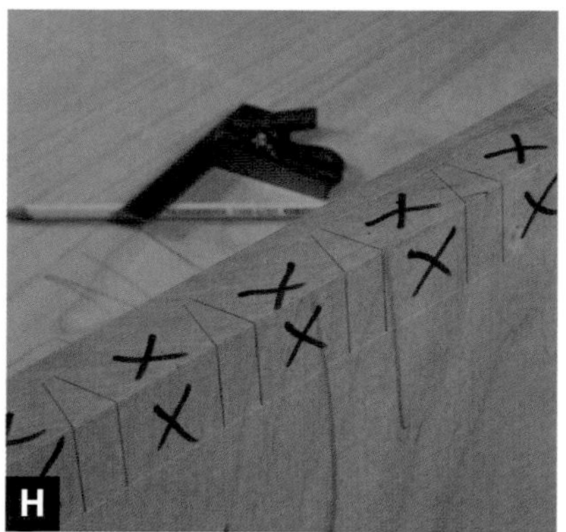

H

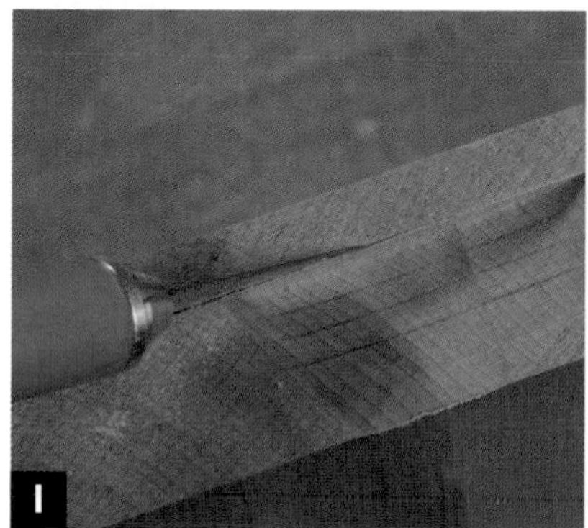

I

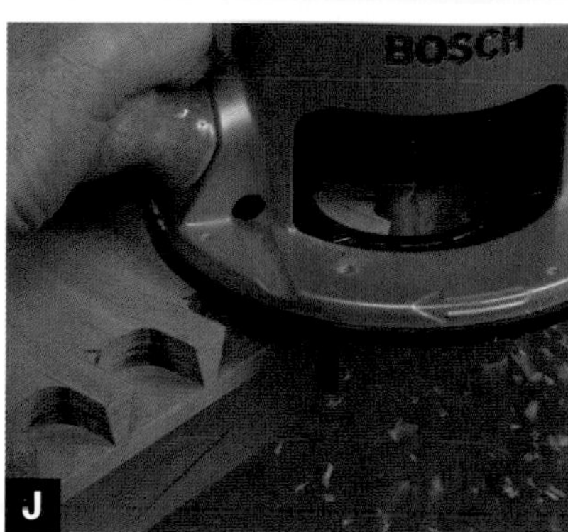

J

K

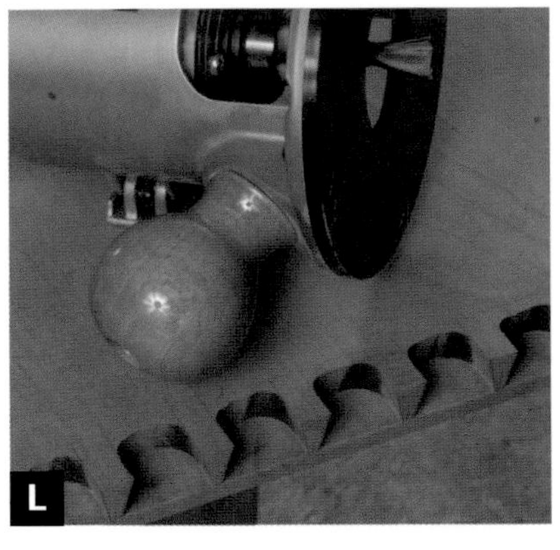
L

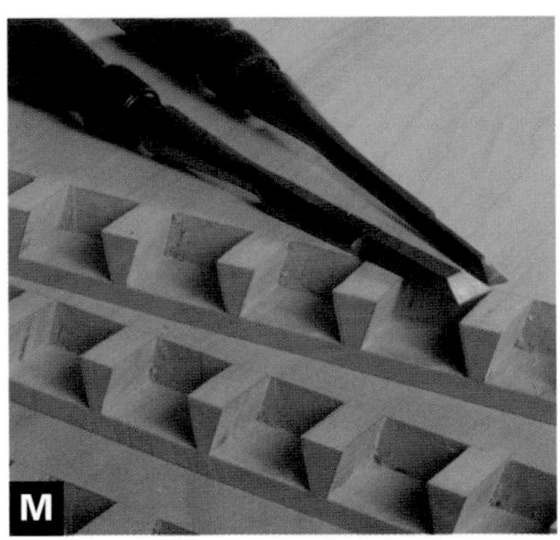
M

N

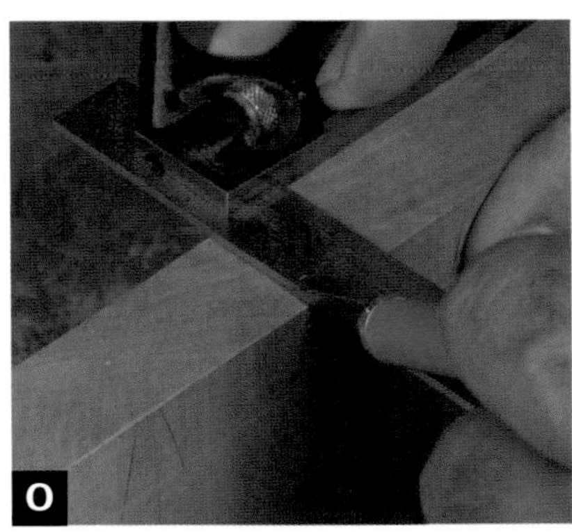
O

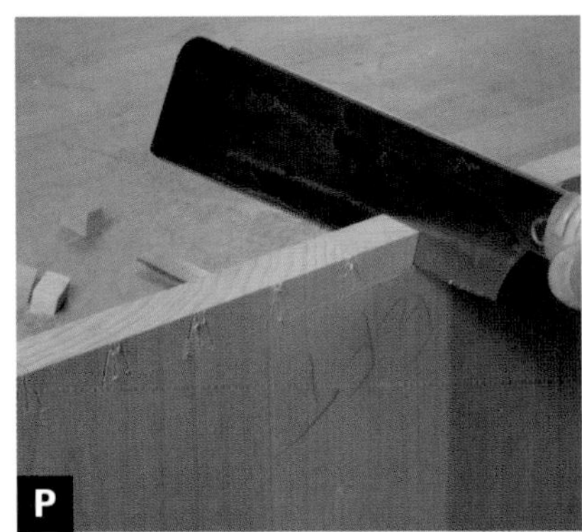
P

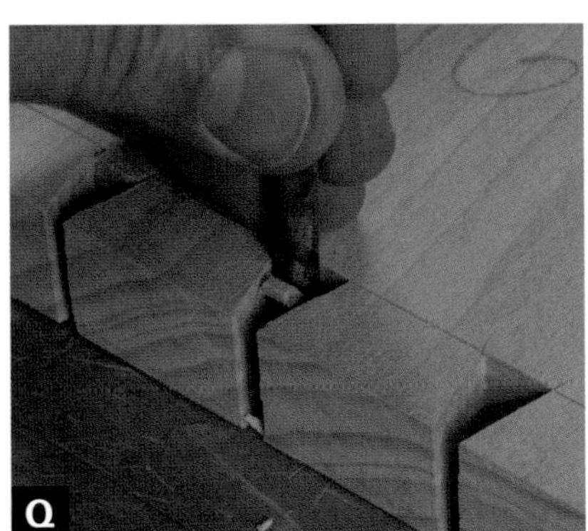
Q

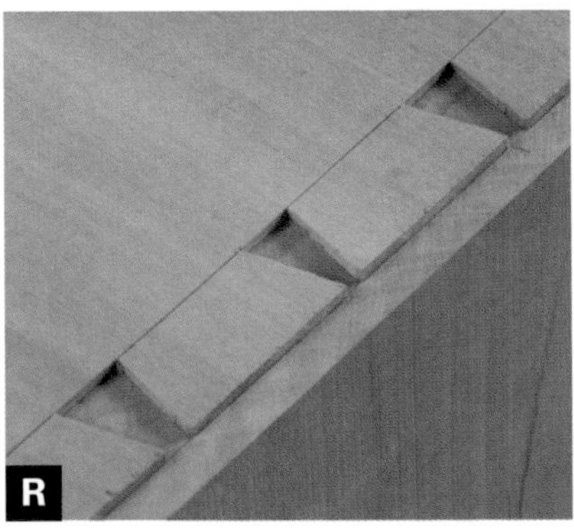
R

S

bit leaves the back of each space rounded **(L)**. The next step is to square the corners to the baseline with a chisel and mallet **(M)**.

Now you're ready to create the tails. Position the routed pin board over the tail board adjacent to the base line. Use a sharp knife to mark the tails from the pins **(N)**. Complete the layout by transferring each mark around the end of the board **(O)**.

With the layout complete, you're ready to begin sawing. Angle the saw to follow the 14-degree slope of the router bit and saw to the baseline **(P)**. Next, remove the waste between the tails with a sharp chisel **(Q)**.

As you assemble the joint, look carefully for tight spots and pare them away **(R)**. Assemble the completed joint with gentle taps of a mallet **(S)**.

Shopmade Dovetail Jig

All woodworkers want to make the dovetail joint a part of their work, and for good reason; the dovetail joint is undoubtedly the strongest, most beautiful method for joining the sides of casework and drawers **(A)**. And although the through dovetail is faster and easier to cut than the half-blind version, it's the half-blind form that's typically used for drawers and casework.

One method for easing the tedium of chopping all those tail sockets is to rout them out first using a jig to guide the router **(B)** and then square up the corners with a chisel and mallet. Once the sockets are cut out, the tails can be scribed from the sockets and sawn to fit.

However, be aware that with this jig, you'll still need to learn two important aspects of dovetailing: sawing and chiseling to a line. But the jig will quickly and accurately remove much of the excess stock so that you can instead focus your efforts on the finer details.

The bottom line is this: The jig in this essay makes quick work of creating the pins on a half-blind dovetail. And if you're making multiple boxes the same size, the jig is especially worth the few minutes that it requires to construct.

Once you've constructed the jig, select a dovetail bit, and mount a guide bearing on the shank **(C)**. In order to secure the bearing in place, this process requires a bit with a flange at the top of the shank above the cutter.

➤See *"Changing Bearings,"* on p. 49.

Next, lay out the joint as usual by marking the baseline on the end **(D)** and the face of the stock **(E)**. Place the pin board in the jig with the inside

(Text continues on p. 154.)

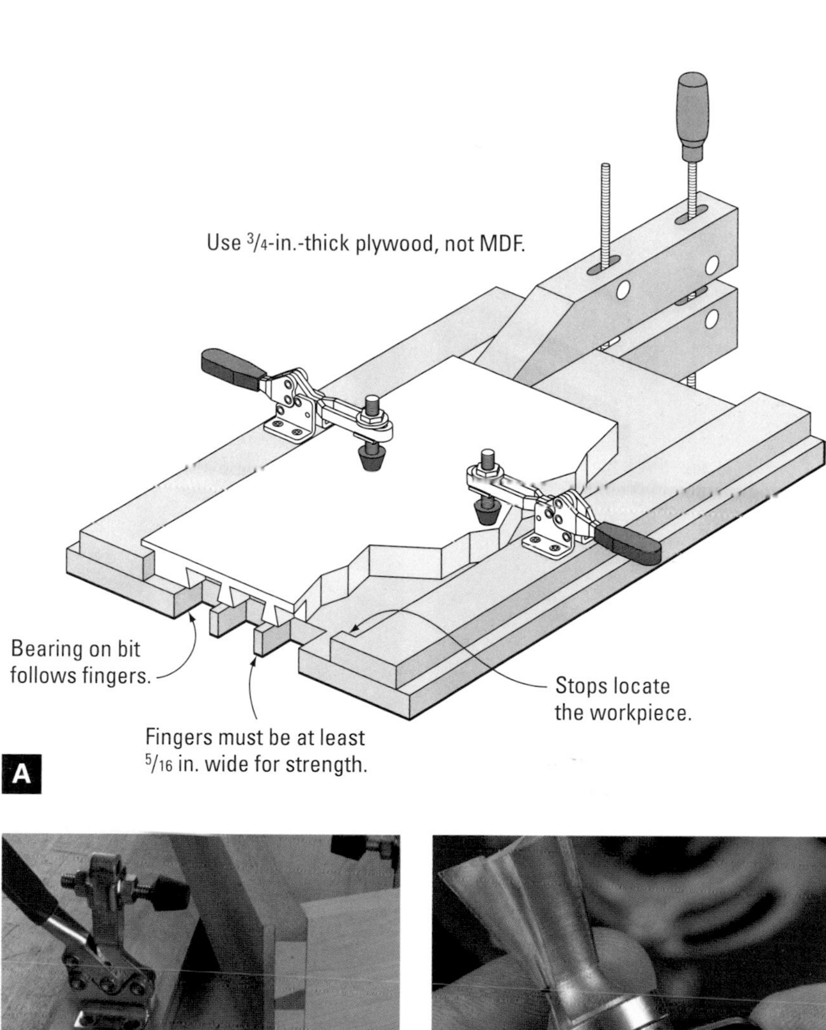

A

B

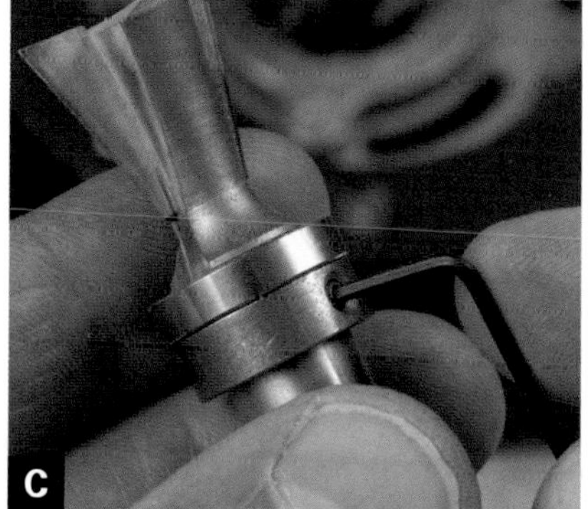
C

D

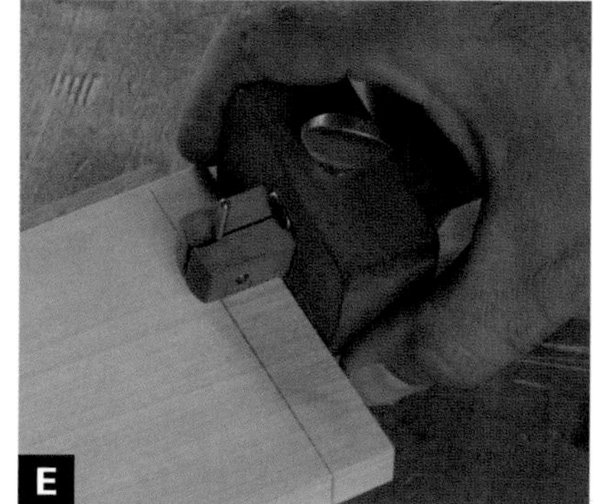
E

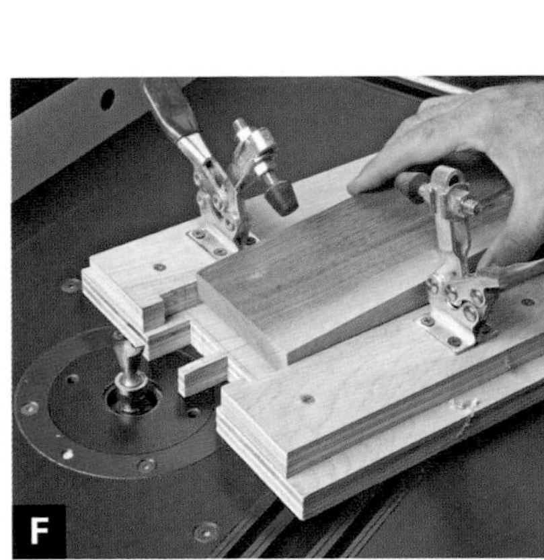
F

G

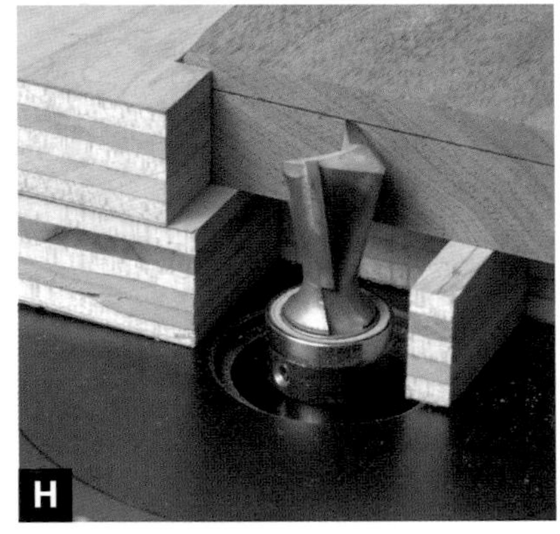
H

I

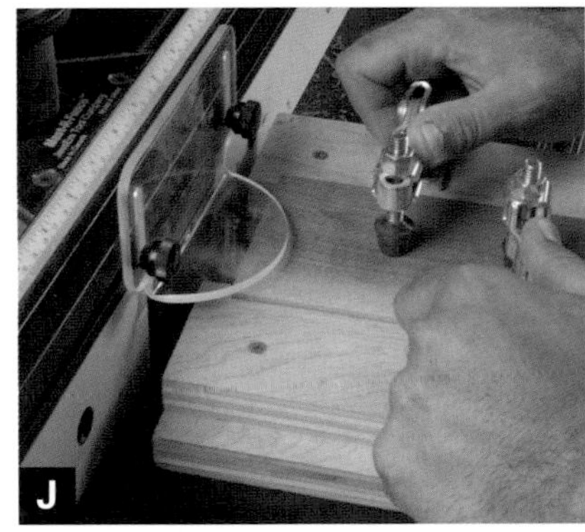
J

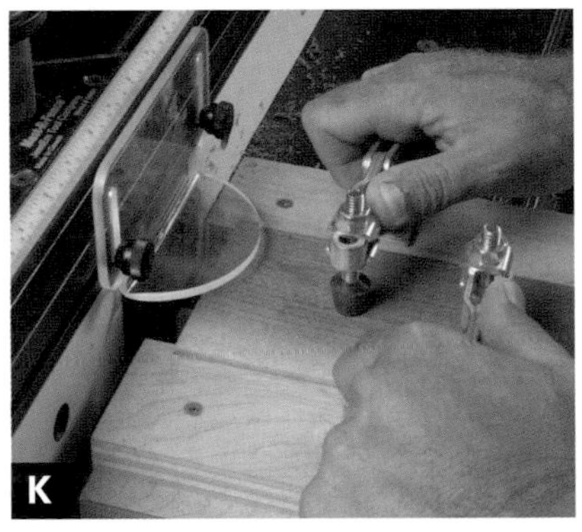
K

L

M

facing down **(F)**. Secure the workpiece with toggle clamps and put a clamp at the opposite end to lock it in place **(G)**.

Now use the baseline on the pin board to adjust the height of the bit. Place the jig adjacent to the bit and adjust the height until the corner of the bit grazes the baseline **(H)**. When the bit is accurately positioned, there will be none of the tedious hand work that is typically required to clean up the bottom of the space between each tail!

The router table fence isn't actually required for use with this jig, but it's a good idea to position it near the bit anyway. It will prove useful by providing a hookup for dust collection and, most importantly, a place to fasten a guard **(I)**.

Now you're ready to rout the tail sockets, which creates the pins. Begin on the left corner of the workpiece **(J)** and work toward the right **(K)**. If your bit depth is set correctly, the cut should reveal a tiny line of burnished surface at the very end of the socket, created when the marking gauge pin scribed the baseline across the end grain **(L)**.

Once you've completed the routing, most of the work on the pin board is complete; all that remains is to square the inside corners. As you chisel back to the baseline scribed across the face of the workpiece, again look for the tiny burnished area to remain, indicating that you have split the baseline in two.

When squaring the corners, use a narrow chisel (such as a 3/8 in.), grasping it as you would a pencil **(M)**. This method will provide you with the greatest control. Although conventional wisdom would dictate using a wide chisel, it isn't needed because the scribed baseline keeps the chisel in a straight path. And a narrow chisel is easier to control because it has less resistance than a wide one.

Also, as you're chopping out the corners, it's a good idea to undercut the back wall slightly **(N)**. Because this surface is end grain, it's not really useful as a glue surface, and a small degree of undercut will make it easier to assemble the joint. As you make each cut, remember to position the chisel on the baseline **(O)**.

Once you've squared the corners, the next step is to lay out and cut the tails. First position the pin board over the tail board and clamp it in place. Then mark the tails with a sharp knife **(P)**. Now carefully saw to the layout line **(Q)**. After sawing the tails, use a chisel to remove the waste **(R)**.

Finally, slide the tail board into the pin board and admire your work **(S)**.

N

O

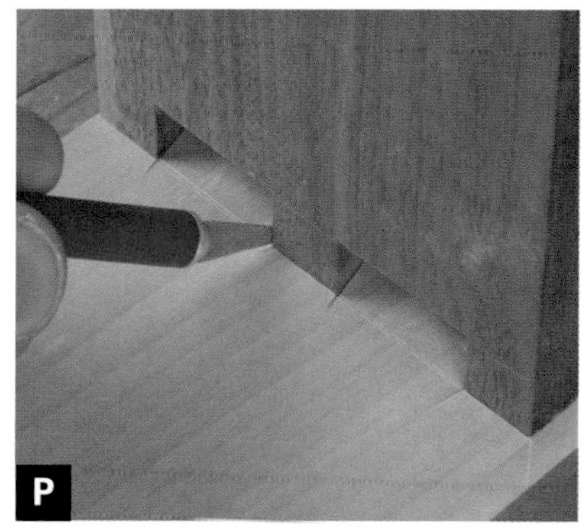
P

Q

R

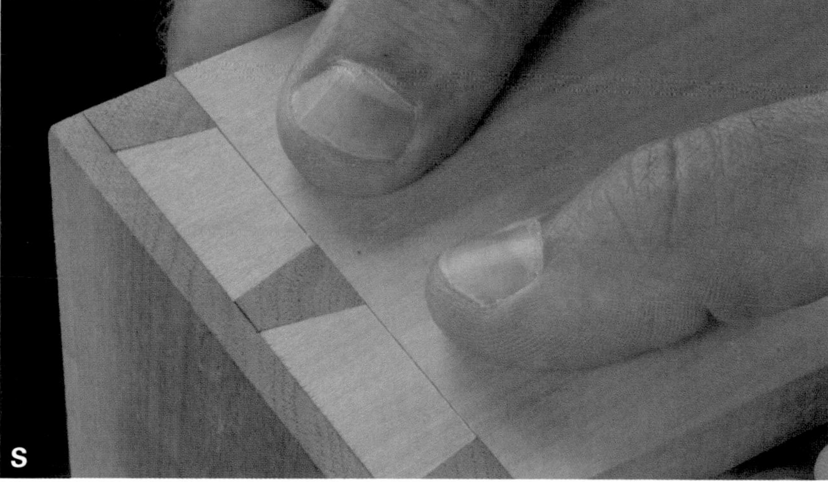
S

Sliding Dovetail

Unlike a row of dovetails, which is used to join the sides of drawers and casework, the sliding dovetail is most often used to join drawer dividers to the sides of the case **(A, B)**. This process involves both handheld routing and the router table.

Begin by routing the dovetail sockets in the case side **(C)**. Thin plywood guides ensure uniform spacing and the correct position of each socket. Next, mount the dovetail bit in the table **(D)** and reduce the table opening to maximize stock

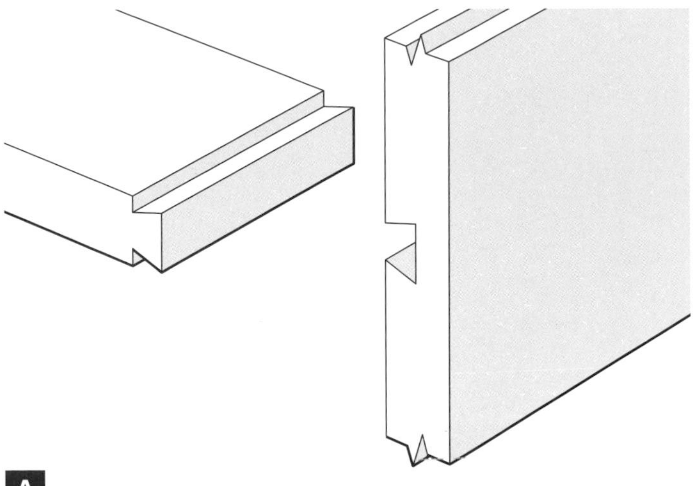

A

B

C

D

support **(E)**. Set the height of the bit to the socket depth **(F)** and reduce the fence opening **(G)**.

Now clamp a board to the workpiece at 90 degrees to provide stability as you make the cut. Remember to distance your hand from the bit by using a push block **(H)**.

E

F

G

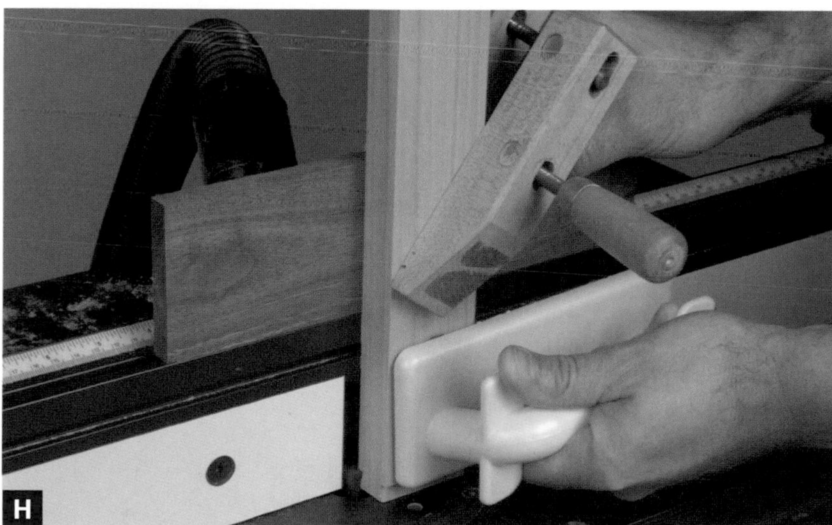
H

Half-Blind Dovetails with Porter Cable Omnijig

This Porter Cable Omnijig® can cut a number of variations from through to sliding dovetails **(A)**. Like many jigs, it cuts both members of a half-blind dovetail joint simultaneously. In order for the process to work effectively, the mating members of the joint must be mounted offset to each other—in this case by 3⁄16 in.

Begin by marking the end of the drawer front 3⁄16 in. from the edge **(B)**. Next, position the drawer side in the front of the jig and lock it in place with the clamp **(C)**. Now position the drawer front in the top of the jig so that the 3⁄16 in. layout mark aligns with the drawer side **(D)**. Position the stop bars against the stock and lock them in place **(E)** for use on subsequent cuts.

Now position the half-blind dovetail template so that the bottom of the gullet midway between the fingers is 19⁄32 in. from the end of the drawer front **(F)**. Photo **(G)** shows the stock correctly positioned in the jig and ready for the cut.

To set up the router, attach a 5⁄8-in.-dia. template guide to the router baseplate. Then secure a 1⁄2-in.-dia. dovetail bit in the collet and adjust the height to 19⁄32 in. **(H)**.

To use the jig, always slide the router in from the front and feed it from left to right **(I, J)**. Remember, never attempt to lift the router directly from the jig. Instead, slide it out from the front.

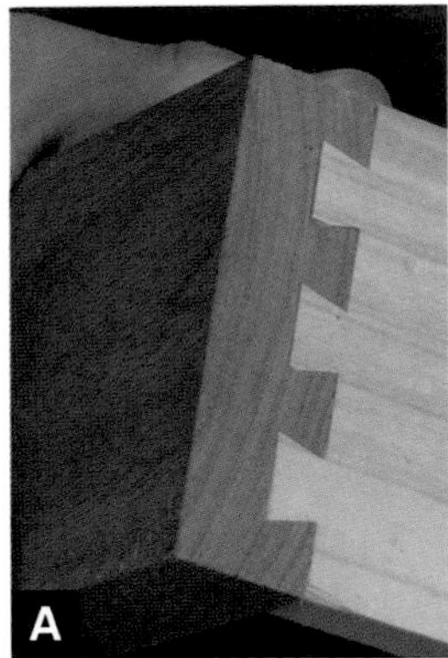
A

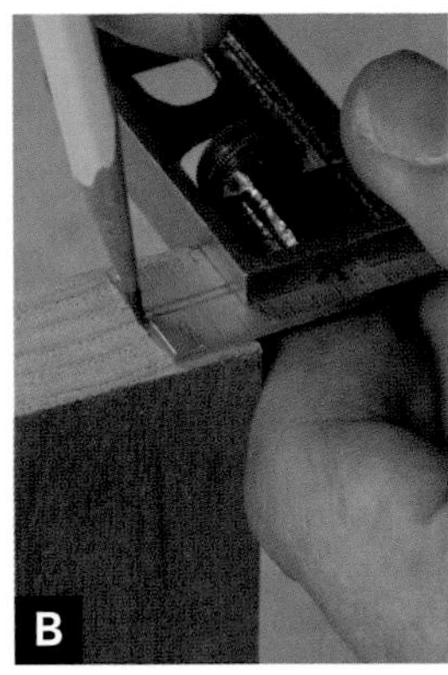
B

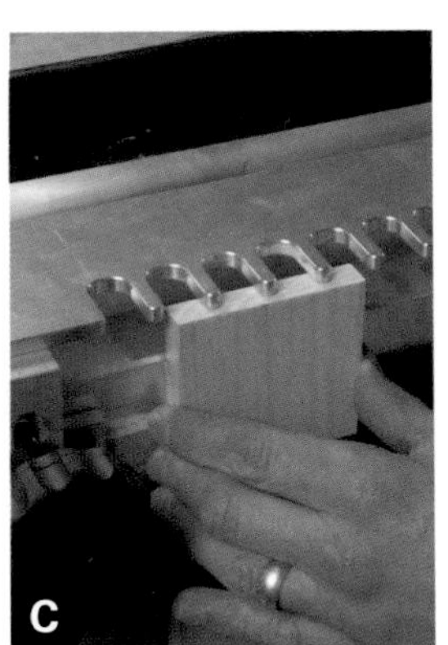
C

D

E

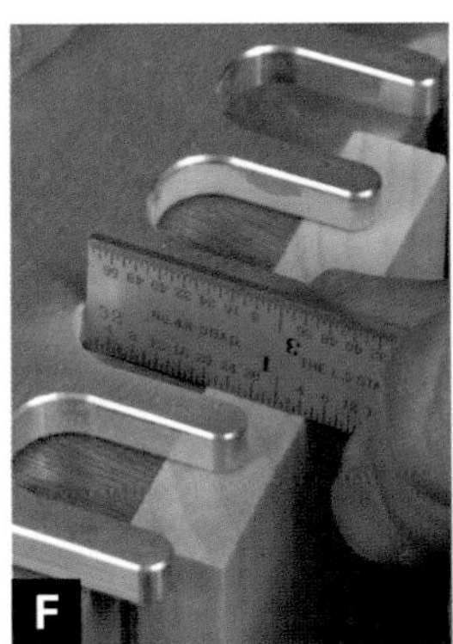
F

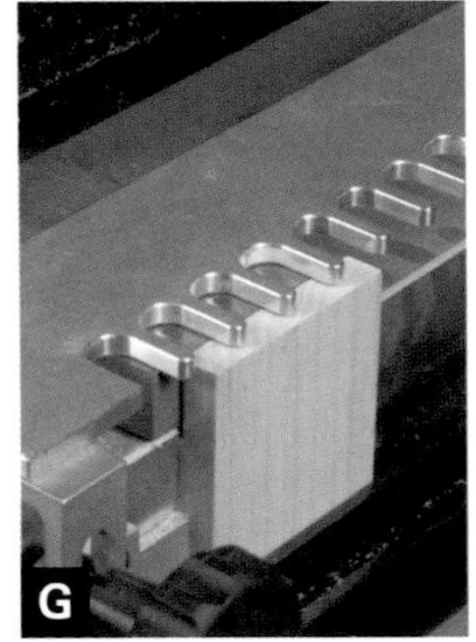
G

H

I

J

Through Dovetails with Katie Jig

Among dovetail jigs, the Katie is one of the least complex to set up. And it does have adjustable guides so that you can vary the spacing to suit your taste and the job at hand. Each guide has two ends, one for the pins and the other for the tails **(A)**. The jig is designed so that the tails and pins on the completed joint will protrude. The idea is that you can flush-trim the joint after assembly. Of course it's important to account for the loss of material when you're milling the stock to size. In this photo-essay I show how to create the joint so that the mating surfaces are flush, which I prefer.

Beginning with the pin board, adjust the guides **(B)** so that the joint will begin and end with a pin **(C)**. Next, position the edge stop against the workpiece and lock it in place **(D)**. The edge stops will align the boards in the jig for subsequent cuts. Position ¼-in.-thick plywood as spacers between the stock and the guides, and then clamp the stock firmly in place **(E)**. Now remove the plywood spacers **(F)**.

(Text continues on p. 160.)

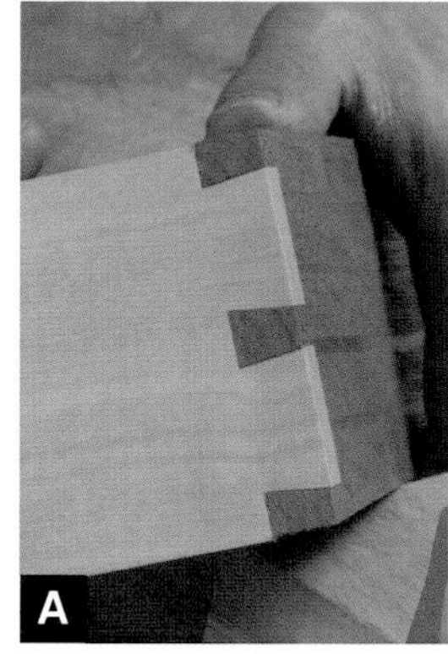
A

B

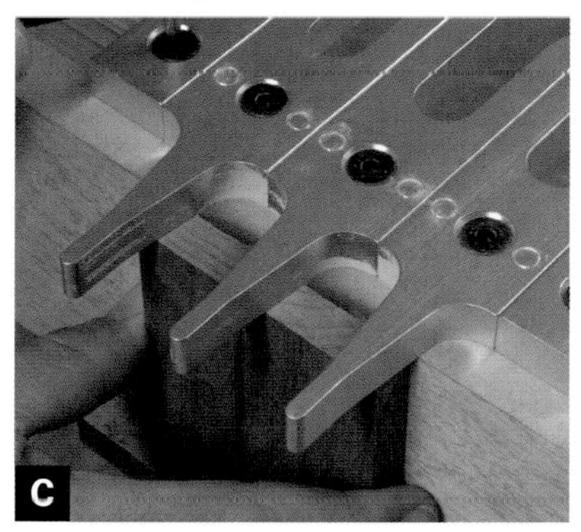
C

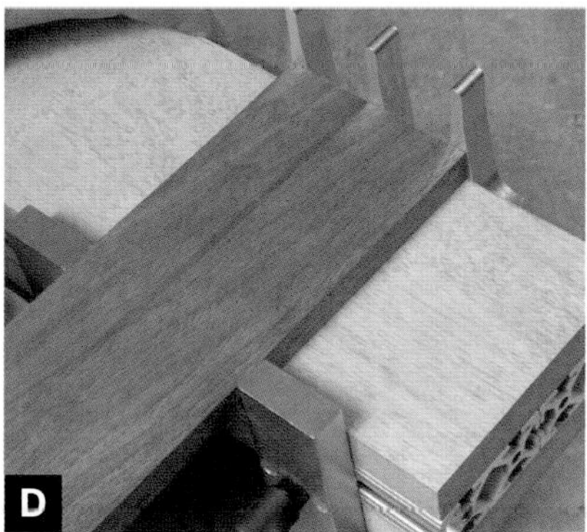
D

E

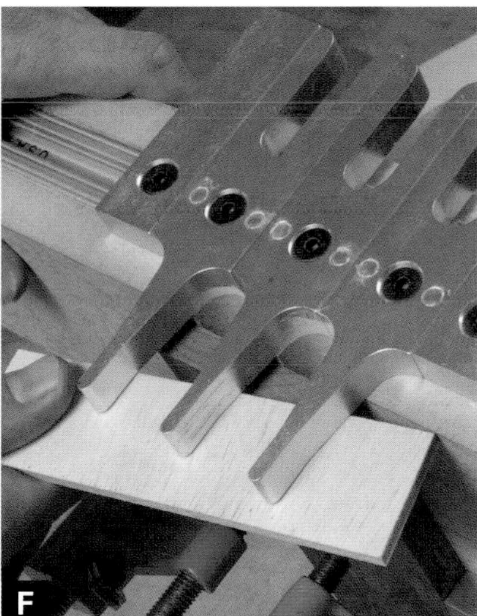
F

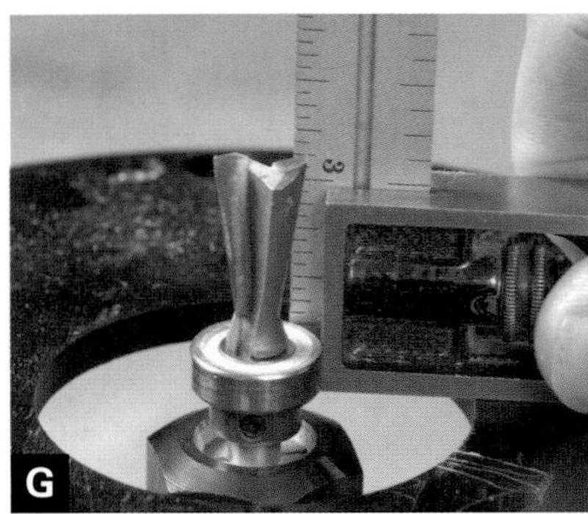

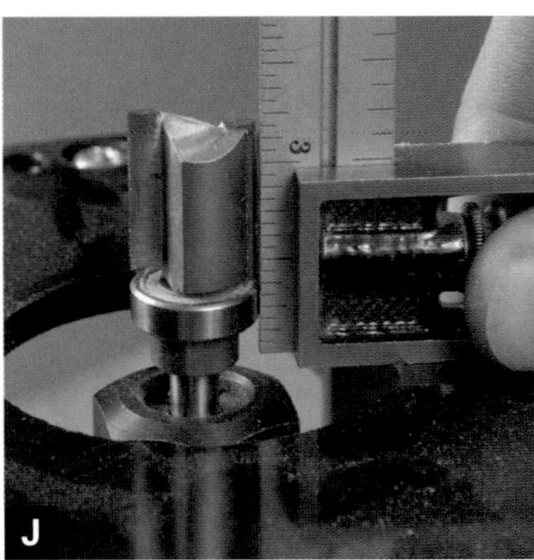

To set up the router, lock the bit in the collet and adjust the cutting depth **(G)**. The depth equals the sum of the pin board thickness, guide thickness, and the spacer. Using the straight end of the guide fork, cut the tails **(H)**. Always feed the router from left to right as you're facing the tail board **(I)**.

Before routing the pins, you'll need to switch to the straight bit. The cutting depth should equal the sum of the tail-board thickness, the guide thickness, and the spacer **(J)**. Finally, make the cut **(K)**.

Half-Blind Dovetails with the Akeda Jig

Among dovetail jigs, the Akeda® is a relative newcomer **(A)**. It will cut both half-blind and through dovetails. Begin by locking the first tail guide in position ⅛ in. away from the reference mark **(B)**. Position the remaining guides and mark their locations on the jig **(C)**. The first and last guides should slightly overlap the edges of the pin board **(D)**. Once the first and last guides are in place, snap the remaining guides into position **(E)**. Next, position the tail board in the front of the jig firmly underneath the guides and clamp in place **(F)**. Now set the depth of the bit **(G)**

(Text continues on p. 162.)

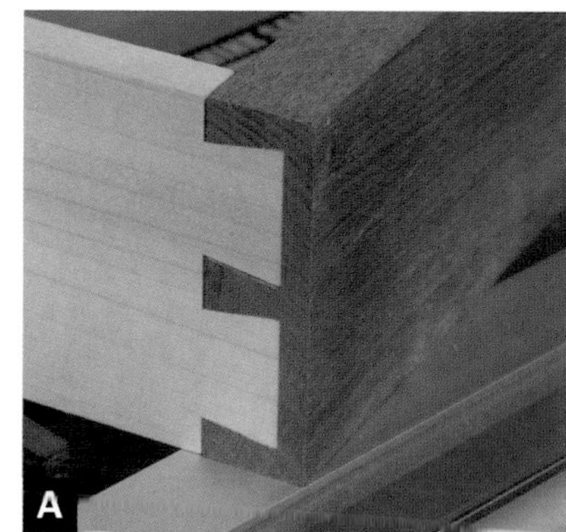
A

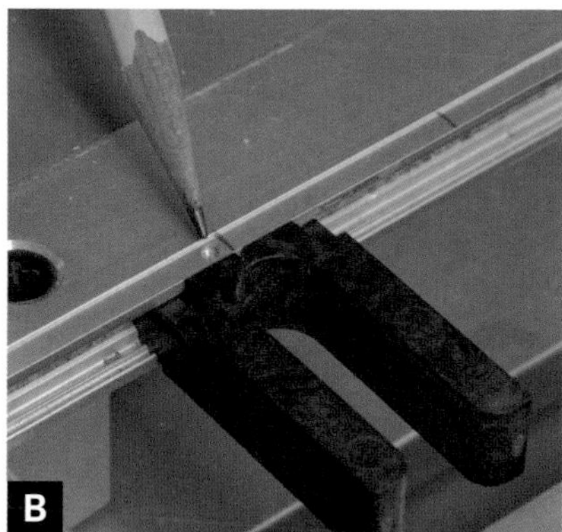
B

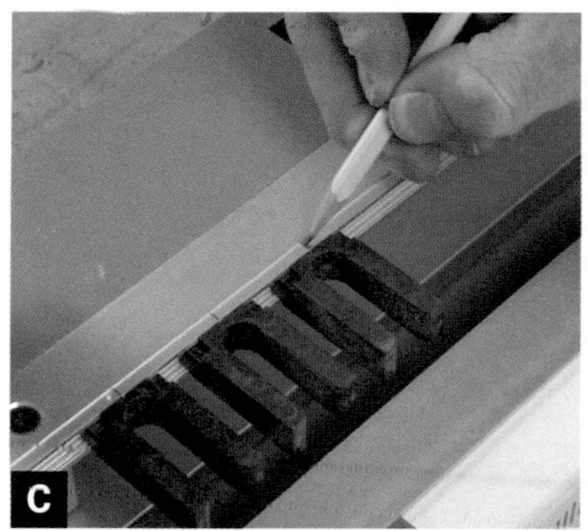
C

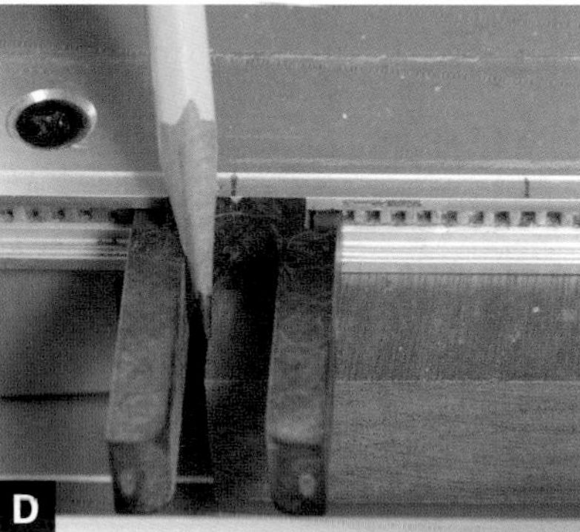
D

E

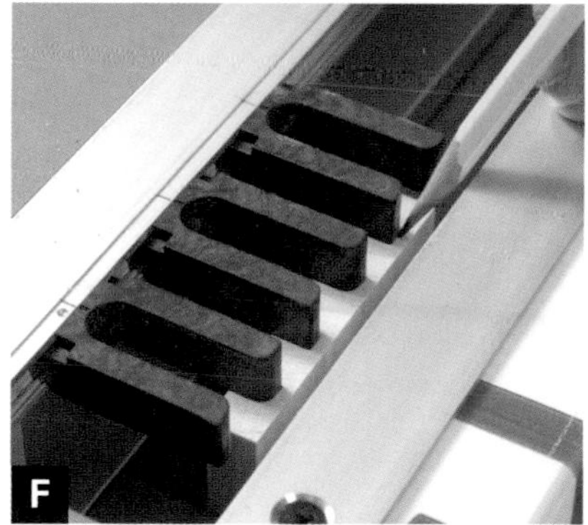
F

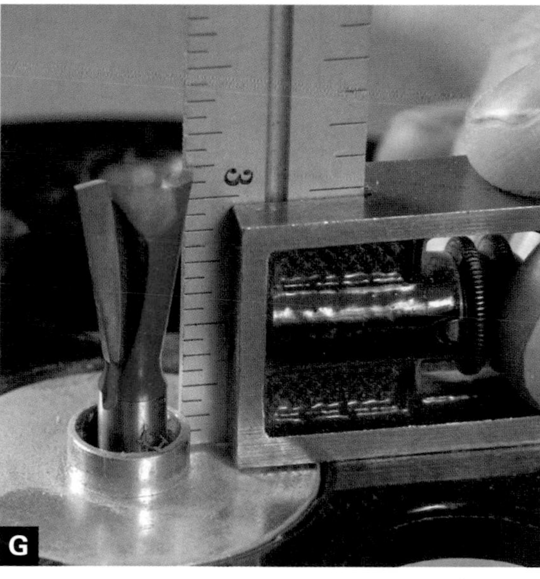
G

and cut the tails **(H)**. As you rout, be very careful not to cut the area between the guides **(I)**.

To cut the pins, first remove the tail guides and then put the pin guides in the same location according to the layout marks that you made previously **(J)**. Now place the pin board in the top of the jig. It should extend beyond the pin bar a distance equal to the thickness of the tail board. For the greatest accuracy, I use a small cutoff from the tail board as a gauge **(K)**. Make the cut on the pin board **(L)** and assemble the joint **(M)**.

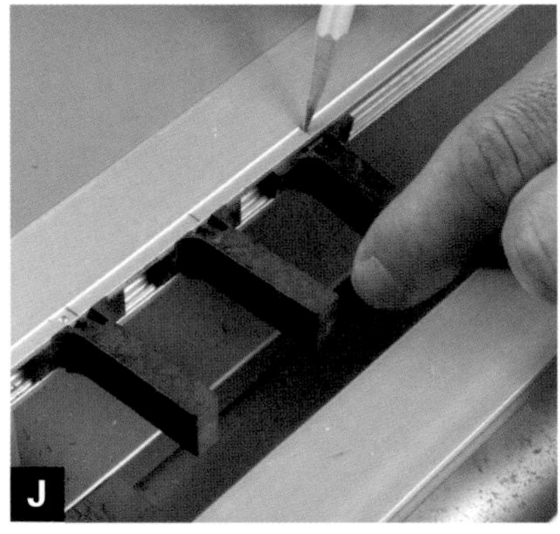

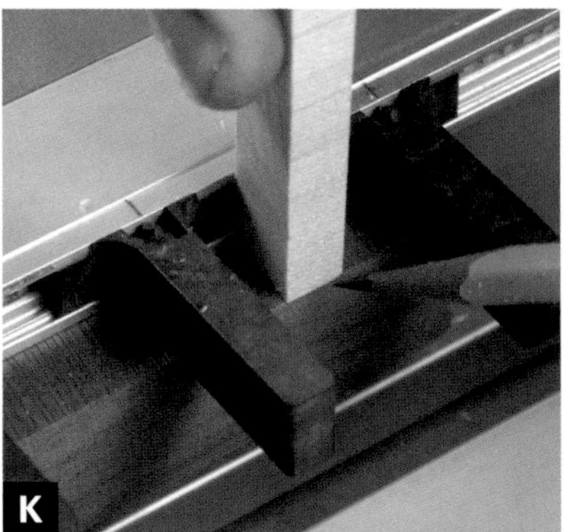

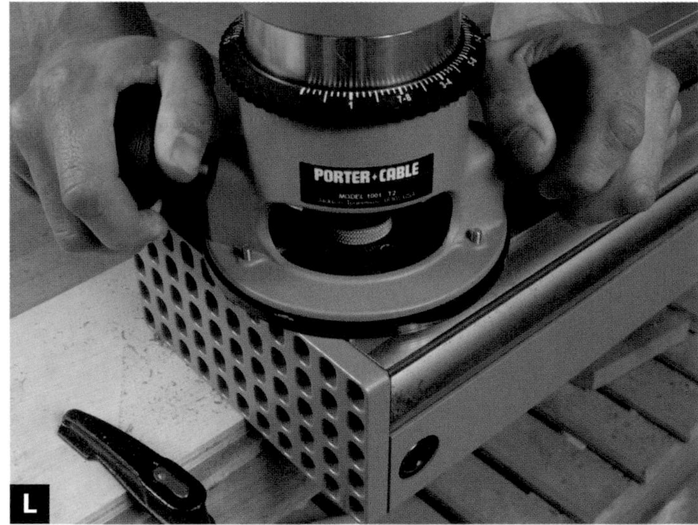

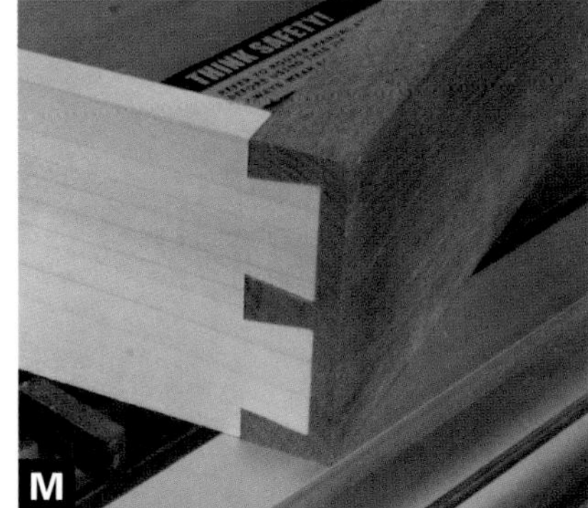

Glue Joint

When two boards are glued edge to edge, the joint is actually stronger than the surrounding wood. Pre-cutting the edges with a glue joint bit can help with alignment **(A)**.

Begin by adjusting the bit height to cut precisely in the center of the stock thickness **(B)**. Next, reduce the fence opening to increase safety and support of the stock as it is cut **(C)**. To accurately locate the fence position, place it tangent to the smallest cutting circle on the bit **(D)**. This is a large bit, so remember to use a guard to shield your hands **(E)**. Now you're ready to make the cut **(F)**.

A

B

C

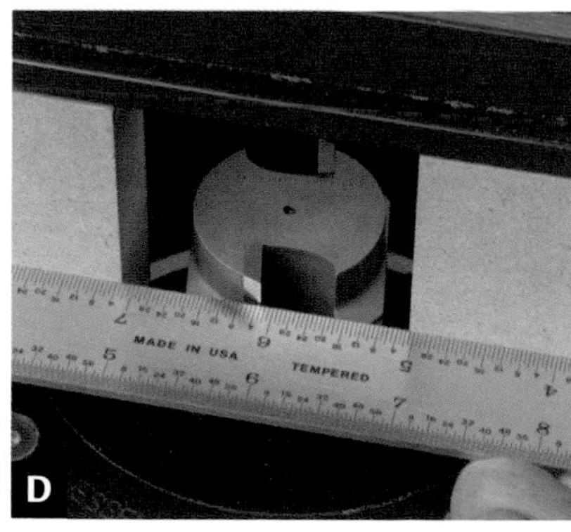

D

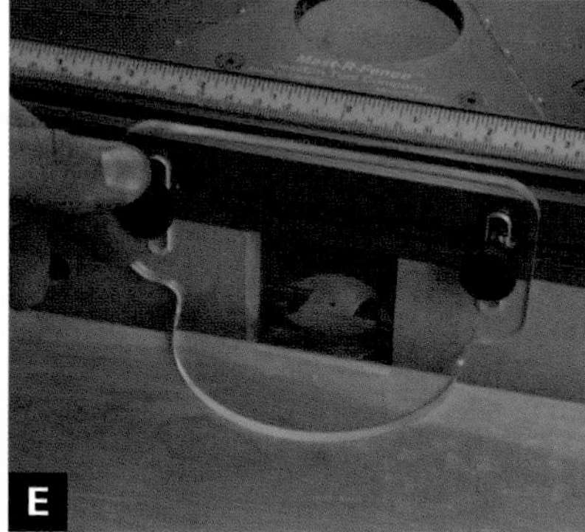

E

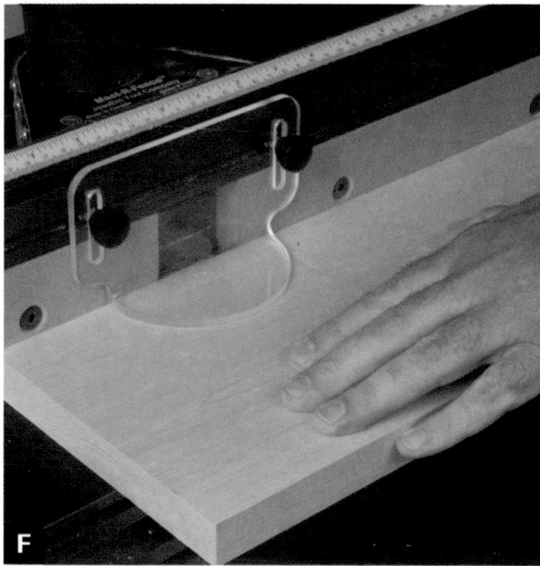

F

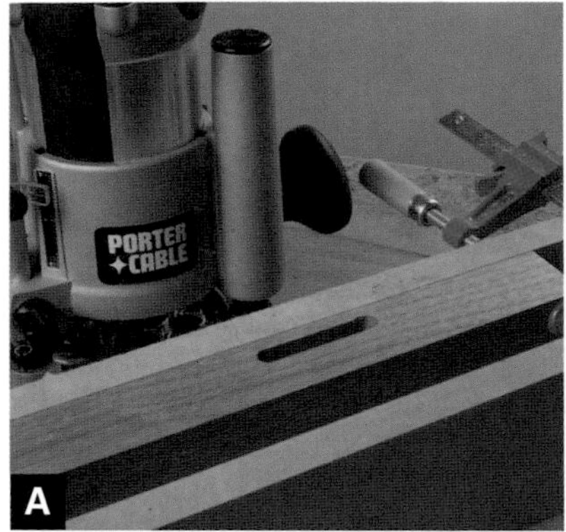

A

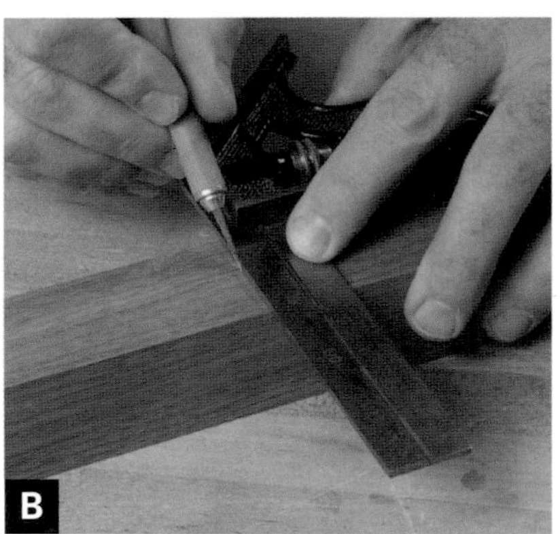
B

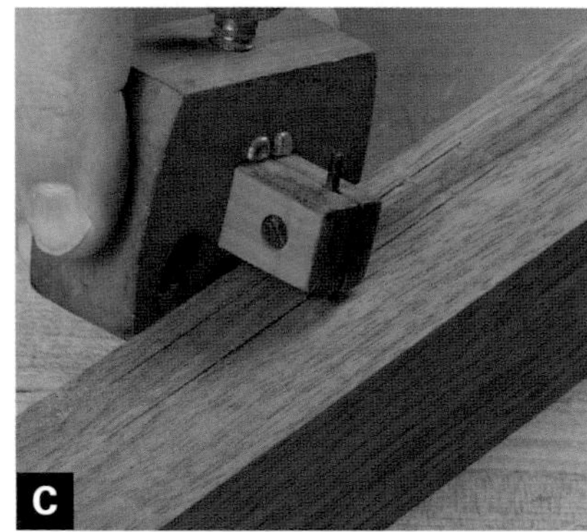
C

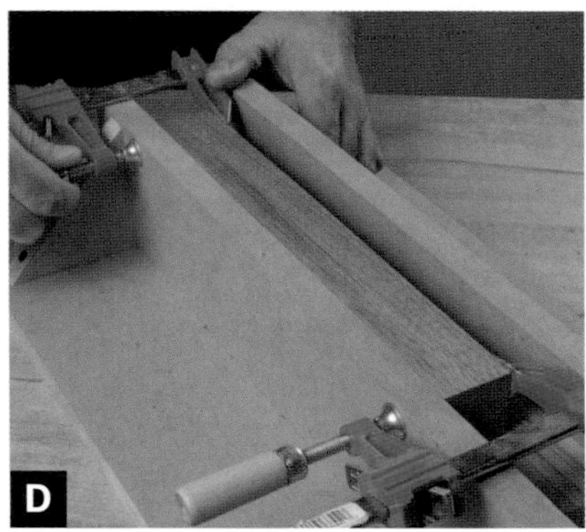
D

E

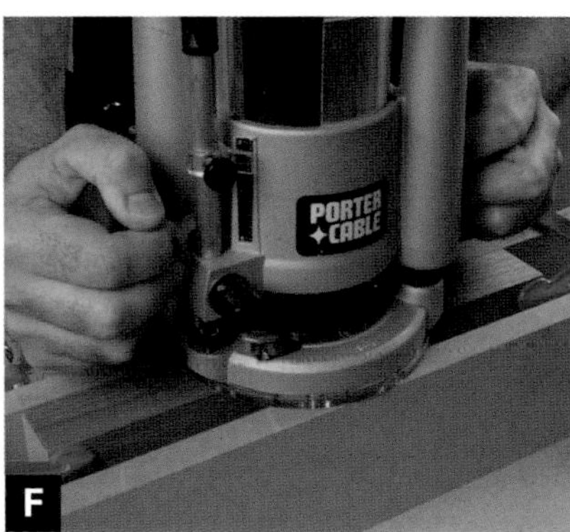

F

Mortise

The mortise-and-tenon joint is undoubtedly the strongest method for joining frame members **(A)**. One approach to cutting the mortise is with a router and a straight bit. Although an ordinary straight bit will work, it tends to cut slowly and overheat. Also, most straight bits are not designed for plunging. A much better choice is an upcut spiral bit, whose spiral flutes eject the chips from the mortise. But you'll first need to construct a jig to hold the workpiece and provide stability to the router.

Begin by measuring **(B)** and marking the mortise location **(C)**. Next, position the work in the jig and secure each end with clamps **(D)**.

To cut the mortise, you'll first need to set the cutting depth on the plunge router. Next, position the router guide against the edge of the jig **(E)**. Now, plunge the bit into the workpiece and feed it to the opposite end of the mortise layout **(F)**.

Tenon with Jig

One of the most important joints a woodworker can choose is the mortise-and-tenon joint. The joint has tremendous strength due to the mechanical interlock between the mating parts, the large long-grain gluing surface, and the shoulder, which resists racking forces. There are a number of methods for cutting the joint, but undoubtedly one of the fastest ways is with a router. As always, it's best to cut the mortise first, because it's easier to cut the tenon to fit the mortise than vice versa.

This method uses a router jig to hold the workpiece and guide the router in a straight path across the stock **(A)**. The first step is to use a gauge and lay out the tenon on a sample piece. Next, use the gauge line to adjust the cutting depth of the router bit **(B)**. A stick placed into the jig serves as a stop to limit the length of the tenon **(C)**. Slide the workpiece under the router guide and secure it in position with a toggle clamp **(D)**. With the workpiece secure in the jig, you're ready to make the first cut. Begin by cutting at the end of the tenon so that the router will gain additional support from the portion of the stock that remains uncut **(E)**. After each pass, reposition the router closer to the tenon shoulder

(Text continues on p. 166.)

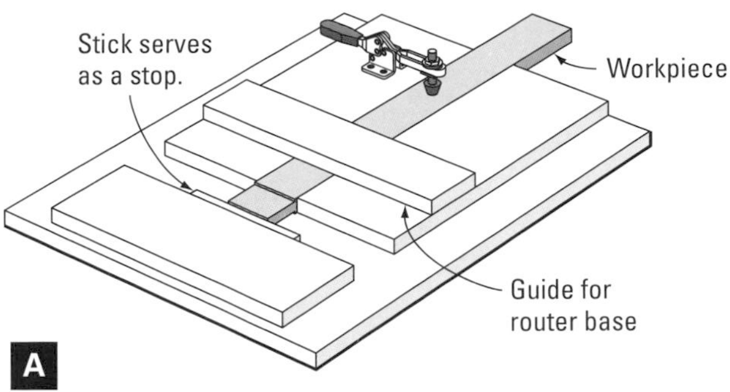

F

G

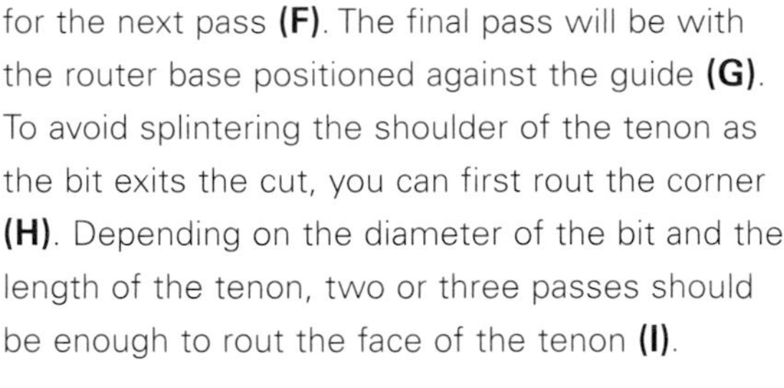

for the next pass **(F)**. The final pass will be with the router base positioned against the guide **(G)**. To avoid splintering the shoulder of the tenon as the bit exits the cut, you can first rout the corner **(H)**. Depending on the diameter of the bit and the length of the tenon, two or three passes should be enough to rout the face of the tenon **(I)**.

Now repeat the process on the opposite side of the stock **(J)** to complete the tenon **(K)**.

H

I

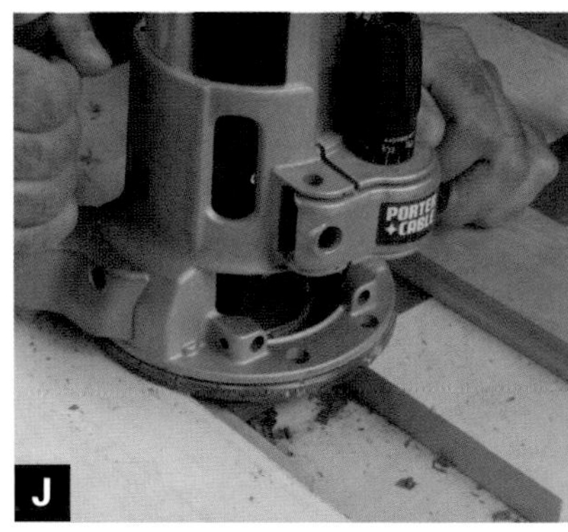

J

K

Tenon on the Router Table

A router table is a great alternative to a jig for cutting tenons. The router table is fast and easy to set up, especially if your table is equipped with a lift. Router lifts have built-in micrometers that allow you to adjust the bit height to within .001 in. with no backlash. The precision of a lift is a significant advantage for routing precise interlocking joints.

When cutting tenons on the router table, it's important to use both the fence and the miter gauge. If your table lacks a miter-gauge slot, you can use a shopmade sled that rides along the table edge.

➤See *"Making a Sled"* on p. 75.

The fence serves as a depth stop to control the tenon length, while the miter gauge is used to guide and support the stock. Make sure to use a guard to provide a barrier between your hands and the spinning bit.

Mount a large-diameter straight bit in the router, lay out the tenon on a sample piece, and adjust the bit height to the layout line **(A)**. Before cutting, be certain that the miter gauge is locked at exactly 90 degrees. Make the first pass along the end of the stock **(B)** and then take as many additional passes as necessary, working toward the shoulder. For the last pass, place the end of the stock against the fence and make the cut along the shoulder **(C)**. A backing board fastened to the miter gauge will eliminate splintering at the end of the cut.

Invert the stock and repeat the process on the opposite face **(D)**. Several passes will complete the tenon **(E)**. I always check the setup on a sample piece to ensure a snug fit between the tenon and the mortise **(F)**.

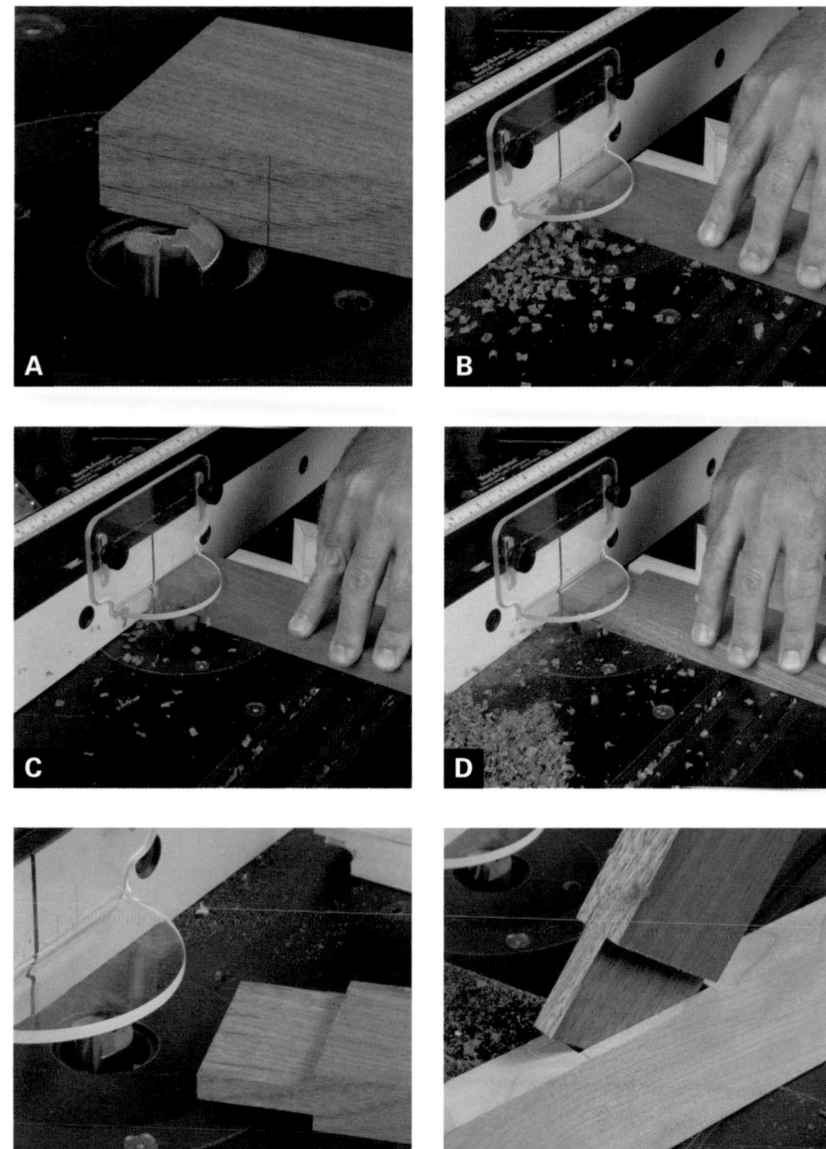

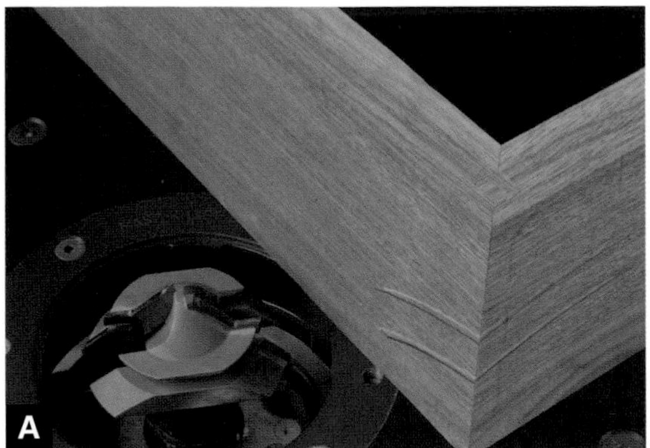

Lock Miter

To make grain "turn the corner" without a visible seam, the miter joint is a good choice. But cutting and fitting a perfect miter can be tricky. As you assemble the joint, the two halves can easily become misaligned as a result of the lubricity of the glue. One solution is to use a lock miter. This unique joint features an interlocking tongue and groove to create a flawless 45-degree miter **(A)**. To make the grain continue around the corner, mill the two halves of the joint from the same board **(B)**.

Begin by adjusting the bit height **(C)**. Because of the large bit diameter, it's important to increase stock support and safety by creating a zero-clearance opening **(D)**. The next step is to adjust the fence. Because the miter gauge is used in this process, you'll need to adjust the fence to be parallel to the miter-gauge slot **(E)**. Position

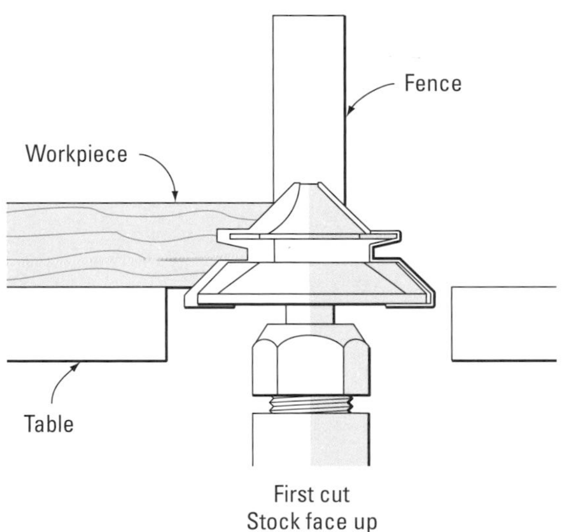

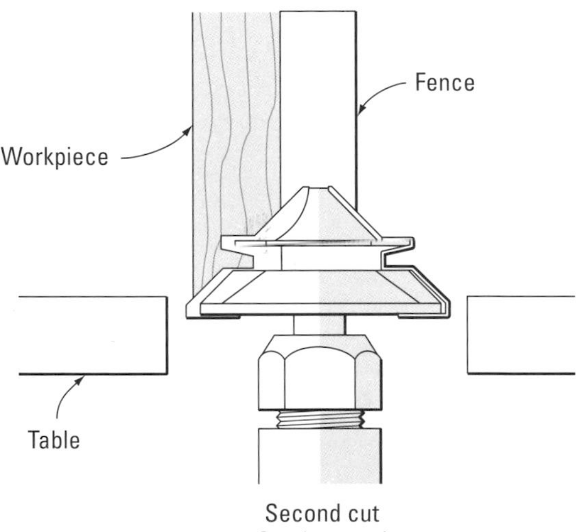

C

a guard over the bit **(F)**. To complete the setup, attach a backing board to the miter gauge **(G)**.

Now cut the first half of the joint. Position the stock on the table with the outer face up and make the cut **(H)**. The mating half of the joint must be positioned on end. For support, clamp a board to the stock at 90 degrees and use a featherboard **(I)**.

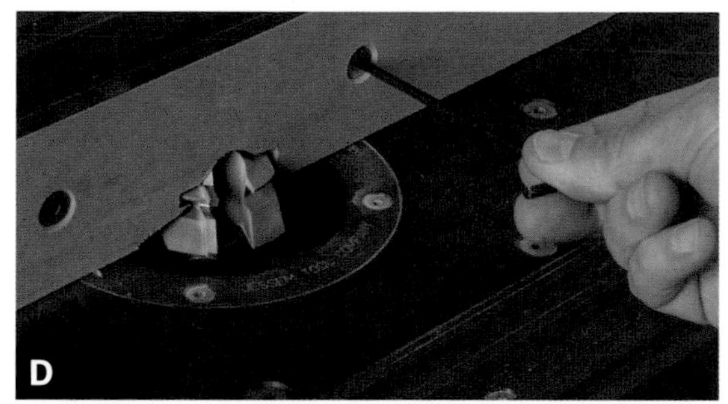
D

E

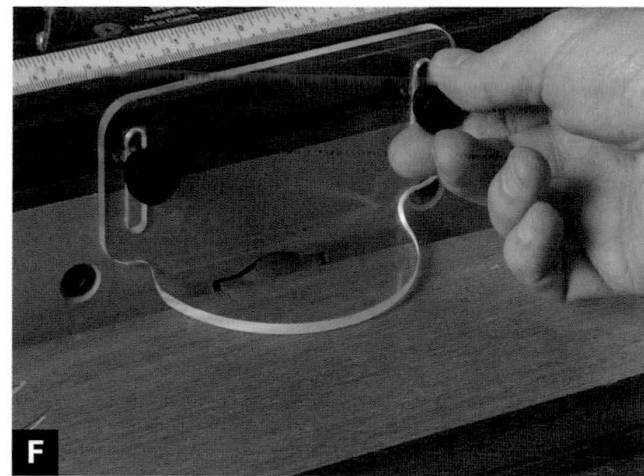
F

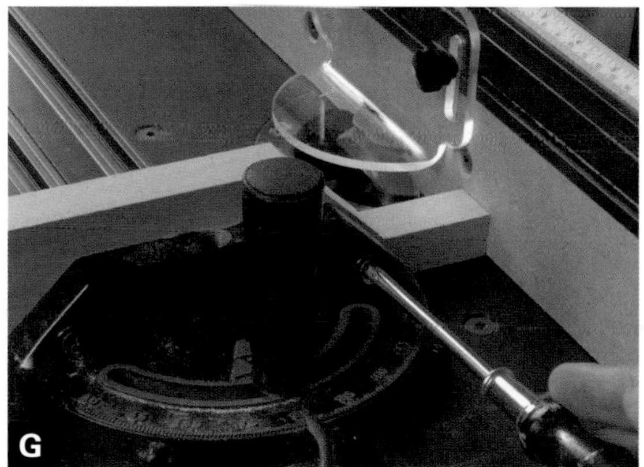
G

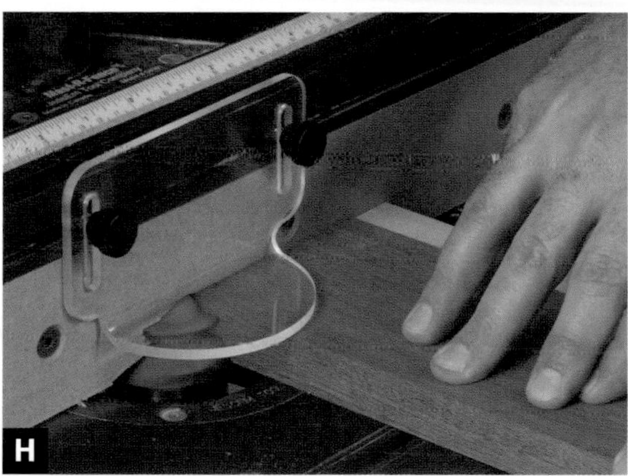
H

I

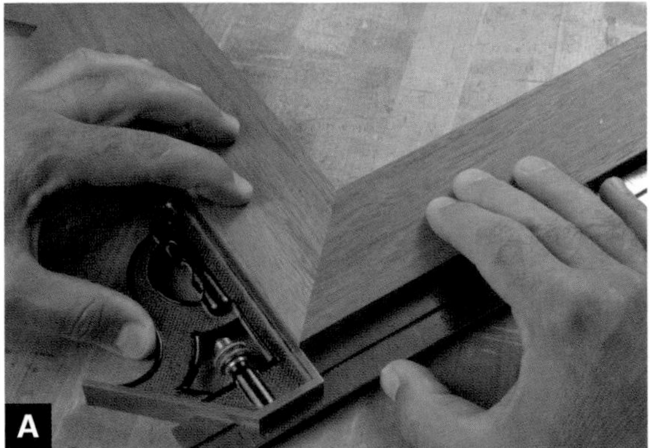

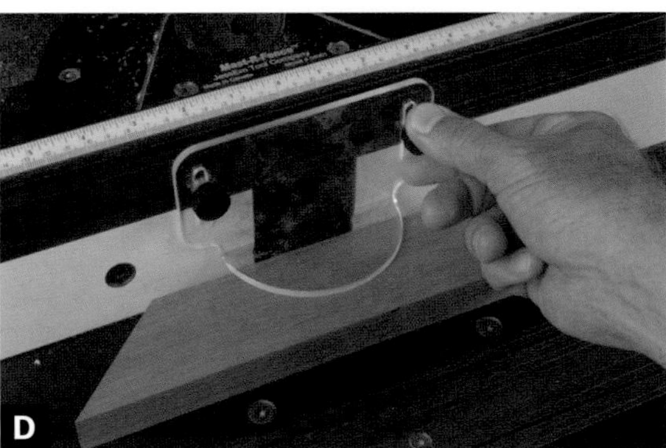

Splined Miter

Miters are used whenever the goal is to hide end grain. The miter is a simple yet elegant way to change directions, whether at 90 degrees or some other angle. The only real downside to the miter is that it is inherently weak, because the joint primarily consists of end-grain contact. The traditional method of reinforcement is to add a spline. The spline is simply a third piece of wood incorporated into the joint to create long-grain surface area for glue. From an aesthetic standpoint, you can downplay the spline by making it from the same wood as your primary pieces. Alternatively, you can emphasize the spline by making it of a contrasting wood. However, the most important consideration when making the joint is to run the grain of the spline perpendicular to the joint line. If the spline grain runs parallel to the joint line, the joint will be weak.

To make the joint, begin by sawing the miter and checking it for accuracy by fitting the parts together within the legs of a square **(A)**. Next, install a grooving bit in the router table and adjust the fence tangent to the guide bearing on the bit **(B)**. For the greatest safety and accuracy, close the fence halves as much as possible **(C)**. Also, position a guard above the bit **(D)**. It's important that the cut be centered exactly across the thickness of the stock; otherwise, you'll need to make half the cuts with the miter gauge turned away from the fence. It's actually easier and much less awkward to adjust the bit height to center on the stock. One method is to measure with a square set as a depth gauge **(E)**. However, using a dial caliper is more accurate **(F)**.

Once you're satisfied that the setup is accurate, you're ready to cut the grooves for the spline. Rotate the head of the miter gauge to 45 degrees, and make the cut **(G)**. To complete the joint, size the thickness of the spline for a snug fit within the groove **(H)** and then assemble the joints with glue **(I)**.

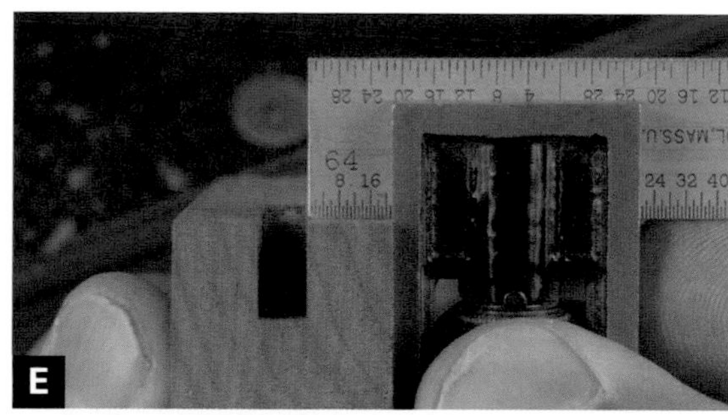
E

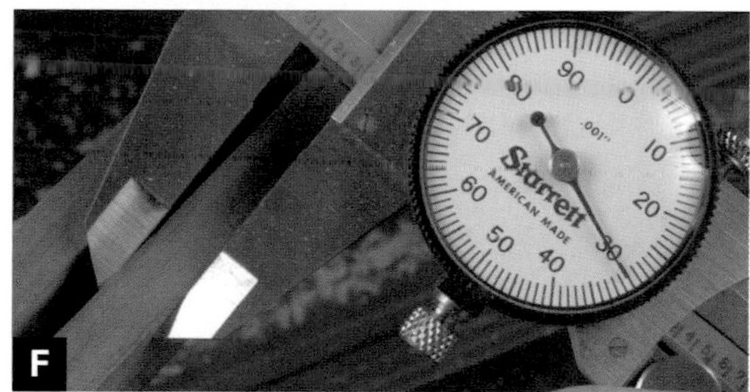

F

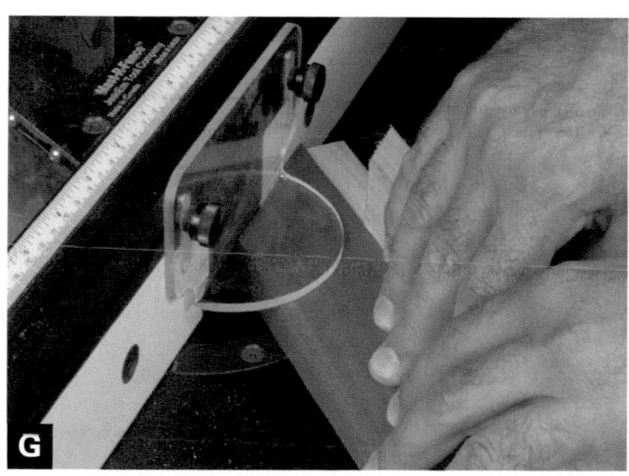
G

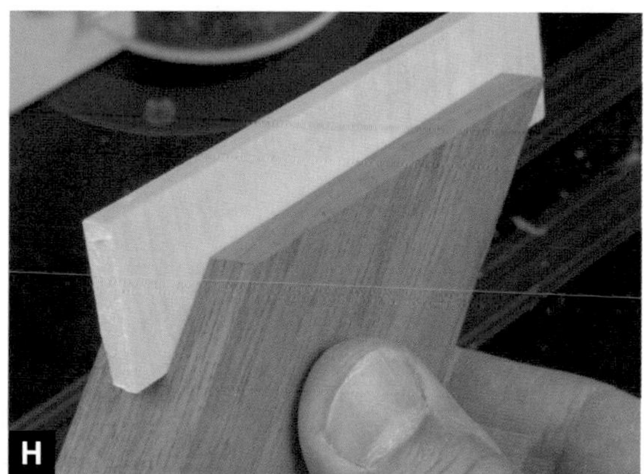
H

I

A

Bird's Mouth

A bird's-mouth joint is essentially a mitered tongue-and-groove joint. A 90-degree V cut in the first piece joins with a point on the end of the mating piece to create a joint that is both strong and attractive **(A)**.

Begin by routing the V groove **(B)**. The depth of the groove is less important than the width; it must equal the thickness of the mating piece **(C)**. To cut the point, the best choice is a 45-degree chamfer bit; the cutting geometry cuts cleaner than the groove bit used for the V **(D)**.

B

C

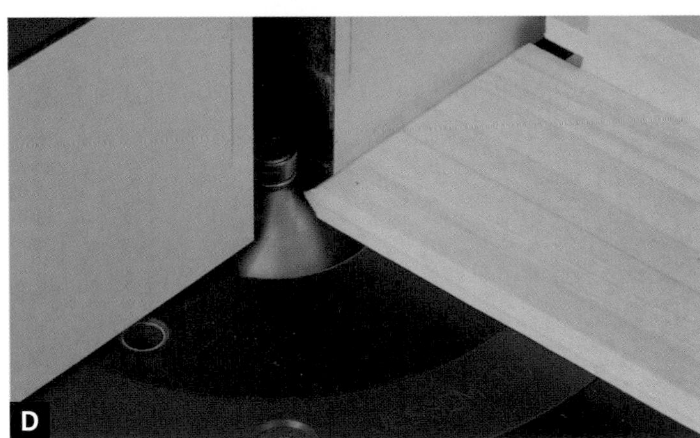
D

Box Joint

The box joint comprises rows of interlocking "fingers." Like the dovetail, the box joint gets its strength from its mechanical interlock as well as the large amounts of long-grain glue surface area **(A)**. Because a box joint lacks the tapered interlock of a dovetail joint's tails and pins, it's not quite as strong. However, it more than makes up for this by its ease of construction.

Although you can cut the box joint with a tablesaw, it has a much better appearance when cut with a router. That's because a router bit creates a square, smooth bottom between the fingers, as opposed to the slightly jagged surface created by a saw blade.

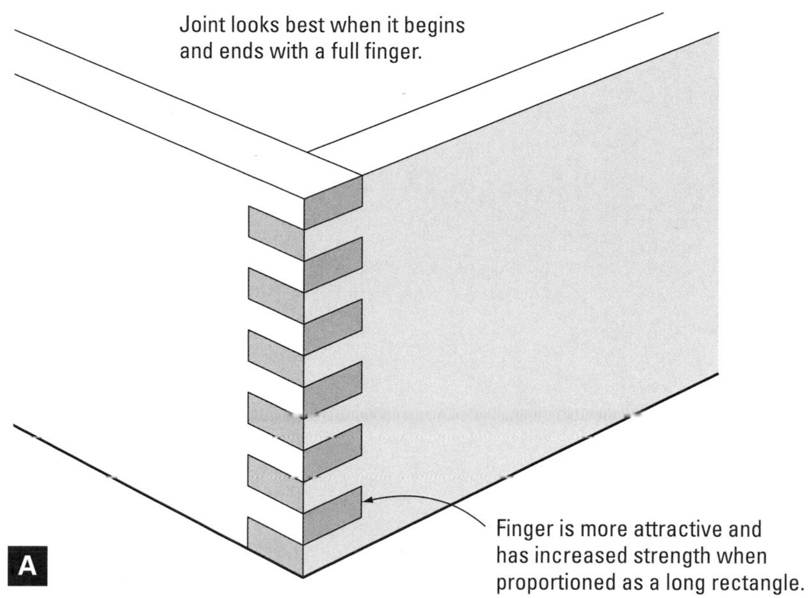

The key to making strong, snug-fitting box joints is to use a simple jig that ensures perfect spacing **(B)**. Although you can purchase a jig, it's easy to make your own. Begin by selecting a straight bit to cut the space between the fingers. I select a bit with a diameter that is three-fourths of the thickness of the stock. For example, in this photo-essay I'm using a 3/8-in.-dia. bit on 1/2-in.-thick stock. This creates a finger with the proportions of a long rectangle, as opposed to a square. Besides being stronger than a square due to its larger glue surface area, the rectangle is more eye-pleasing.

Adjust the height of the bit so that it is slightly greater than the stock thickness. This will cause the fingers to protrude slightly from the stock surface once the box is assembled. After assembly, the fingers are sanded flush. Of course it's important to account for this loss of stock when sizing the parts for the box. Otherwise the completed box will end up smaller than you intended.

To make the jig, first mill a piece of stock to serve as a backing board. The length of the stock should be at least twice the width of the material used

(Text continues on p. 174.)

C

D

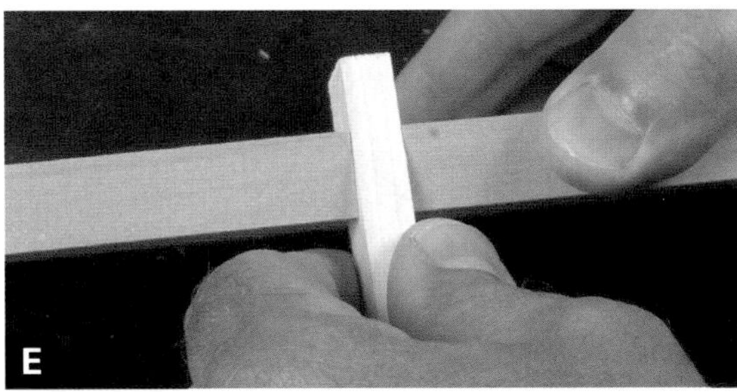
E

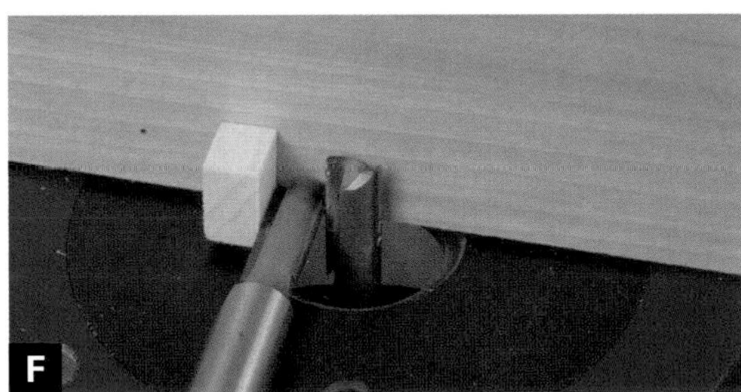
F

G

to create the box joint. This will provide plenty of support as the joint is cut into the workpiece. Securely clamp the backing board to the miter gauge **(C)** and feed it into the bit to create a slot **(D)**. Now carefully fit a stick into the slot **(E)**. The slot and stick will serve as a spacer to locate the position of each cut.

As each notch is cut, it is slipped over the stick to locate the correct position for the subsequent cut. Therefore, it is important that the stick be positioned from the router bit at a distance that is equal to the bit diameter. This is the trickiest part of the setup. However, there is an easy way to ensure perfect spacing. Just use a second bit that is the same diameter as the first. Position the second bit between the stick and the bit in the router **(F)**. Fasten the backing board to the miter gauge **(G)**. Now you're ready to begin cutting the joint.

On the first half of the joint, position the stock against the stick for the first cut **(H)**. This will start the board with a finger; the mating board will begin with a space. Now make the first cut **(I)**. Slip the freshly cut space over the stick and make the next cut **(J)**. Now continue the process across the end of the stock.

Of course the next step is to rout the second half of the joint. Remember, this half must begin with a space, which will interlock with the finger on the first half of the joint. To accurately make the first cut, just align the edge of the stock with the void in the backing board **(K)**. Now, rest the cut against the stick to align the stock for the next cut **(L)**. The remaining cuts are now made by slipping each previous cut over the spacing stick **(M)**. Apply glue to the fingers and slip the joint together **(N)**.

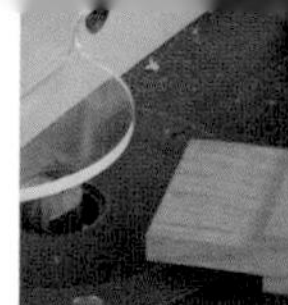

H

I

J

K

L

M

N

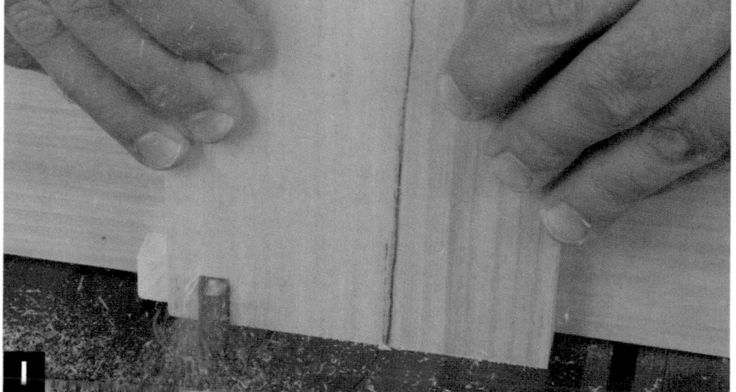

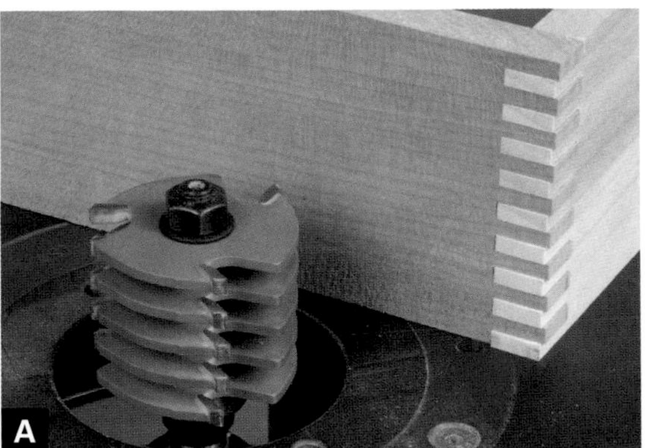

A

B

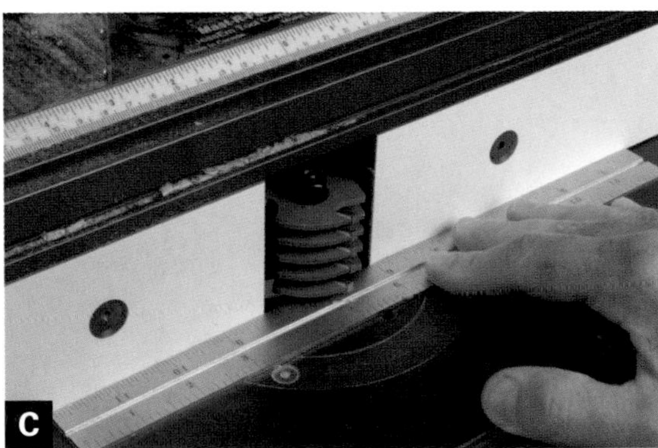

C

D

Box Joint Bit

As the name implies, the box joint is primarily used for joining the corners of boxes. Like the dovetail, the box joint gets its strength from lots of long-grain gluing surface, as well as the mechanical interlock of the adjoining halves **(A)**. Unlike the dovetail, the box joint does not have the wedging action of the angled tails and pins, so it is not nearly as strong. Also, it's not practical to cut box joints on full-sized casework. Because of these issues, I limit the use of the box joint to small boxes.

To cut a box joint, you can use multiple passes of a straight bit along with a jig to guide the stock and control the spacing of each cut. Or you can opt to use a finger joint bit like the one in this essay. Making box joints with this special bit is more efficient; the setup is fast, and each corner of the box is quickly cut in one or two passes, instead of a separate pass for each individual finger.

When designing your box joints, remember that one half of the joint must begin with a full socket; the mating half must end with a matching finger. To avoid confusion, it's a good idea to first position the parts on the bench in the order of assembly and label the cuts. Also, when sizing the stock, remember to rip it to a width that is a multiple of the finger/socket width.

Begin by adjusting the bit height so that the first cutter in the stack is flush with the lower edge of the stock **(B)**. Next, position the fence tangent to the guide bearing **(C)**. As you lock the fence in place, make sure that it is parallel with the miter gauge slot **(D)**. Minimize the fence opening to provide support for the workpiece and to create a barrier around the bit **(E)**. Also, fasten a backing board to the miter gauge **(F)**.

With the setup complete, you're ready to make the cuts on all the parts. Remember to position each part according to the labels that you made earlier. This is a large bit, so don't attempt to hold the workpiece with your hand. Instead, clamp it securely to the backing board and make the cut **(G)**.

Also, if you're cutting a joint on stock that is wider than the bit height, you'll need to invert the stock for a second pass. But first adjust the bit so that the cutter aligns with the first cut **(H)**. This will ensure alignment during assembly.

E

F

G

H

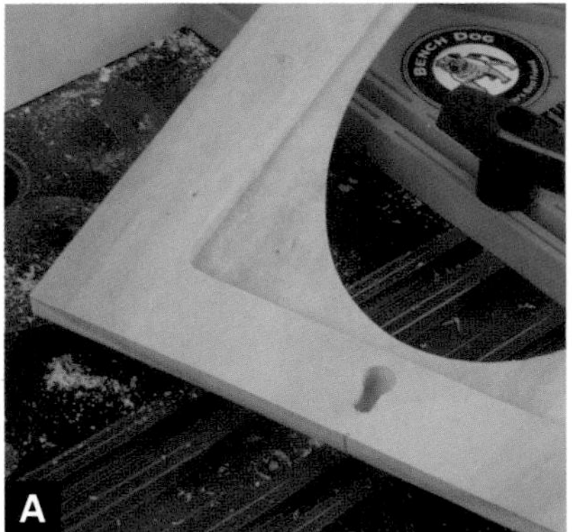
A

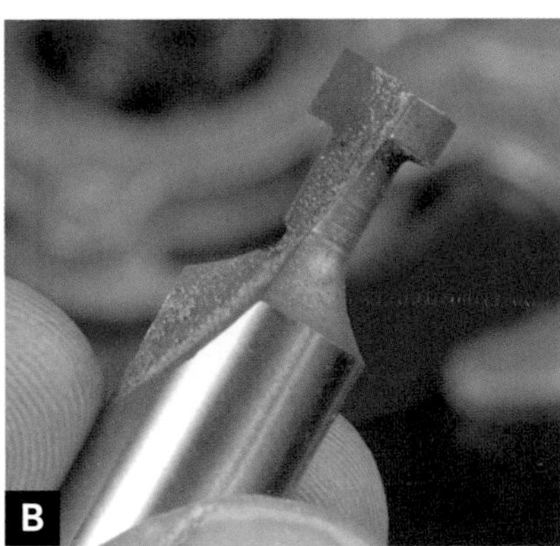
B

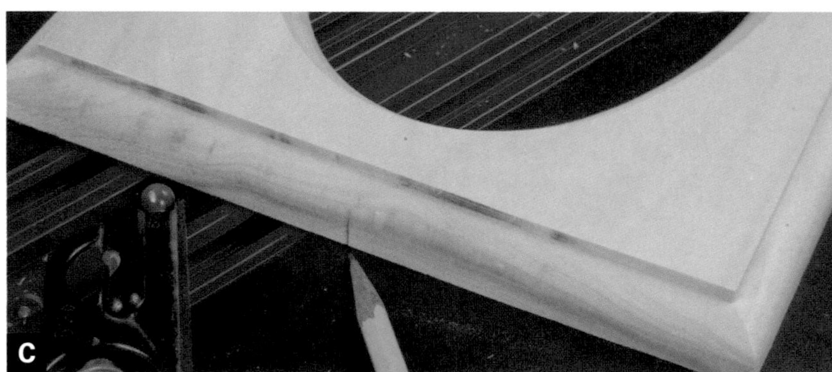
C

D

Rout a Keyhole

A keyhole bit isn't really for routing a true keyhole but for a small, elongated hole in the back of a frame or shelf for ease of hanging **(A)**. Once plunged into the stock, this unique, large-diameter bit creates an undercut hole designed to capture the head of a nail or screw **(B)**.

Begin by marking the desired location of the keyhole **(C)**. Small frames, such as the one pictured here, typically require only one hole. However, a large item, such as a shelf, will require at least two appropriately spaced holes. Position the fence near the bit, and use stops to position the layout line over the bit **(D)**. By trapping the frame on three sides, you can easily plunge the frame onto the spinning bit and pull it away from the fence to elongate the keyhole. But first, mark a line to indicate the stopping point of the elongation **(E)**.

Position the frame between the stops and against the fence, and plunge the frame into the bit **(F)**. Now pull the frame away from the fence until it aligns with the layout mark that you made earlier **(G)**.

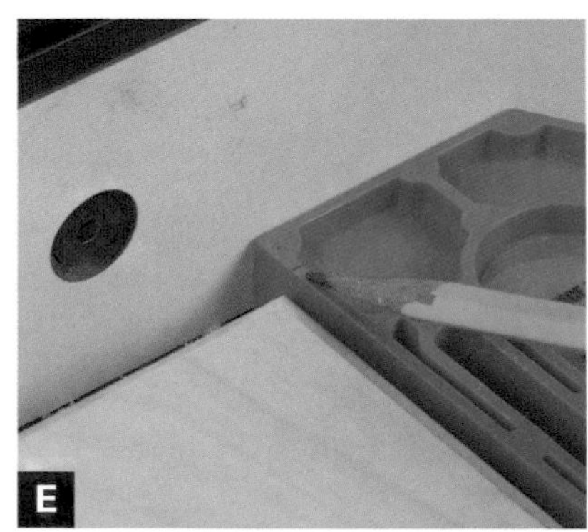
E

F

G

Rule Joint

Rule joints are used for drop leaves on tables **(A)**. A cove is cut on the lower edge of the leaf to mate with a thumbnail profile on the table edge. The result is both beautiful and functional. When the leaf is dropped, the two profiles mesh to create an attractive ovolo profile **(B)**. Conventional wisdom is to locate the hinge barrel directly below the fillet. I prefer to position the barrel an additional 1⁄64 in. toward the edge to prevent the finish from wearing away each time the leaf is raised or lowered.

For this unique movable joint to function properly, it is important that the cove and thumbnail profiles match.

You can cut the profiles with molding planes if you are fortunate enough to have a matching pair. Or you can shape the profiles with router bits. Choose a radius that will leave a 1⁄4-in. fillet; anything heavier tends to look clumsy. For the example in these photos, I'm using 1⁄2-in. radius bits with a 3⁄4-in. top and leaf thickness. Also, before you jump in to this process, you'll need special drop-leaf hinges; one leaf is longer than the other.

After shaping the cove and thumbnail, mark the hinge position with a knife **(C)**. Next, mortise for the hinge thickness. I speed this up with a small router and a straight bit **(D)**. After squaring the mortise with a chisel, cut a recess for the hinge barrel and fasten the hinges in place **(E)**. Photo **(F)** shows leaf in position.

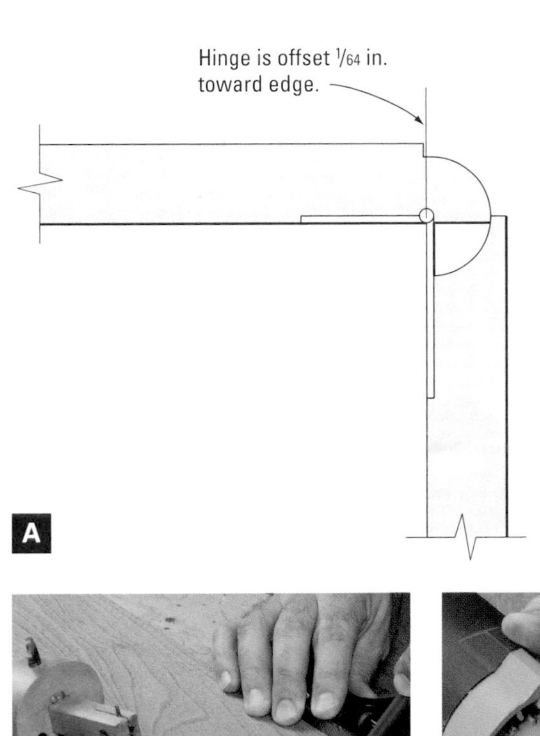

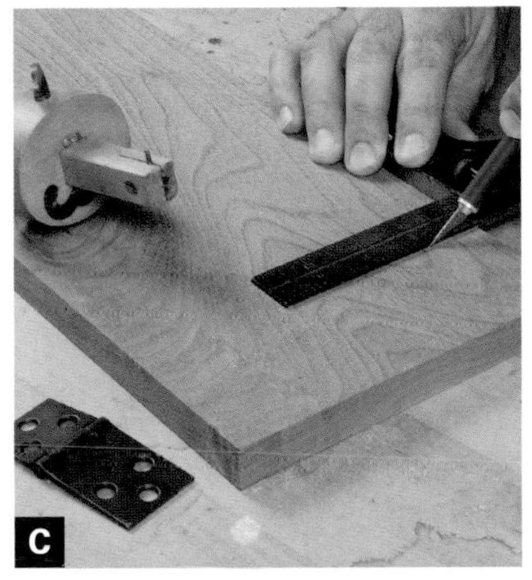

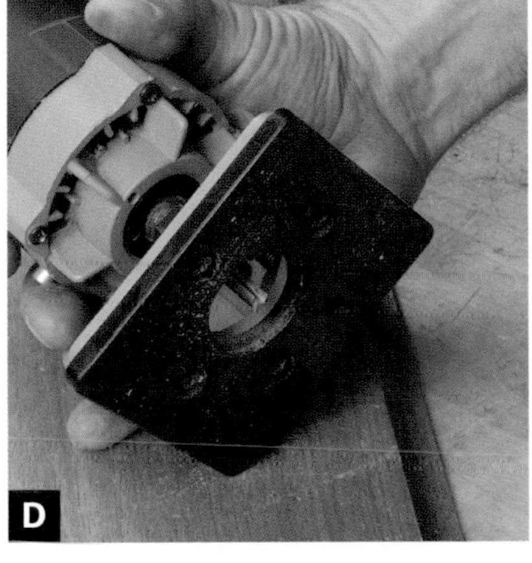

Doors and Drawers

Frame Joinery

Panels

Door Details

Drawer Joinery

FRAME-AND-PANEL construction is one of the most important design elements in furniture making. A frame-and-panel assembly can span a broad expanse while accommodating seasonal dimensional changes. Frame-and-panel doors fit year-round because the seasonal expansion and contraction takes place within the frame. By changing design elements, such as wood, finish, proportions, and panel details, you can use the frame-and-panel in virtually any style of furniture or architecture. In fact, the frame-and-panel is used for room paneling and even casework, such as paneled chests and roll-top desks.

Frame-and-Panel Design

The frame-and-panel looks best as a long rectangle, either horizontal or vertical, as shown in the drawing on the facing page.

FRAME-AND-PANEL CONFIGURATION

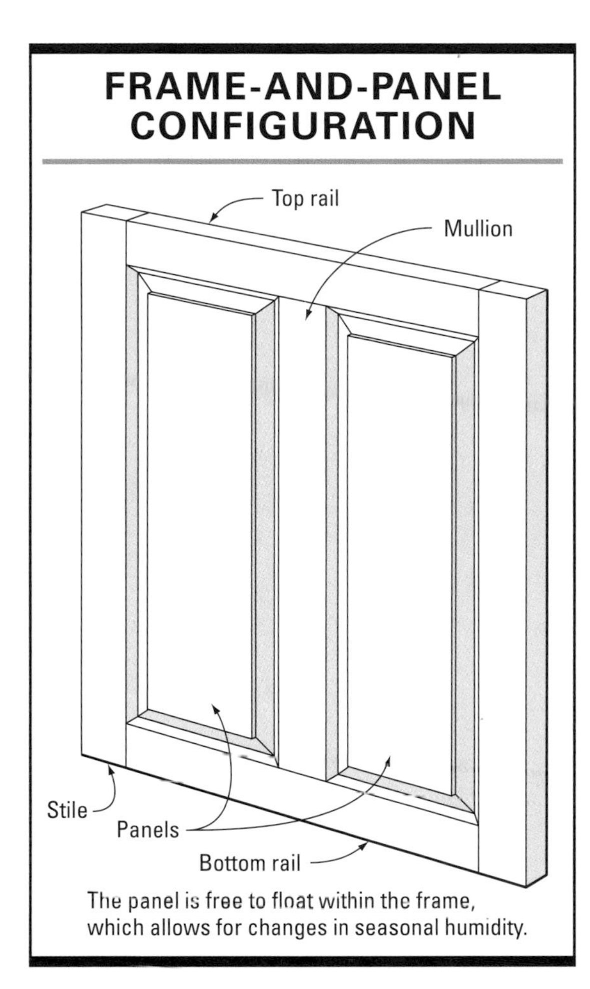

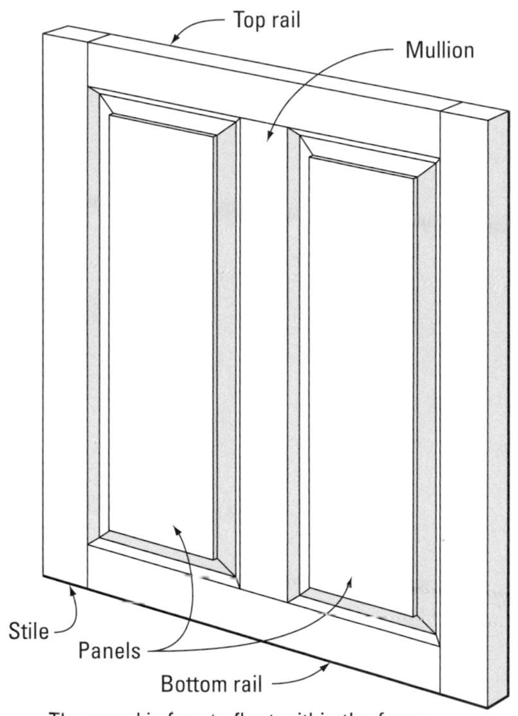

The panel is free to float within the frame, which allows for changes in seasonal humidity.

The vertical frame members are called stiles, and horizontal members are referred to as rails. The rails typically fit between the stiles.

Although the inside edges of a door frame can be square, they're often shaped with a simple decorative profile—usually a thumbnail, ovolo, or ogee. This profile, which is referred to as sticking, can actually be part of the frame joinery. In that case, it's called cope-and-stick joinery because the sticking profile on the stiles mates against a complementary cope cut on the ends of the rail. Although the profiles are usually cut with a matching set of separate router bits, you can instead use a reversible bit that changes profiles by inverting sections of the cutter.

Flat-panel doors can be made using panels no thicker than the panel groove in the frame. However, thicker panels are often used, although they're generally thinner than the frame, and commonly range from 1/2 in. to 5/8 in. thick. The edges of thick panels are beveled to fit within the groove in their frame, creating raised panels.

Some raised panels are beveled on the inside face of the door (exhibiting the look of a flat panel on the exterior face), but most panels are beveled on the outside face. The most common profile for a bevel is flat, but bevels can also be cove- or ogee-shaped.

The thickness of the shaped panel edge is important. It should be thin enough to slip easily into the frame groove, but snug enough that the panel doesn't rattle each time the door is opened. Of course, the panel's width should allow for cross-grain panel expansion during the humid season. As a rule of thumb, I allow for 1/16 in. at the bottom of each stile groove, which provides 1/8 in. space overall. This is plenty of room for even large cabinet door panels to expand during summer.

Bits for Doors and Panels

With the selection of router bits available today, it's possible to make all the shaping and joinery cuts for a paneled door on your router table. Cope-and-stick bits make construction of the frame flawless and efficient. A sticking bit is used to shape the decorative profile along the inside edges of the panel frame. As it cuts the sticking, it simultaneously cuts the panel groove. The cope bit cuts a reverse profile on the ends of the rails, along with a short tenon that fits within the

Cope-and-stick bits greatly simplify door making.

COPE-AND-STICK JOINERY

Sticking

Cope

Rail

Stile

Offset shoulders on rail.

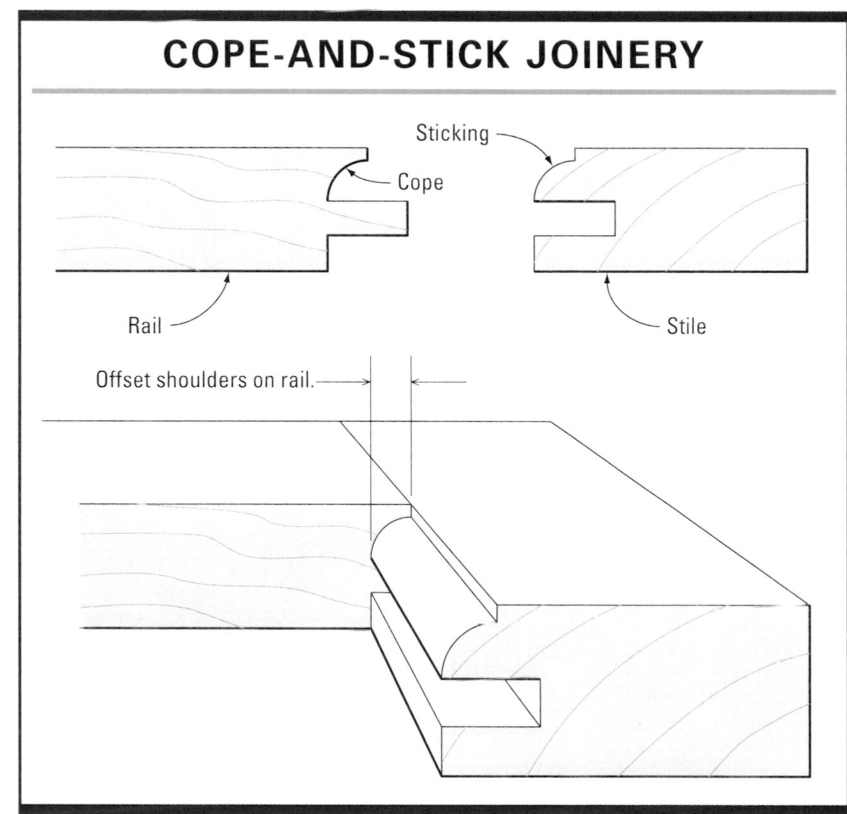

panel groove. These bits can quickly produce a kitchen full of doors.

To substantially increase the strength of a door, consider using a plywood or MDF panel and gluing it into the frame. Don't attempt this with a solid wood panel, as the seasonal expansion and contraction would cause the panel to split if it were glued in place. Instead, you can reinforce the corners of a solid-panel door frame by incorporating long tenons.

➤ See *"Coped Mortise-and-Tenon"* on p. 190.

When shopping for cope-and-stick door bits, there are two types to consider: matched sets and reversible bits. Most woodworkers use matched sets, in which one bit cuts the cope and tenon simultaneously, while the complementary bit cuts the sticking and panel groove. As an economical alternative, you can purchase a "reversible" bit. Rearranging the sections on this bit allows you to cut the cope and sticking in turn. Of course it takes more time to set up a reversible bit, and the design is limited to simpler profiles that are easily reversed. But for the woodworker who only needs to make an occasional door, reversible bits are a good option. If you're using a plywood panel, some bits adjust for the plywood thickness (see the top left photo on the facing page).

There are two types of bits for panel raising: horizontal and vertical. The most common are the large, horizontal two-wing

A reversible bit will cut both the cope and the sticking.

This unique cope-and-stick set adjusts to accommodate undersized plywood.

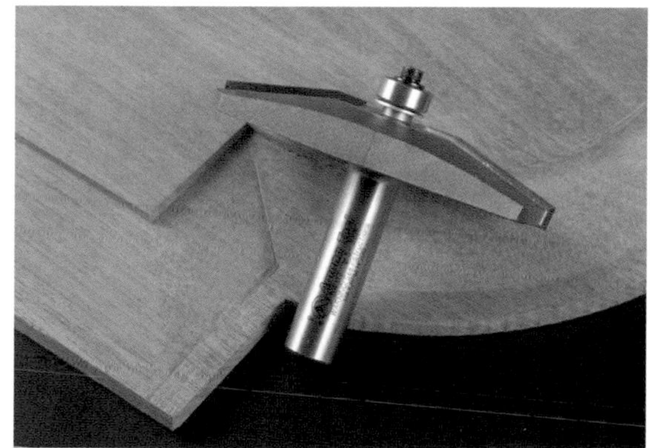

With this bit, you can create raised-panel doors on your router table.

cutters. These cutters are my first choice because their large diameter offers more effective cutting geometry than that of vertical bits, resulting in a smoother cut. The only drawback of wing-type panel-raising bits is that spinning them safely requires a 3-hp or larger router.

For those woodworkers who have not yet purchased a big router, vertical bits

WARNING Never attempt to use any of these door or panel bits in a handheld router. They should only be run in a table-mounted router.

The reversible sash bit cuts both the cope and the sticking.

To safely shape narrow sash mullions, you'll need to construct a jig.

are a good option. The small diameter of these bits allows you to use them effectively in smaller routers. Just be aware that the smaller diameter also means a less effective cutting geometry, resulting in a less cleanly cut surface.

Sash bits allow you to construct sash-type doors with your router. Like cope-and-stick frame bits, sash bits are available in a two-piece set or as a reversible bit. And like the cope-and-stick bits, sash bits cut a cope on the ends of the stock and a matching sticking profile on the edges. However, instead of a panel groove, these bits cut a rabbet for glass. When shaping the narrow bars or mullions on a sash window, it's important to construct a jig to distance your hands from the bit, as shown in the drawing on p. 196.

A

Door Bit Set

Stile-and-rail bit sets have greatly simplified door construction **(A)**. One bit cuts the cope, along with a short tenon that fits within the panel groove of the adjoining frame member. The other bit cuts the sticking profile, which meshes with the cope cut to create a neat, mitered appearance **(B)**.

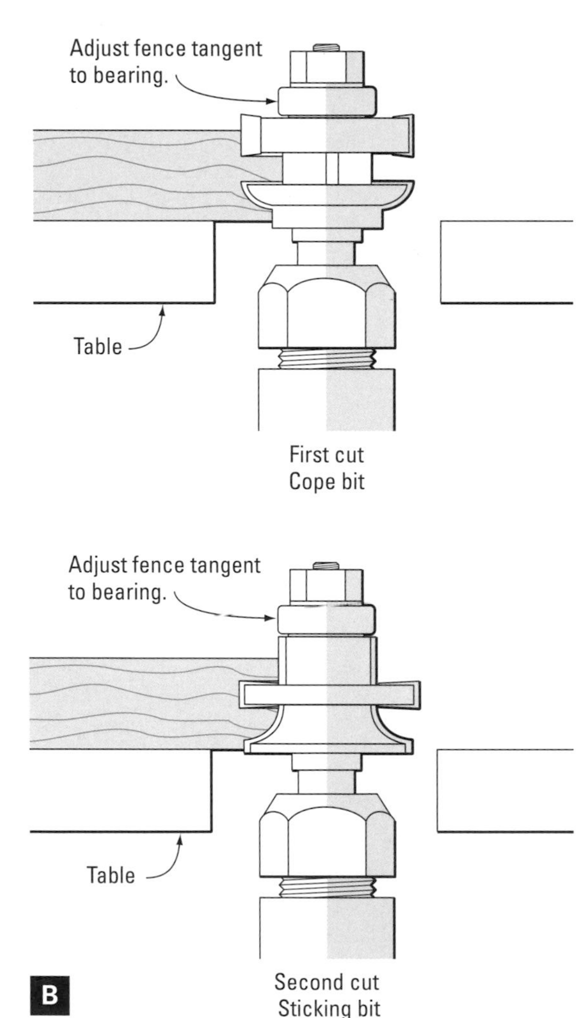

Begin by installing the coping bit and adjusting its height to create a small fillet at the top of the sticking profile **(C)**. Next, position the fence tangent to the guide bearing on the bit **(D)**, and make certain that the fence is positioned parallel to the miter gauge slot **(E)**. Reduce the fence opening as much as possible **(F)** and position

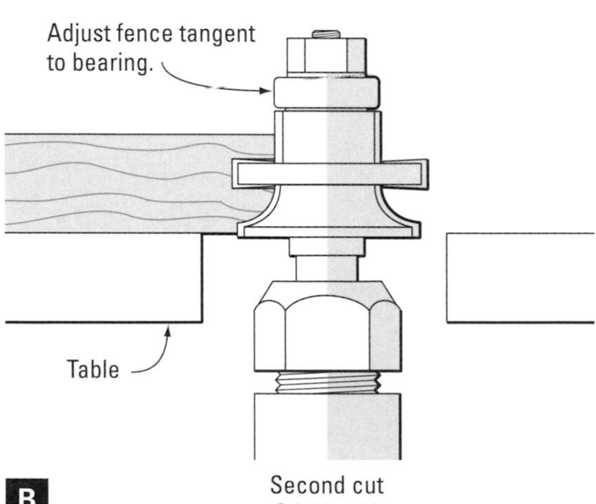

B

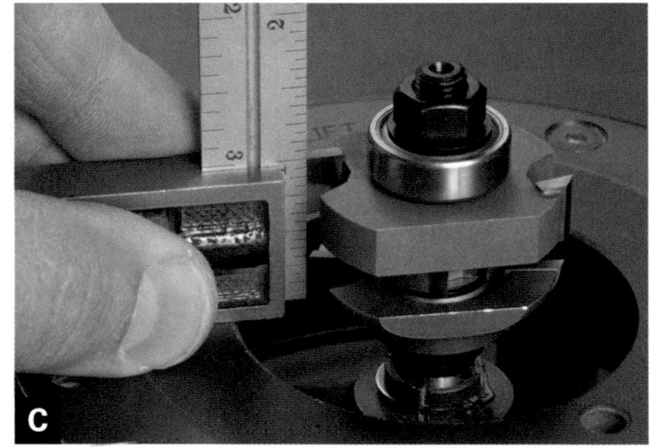
C

D

a guard over the opening **(G)**. To complete the setup, fasten a backing board to the miter gauge **(H)**. Now make the cope cut on the ends of the rails **(I)**.

To cut the sticking and groove, secure the sticking bit in the router and adjust the height to match the cope cut **(J)**. Next, position the fence tangent to the bearing **(K)**. A featherboard can be used to hold the stock to the fence. Use a push stick to distance your hands **(L)**.

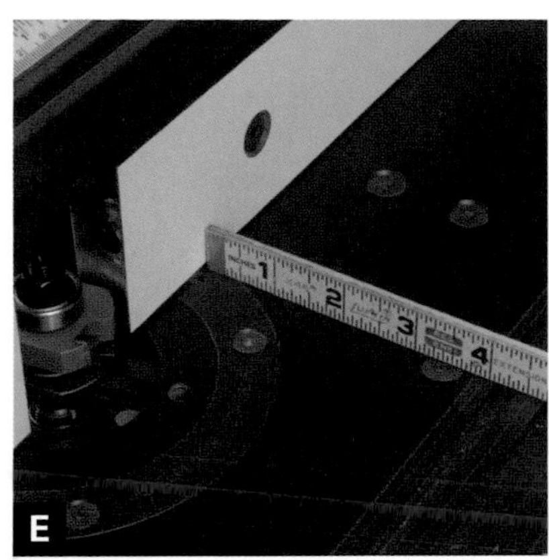
E

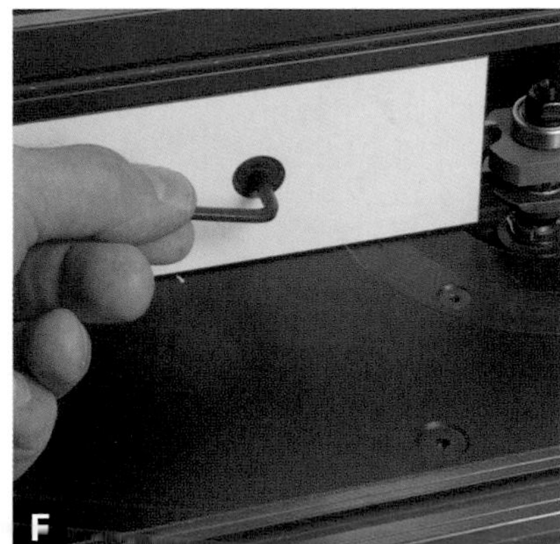
F

G

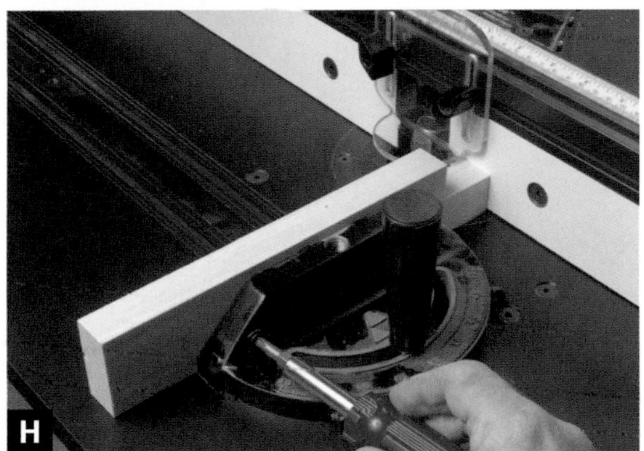
H

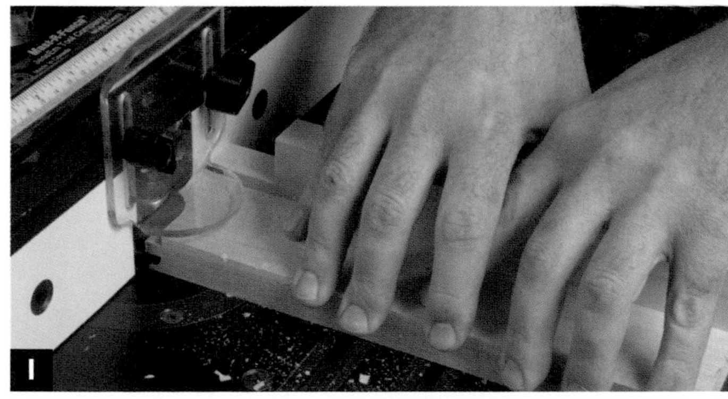
I

J

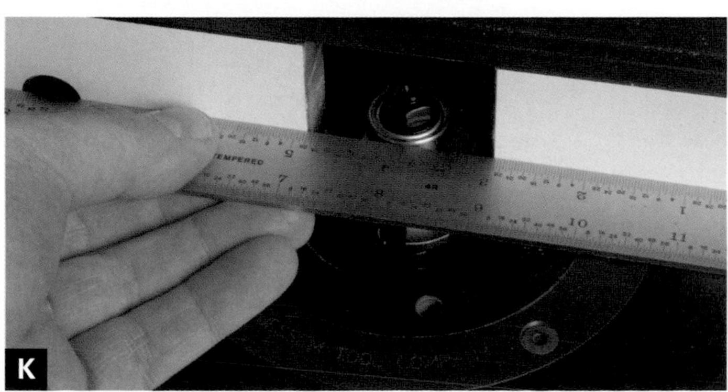
K

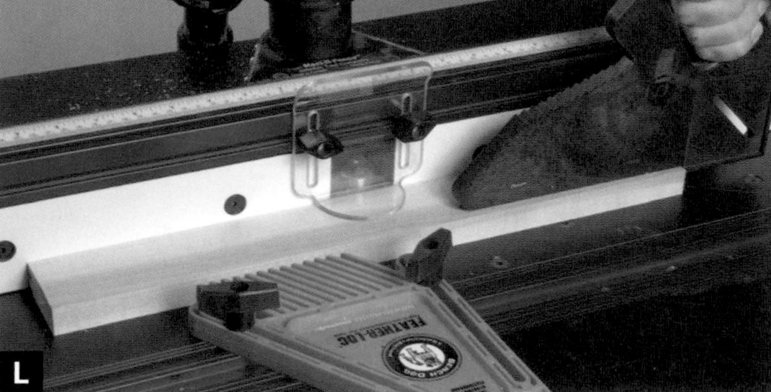

L

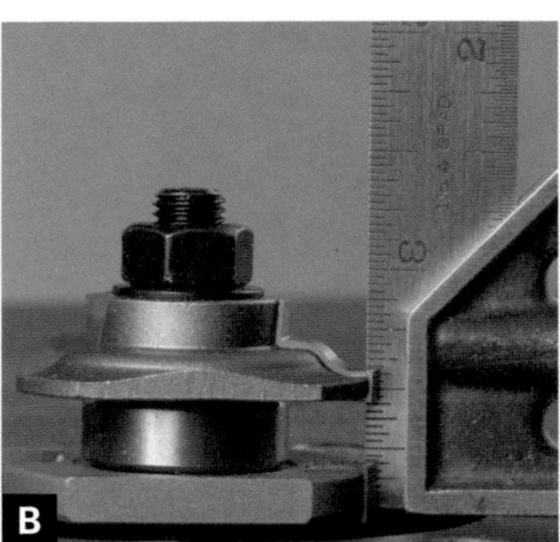

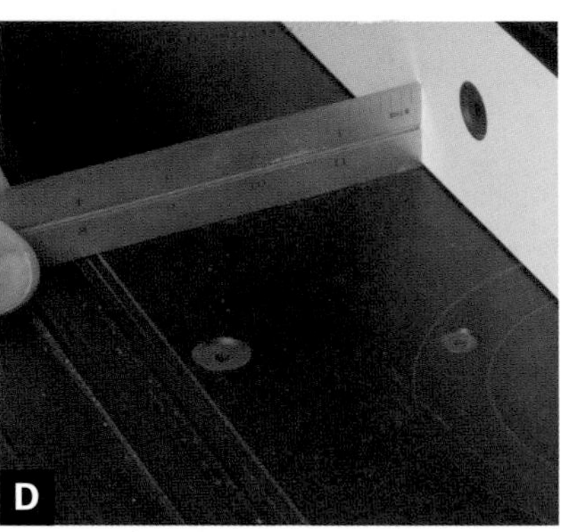

Reversible Door Bit

If your woodworking budget is limited and/or you only need to make an occasional door, then you'll probably want to consider using a reversible cope-and-stick bit **(A)**.

After you mill the stock for the frame, the first step is to cut the cope on the ends of the rails. Begin the setup process by adjusting the height of the bit so that a small "fillet" or step is created above the sticking profile **(B)**. Next, position the fence tangent to the bearing on the bit **(C)**. As you position the fence, make certain that it is parallel to the miter-gauge slot **(D)**. Next, reduce the fence opening **(E)** and position a guard over the bit **(F)**. The final step of the setup is to attach a backing board to the miter gauge for additional stock support **(G)**. Now make the cope cut on the ends of the rails **(H)**.

To cut the sticking profile and groove, you'll first need to rearrange the parts of the bit on the arbor. First, remove the arbor nut. To safely remove the nut without damaging the bit, secure it in the router collet **(I)**. Next, place the parts on a table to familiarize yourself with them **(J)**. Now, stack the parts on the arbor according to the manufacturer's instructions and secure the assembly with the arbor nut.

Next, adjust the bit height to match the cope profile that you cut earlier **(K)**. Lock the fence in place tangent to the guide bearing. Now, for your personal safety, secure a guard over the bit and position a featherboard to hold the stock against the fence. When making the cut, remember to use a push stick to distance your hands **(L)**.

Mast-R-Fence
JessEm Tool Company
F

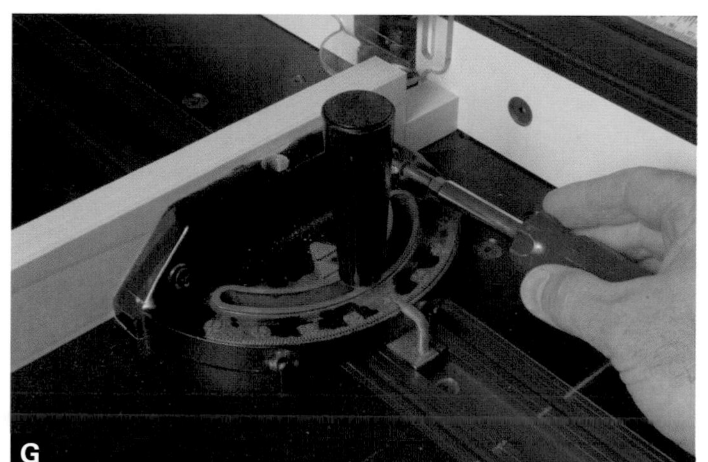
G

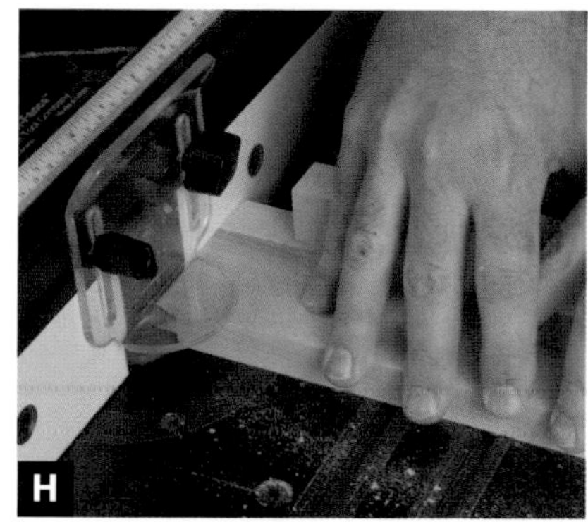
H

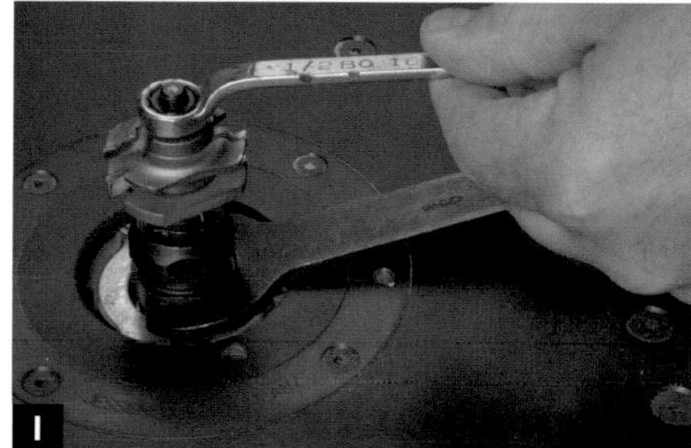
I

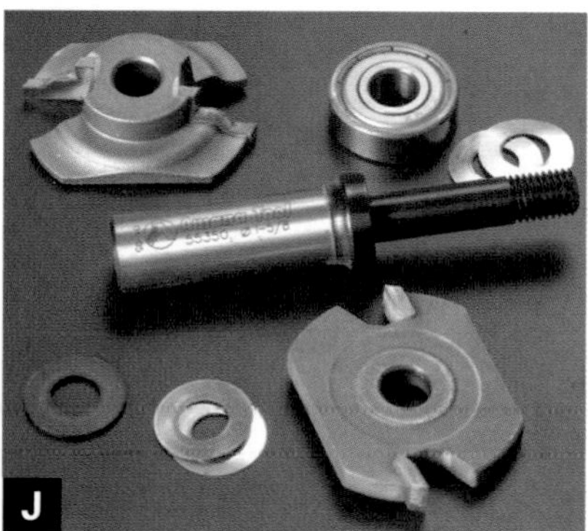
J

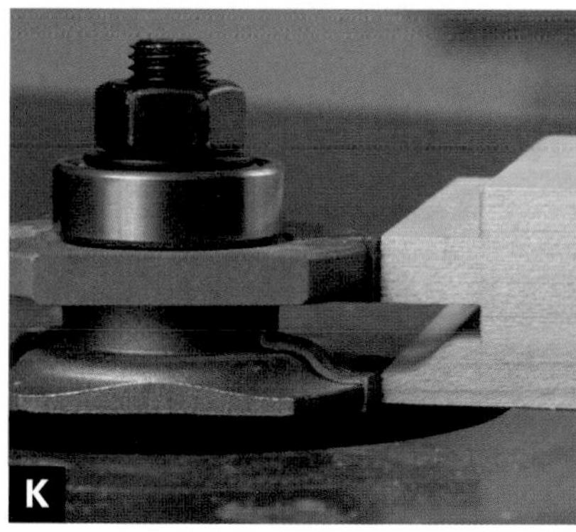
K

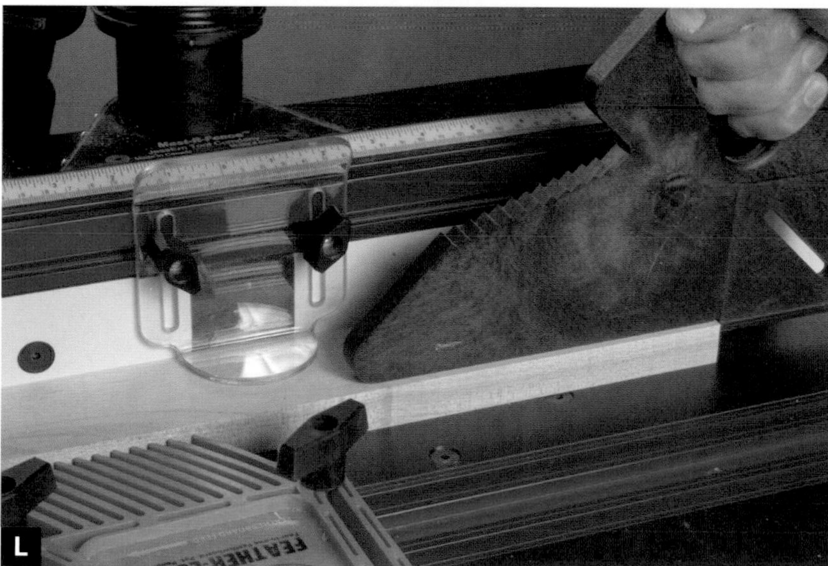
Mast-R-Fence
L

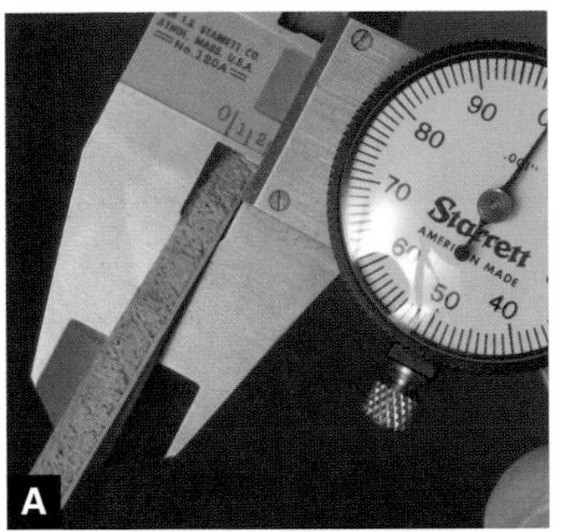

A

B

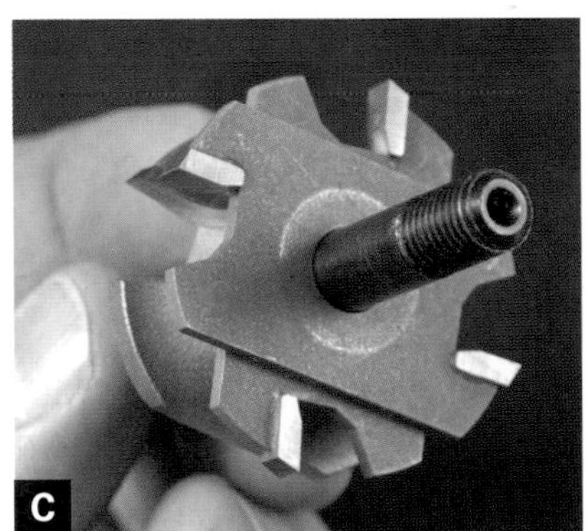

C

D

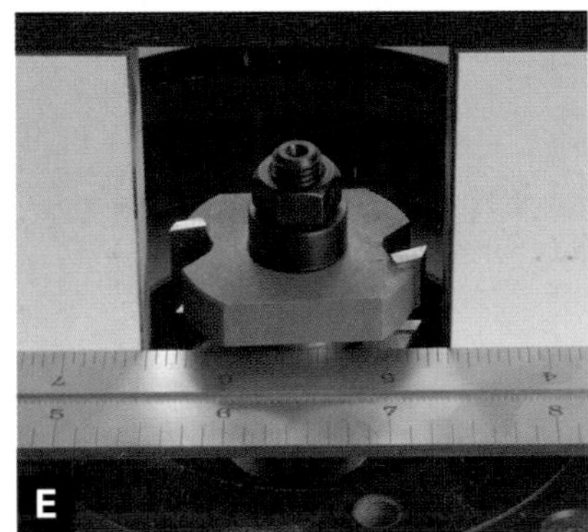

E

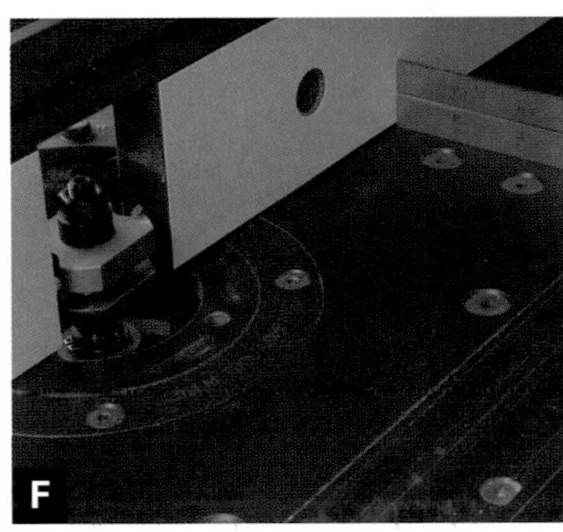

F

Adjustable Door Bit

When you're making frame-and-panel doors, a good method for adding strength to the assembly is to use plywood for the panel and glue it into the frame groove. To compensate for the undersize plywood that is so common today, some bits are adjustable. These bits feature stacking cutters and shims that allow you to fine-tune the groove to fit the plywood.

As with any cope-and-stick bits, you'll want to first cut the cope on the ends of the horizontal frame members or rails. Begin by measuring the thickness of the plywood with a dial caliper **(A)**. Next, secure the cope bit in the collet and loosen the arbor nut **(B)**. Following the manufacturer's instructions, stack the parts to achieve the required spacing. As you stack the parts, remember that the cutters must face counterclockwise when viewed from the threaded end of the arbor **(C)**.

Replace the arbor nut and adjust the bit height to create a small fillet, or step, at the top of the profile **(D)**. Now position the fence tangent to the guide bearing **(E)**. As you secure the fence to the table, be certain that it is parallel to the miter-gauge slot **(F)**. Now reduce the fence opening **(G)** and position a guard over the bit **(H)**. To complete the setup, fasten a backing board to the miter gauge **(I)**. Now cut the cope on the ends of the rails **(J)**.

Before cutting the "sticking" along the edges of the stock, adjust the bit to match the thickness of the plywood. Next, mount the bit in the collet and adjust the height to correspond to the cope cut **(K)**. Position the fence tangent to the guide bearing and cut the profile on all the frame members **(L)**.

G

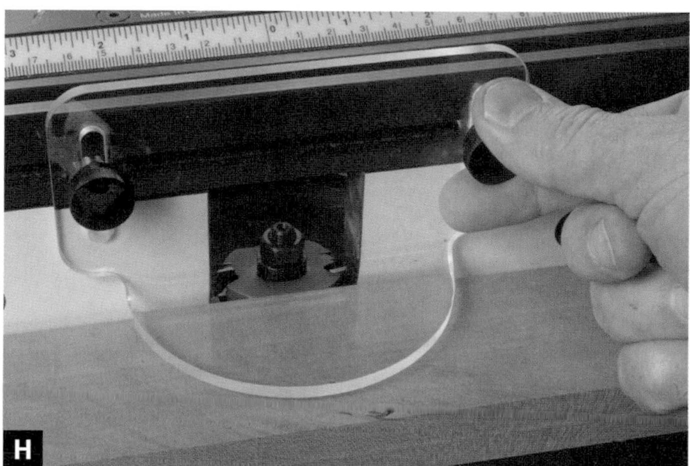
H

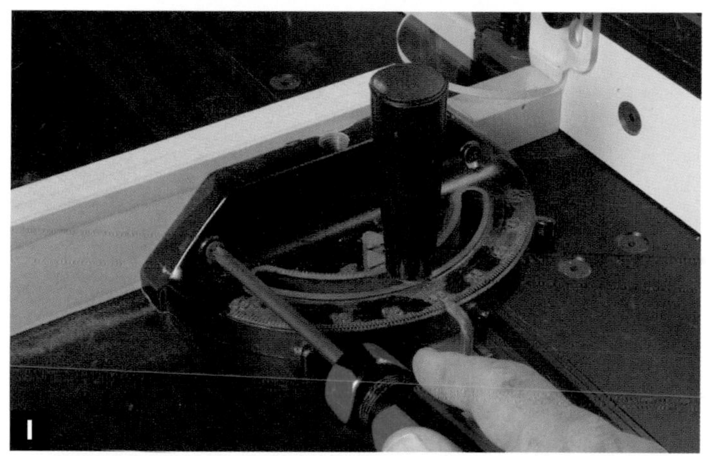
I

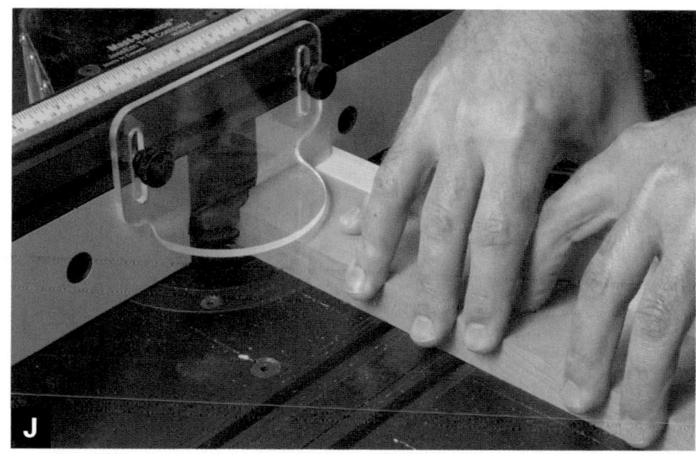
J

K

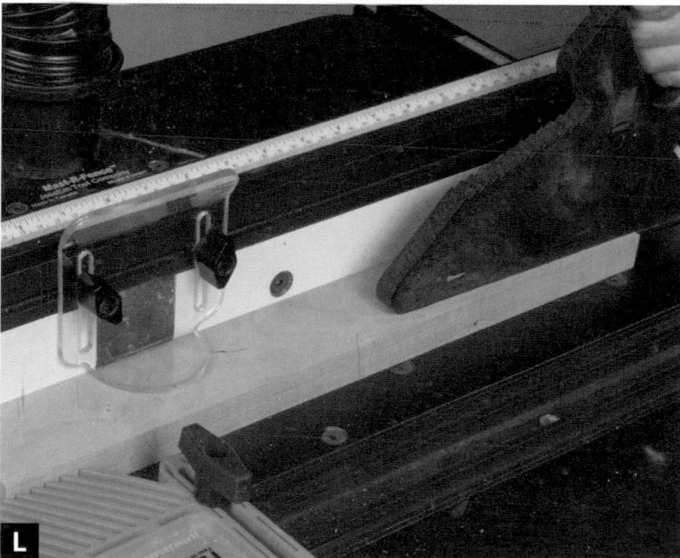
L

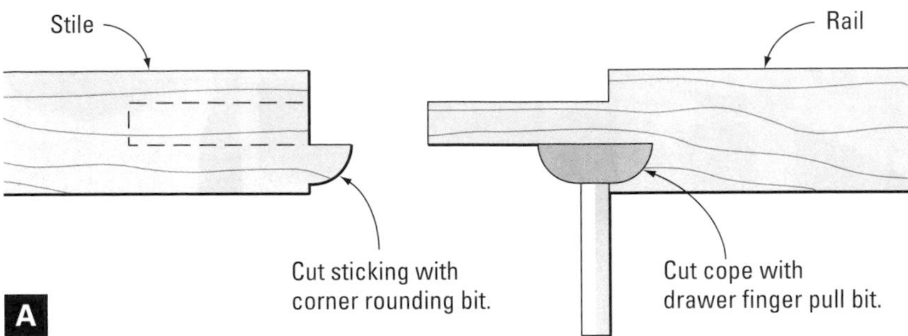

B

C

Coped Mortise-and-Tenon

Mortise-and-tenon joints are commonly used to join rail-and-stile framework for doors **(A)**. Sometimes a simple molding profile is shaped along the inside edges of the frame as an embellishment. There are number of cope-and-stick router bit sets for efficiently producing doors, but they create a short tenon rather than the long tenon associated with traditional work. While cope-and-stick bits make door construction fast and easy, the stubby tenon created by these sets lacks the strength and longevity of a true mortise-and-tenon joint. A much stronger method is to use a long tenon and cope the tenon shoulder with a bit that allows the tenon to pass unobstructed over the top of the bit.

In this example, I'm using a 3⁄8-in. roundover bit to create the decorative sticking along the interior frame edges, and a 3⁄8-in.-radius "finger pull" bit to cope the shoulder **(B)**. Although this bit was designed to cut a finger pull along the lower edge of a drawer front, it is ideally suited for coping the shoulder along a tenon. This method is a unique way to create an authentic cope-and-stick joint with the strength and longevity of a traditional mortise-and-tenon. Here, I'm cutting a rabbet for glass or screen, but another option is to cut a groove for a panel.

Begin by laying out and cutting the mortise-and-tenon joints on the frame. The next step is to cope the shoulder of the tenon. Mount the finger-pull bit in the router table and adjust the bit height so that it just grazes the underside of the tenon **(C)**. Close the fence opening, as the fence will be used to support the end of the tenon and correctly locate the cut. Position the fence so that the bit produces a quarter of a circle when the cope is cut. Because the bit is not between the fences, it's important to position a guard over the bit to provide a barrier for your hands. Now use the miter gauge to support the stock and cut the cope **(D)**.

The next step is to shape the sticking profile with the 3/8-in. roundover bit. It's critical to adjust the height of the bit so that the cut from the roundover bit intersects the cope cut to create the appearance of a miter **(E)**. It's a good idea to make test cuts on sample stock to arrive at the final setup **(F)**.

The last step is to cut a rabbet along the inside edges of the framework. The rabbet forms a recess to accept glass or perhaps screen for a window or door. First, adjust the height of the rabbeting bit to cut just below the sticking profile **(G)**. The depth of the rabbet should be 3/8 in., which is equal to the size of the sticking bit. Now cut the rabbet **(H)** and assemble the joint **(I)**.

D

E

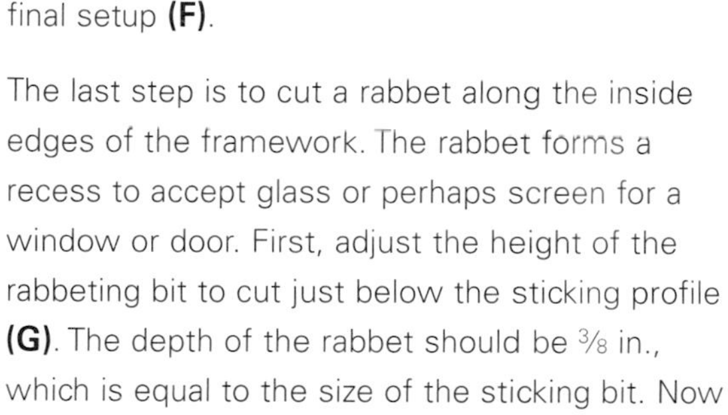

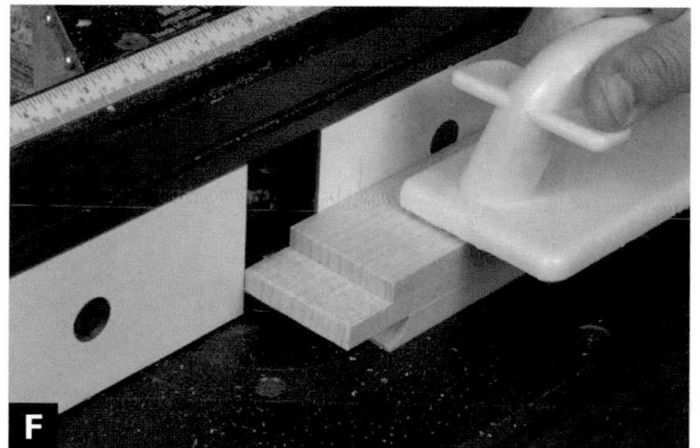
F

G

H

I

A

B

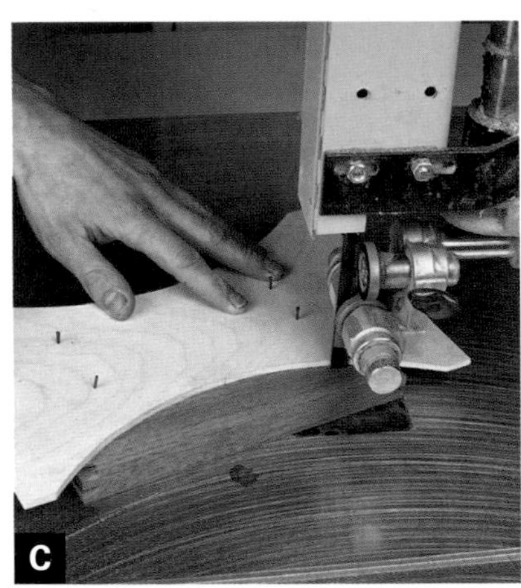
C

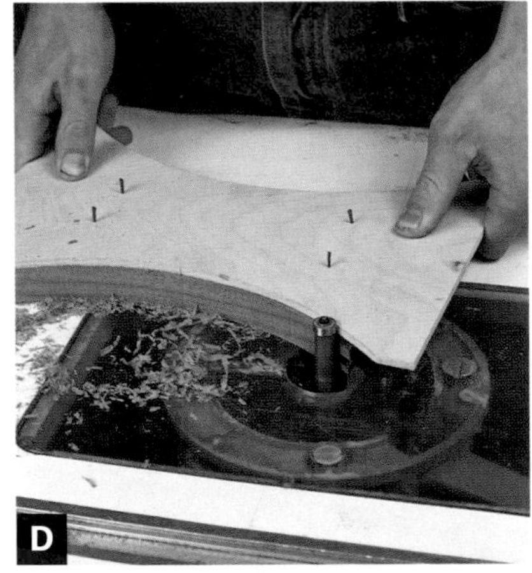
D

E

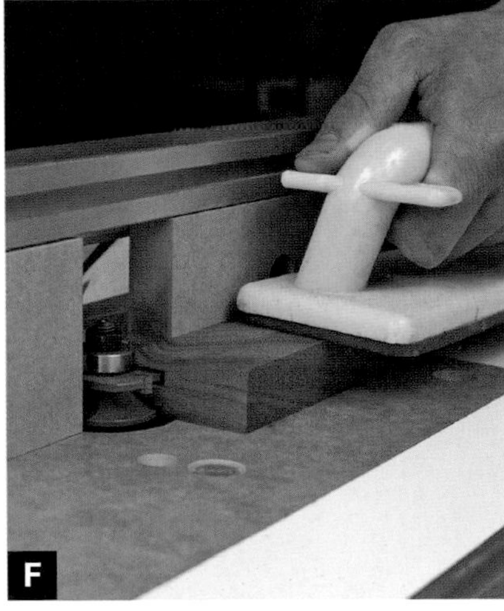
F

Arched Door with Cope-and-Stile Bits

It may seem that making an arched door with a frame that matches the panel is complicated—but it's really not. The key is making an accurate, full-scale layout.

Begin by drawing a rectangle to represent the outside dimensions of the door.

Next, use a compass to draw an arch to represent the top rail. Then, using the same center point, shorten the compass setting and draw an arch to represent the top edge of the panel. When you're satisfied with the drawing, mill the frame parts.

The next step is to set the bit height **(A)**; then you're ready to shape the cope on the rail ends **(B)**. Use a miter gauge for support.

Now bandsaw the arch in the top rail **(C)**; use your drawing to determine the radius. Next, fasten a template to the rail and trim it flush with the router table **(D)**; then switch router bits and mill the sticking and groove while the template is still attached **(E)**. Remember to shape the stiles and bottom rail as well. Because the stock is straight rather than curved, it makes sense to use the fence **(F)**.

With the frame completed, turn your attention to the panel. First, mill the panel to size. Then bandsaw the arch and trim it flush with the template **(G)**. When fastening the template, drive the nails in the edges of the panel where they will be shaped away.

Now you're ready to shape the panel. Remove the template and begin with the arch. Use a box fence for safety. Position the arch against the fence **(H)** and pivot it into the spinning bit **(I)**. Next, shape the opposite end and then the edges **(J)**.

The last steps are to sand the panel and assemble the door **(K)**.

G

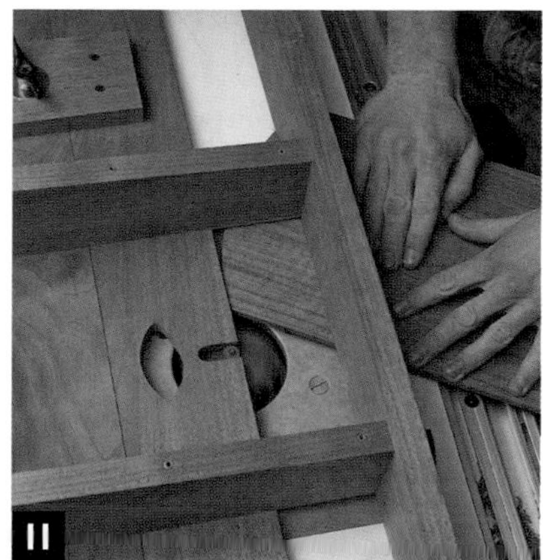

H

I

J

K

A

Table

First cut
Cope setup
Stock face up

Table

Second cut
Sticking setup
Stock face down

B

C

Sash Door

A sash is a traditional framework for glass panes. As with a paneled door, the outer frame members are called rails and stiles. The narrow bars that divide the glass into smaller, individual panes are called mullions. The intersections at each corner are coped, which creates the appearance of a miter **(A)**.

To make a sash door, it's best to begin with a drawing that shows the overall size as well as the dimensions of the individual frame members. When milling the stock, cut the material for the mullions oversized in width. This will make it easier to work. After coping, you can rip it to final width.

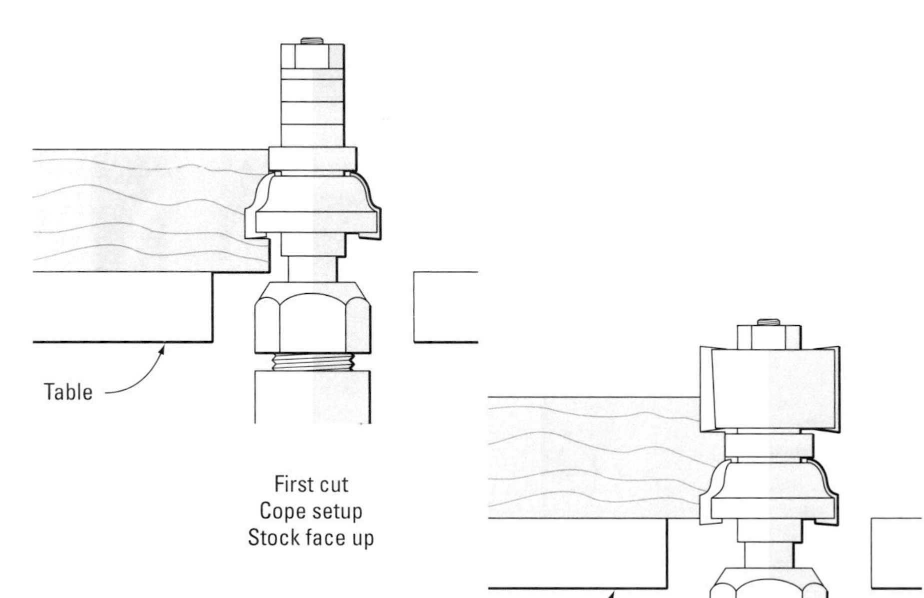

The bit used in this photo-essay is reversible **(B)** and was used to rout both the cope and stick profiles. To use a reversible bit, you'll need to disassemble it and rearrange the cutters for each sequence of cuts. Since it's best to begin with the cope cut, you'll want to arrange the cutters for that profile first. To remove the arbor nut, first mount the bit in the router collet **(C)**. After rearranging the parts on the arbor, adjust the bit height **(D)**. Next, position the fence tangent to the guide bearing on the bit **(E)**. Also, check to see that the fence is parallel to the miter gauge slot **(F)**. To provide optimum support for the workpiece, reduce the fence opening as much as possible **(G)**.

Attach a backing board to the miter gauge **(H)**. The backing board will support the stock close to the bit and prevent tearout on the trailing edge of the workpiece. Also remember to place a guard in position over the bit **(I)**.

(Text continues on p. 196.)

D

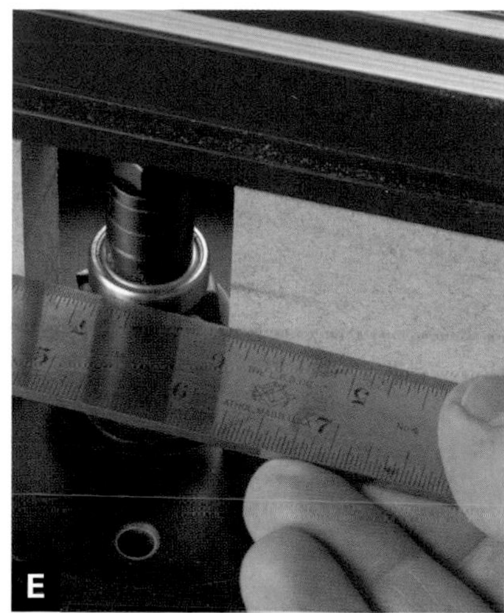

E

F

G

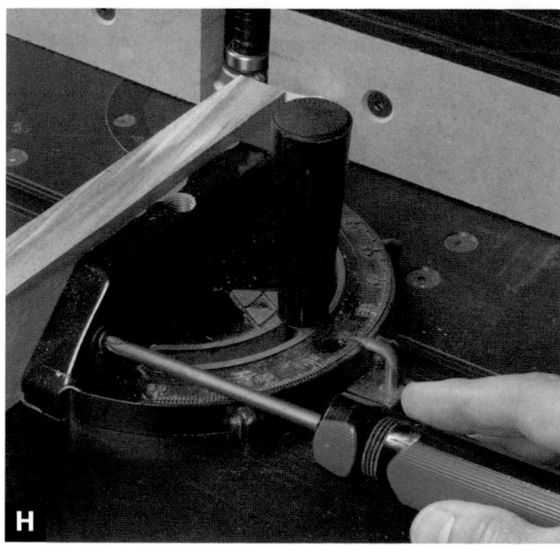

H

I

J

K

Now cut the cope on the ends of the rails and mullions **(J)**.

Next, refer to the drawings from the manufacturer and rearrange the bit for the sticking profile. Remember, as you stack the cutters on the arbor, they should face counterclockwise when viewed from the end **(K)**. To find the correct height, position the coped profile next to the bit **(L)**. Set the fence tangent to the bearing **(M)**. Now use a push stick and make the cut on the rails and stiles **(N)**. Use the jig shown to safely shape the narrow mullions **(O, P)**.

L

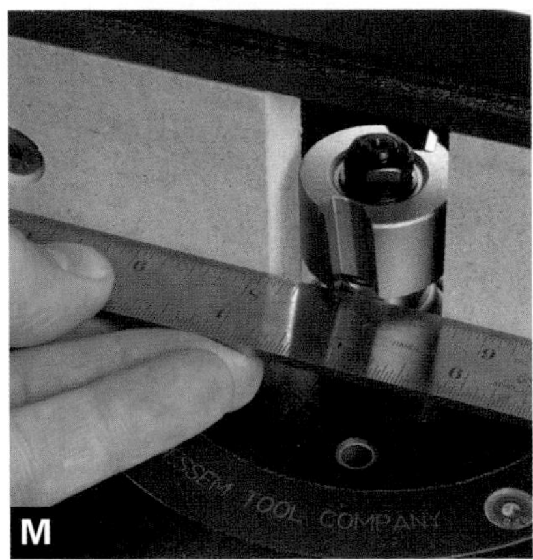
M

N

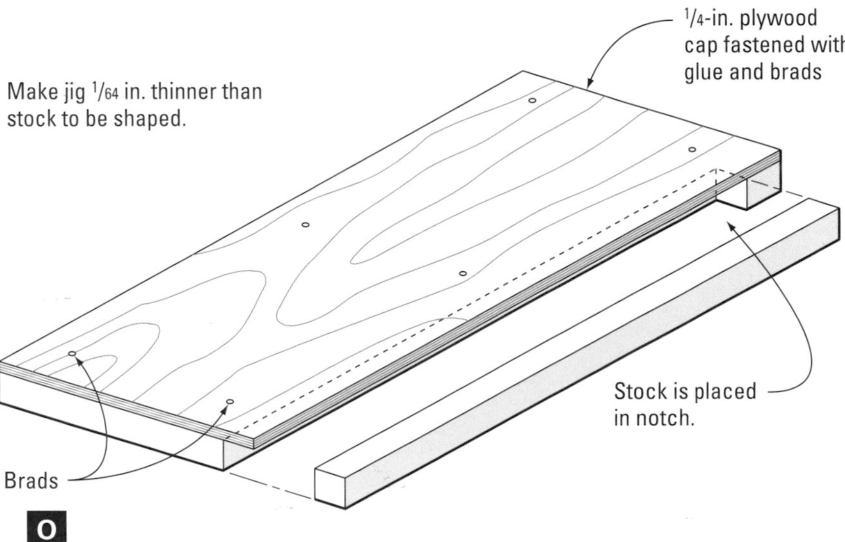

O

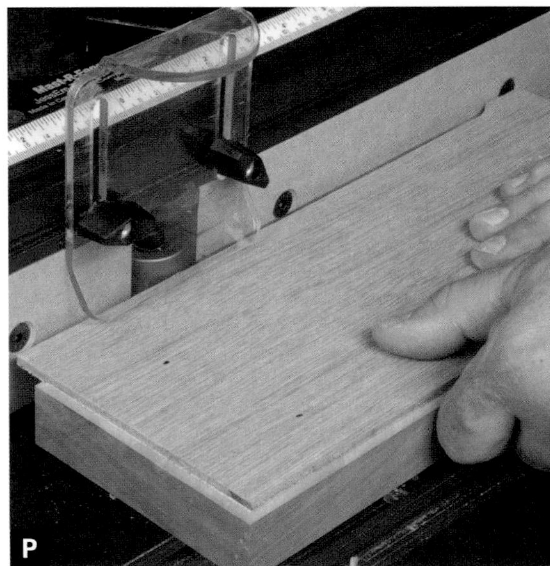
P

Arched Light Sash Door

Constructing a sash-type door with interlocking bars is another variation on the cope-and-stick construction shown on p. 182. The key is accurate layout and machine setup.

Check the fit frequently and make any necessary adjustments.

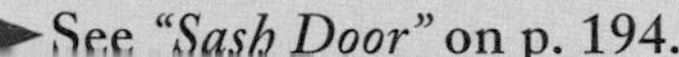

➤ See *"Sash Door"* on p. 194.

Begin by accurately milling the stock. Make the stock for the bars wide enough for two; this makes feeding the work through machines safer and more accurate. For greatest accuracy, clamp matching pieces together and transfer the lines **(A)**.

The location of the mortise in relationship to the sticking is critical. For this reason, shape the sticking on the stiles first **(B)**. Then cut the mortises with a hollow chisel according to the layout **(C)**. When correctly positioned, the mortise falls just on the edge of the sticking **(D)**.

Next, cut the tenons. Since the tenon shoulders are offset, cut the face of each tenon **(E)**, and then adjust the setup for the second shoulder **(F)**.

Before bandsawing the curves, cut the cope on the tenon shoulder **(G)**. Then bandsaw the arches in the top rail **(H)** and smooth them with a spindle sander.

(Text continues on p. 198.)

[TIP] Remember to check the cope for fit to the sticking; it may be necessary to adjust the cutter height, fence position, or both.

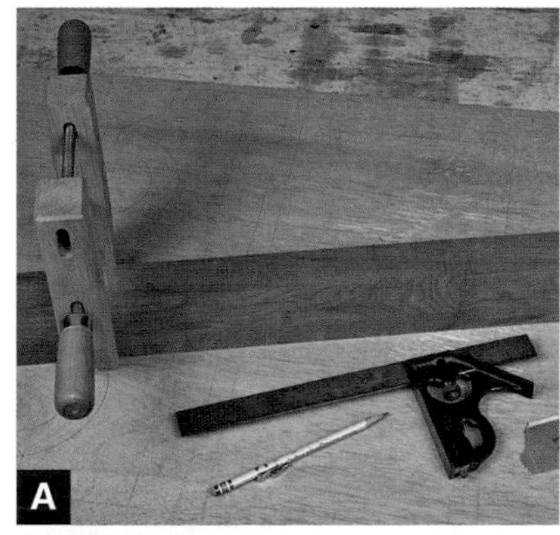
A

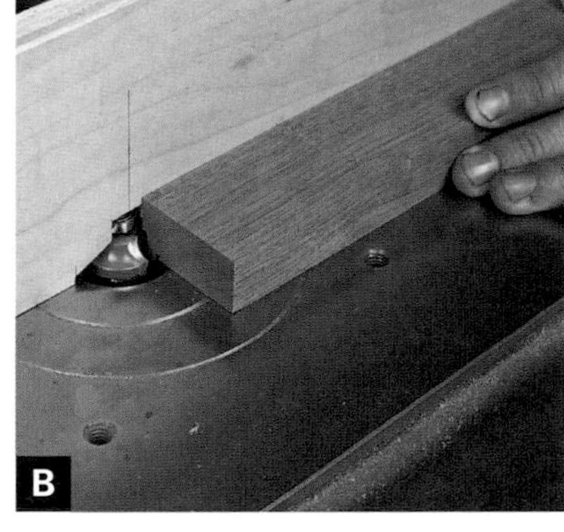
B

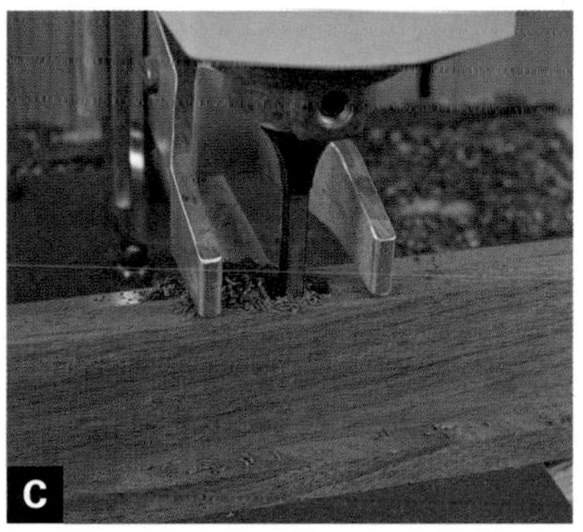
C

D

E

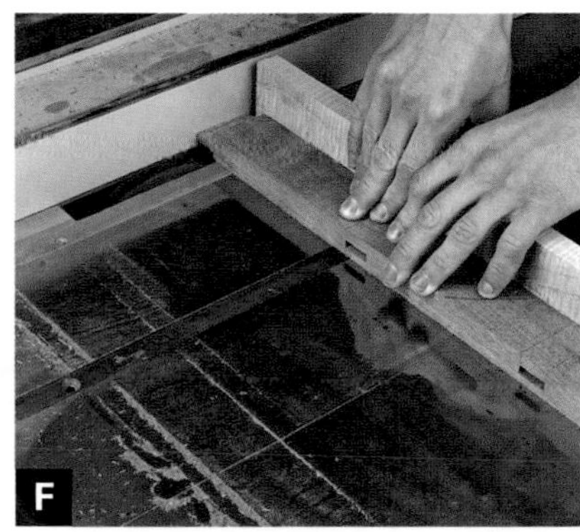
F

G

H

I

J

The last two steps are to shape the sticking and the rabbet. But first you'll need to rip the narrow sash bars to final width. To shape the bars safely, take a few extra minutes to shape the jig shown on p. 196. This jig will add much-needed mass to the otherwise narrow stock **(I)**. When cutting the second rabbet, fill the first rabbet with a stick tacked into the jig **(J)**. To shape the sticking and to rabbet the arches, it's necessary to use a starting pin or block as a fulcrum when entering the cut **(K)**.

Once all the cuts are made, fit each joint individually and check the fit. To assemble the framework, fit the sash bars into the rails first **(L)** and then the stiles. Gently tap the joints together with a mallet **(M)**. Finally, clamp the door and set it on a flat surface while the glue dries **(N)**.

K

L

M

N

Raised Panel

If you wanted to create raised-door panels years ago, you would need to do it by hand or purchase a shaper. Nowadays, panel-raising bits are available for use with the router **(A)**. But first a word of caution: Bits for shaping raised panels are very large and should only be used with a guard. Additionally, never exceed the manufacturer's recommended rpm. Also, routers simply lack the power of shapers, so you'll need to make the cut in several passes to avoid stalling the router.

Begin by mounting the bit securely in the collet. Insert the bit fully and then back it out 1⁄16 in. **(B)**. Next, adjust the bit height to the depth of the finished profile **(C)**, and reduce the opening at the fence as much as possible **(D)**. The final

(Text continues on p. 200.)

A

B

C

D

E

position of the fence should be tangent with the guide bearing **(E)**. Next, lower the bit for the first pass, and position a guard such as the Bench Dog Panel-Loc over the bit **(F)**.

Now you're ready to make the cut. Always begin with the end grain **(G)** and finish the process with the long grain **(H)**.

F

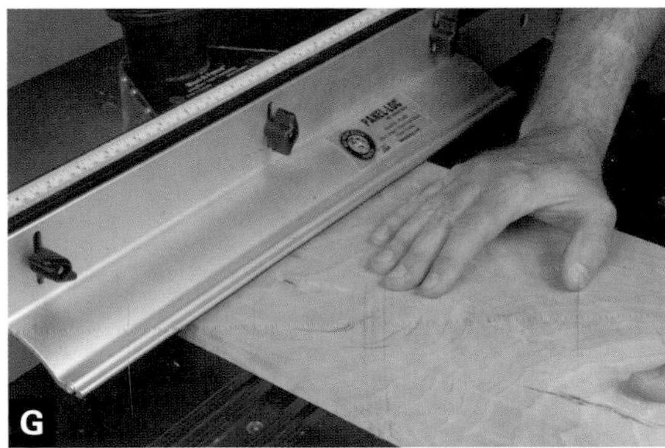

G

H

Raised Curved Panel

Raising a curved panel requires a vertical router bit and a curved fence to guide and support the workpiece **(A)**.

First, bandsaw a curve into wide stock for use as a fence. After cutting a small opening for the panel bit, attach the fence to the router table fence.

To make the cut, feed the panel slowly and keep it firmly against the fence **(B)**. After shaping the curved ends, shape the edges with the same bit and a straight fence. To maintain the correct angle while shaping, feel the panel between the fence and a stick clamped to the table **(C)**. Pushing the panel face against the fence wedges it between the fence and the stick. This prevents it from rocking or tilting as it passes the router bit.

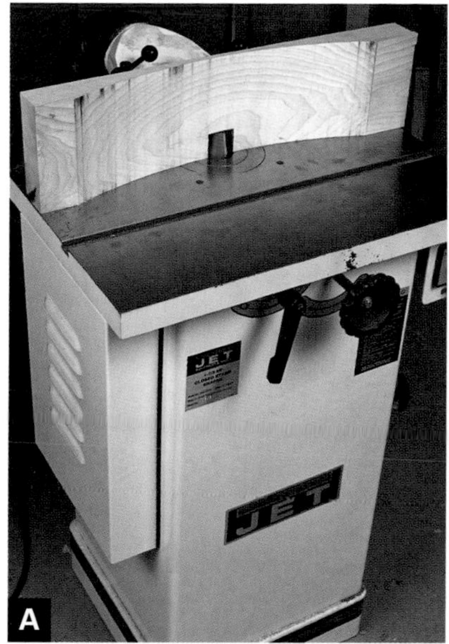

A

B

C

B

Shaping a Lipped Door Edge

Unlike an overlay door that closes against the cabinet face, a lipped door looks refined. That's because most of the door's thickness fits inside the cabinet and the remaining lip is shaped with a delicate thumbnail profile.

The example I'm using here is the pendulum door from the waist of a tall clock. The top of the door has a decorative cutout. After bandsawing the top of the door, use a flush-trimming router bit and a template to remove the bandsaw marks **(A)**. Then carve the inside corners where the router bit didn't reach **(B)**. Next, use a roundover bit to shape the thumbnail profile around the perimeter of the door **(C)**. Set the height of the bit to create a $\frac{1}{16}$-in. fillet next to the thumbnail profile. This fillet is important; it creates another fine detail to capture light and create a shadow line.

After the thumbnail, shape the rabbet that allows most of the door to fit within the opening. The bearing on the rabbeting bit can ride along the thumbnail without damaging it; just don't press too hard **(D)**.

[TIP] A fence can be used to limit the rabbet's depth along the straight portions of the door.

Afterward, carve the inside corners on the top of the door to complete the thumbnail profile **(E)**.

Lock Mortise

All doors require hardware—and the most efficient way to cut the recess for a hinge or lock is with a router. In fact, a laminate trimmer is the best choice. Its compact size makes it easy to control, yet it has plenty of power for the task.

For this essay, I'm using a half-mortise lock. This traditional lock is a good example because it actually requires two mortises: A deep mortise for the lock mechanism and a shallow mortise for the thin brass backplate.

Begin by laying out and drilling the hole for the key **(A)**. Next, lay out the pattern for the lock body and backplate **(B)**. Now set the cutting depth of the bit to the thickness of the lock **(C)**. As you rout the mortise, be careful not to exceed the layout lines **(D)**. Now use a chisel to square the corners of the mortise **(E)**.

(Text continues on p. 204.)

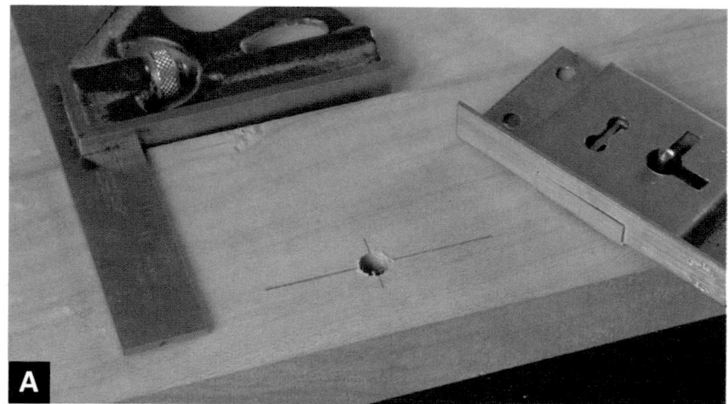

A

B

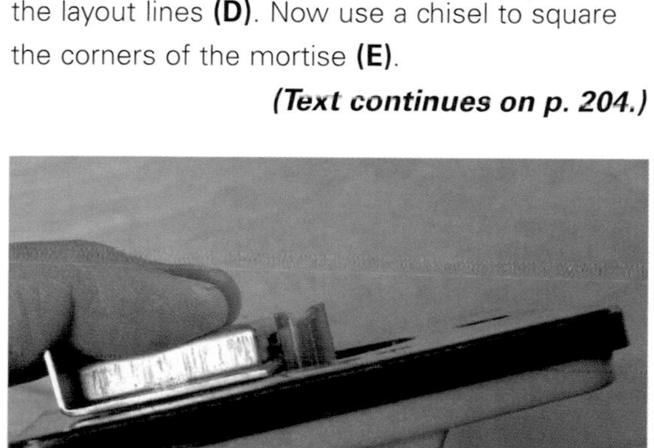

C

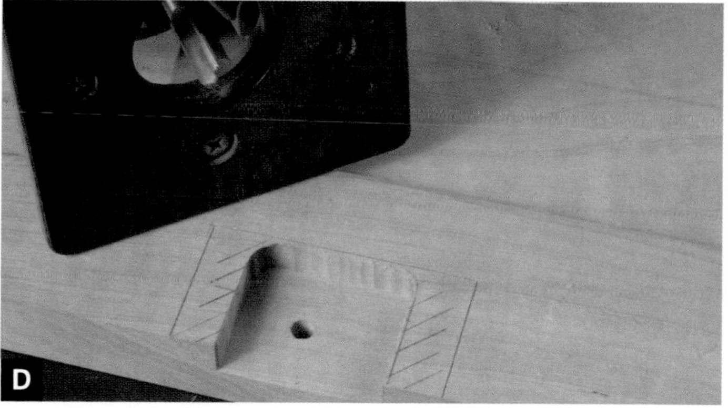

D

E

F

G

H

The next step is to rout the shallow mortise for the backplate. First, set the cutting depth to the backplate thickness **(F)**. Now carefully rout the mortise, taking care not to rout beyond the layout lines **(G)**. Now square the corners and clean up the edges with a chisel to complete the job **(H)**.

Sliding Dovetail Drawers

If you'd like to make a kitchen full of drawers but don't want to take the time to cut rows of dovetails, then the stopped sliding dovetail is a great choice **(A)**. The joint is strong and can be quickly and easily cut on the router table. Setup takes a few minutes, but once it's complete, you can rout an entire set of drawers for a shop or kitchen in short order **(B)**. Best of all, the sliding dovetail is strong, yet hidden from view, resulting in sturdy, attractive drawers that will stand up to the rigors of hard use.

To make the drawer, dovetail sockets are first cut into the back surface of the drawer front and then mating dovetails are cut on the ends of the drawer sides. All that remains is to rout dadoes to accept the back, and grooves to accept the drawer bottom.

Begin by mounting a 1/2-in.-dia. dovetail bit into your table router, adjusting the bit height to 3/8 in., which is approximately one-half the thickness of a typical drawer front **(C)**. The resulting 3/8-in.-deep socket will create a strong joint without weakening the drawer front. When using thicker or thinner drawer front stock, adjust the socket depth to suit.

Close the fence opening completely **(D)** and then position the fence the correct distance from the center of the bit **(E)**. As seen in the drawing, **(F)** a distance of 1 1/16 in. from the fence to the center of the bit allows 1/2 in. of space to accommodate a typical commercial drawer runner, plus 1/2 of the bit diameter, plus 1/4 in. of overlay on the cabinet face. Careful measurements are critical if the drawer slides are to work smoothly. Remember that the length of the drawer front is critical, because the position of the socket

(Text continues on p. 206.)

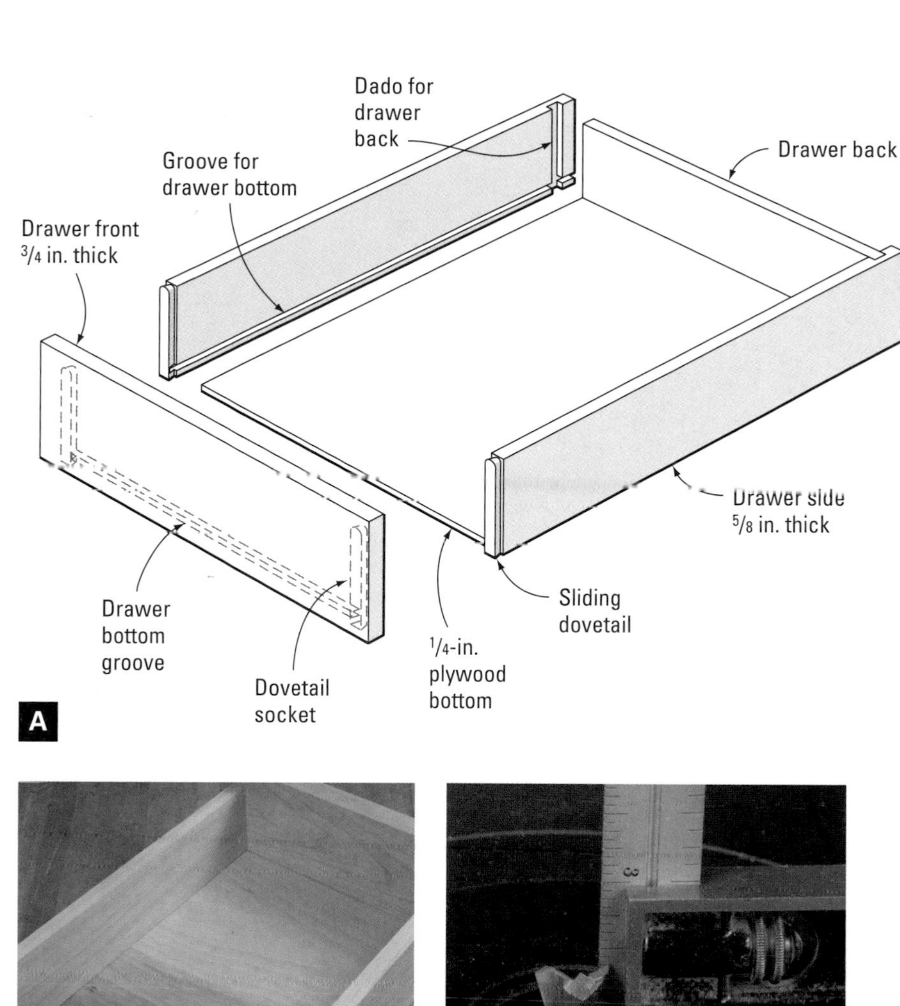

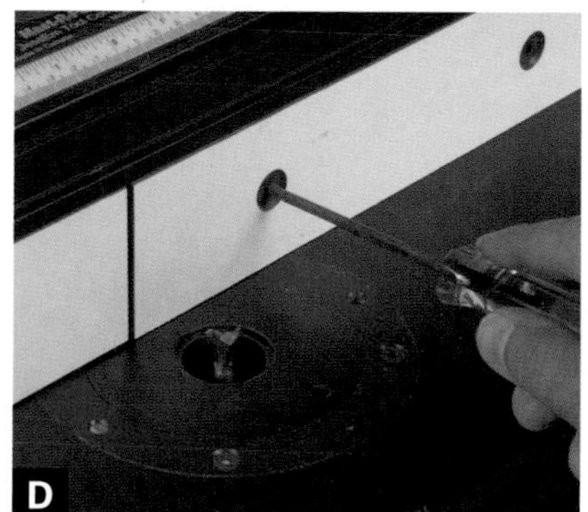

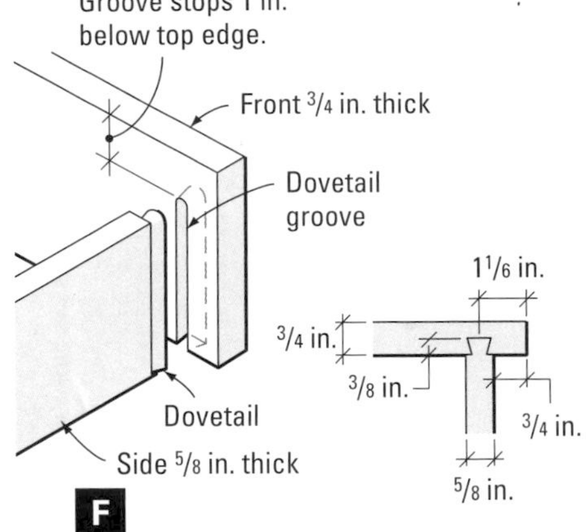

is registered from the end of the drawer front. Because a miter gauge is used to feed the workpiece, it's necessary to position the fence parallel to the miter-gauge slot **(G)**.

The socket begins at the bottom edge of the drawer front and stops an inch from the top. Because you're making a stopped groove, it's necessary to mark the stopping points on the fence. Use a block of wood to mark the fence to indicate the diameter of the bit **(H)** and then mark the stopping point of the socket on the stock **(I)**.

Begin by routing the left-hand socket. Clamp the stock to the miter gauge and feed it in the usual manner, from right to left **(J)**. Stop feeding when the layout marks on the fence and the workpiece align **(K)**. To cut the right-hand socket, you'll need to feed the stock from left to right. To prevent the bit from pushing the stock away from the fence and spoiling the cut, it's important to clamp the stock securely to the miter gauge **(L)**.

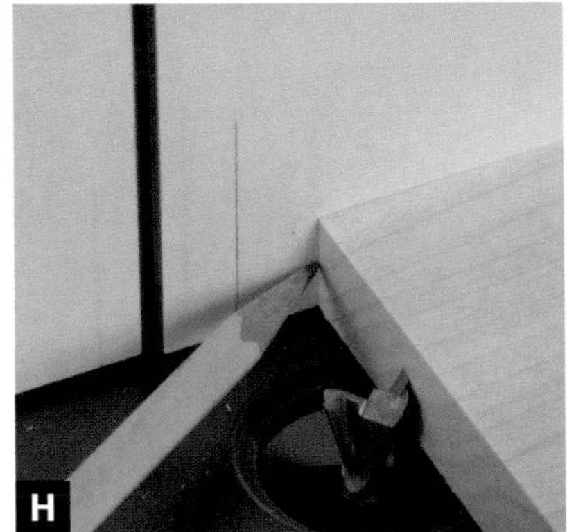

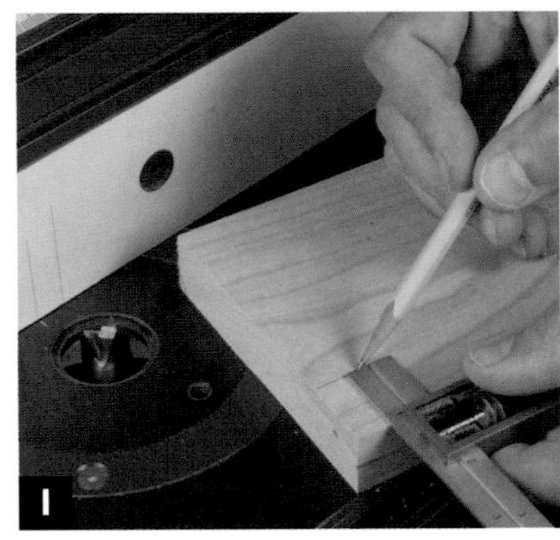

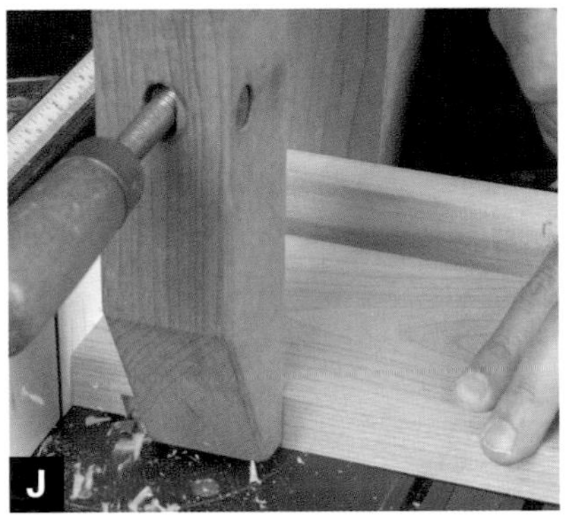

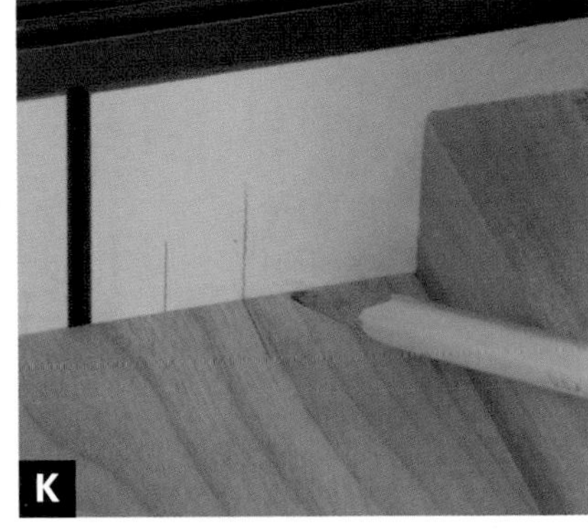

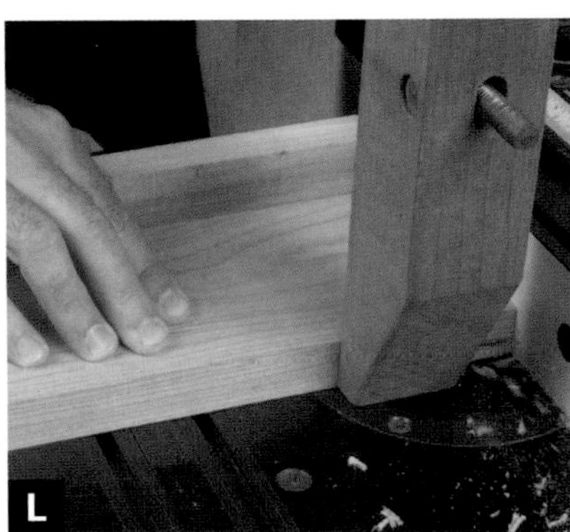

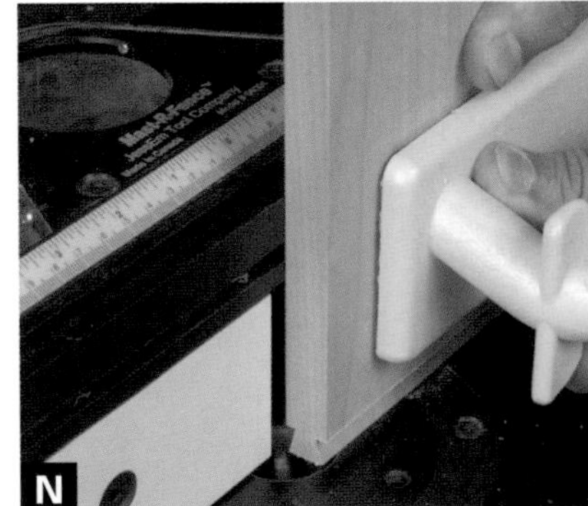

The same dovetail is now used to cut the tail. First, position the bit within the fence opening **(M)**. Next, stand the stock on end and feed it past the bit **(N)**. Two passes, one on each face, will complete the tail. The deeper the cut, the smaller the tail will be and vice versa. Test the setup with a sample board before routing the actual workpieces. Finish up by rounding the corner of each tail to correspond to the rounded end of the socket **(O)**.

The next step is to rout the groove for the drawer bottom. Close down the fence opening, mount a ¼-in.-dia. straight bit in the router, and position the fence ¼ in. from the bit. Then rout the grooves **(P)**, remembering to orient the parts as necessary to create a left-hand and a right-hand drawer side **(Q)**. When making the groove in the drawer front, don't rout beyond the dovetail sockets **(R)**.

To rout the dadoes for the drawer back, use the fence to position the cut. A push block will make it easy to maintain contact with the fence while keeping your hands positioned a safe distance from the bit **(S)**.

To assemble the drawer, apply glue and slide the parts together **(T)**. Next, measure between the drawer sides at the drawer front and add twice the depth of the drawer back dado to determine the length of the drawer back. After making the back, apply glue to the rear joint and slide the back into place **(U)**. A couple of small nails through each side will reinforce the joint **(V)**. The last step is to cut a piece of ¼-in.-thick plywood for the drawer bottom and slide it into place **(W)**.

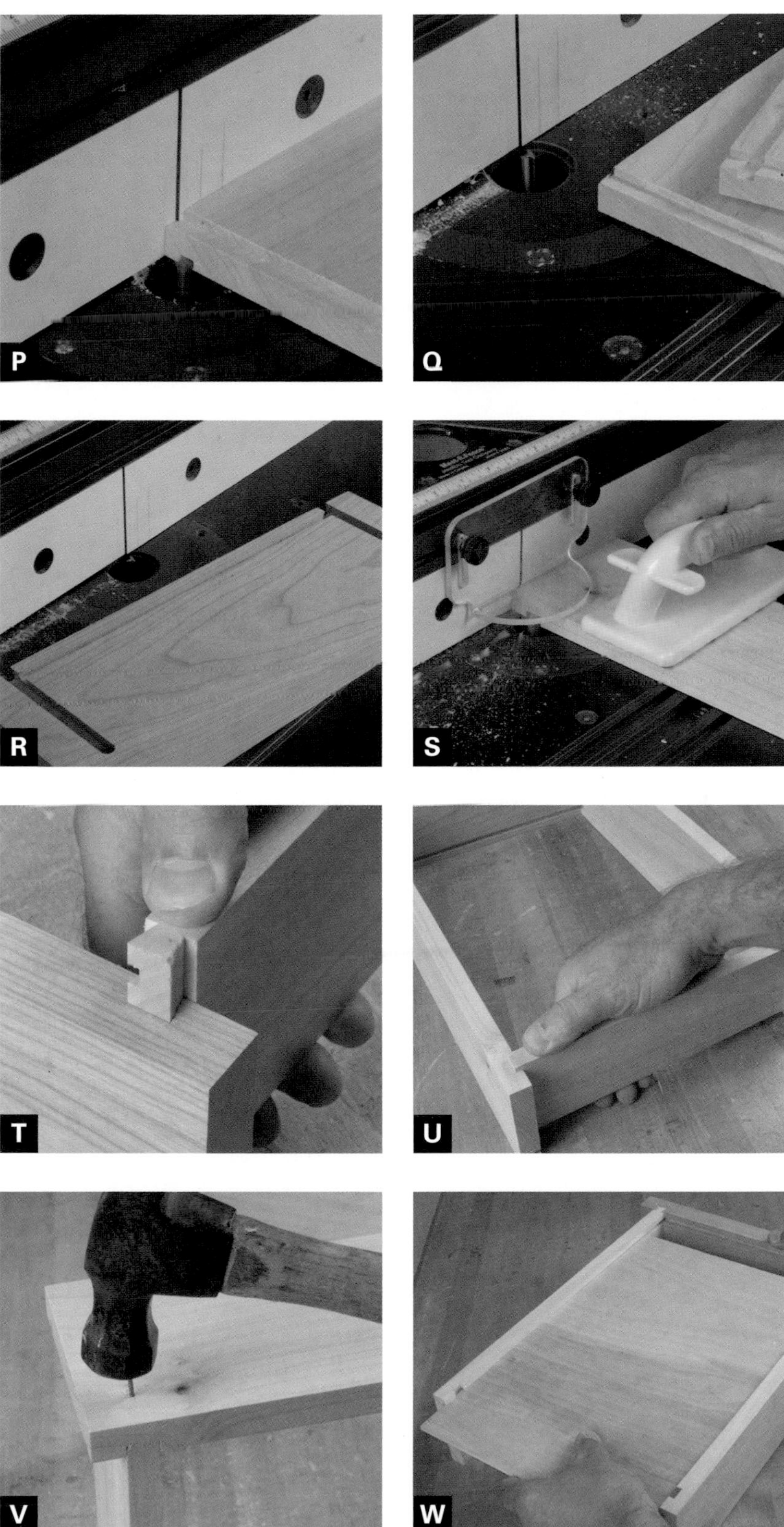

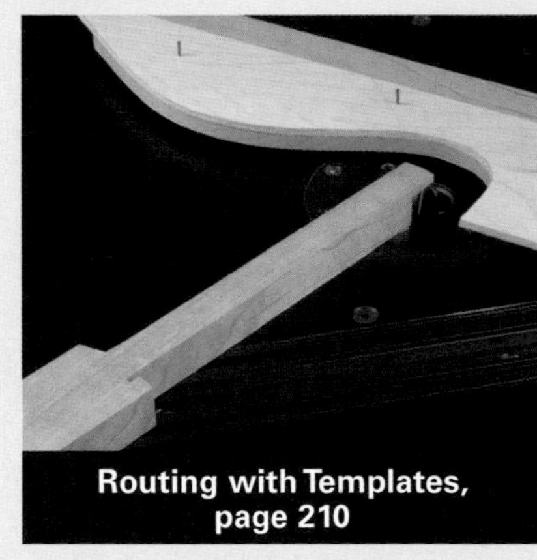
Routing with Templates, page 210

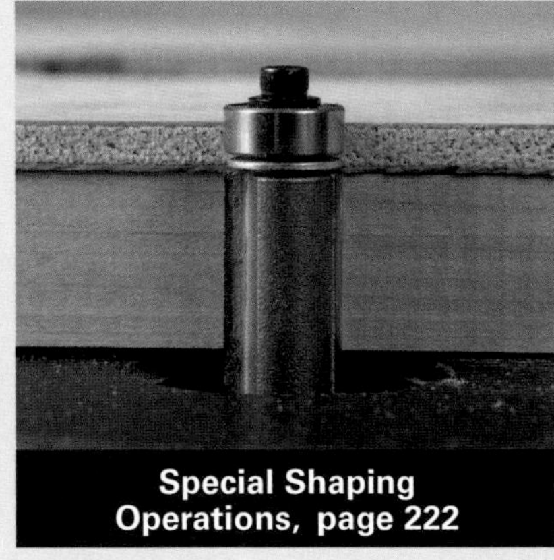
Special Shaping Operations, page 222

PART FOUR

Special Shaping

THERE'S NO FASTER METHOD for making multiple workpieces than using a template, and the router lends itself perfectly to this particular task. As you'll see in this part of the book, template-routing involves attaching a template to the workpiece in order to guide either a bearing on the router bit or a sleeve-shaped bushing that's mounted to the router base. When pieces are cut out using a template and a guide, they'll all be identical, whether you're making two pieces or twenty. The technique is often used to clean up bandsaw marks after you rough-saw curved pieces like table legs. And it can even be employed to cut a profile completely across the edge of a tabletop or other projecting surface.

In this part, I'll also address fluting and dishing operations, which are both decorative processes that can add a very distinctive touch to your furniture.

Routing with Templates

Using a Bearing

Using a Bushing

Without a doubt, one of the most efficient and productive woodworking techniques is routing with a template. With this method, a template is fastened to the workpiece to provide a guide for a bearing or bushing to follow as the bit shapes the profile, as shown in the drawing on the facing page. Template routing allows you to produce identical pieces, whether two or twenty, and eliminates the tedium of smoothing bandsaw marks with a sander or file. It's a particularly good method to use when you need to shape away the entire edge of a curved workpiece (see the bottom drawing on the facing page).

Curves with Templates

Curves—such as the arched moldings used in doors, clocks, and many case pieces—add beauty and visual interest to furniture. They capture the imagination and draw you in for a closer look. For practical purposes, curves can be divided by type—circles, ellipses, freeform or S curves, and arcs (an arc being a segment of a circle).

Curves and arcs are easily shaped with a template, as shown in the top photo on the facing page. After the curve is bandsawn slightly oversized, a template and straight bit are used to smooth away the saw marks. Afterwards, the profile can be shaped with

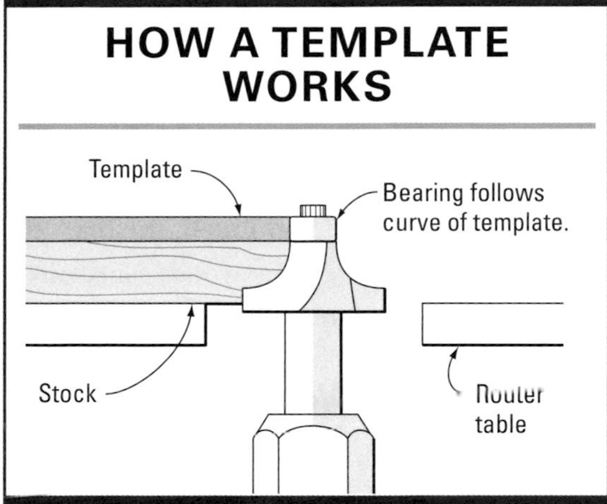

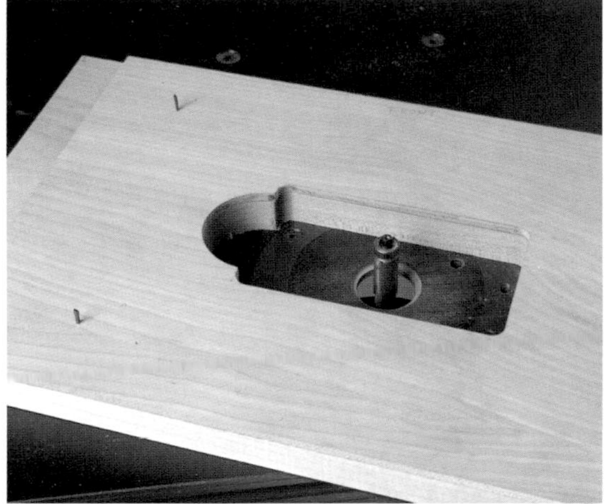

Circles, arcs, and ellipses are easily shaped with templates.

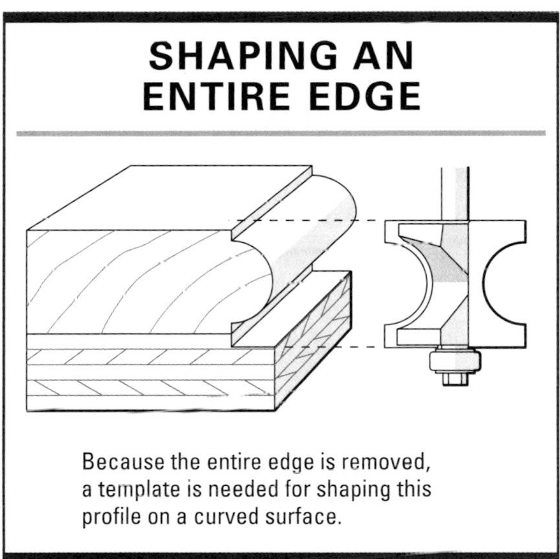

Among other things, templates allow you to shape freeform curves.

the workpiece as a guide, or if the entire edge is to be shaped, a template can be used as a guide for the bit bearing.

An S-curve molding—usually referred to as a gooseneck—can be among the most difficult moldings to shape. Routing a gooseneck molding requires an S-shaped template and an overarm pin guide for your router table. In this case, the workpiece is fastened to the template, which contacts the overhead pin in order to guide the workpiece past the bit.

➤ **See *"Curve with Template"* on p. 215.**

An unfortunate drawback to template routing is that you cannot completely shape a sharp inside corner due to the rounded cut that a spinning bit creates. One solution is to eliminate sharp inside corners from the design, but I prefer to carve the corners by hand after routing, as shown in the top photo on p. 212. Sure, the second option takes a few more minutes, but it will separate your work from the rest.

The rounded inside corner (right) created by a router bit can be hand-carved after routing to produce a distinctive square detail (left).

As a template material, ¼-in.-thick cabinet-grade plywood is ideal.

Preparing the Template and Workpiece

A router will faithfully duplicate a template profile for better or worse. Any bumps or irregularities in the template will be transferred to the workpiece, so it's essential to create clean, smooth template edges. You can smooth bandsawn curves carefully with a spindle sander or a file.

Templates can be made from any smooth, stable material, but I prefer to use 1/4-in.-thick plywood, which is much more stable than solid wood. I use cabinet-grade plywood because it is free of the voids that can snag a guide bearing and spoil the work. Plywood is also easy to work with tools typically at hand.

Work to be routed with a template should be sawn slightly oversized. There should be just a little material left to rout away cleanly. For the smoothest possible surface, I leave only 1/32 in. or so of material outside the cutline. If there is too much, the bit can splinter or tear out the wood, especially when routing a curve.

Securing the Workpiece

There are three common methods for securing a workpiece to a template: using toggle clamps, fasteners, or double-sided tape.

Toggle clamps are used along with the template to make a jig. Stop blocks are located on the jig to position the workpiece and counteract the forces of the spinning router bit, as shown in the photo on p. 128. Toggle clamps are a good option when the work is only routed along one or two edges. However, if the workpiece is to be shaped around the entire perimeter, they will obstruct the cut.

Fasteners, such as nails and screws, hold the workpiece firmly to the template and are quick to install and remove. Although fasteners will obviously leave ugly holes in the work, they can often be positioned so that the hole won't be seen in the finished work. Always remember to position a fastener well out of the path of the router bit.

Another good option for securing a workpiece to a template is double-sided tape. Tape doesn't leave an unsightly hole, and the grip is surprisingly strong. However, I caution you to use only cloth woodturner's tape, and not the inexpensive paper or foam carpet tape. Also, I never use tape when making heavy cuts with large bits.

Guiding the Bit

There are three methods for guiding the bit: using a guide bearing on the bit itself, a bushing (also called a template guide), and the router base. The most common method for guiding the cut when routing with a template is to use the guide bearing on the bit. This method is also the most straightforward, because you don't have to calculate an offset, as you do when using the router base or a bushing. Simply make the template the size of the desired workpiece. It's also an advantage that a bearing is always concentric with the bit, which isn't true with guide bushings or router bases. The precision that is built into a router bit and its guide bearing ensures much more accurate results than you'll achieve with the other two methods.

But how about when the template is placed between the router base and the workpiece? Today, more than ever before, there are bits available with a top bearing, which is slipped over the bit shank and held in position with a small stop collar.

However, there are times when the desired router bit isn't available with a top bearing, and it just isn't practical to position the template below the workpiece. One option is to use the router baseplate to guide the bit. Alternatively, you can use a bushing that is fastened to the center opening of the baseplate.

Using the baseplate as a guide is pretty simple, but you'll first have to calculate the offset distance before making the template. Just subtract the bit diameter from the router base diameter and divide the result by two. When routing with this method, it's important to realize that the base is probably not concentric with the bit. So, if you inadvertently rotate the router during the process, the cut will not be accurate. The solution is to make a mark on the base of the router and always keep the mark adjacent to the template.

When the diameter of the router base is too large to follow the curve of the template, the solution is to use a bushing. A bushing is a metal sleeve that mounts to the opening in the router base. Bushings are available in various lengths and diameters to suit the template and the router bit. As when using the base as a guide, you'll need to first calculate the offset between the bit and the bushing (see the sidebar above), and then keep the same area of the bushing against the template to compensate for the fact that the bushing isn't concentric with the bit.

CALCULATIING BUSHING OFFSET

When using a template guide, or bushing, you'll have to calculate the offset between the bit and the bushing in order to make an accurately sized template. To determine the correct amount to offset the template, simply subtract the diameter of the bit from the outside diameter of the bushing; then divide the remainder by two.

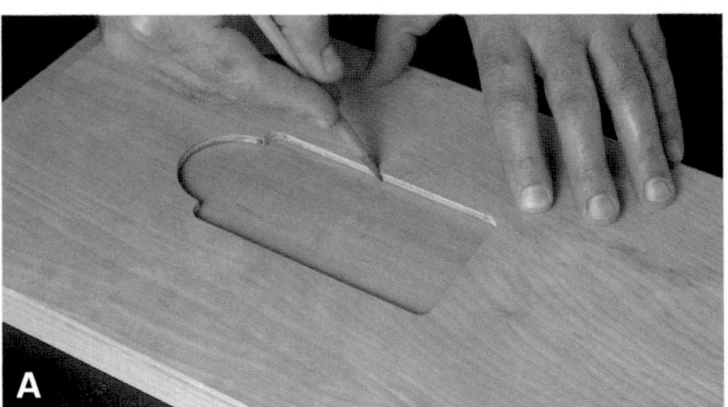

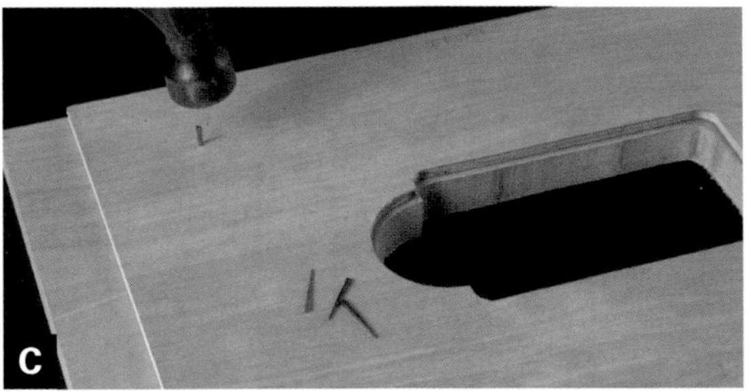

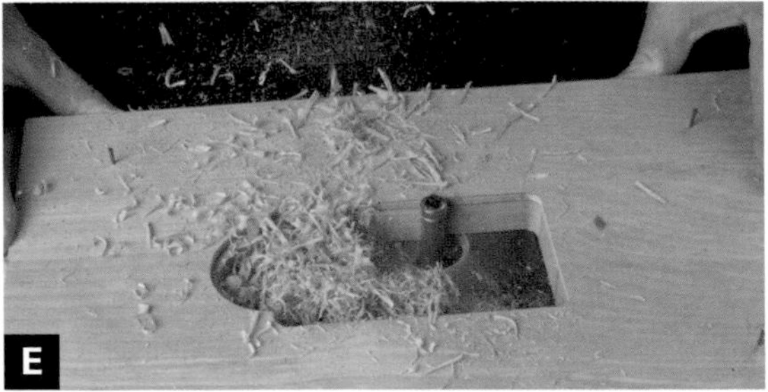

Internal Cut

Internal cuts involve laying out the opening, drilling a hole, and then cutting away most of the interior using a scrollsaw, jigsaw, or coping saw. As discussed previously, leave about ⅓₂ in. of material to be removed by a template-guided router, which is without a doubt the fastest method for smoothing away the saw marks.

For this example, the workpiece is the side of a tall case clock hood. Begin by using the template to lay out the opening **(A)**. Next, saw along the layout lines, staying approximately ⅓₂ in. inside the line **(B)**. Then attach the template to the workpiece **(C)**. As shown here, you can use nails if the nail holes will not be visible on the inside of the completed piece. However, cloth woodturner's tape could be used instead. Adjust the height of the flush-trim router bit so that the bearing contacts the template with the cutter set to engage the entire workpiece edge **(D)**.

To make the cut, push the stock along the bit, feeding it against the bit rotation. Remember that for an internal cut, the workpiece will be fed clockwise around the bit **(E)**.

Curve with Template

Making curves in furniture is always a challenge, but it's worth the extra effort for the detail it adds. In this example, I'll show you how to make a curved piece with smooth edges and then how to rout a profile on the edge **(A)**.

Begin by sketching the curve onto the template stock and sawing it to shape. When making the template, include an extra inch or so at each end so that the bit bearing will have contact with the template before and after the cut. Next, use the template to trace the curve onto the stock **(B)**. Bandsaw the curve approximately 1⁄32 in. proud of the line **(C)**. To smooth away the saw marks, attach the template to the stock and then begin the cut with the bearing contacting the overhanging end of the template. This will ensure smooth entry into the cut **(D)**. Feed the workpiece against the rotation of the bit **(E)**.

Once the curve is smooth, you're ready to add the molding profiles. The first molding cut here is made with a core box bit, which has no bearing. Therefore, you'll need to use a simple jig to guide the template **(F)**. The jig is simply a stick

(Text continues on p. 216.)

A

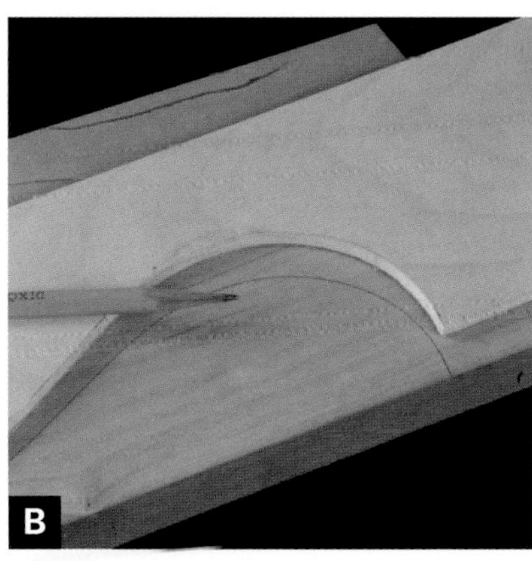

B

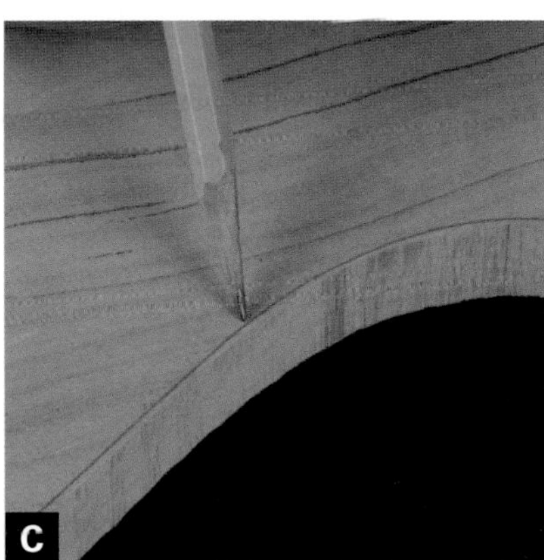

C

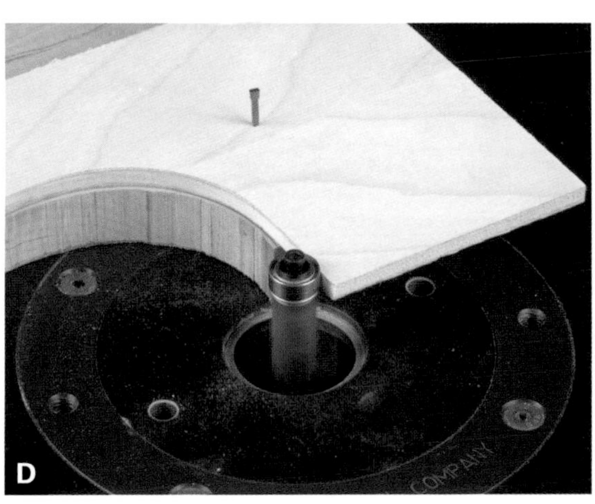

D

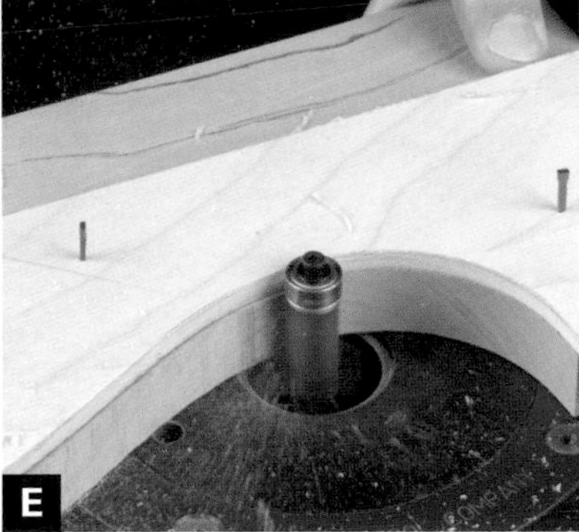

E

F

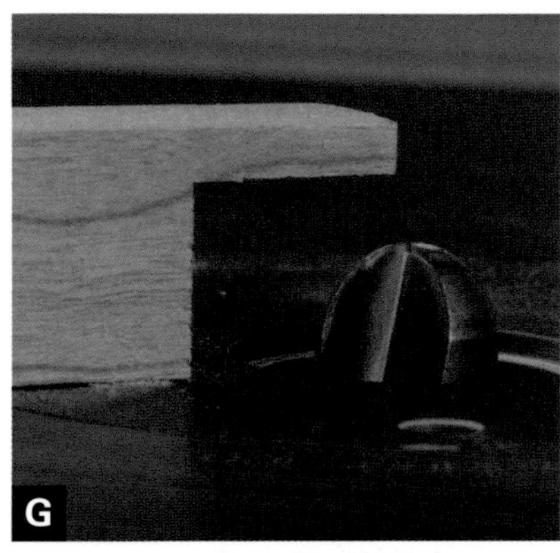
G

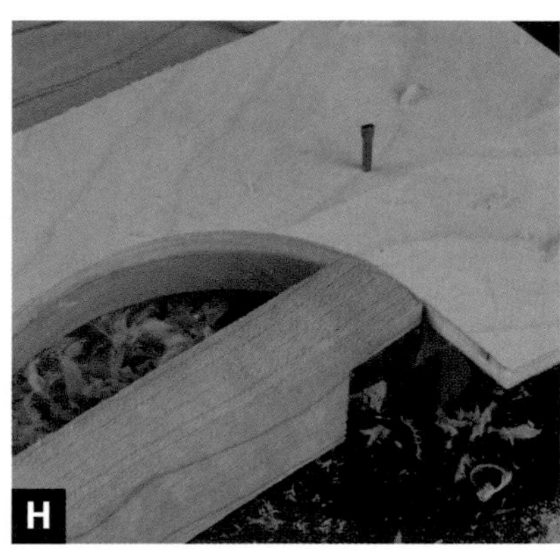
H

I

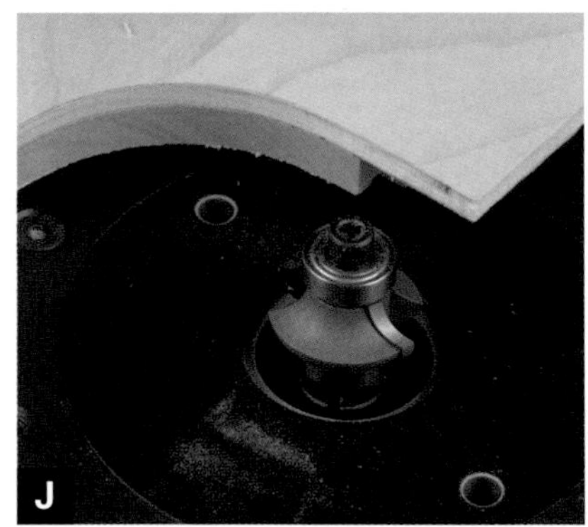
J

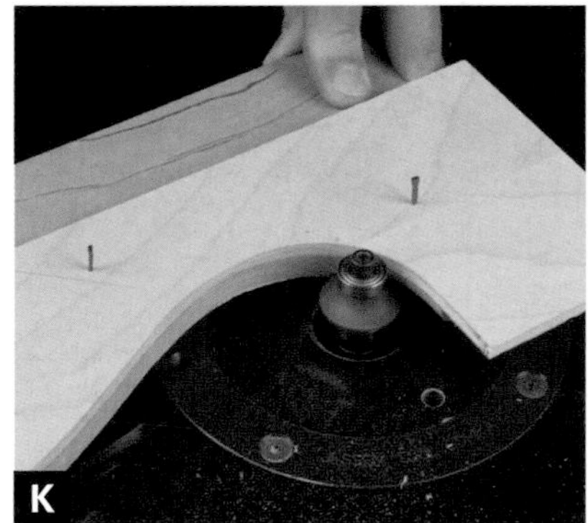
K

L

with a rounded end that overhangs the bit **(G)**. After setting the bit height for a light cut, begin by routing at the end **(H)**. As you rout, feed the stock from right to left with the workpiece between you and the cutter **(I)**. Follow up with a series of successively deeper cuts until the full depth of the profile is reached.

The next bit used for this molding is a roundover **(J)**. The profile is small enough to take the cut in one pass **(K)**. As always, remember to feed the stock against the bit rotation **(L)**.

Flush-Trimming Tight Curves in Small Stock

The small workpiece in this example, a drawer front from a desk, presents unique problems. The stock is small, and the cut is somewhat heavy because of the stock thickness. Also, the entry and exit portions of the cut are on end grain, which is tough and doesn't cut easily. As the bit exits the cut, tearout can occur on the drawer face.

To overcome the problem of the small stock size, use a jig **(A)** that positions the toggle clamps in the back, away from the cut. Blocks on the face of the jig counteract the clamp force and help prevent tearout as the bit exits the work.

[TIP] Use a spiral bit; it cuts much cleaner than an ordinary straight bit and with minimal tearout.

Begin by bandsawing the stock just outside the layout line **(B)**. Secure the work in the jig **(C)**. Make the first cut **(D)**, and then raise the bit for the second cut **(E)**. During the second cut, the bearing follows the surface created by the first cut instead of the template.

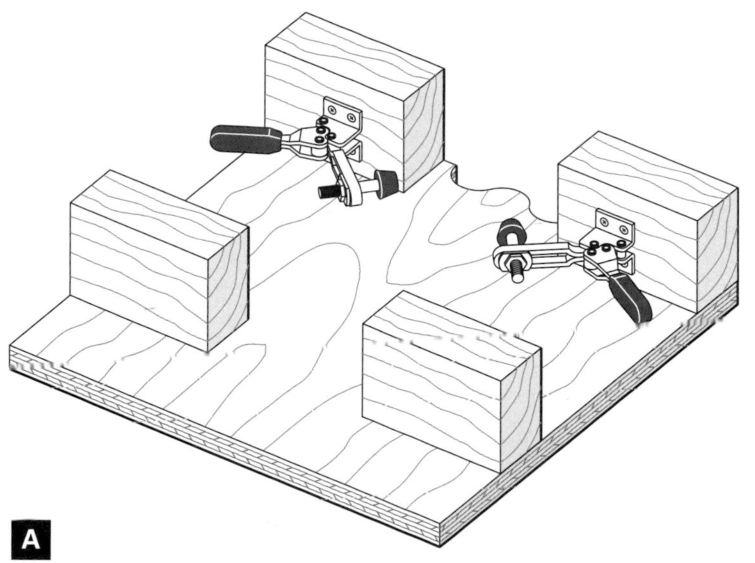

A

B

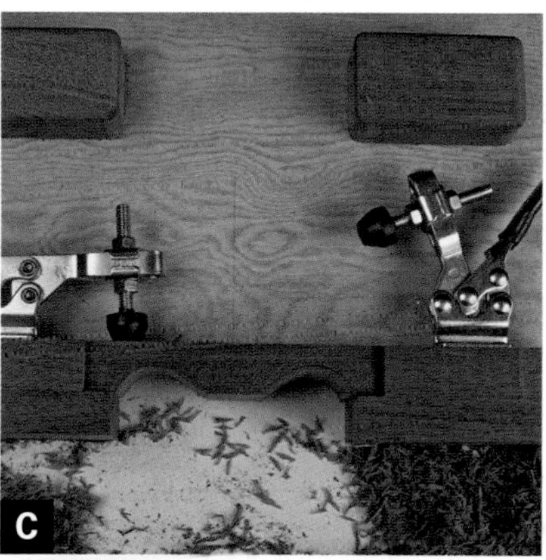

C

D

E

A

B

C

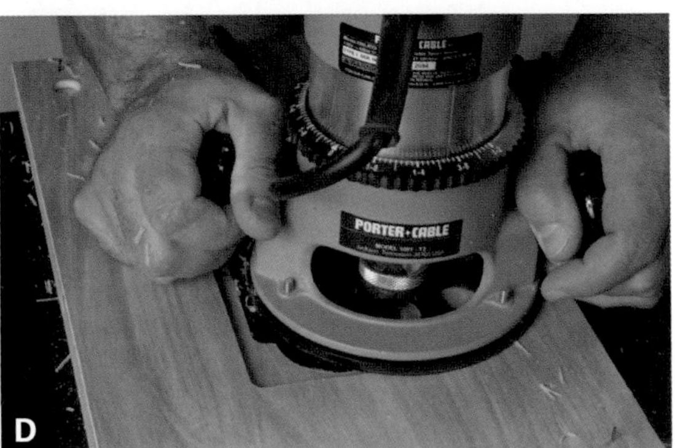

D

Internal Rabbet with Template

When routing a rabbet on the router table, you can usually guide the stock against the fence, but that method does not work with an internal cut. This internal rabbet is a perfect example of a case in which you'll need to use a template and guide bushing. The rabbet shown here houses a small pane of glass inside a clock hood window.

The first step is to attach a rectangular template to the workpiece **(A)**. When sizing the template, remember that it must allow for the offset between the bushing and the bit. Attach the bushing to the router base and adjust the cutting depth of the bit **(B)**. Now you're ready for the cut. Position the bit in the opening and feed the router toward the perimeter until the bushing contacts the template **(C)**. Now push the router along the template against the bit rotation, which is clockwise inside the opening **(D)**.

Corner Shelf

One of the most efficient methods for routing multiple workpieces is to use a template and a guide bushing. The technique has broad applications, which include routing identically shaped cabinet shelves, or routing shallow mortises in a stair stringer to accept the ends of the treads.

In this photo-essay I'll show how to rout a corner cabinet shelf to size. The unusual shape of a corner cabinet shelf makes it a great candidate for template routing using a bushing, because the technique can effectively produce multiple identical shelves.

After selecting a straight bit and bushing **(A)**, mount the bushing in the base of the router **(B)**. Make a template the same size as the shelf, minus the amount of bushing offset.

In order to minimize the strain on both the bit and the router, it's best to first remove as much excess stock as possible. Using the template as a guide, trace around the workpiece using a spacer stick between the pencil and workpiece to account for the bushing offset **(C)**. Next, saw away the excess stock.

Fasten the template to the workpiece. In this case, double-sided woodturner's tape is the best approach **(D)**, because nails or screws would leave holes in the finished piece, and toggle clamps would obstruct the path of the router. When using tape, apply pressure with a clamp or a mallet to ensure good adhesion **(E)**.

(Text continues on p. 220.)

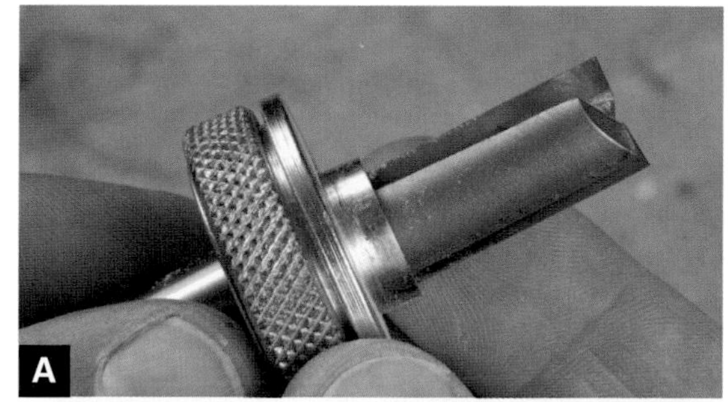
A

B

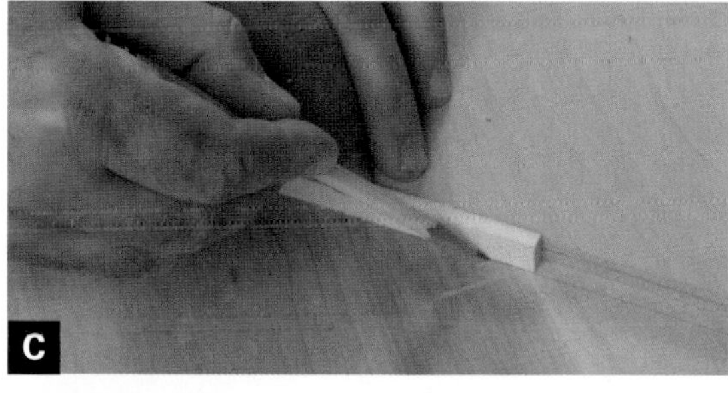
C

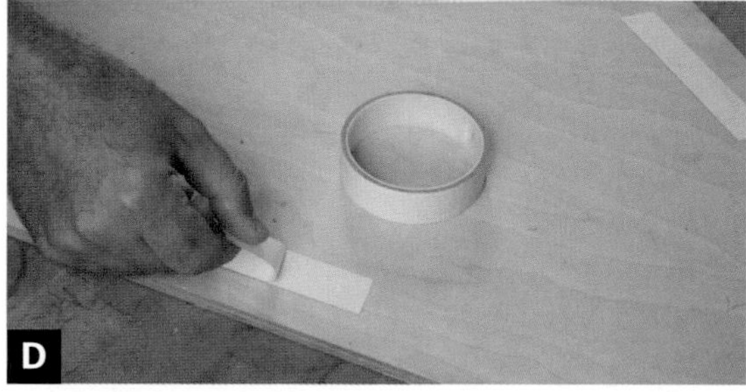
D

E

F

G

H

I

To make the cut, guide the router along the edge of the template in a counterclockwise direction **(F)**. The bushing will duplicate the template exactly **(G)**, so make sure that the template is precise and free of voids or irregularities.

Another option is to use the router table, if the top accepts a bushing **(H)**. For safety, position the fence adjacent to the bit and use a guard **(I)**.

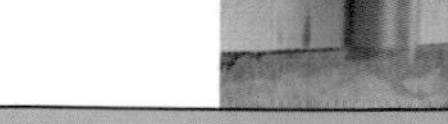

Scalloped Top on the Router

Anytime you shape a curved surface with a router, the rub bearing on the bit must follow a curve to guide the bit and limit the cutting depth. When only part of the edge is shaped, the portion that remains can serve to guide the bearing. However, when the entire edge is shaped, a template is needed to guide the cut **(A)**.

After making the template, trace it onto the workpiece. Now saw the outline slightly proud of the line, which will provide extra stock to be removed by the router bit. If the top is large and your bandsaw is limited in size, you may opt to use a portable jigsaw **(B)**. If so, clamp the work to the bench to keep it stationary while sawing.

Next, attach the template to the underside of the top with screws **(C)**. The screw holes will later be hidden, but make certain that the screw doesn't penetrate the full thickness of the top.

Before shaping, set the bit height with an offcut from the top **(D)**. Now you're ready to make the cut. To have complete control of routers and shapers, it's important always to feed in the opposite direction of the cutter rotation **(E)**. When hand feeding a router, move it counterclockwise around the top's perimeter.

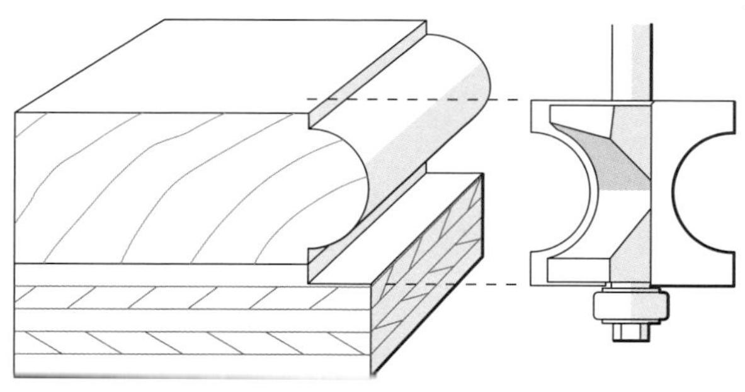

A Because the entire edge is removed, a template is needed for shaping this profile on a curved surface.

B

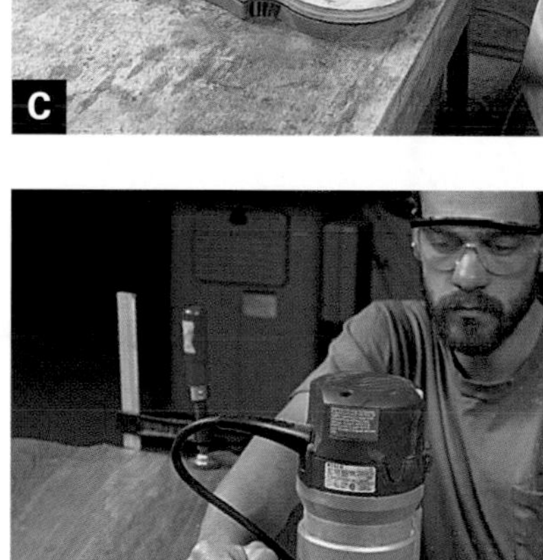

C

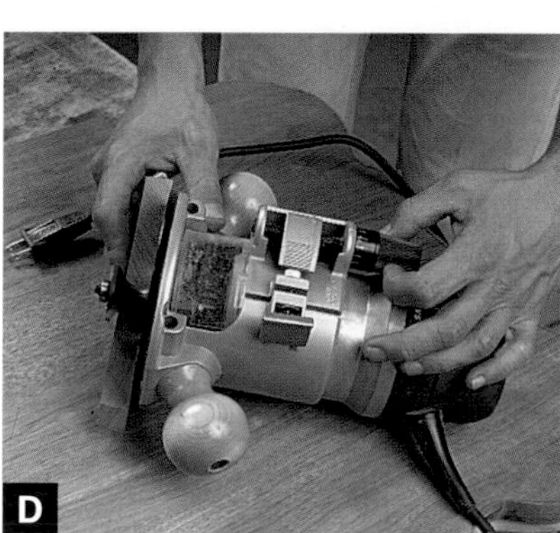

D

E

Special Shaping Operations

Fluting

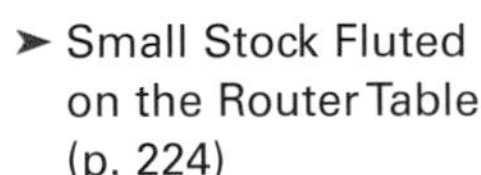

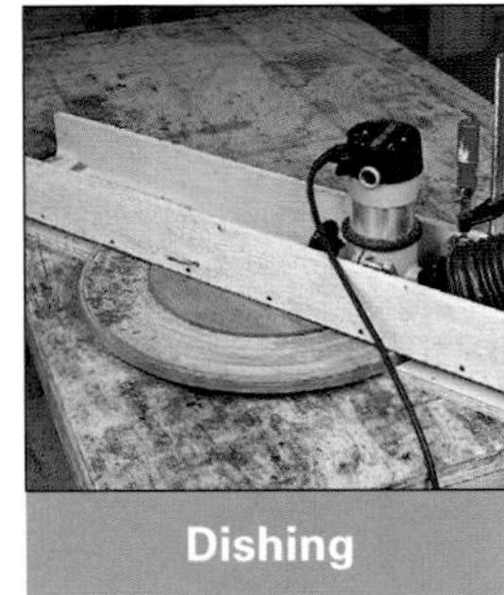

Dishing

A NUMBER OF routing operations can add tremendous detail to your work with just a small amount of effort. Fluting is a good example. The narrow grooves used on the surface of pilasters and columns trace their roots back to the times of the ancient Romans and Greeks. Today, woodworkers can use this simple detail to add an architectural element to any number of projects, ranging from fine furniture to kitchen cabinets.

Another distinctive furniture treatment is a dished tabletop. This dishing and the resulting raised-edge molding can be performed on the outboard end of a lathe, but the process can take several hours and requires a large, heavy-duty lathe. However, you can use your router along with a specialized shopmade jig to rout and dish a tabletop in a fraction of the time.

➤ **See *"Routing a Dished Tabletop"* on p. 228.**

After you true the perimeter of the top with a straight bit, the interior is dished and the molding profiles shaped.

Large Pilaster Fluted with a Handheld Router

Fluting lengthy stock, such as this pilaster for a corner cabinet, can be awkward when the stock is passed across the short top of a router table. In situations such as this, it's much easier to pass the router over the stock. Before you begin, you'll need a guide accessory, which attaches to the base of your router. Or you can make a guide, as I did here **(A)**.

After attaching the guide, adjust the cutting depth of the bit **(B)**. Next, mill the stock for the pilasters. If you mill it oversize in length, you'll have an area on which to lay out the flutes and check each router setting **(C)**.

After layout, clamp a stop block at each end to keep the flutes uniform in length. Begin by routing the center flutes and work outward **(D)**. Afterward, cut two flutes with each new setting **(E)**. Each time you start a new flute, position the router base against the stop block **(F)**.

A

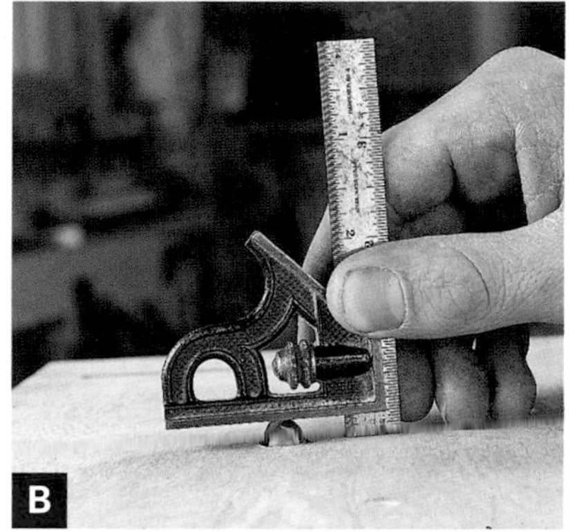
B

C

D

E

F

A

B

C

D

Small Stock Fluted on the Router Table

A router table will dramatically increase the versatility of your router. Here's a good example. This small fluted plinth is narrow, which makes it difficult to keep the router steady if it's handheld.

Begin with layout. You'll want to be accurate with the spacing, because it's used to set up the router. Also, mark the position of the end of the flute **(A)**. Next, set the cutting depth of the bit and position the fence to cut the center flute. Finally, set stops at each fence to control the length of the flutes and keep them consistent. Now you're ready for shaping.

Position the workpiece against the infeed stop and lower it onto the spinning bit **(B)**. Then push the stock to the next stop **(C)**. Feed the stock slowly to avoid a fuzzy, torn surface; small-diameter bits have a relatively slow rim speed even at higher rotations per minute (rpms).

For each successive cut, move the fence closer to the bit **(D)**. For each side of the center flute, each fence setting will make two flutes; simply turn the stock end for end.

Fluted Quarter Columns

Quarter columns, as the name implies, are one-quarter of a full circle. Typically fluted, the columns are inset within the front corners of casework such as desks, chests, and clocks. Like full-round columns and pilasters, quarter columns require a base and capital to complete them visually. Once complete, quarter columns provide a formal architectural look and additional detail.

To create quarter columns, you must glue four strips of wood together with heavy paper in the glue joints. After turning and fluting, the column is easily split into four segments, because the heavy paper in the joints allows the pieces to separate.

Begin by drawing a cross section of the column full-scale **(A)**. Columns typically have a 1¾ in. diameter, which yields a quarter column that's ⅞ in. across when viewed from the front of the case. Next, draw the flutes in place. The size and spacing of the flutes must look proportional to the column; spacing is determined by the index head on your lathe. More specifically, the number of flutes must divide equally into the number of divisions on the index head of your lathe.

The next step is to mill the stock for the columns. If you mill it slightly oversize, you'll easily be able to turn the column to the required diameter. After milling, you must glue the four sections together to create a full column. However, before you begin, remember that joint alignment is critical; the four seams must align perfectly. Otherwise the separate columns will not be exactly a quarter circle. Starting with the ends, align the joints with pressure from opposing clamps **(B)**. You can check the alignment by examining the joint at the end of the assembly **(C)**. After aligning the ends, clamp the remainder of the work. For safety reasons, allow the glue to dry overnight before turning.

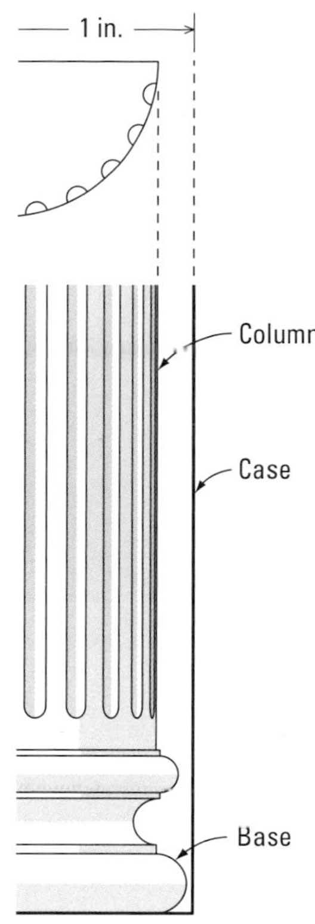

A

B

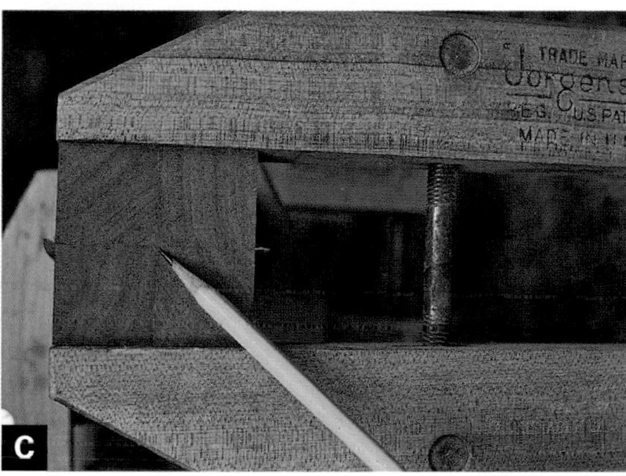
C

D

E

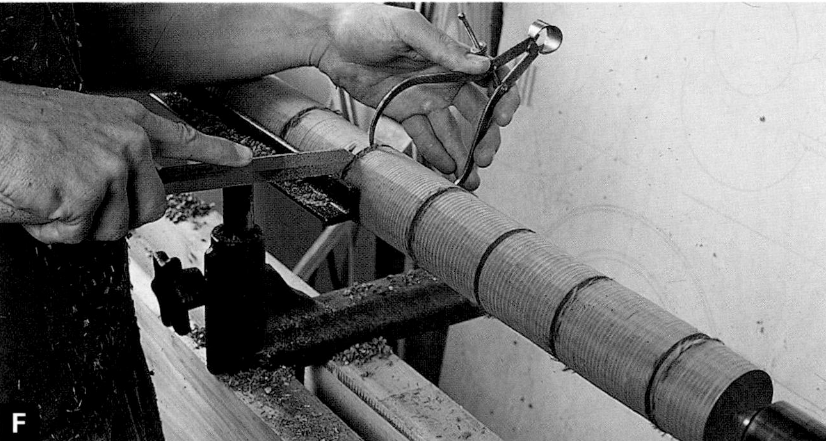
F

G

H

The next step is to turn the square to a uniform cylinder. Begin by squaring the ends of the turning blank. Then mark the centers for mounting in the lathe. Once again, alignment is critical. Mark the exact location with the point of an awl **(D)**. Afterward, mount the blank securely in the lathe for turning.

Turning a straight, uniform cylinder isn't difficult if you follow a few easy steps. First, turn the blank round with a roughing gouge **(E)**. Then carefully turn it to the required diameter. You can accomplish this by cutting to the diameter at several locations with a parting tool. As you lever the tool into the spinning stock with one hand, gauge the diameter with spring calipers in the other hand **(F)**. Then turn the remaining portion of the cylinder to diameter with the roughing gouge. Afterward, smooth the cylinder with a block plane. Support the plane on the tool rest and push it slowly down the length of the slowly spinning stock **(G)**. This is a great technique! The plane cleanly shears away the high spots to create a perfectly smooth, uniform surface **(H)**.

The next step is to rout the flutes. But first you'll need to build a jig **(I)**. The jig is actually a box that mounts to the bed of the lathe to support the router during the fluting process. Next, mount the box under the workpiece and, if necessary, attach a square base to your router to fit within the sides of the box **(J)**. Finally, set the cutting depth of the bit and lock it in position.

Before you begin routing, remember that the flutes must be spaced equally around each quarter column; the first and last flute on each quarter column should be adjacent to a glue joint. For this spacing to occur, it may be necessary to reposition the cylinder between the centers.

Lock the cylinder in place with the pin on the index head **(K)**; then make a very short test cut on one end of the cylinder. If the flute falls next to the glue joint, fine. If not, release the pressure slightly at the tailstock and rotate the column to bring the router bit into alignment. Now tighten the handwheel at the tailstock and make a second test cut.

Once the column is aligned for the first flute, successive flutes will be correctly positioned in relation to the glue joints. Once the setup is complete, route the flutes **(L)**. If you choose to stop the flutes, tack a wood block to the jig to act as a stop.

When fluting is complete, remove the column from the lathe and carefully split it into corners by placing a wide chisel at one end and tapping it gently **(M)**.

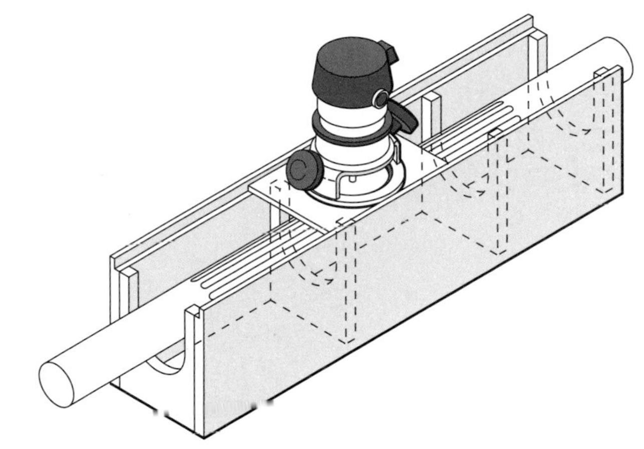

I

J

K

L

M

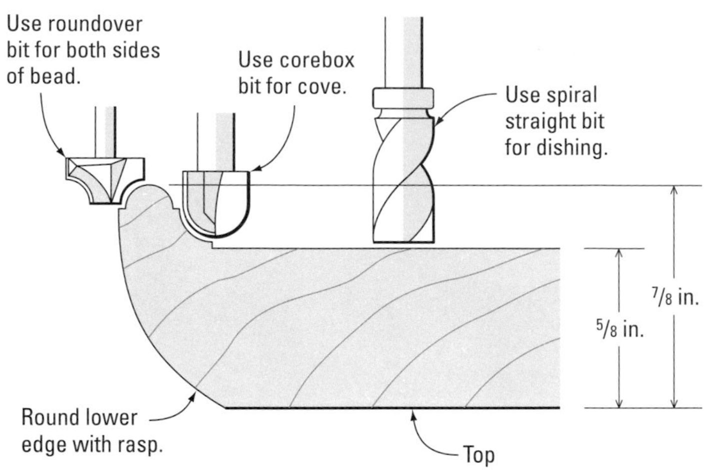

Routing a Dished Tabletop

A dished tabletop has a molded rim that sits slightly above the rest of the table surface **(A)**. The molding is small and refined, and the effect is dramatic as it reflects light and casts shadows. The design is a classic one, but the router technique for producing it is relatively new. The router is suspended over the top, which rotates on a hub. To use the technique you'll first have to build a jig.

[TIP] A one-board top looks best, but if you must use two boards, take care when matching the grain and color.

Begin by milling the stock for the top. Now draw the radius of the top **(B)**. Next, bandsaw the top perimeter and glue the hub to the center **(C)**. If you sandwich a layer of heavy paper between the top and the hub, it is much easier to remove the hub after the process is complete.

After the glue has dried, mount the top in the jig **(D)**. Before shaping the molding, it's necessary to true the edge of the top. A spiral straight bit cuts cleaner and with less chatter than an ordinary straight bit **(E)**.

Once the bit is mounted, you're ready to begin. Never attempt to start the router when the bit is in contact with the stock. Instead, start the router, slide it along the rails until it touches the top, clamp the router in position, and rotate the top. Always rotate the top clockwise against the bit rotation **(F)**.

WARNING **A dust collector is a must. Otherwise this process produces a choking cloud of fine dust and chips.**

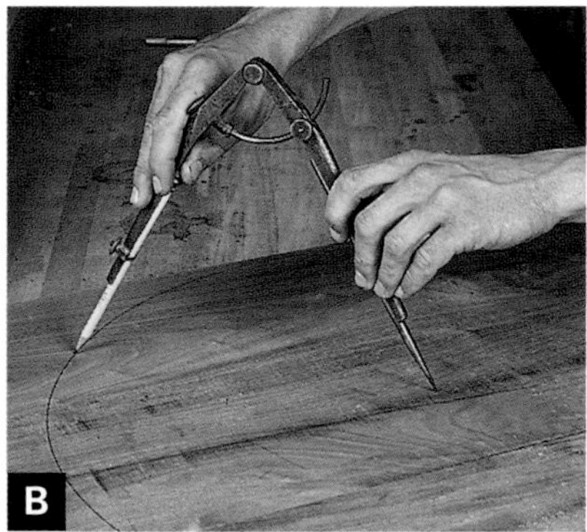
B

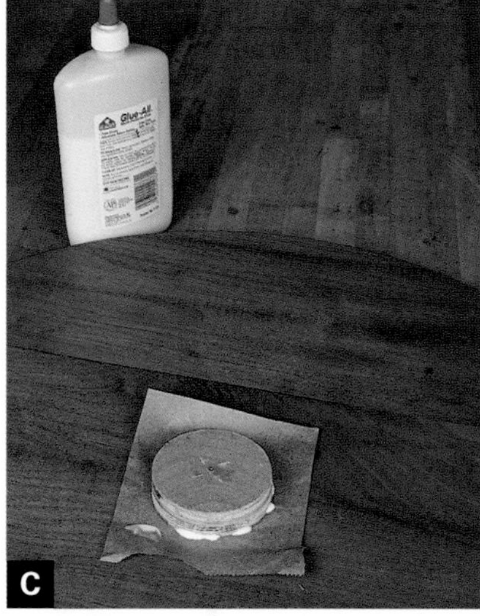
C

D

E

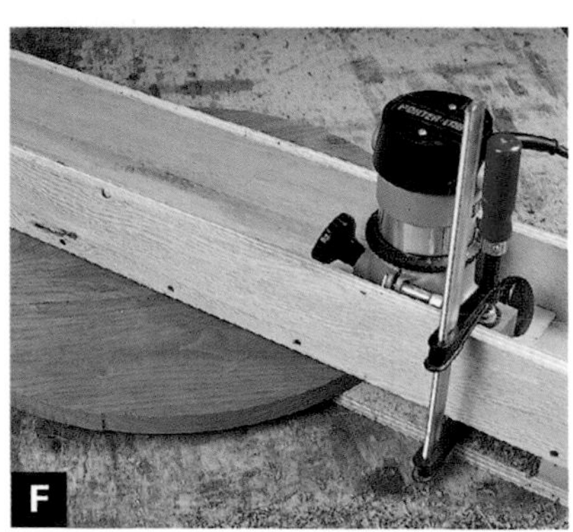
F

Next, switch to the roundover bit to create the bead. If you're not able to find a bit without a bearing, it's easy to remove the bearing and grind away the bearing stud. To adjust the bit depth, use a block of plywood from the jig **(G)**.

Shaping the molding is much the same as truing the perimeter: Start the router, clamp it in position, and rotate the top **(H)**. To ensure that the molding isn't squeezed, begin from the outside edge and work inward **(I)**. The molding is shaped in three steps: outside edge of bead; inside edge of bead; and cove, which is shaped with a bullnose bit.

Once the molding is complete, switch back to the straight bit to dish the top **(J)**. This process goes quickly, because there is no careful positioning of the router as there was with the molding. If you have a helper, one of you can hold the router while the other rotates the top, which sidesteps the process of clamping the router for each cut.

With the router work completed, you're ready for the handwork. Clamp the top to the bench and scrape the surface smooth **(K)**. Use care to avoid scarring the molding. After you smooth the top, the edge will need shaping along the underside to remove the square corner. This step also gives the top a thin, refined appearance. A rasp works well for this process, but first draw a line with a compass for use as a guide. Now secure the top in the vise and rasp the edge **(L)**. Work the surface from the fillet at the bead to the layout line. When you're satisfied, smooth the edge with a file, a scraper, and then sandpaper.

G

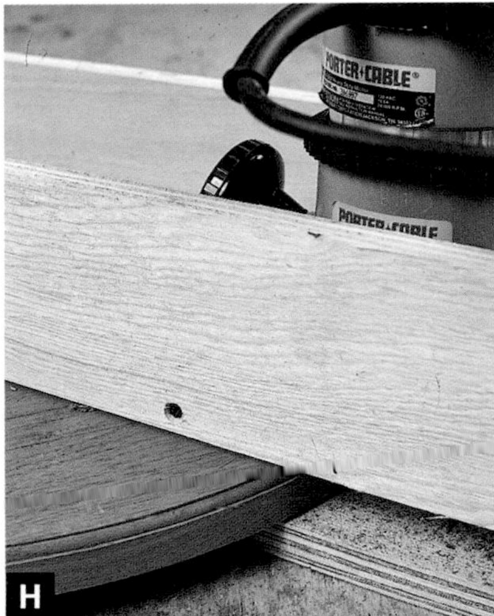

H

I

J

K

L

Index

S

T

U

V

W

Z

Other Books in the Series:

HARDCOVER

The Complete Illustrated Guide to Joinery
Gary Rogowski
ISBN 978-1-56158-401-7
Product #070535
$39.95 U.S.
$52.95 Canada

The Complete Illustrated Guide to Furniture and Cabinet Construction
Andy Rae
ISBN 978-1-156158-402-4
Product #070534
$39.95 U.S.
$52.95 Canada

The Complete Illustrated Guide to Shaping Wood
Lonnie Bird
ISBN 978-1-56158-400-0
Product #070533
$39.95 U.S.
$52.95 Canada

Taunton's Complete Illustrated Guide to Finishing
Jeff Jewitt
ISBN 978-1-56158-592-2
Product #070712
$39.95 U.S.
$52.95 Canada

Taunton's Complete Illustrated Guide to Sharpening
Thomas Lie-Nielsen
ISBN 978-1-56158-657-8
Product #070737
$39.95 U.S.
$52.95 Canada

Taunton's Complete Illustrated Guide to Using Woodworking Tools
Lonnie Bird
ISBN 978-156158-597-7
Product #070729
$39.95 U.S.
$52.95 Canada

Taunton's Complete Illustrated Guide to Turning
Richard Raffan
ISBN 978-1-56158-672-1
Product #070757
$39.95 U.S.
$52.95 Canada

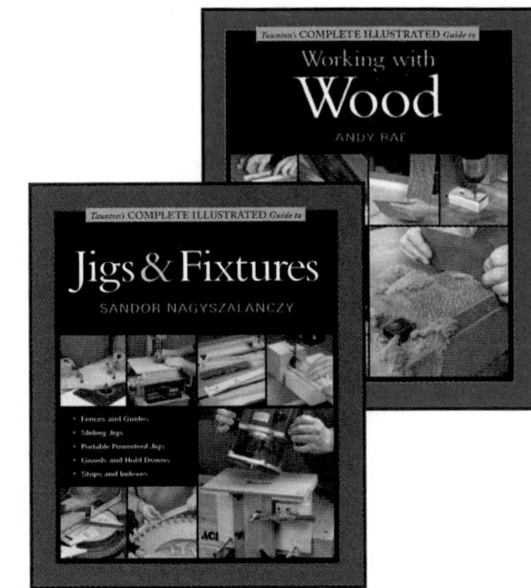

Taunton's Complete Illustrated Guide to Working with Wood
Andy Rae
ISBN 978-1-56158-683-7
Product #070765
$39.95 U.S.
$52.95 Canada

Taunton's Complete Illustrated Guide to Jigs & Fixtures
Sandor Nagyszalanczy
ISBN 978-1-56158-770-4
Product #070832
$39.95 U.S.
$52.95 Canada

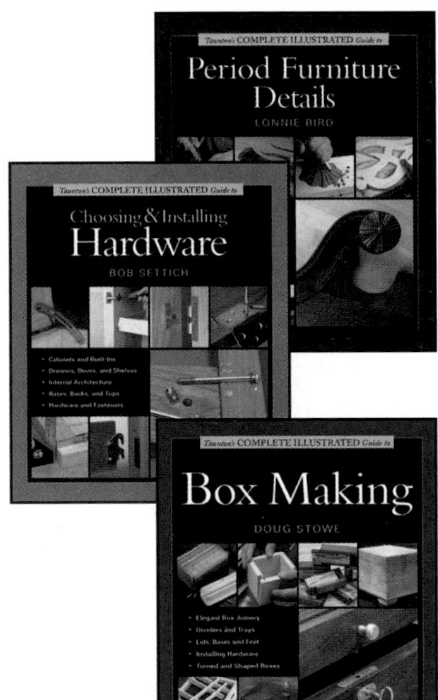

PAPERBACK

Taunton's Complete Illustrated Guild to Period Furniture Details
Lonnie Bird
ISBN 978-1-56158-590-8
Product #070708
$27.00 U.S.
$36.00 Canada

Taunton's Complete Illustrated Guild to Choosing and Installing Hardware
Robert J. Settich
ISBN 978-1-56158-561-8
Product #070647
$29.95 U.S.
$39.95 Canada

Taunton's Complete Illustrated Guild to Box Making
Doug Stowe
ISBN 978-1-56158-593-9
Product #070721
$24.95 U.S.
$32.95 Canada